Disintegration

Studies in Critical Social Sciences Book Series

Haymarket Books is proud to be working with Brill Academic Publishers (www.brill.nl) to republish the *Studies in Critical Social Sciences* book series in paperback editions. This peer-reviewed book series offers insights into our current reality by exploring the content and consequences of power relationships under capitalism, and by considering the spaces of opposition and resistance to these changes that have been defining our new age. Our full catalog of *SCSS* volumes can be viewed at https://www.haymarketbooks.org/series_collections/4-studies-in-critical-social-sciences.

Series Editor
David Fasenfest (Wayne State University)

Editorial Board
Eduardo Bonilla-Silva (Duke University)
Chris Chase-Dunn (University of California–Riverside)
William Carroll (University of Victoria)
Raewyn Connell (University of Sydney)
Kimberlé W. Crenshaw (University of California–LA and Columbia University)
Heidi Gottfried (Wayne State University)
Karin Gottschall (University of Bremen)
Alfredo Saad Filho (King's College London)
Chizuko Ueno (University of Tokyo)
Sylvia Walby (Lancaster University)
Raju Das (York University)

DISINTEGRATION

Bad Love, Collective Suicide,
and the Idols of Imperial Twilight

MARK P. WORRELL

Haymarket Books
Chicago, IL

First published in 2020 by Brill Academic Publishers, The Netherlands
© 2020 Koninklijke Brill NV, Leiden, The Netherlands

Published in paperback in 2021 by
Haymarket Books
P.O. Box 180165
Chicago, IL 60618
773-583-7884
www.haymarketbooks.org

ISBN: 978-1-64259-424-9

Distributed to the trade in the US through Consortium Book Sales and Distribution (www.cbsd.com) and internationally through Ingram Publisher Services International (www.ingramcontent.com).

This book was published with the generous support of Lannan Foundation and Wallace Action Fund.

Special discounts are available for bulk purchases by organizations and institutions. Please call 773-583-7884 or email info@haymarketbooks.org for more information.

Cover design by Jamie Kerry and Ragina Johnson.

Printed in the United States.

10 9 8 7 6 5 4 3 2 1

Library of Congress Cataloging-in-Publication data is available.

For Beck and Eric

Contents

Preface IX
Acknowledgements XXVI
List of Figures XXVII
Abbreviations XXVIII

Introduction 1
1 Marxheimianism and the Return of the Repressed 4
2 Freedom and Anomie 16
3 Dynamism, Alienation and Reification 18
4 Masters and Slaves 21
5 Authoritarianism, Character, and Resonance 28
6 Disobedience and Necessity 33

1 Reflective Determinations 38
1 The Lifeless Universal 38
2 The Judgement 40
3 The Syllogism 44
4 Telos 49
5 The Idea 50
6 Necessity Versus Necessity 53
7 The Commodity 57
8 The Dialectic 59

2 Bad Love 62
1 The House of the Absolute 64
2 The New Economy and the Reign of Tyche 86
3 The Nightmare of Collective Unconsciousness 101
4 Suicide 115

3 The Four Horsemen of the Apocalypse 135
1 Egoism 135
2 Altruism 159
3 Anomie 164
4 Fatalism 181
5 Composite Forces 188
6 Positive Hell and Heavenly Negativities 226

Bibliography 233
Index 280

Preface

Disintegration is the second volume of *Sacrifice and Self-Defeat*, a project which has three broad goals: to articulate the terms and conditions (volume one)[1] under which we may explicate the moral geometry[2] of collective consciousness (combined in the present work and the forthcoming *Ecstasy and Resignation*), in a social system dominated by capital (the final phase of the project). While here we are presently interested in the moral economy of neoliberalism the final, twofold aim of the concluding volume will be the examination of the Calvinistic logic of ascetic labor in a calling as a "vanishing medium" (Karl Rosenkranz, in Hegel 2002: 264) clearing the way for the modern epoch and, secondly, extending the idea of a moral geometry in an effort to reconstruct and expand Marx's general formula for capital that provides a fresh view of the commodity.

We pick up where *The Sociogony* concluded by articulating the generation of a current of assemblage energy and the solidification[3] of that current into a geometric core[4] represented by the image of something like a 'wobbly

---

1 *The Sociogony* (volume 128 in the *Studies in Critical Social Sciences* series, Brill).
2 By 'geometry' I am playing off the original meaning of the word: the measuring and surveying of a ground with an eye toward pulling various, disconnected determinations into formal relations with one another. Where there is rationalism and universal thought there is a "geometry" even though it remains, "simple," abstract and untrue (Durkheim 1961: 279). For us, 'geometry' is the teleological work of the concept in giving a form or shape to things such that they stand out as moments within an integrated constellation of synthetic *a priori* judgments. Further, whenever we are in the presence of untrue representations of the sacred we also encounter geometry: lines, circles, spirals, cubes, and so on (Durkheim [1912] 1915: 148–49). The bare minimum seems to be the straight line (e.g., the gospels of the New Testament). Galileo is famous for making geometry a prerequisite for comprehending the universe (see Hodgkin 2005: 133) but the triangle, for example, is a concept projected into nature, not nature directly imposing itself upon the intellect.
3 In social-psychoanalytic terms we are referring to a hypercathexis process where energy is invested in a representation that results in separations and oppositions (a primordial dialectic). The setting of one representation apart creates an irresistible yet simultaneously dreadful object that stimulates a collective (symbolic) economy of desire (cf. Fink 1997: 188–91). Our lack in the real is, once we have the collective representation, doubled in the symbolic domain *qua* the contamination of the group emblem with black holes and impure corruptions.
4 "Ideas which yesterday were held sacred, which a small number of spiritual men still prize and try to live by, may tomorrow be utterly discredited and forgotten — all but an indestructible core which must serve as the leaven for any renewal. As long as there are men, that core will never be lost, it is man's one 'eternal' possession" (Hesse 1971: 132).

sphere' that, when it can no longer hold itself together due to internal defects, or where it encounters a more powerful externality or necessity, disaggregates in the direction of its primal form, something that resembles a Möbius band; we could use the lemniscate (∞) or an 'eight curve' (the 'Gerono lemniscate') to represent this strange ribbon. The advantage of the lemniscate is that it can also be constructed as an "envelope" of a rectangular hyperbola. These metaphors should not be taken too seriously; though, they are not pointless either.[5] The representations of becoming are different than the images of being where we are confronted with the classical juxtaposition between names without a corresponding existence, *nomina*, or existing beings lacking a signifier out there somewhere beyond comprehension, *numina* (cf. Durkheim [1912] 1915: 101). When society suffers an inevitable downfall, a void opens (Durkheim [1897] 1951: 377) in the place where there had once been a constellation of particular realities and facticities striving for conceptual unity. However, unlike individuals and institutions, the Idea does not simply vanish altogether. Even the "polar night of icy darkness" in which a great nothingness swallows pride and rights gives way to the positing of new subjective and objective possibilities (Weber 1946: 128). Tormented by the 'phantom limb' of an unconscious Idea that haunts the post-apocalyptic world, Spirit surreptitiously dissolves existing frameworks in a virtually infinite series of moments along its historical odyssey.[6] In this book, we will go no further than the point of a thing tearing itself apart and attempting to fill the void (positivize the hole) with negative elements such as magic, mystique, specious desires, unrealistic dreams, doom, resignation, taboos, ecstasy, scapegoats and demons. If miracles were real, any number of these dead ends could lead to life. Lacking miracles, another concept would have to counteract the energies of the moral whirlpool.

---

5 On the other hand, the metaphors are deadly serious. If society is a conceptual being, both a personal and impersonal being that is conscious of the whole (Durkheim 1961: 277) then it is a being, and at some point, every being decides to be or not to be. This extravagant statement does not presuppose spooky ontology or a stand-in for a suicidal god, far from it, but it does take Hegel and Durkheim seriously that the absolute is an autonomous being that has its own 'agenda' that one cannot locate in abstracted empirical consciousness (Durkheim 1961: 277). Individuals have suicidal thoughts all the time; why would collective consciousness be any different? If the sacred pure entails life and sacrifice, the sacred impure, the domain of filth and horror, concerns itself with death and murder. And what is suicide but self-murder?

6 In the next volume we will further explore the notion of the apocalypse of the Idea as (a) revelation; (b) cataclysm; and (c) return.

In *The Sociogony*, many concepts that critical theory finds repulsive or obsolete, such as social facts,[7] repression,[8] authority, alienation, faith, ambivalence, projection, externality,[9] Spirit, and especially the absolute, were reconsidered and found to be non-disposable aspects of the teleological process.[10] To wag one's finger at the 'social fact' is an infantile and self-defeating wish to bring

---

7   Facts are representable "deeds" (Kant) that form the ground of teleological activity, i.e., praxis, as moments in the odyssey of the concept's self-realization. Facts are not true but radical theorists who pine for a world lacking facticity can, at this point, choose only between a psychology and the thing-in-itself (Kant 1991: 176). The pseudo-radical negation of facticity amounts to a suspension of telos whereby externality is revealed to be an alien representation of our acting, thinking, and feeling. To eject 'fact' from our lexicon means simply that the goal of the Idea is not worth the trouble and that we might as well backslide into the abyss of pragmatic indifference, crude materialism, or Stoic self-absorption, etc.

8   Drive inhibitions have the "functional advantage" of generating "permanent ties," i.e., group solidarity (Freud [1921] 1959: 91). Hyper-repression is usually what is meant by 'repression' but hypo-repression is also pathological and leads to death (Durkheim [1897] 1961: 37/1-71). As we will see in the next chapter, perhaps the most important aspect attaching to repression is in surmounting magic and putting Spirit on the road to the concept. Progressive types who have no place for repression also have no theory of solidarity and probably do not care anyway.

9   "[W]hat seems to happen outside of [Spirit], to be an activity directed against it, is really its own doing" (Hegel [1807] 1977: 21). The radical negation of externality unconsciously presupposes the negation of subjectivity. The "external" or "outward" is only the expression and manifestation of the "internal" or "interior" of subjectivity (Durkheim [1912] 1915: 239; Durkheim [1912] 1995: 210). If one gives the matter a moment of thought, it is obvious (unless one is a follower of Bertrand Russell) that where one dwells on individuals in relation to causes, *everything* is external (cf. Brinton 1902: 86; cf. Marx [1867] 1976: 165). Where causality and externality have been abandoned we know we are in a place where the abstracted ego, debilitated by crude materialist reductions, has set itself up against society in a "sterile independence" and acting as moral plague on the body social (Durkheim 1978: 97). The external has the capacity for re-internalization, e.g., Marx and "the act of seeing" ([1867] 1976: 165) but without the external we would not even be fit as animals; lacking instincts we need a conscience we are not born with and, consequently, must acquire from society (Freud 1965: 77). Lacking the quality of even an untrue externality, we would also therefore lack morality: society would submerge in the unconscious and subjectivity would be even more enslaved than if it wrestled externality with the powers of reason and reflection. Freud credits morality with a periodicity or non-continuousness but what this means, sociologically, is that morality is a relation, a fact that emerges from society and asserts itself in our associations with others. Personal conscience is fluid and temporary whereas law (not in the lifeless and schematic sense) is the continuous crystallization of conscience.

10 'Spirituality' denotes an autonomous and irreducible creative power of human consciousness in contrast to lower, animal forms of thinking and life in common (Durkheim [1893] 1984: 275, 284).

praxis to a halt. The consequence would be forsaking the absolute as a bad dream. If William "Damn the Absolute!" James can come around there may still be hope: "The absolute is not the impossible being I once thought it. Mental facts do function both singly and together, at once, and we finite minds may simultaneously be co-conscious with one another in a superhuman intelligence" (1909: 292; cf. Hocking 1926: 353).[11] However, to be "co-conscious with one another in a superhuman intelligence" means that association is built on more than pragmatic agreements. There must also be a reconciliation with necessity itself and a will to share a faith in some regulative thing, a general ground of unity that imposes hard limits (Hegel [1812] 1969: 530). The status of the absolute, and our faith (or, lack of faith) in it, is tricky and to approach it means being exposed to many traps.

Žižek wants his cake and to eat it too when it comes to the absolute: the absolute does not exist, *but when it does*, it is contradictory which amounts to identifying the defects of understanding with reason (2014b: 20–23).[12] Since everything is contradictory we cannot act on the basis of reason and reflection, rather, we pick and choose the reasons that are convenient for our actions or, what amounts to the same thing, just act upon our desires and rationalize as we go. Here, reason does not exist but is merely a word that signifies nothing more than a retroactive construction, or, is a function of *ex post facto* critique.[13] Žižek makes clear that what we call 'reason' is an illusion or, what amounts to the same thing, reason is the realization that there is nothing that corresponds to the concept of reason, only the mere understanding, which itself rests on a foundation of misunderstandings and miscommunications. Anthropologically, this confusion or, really, obliteration of the distinction between

---

11 James did not find his way to a sociological concept of the absolute. He tried to remedy his intellectual bankruptcy by investing in Bergson's mysticism. This should come as no surprise: personalism leaves James susceptible to the 'magnetic' charms of the charismatic leader (Mills 1966: 269). James also says, "It is only the extravagant claims of coercive necessity on the absolute's part that have to be denied by *a priori* logic" (1909: 292) and, as such, it is "onward ... with Fechner and his method, rather than with Hegel, Royce, or Bradley" (Ibid: 293). James and pragmatism lead backwards toward nominalism, instincts, habit, anomie, and social disintegration (Mills 1966: 268–72) and, in the final analysis, pragmatism attempts to bring teleological activity to a halt via indifference.

12 "The universal does not exist. We must have the universal. The universal is impossible. The universal is necessary" (Breckman 2013: 219). It might seem odd to worry about Žižek today, however, as of April 2019 there has been more interest in Žižek than in the previous 15 years due to his high-profile 'debate' with Jordan Peterson. Just when it appears that his star has finally burned out, he stages another comeback.

13 "It is rationally knowable where an unleashed, self-escaping rationality goes wrong, where it becomes true mythology" (Adorno 1973: 148).

two dimensions of thought (equivalent to the annihilation of the line between the sacred and the profane) is nothing less than a magical degradation of the universal and the social for purely egoistic and pragmatic ends. The denial of society, the absolute, and reason, is essentially mental suicide and Žižek is the Pied Piper of the walking dead.

With Hegel, the regression from reason to understanding amounts to nothing less than mental illness in need of therapy (1984: 407). However, the 'postmodern' incorporation of psychoanalysis does not liberate the psyche from contradictions but attempts to reinstall the ego within more enjoyable coordinates. It is true that the understanding can never rid itself of contradictions but when it comes to the concept of contradiction, contemporary thought is plagued by a basically anti-scientific regression into mythology (cf. Durkheim [1912] 1995: 12). If Hegel is correct that the resources available to the understanding are insufficient to grasp the enigma of the absolute then we have not much more than an old, Kantian form of critical theory that does not so much dispose of things that resist understanding as preserves them in the hardened amber of an inaccessible dimension.[14] If transcendentalism corresponded with reality we would be in a far better position since the universal could safeguard "its treasures beyond the reach of the destroyer" (Sullivan 1871: 42). But we will have to safeguard our own treasures. What is a contradiction for the understanding is not necessarily one for reason. Indeed, even "monstrous" contradictions often do no damage whatsoever to rational unity (Hegel 1988: 457). In a well-ordered society glaring contradictions that exist for the external understanding pass for centuries without comment (Durkheim [1912] 1995: 54).[15] Where contradictions are incapable of being resolved society has broken down at important points via the intrusion of powerful externalities. The understanding can pinpoint these contradictions, but it is the work of reason that negates and positively resolves these antinomies.[16]

---

14   This problem occurs in mathematics as well. An infinite set can be disposed of by declaring it to be nothing more than a word or just a fanciful object that has no empirical verifiability, or, alternatively, mathematicians can set aside the problem of contradiction and regard the infinite number as an entity that is "so abstract and strange it doesn't conform to math's normal rules and requires special treatment" (Wallace 2003: 40). Attempting to grasp the social absolute with the understanding yields nothing more than the grizzly spectacle of the 'conservative intellectual' trapped in a linear universe of common sense that leaves the absolute untouched, unexplained, ignored, or denied.

15   Myths have the power to erase or lessen "the logical scandal" of contradictions (Ibid: 157).

16   So far from contradictions serving merely to prove the ontological inconsistency of the absolute they can just as well be the proof of the exact opposite. "Now in order to maintain itself, society frequently finds it necessary that we should see things from a certain angle and feel them in a certain way; consequently it modifies the ideas which we would

Prior to the First World War it was rare for social thinkers to retreat from positivity and an orientation toward a necessary order to the world, but contemporary critical trends (espousing pure negativity at the extremities) find only contingent disorder befitting apocalyptic science fiction. With the exception of orthodox Marxism, objectivity melted down to nothing in the postwar era and, so far, where it strives for anything beyond nihilism, the critical spirit has managed to work itself back up to a limp pragmatism. Critical sociology cannot devolve to the point where it is concerned with interpersonal agreements; the sacred, the absolutely different, has as its minimum two related groups in opposition to one another. The distance that separates agreements between people and the moral economy of groups is infinite. In simplistic terms, psychology deals with a single syllogism; along with other sciences, sociology has as its object two syllogisms; the object of absolute sociology is a spiral of three syllogisms.

Subjectivism and makeshift agreements mean that the whole, the absolute, can never be grasped for what it is.

> To Žižek, the difference between Kant and Hegel is not, as is usually thought, that Kant identified a hole at the center of our understanding and concluded that we were incapable of grasping the thing-in-itself directly while Hegel developed a new form of logic which enabled him to get to the thing-in-itself. Rather, Hegel used the same reasoning as Kant but came to a startlingly different conclusion: the hole is part of the thing-in-itself, the totality requires an intrinsic emptiness.
> SCHROEDER 1998: 12

Actually, the situation is different: Hegel developed a new logic and discovered that the thing-in-itself is a misconception. The representations and concepts of the understanding and of the abstract ego do not penetrate the absolute; the void of the absolute is the product of the understanding and the mulching of one-sided perspectives. Where Žižek interrogates abstracted bits of cinema and pop culture, a sociology intent on working beyond the twin dead ends of individualism and transcendentalism reaches out for absolute concepts. For example: Weber's expropriation of the charisma concept and grounding it in immanent processes and social dynamics; Durkheim's analyses of mana and primitive social organization to explain the origins of the categories of human

---

ordinarily make of them for ourselves and the sentiments to which we would be inclined if we listened only to our animal nature; it alters them, even going so far as to put the contrary sentiments in their place" (Durkheim [1912] 1915: 83).

thought; and Marx's reworking of Hegel's concept of Spirit to comprehend the enigma of value-bearing objects within an economic system that revolves around production-for-exchange. Notice that Durkheim makes few appearances in Žižek's writings and, when he does, it is an occasion for a single absurd caricature: Durkheim is an organicist that leaves us in a Kantian deadlock "which cannot be resolved through any higher dialectical synthesis: society as such cannot but appear as a Thing-in-itself, forever out of grasp of our cognitive capacities" (2005: 333). It's as if *Elementary Forms* never existed. Durkheim quite literally does the exact opposite of what is claimed by his critic.[17] If Žižek has little to say regarding Durkheim he has even less use for Max Weber who makes a few appearances only as an accessory to Fredric Jameson's 'vanishing mediator' phrase. One can imagine the concept of *jouissance* as an analog to charisma or mana, but this work remains to be done. If one insists on synthesizing Hegel with Lacan, Freud, Žižek, or any other psychologist, one will search in vain for the whole because, like the value of the commodity (value being the absolute subject-substance of modernity), when the thing is examined analytically, twisting and turning the thing, there is no value. Value is not 'in' the utility of the individual thing, the physical body or finite being, but emerges and endures as a social fact within the exchange relation and only within that relation (Marx [1867] 1976: 148; cf. Durkheim 1974: 57). Psychology and survey research, etc., probe the individual or a multitude and hope to make contact with the social and the infinite and, not surprisingly, find a hole where there should be a whole.[18]

---

17 One can examine the few uninformed, textbook caricatures of Durkheim for oneself, which consist mostly just recycled paragraphs from one book to another: (2000d: 29; 2001b: 102; 2003: 77; 2006b: 26; 2012: 583, 633). When one eliminates the repetitions, Žižek is really left with only one thing to say about Durkheimian sociology and gives the distinct impression he knows nothing about it at all.

18 Schroeder lets us in on a secret: "In sublation, contradictions are not merely negated. They are also preserved. And yet there is always implicitly an unsublated trace, a vanishing mediator, an unaccountable fourth, which implicitly remains after the triadic operation of the dialectic" (1998: 11). This "fourth" is a contradictory leftover or surplus that has become disconnected from the whole but, as we know, will eventually return. The postmodern leftover is the thing that makes the psyche go and keeps the social beehive abuzz. Every theorist that matters has at the center of their thought this problem of the enigmatic surplus: value, charisma, mana, and so on. But postmodern theory is fixated on this quicksilver remainder in the abstract (it makes conferences and books go) while modernists convincingly demonstrate that the "fourth" is really no fourth at all but is a reflection of the 'transcendental' third. The 'leftover' is real, but it is not the mediator that has dropped out of the dialectical process, nor is it an empty signifier or some kind of lack, etc., the way it is paraded about in postmodern theory, but a deformity in the structure of Spirit. The myth of this postmodern fourth is the product of irony and alienated sideways

What all of this means is that the egoist falls backwards into the dichotomy and the identity of universals and individuals with a missing social and institutional substrate or ground that works to unify extremities.[19] Mediation, the middle, is excluded. Žižek follows Adorno in rejecting Hegelian speculative dialectics (unity is a place of negative fictions) as well as rejecting the concept's self-development, hobbled as it is by the obstacle imposed on the concept (2000b: 102). Mediation becomes synonymous with disintegration rather than synthesis (2012: 383). These regressions do not fit with the spirit or letter of Hegel but does jibe with Freud's dismissive comments on speculative philosophy[20] and is in conformity with the pessimistic mood of critical scientific

glances. As Haraway says, "Irony is about contradictions that do not resolve into larger wholes, even dialectically, about the tension of holding incompatible things together because both or all are necessary and true. Irony is about humor and serious play. It is also a rhetorical strategy and a political method, one I would like to see more honored within socialist-feminism" (2016: 5). Irony is associated with postmodern chic as "the only legitimate stance of discourse.... And to the extent that postmodernism denies the possibility of a metanarrative or a totalizing discourse, irony would appear to be its natural medium..." The takeaway is that "we are condemned to fragments of past traditions which we are powerless to reintegrate" (Higgins 1990: 199–200). Let us not overlook that 'irony' is literally *feigning ignorance* and this meaning is reflected in its etymology. The dangers of irony include cynical and iconoclastic mockery, endless reflection, self-satisfaction, empty subjectivity, and the inflation of the self to the point of the absolute (Hegel [1821] 1991: 180–82). Clutching fast to abstractions can lead one to say "precisely the opposite of what he wanted to say" (Hegel [1830] 1991: 273). We will have a more to say about dialectics versus perspectivalism and irony at a later date but, for now, I would ask readers to simply reflect on how Marx 'deconstructs' the general formula for capital to excavate the source of surplus value in surplus labor. What I find interesting about postmodern theory is that most of it reflects a kind of 'paranoid' suspicion that capital is really just a text, i.e., it converts concrete social praxis and history into word strings that are susceptible to infinite analysis. If there's a "fourth," it is merely the leakage of magic back into praxis or the disjointed and enigmatic product of traumatized academics. As Freud surmises, healthy and developed egos trend toward syntheses and unifications whereas neurotics wallow in contradictions and actively resist resolutions due to the psychological premiums gained through persistence (1950: 20, 58–9). And, of course, one cannot rule out the psychotic point of view that negates the absolute through endless textual production and arcane jargon.

19 "The *ratio* recoils into irrationality as soon as in its necessary course it fails to grasp that the disappearance of its substrate — however diluted — is its own work, the product of its own abstraction" (Adorno 1973: 148–49).

20 Through two lines from Heine, who was related to Freud's wife, Martha Bernays (Jones 1961: 67), Freud takes a cheap shot at Hegel (Heine was Hegel's student in Berlin and the references to the nightcap and the dressing-gown leave little room for error). Freud also takes shots at Marx and Hegel in his talk on 'worldviews,' painting speculative philosophy as a vain attempt to logically totalize the entire universe (1965: 198–99). Nonetheless, a few pages later Freud advocates for the dictatorship of reason as if he had not the least bit

thought today.[21] There are sufficient reasons to be pessimistic, but the negative absolute of capital is not all there is, antinomy is incomprehensible apart from universal norms, and negations are meaningless without positivity. Let us take our cue from Durkheim instead. "We don't see why there should be an antinomy rather than a harmony between the mind and things" (Durkheim 2004: 116). This harmony is impossible if we raise ourselves no higher than the understanding and iconoclastic diatribes that 'radical' critique shares with conservatism. Conservative common sense is rightly excoriated by radical critique, yet, the latter usually amounts to nothing more than the playful inversion of common sense, e.g., we do not use money because it *has* value, it 'has' value because we use it as a medium of exchange. This is true insofar as it goes but it does not go beyond intersubjectivist constructions. Magic also likes to enact such inversions as techniques of disruption (Durkheim [1912] 1995: 40).

In the face of a "rising tide" of death (accidental overdoses, suicides, massacres, and ordinary homicide) a disorganized society seems incapable of tackling the problem in a rational manner. Only when problems reach a crisis point of rare strength does the public's attention become "sufficiently absorbed" to the point that the wave of death can "be seen as a whole, coordinated and systematized, and then become the bases of complete theories of life" (Durkheim [1897] 1951: 369–70).

> In fact, in Rome and in Greece, it was when society felt itself seriously endangered that the discouraging theories of Epicurus and Zeno appeared. The formation of such great systems is therefore an indication that the current of pessimism has reached a degree of abnormal intensity which is due to some disturbance of the social organism. We well know how these systems have recently multiplied. To form a true idea of their number and importance it is not enough to consider the philosophies avowedly of this nature, such as those of Schopenhauer, Hartmann, etc. We must also consider all the others which derive from the same spirit under different names. The anarchist, the aesthete, the mystic, the

---

of knowledge regarding Hegel's program and, in *Moses and Monotheism*, Freud does a fair Hegel impersonation on the topic of spiritualization (1939: 146–47).

21 Of course, the bad absolute of the modern world is capital and its law is no law. The lack of regulation in production is synonymous with murder (Marx [1867] 1976: 609). However, a bad absolute, the evil, is by its nature also a finite absolute in contrast to the also-existing and more powerful infinite absolute that, so long as humans remain social, will survive long after capital has passed on and been replaced with a new mode of production and accumulation. Contra C.J. Arthur and Hans-Georg Backhaus, Hudis is correct that the concept of capital is philosophically inadequate to Hegel's absolute Idea (2012: 15, 23).

> socialist revolutionary, even if they do not despair of the future, have in common with the pessimist, a single sentiment of hatred and disgust for the existing order, a single craving to destroy or to escape from reality.
>
> DURKHEIM [1897] 1951: 370

The most comprehensive theory in contemporary critical social philosophy is an offshoot of this same spirit of pessimism and disgust. If simply getting Hegel wrong is Žižek's sin, he is no sinner.[22] But let us not forget that all his brilliance left him slack-jawed and platitudinous in the face of Arab Spring and Occupy,[23] led to an endorsement of Trump's presidential campaign,[24] and finds him hosting a show for a propaganda and disinformation wing of the Russian state. Teachers are in the service of moral forces (Weber 1946: 152) but teachers do not themselves escape the influence of a morally corrupted social system (Durkheim [1897] 1951: 372) so we cannot expect straight guidance to automatically flow from the shapers of opinions, formed as they are by degenerate currents of opinion. Žižek is a cynical opportunist that leads only to more Žižek. Perhaps 'late capitalism' just turns everyone into perverts and that's all there is to it. If for no other reason, this would be cause enough to return (again) to the thinkers of yesterday. Hegel, Marx, Durkheim, Weber, and a few others, endure to various degrees not merely because of academic rituals and deference to tradition but because they are representatives of an important orientation: at a minimum, they all had the concept and the dialectical method for conceptual development.[25] If contemporary sociology has abandoned its faith in society our classical pioneers did not lack faith. One cannot have the concept if one lacks faith in the concept or has exchanged

---

22   "And whoever lacks the capacity to put on blinders, so to speak, and to come up to the idea that the fate of his soul depends upon whether or not he makes the correct conjecture at this passage of this manuscript may as well stay away from science" (Weber 1946: 135).

23   Reflecting upon the exhaustion of Occupy and the Arab Spring in *The Year of Dreaming Dangerously*, Žižek can be found extoling the virtues of the revolutionary *sociopath* (2012c: 124–25).

24   In 2019 Žižek reaffirmed his earlier position on Trump because he believes that one of the results emerging in opposition to Trump is the radicalization of the Democratic Party. He is correct that the Democratic Party is basically corrupt and perverse, serving the interests of oligarchs over the working class, but this is another instance of a long tradition of confusing fragments of rhetoric, platforms, and disgruntlement for genuine 'radicalism.'

25   As usual, our goal of synthesizing the classics is in pretty bad shape. Smith says that "Simmel is an acquired taste, Durkheim a grey eminence, Tönnies an afterthought, and even Marx ... is an embodied Idea, a screen for projection and debate. Only Max Weber is a living presence ..." (2019b).

concepts for lifeless variables. And, rather than abandoning Žižek altogether, let us rehabilitate parts of his work where possible and, where it is impossible, let us confine his thought to the wings of the madhouse we have constructed.

Faith amounts to the will to be allied to your fellow human being and to remain loyal, lawful, and true to them. To know things and to reason is necessary but without the capacity for valuing things ('faith') there is no point in obtaining truth or knowledge; indeed, truth would be worthless without faith. 'Truth' has always meant faith and loyalty "in a service of causes. A cause ... links various human lives into the unity of one life" (Royce 1909: 307). The law is a unity of faith and reason that preserves the personality as an end. We are here at ground zero for sociology: the sublation of the twin axes of solidarity and regulation within collective consciousness (the essence of society). If, as Durkheim says, sociology is ultimately concerned with authority, that is because, at bottom authority is the synthesis of the "communion of thought and adhesion to the rules of the group" (Comte-Sponville 2007: 14). Our problem with regard to the absolute is not the lack of free thought or the 'materials' from which to develop things in the direction of the absolute: the entire "history of the human mind is the very history of the progress of free thought" (Durkheim [1897] 1951: 375). The problem is that the "irresistible" drive of free thought is also consistent with social disintegration and when society disintegrates free thought actually gives way to defensive enclaves. The thing that brings a halt to reflective disintegration, as well as defended outposts, is the syllogism. The word 'syllogism' might sound quaint or outdated, and one might prefer 'dialectic' instead, which is fine, so long as we understand that 'dialectic' is a method with a structure that exceeds its use as an academic buzzword.

The corporate syllogism (Durkheim's proposed restoration and renovation of the ancient guild model into a "single system") is a unified organ integrating productive life at all scales of existence. The reconnection and further construction of "particular" constitutional groups of professions, under the "general influence" of a modest, regulatory state that works to promote organizational solidarity, provides a concrete milieu in which each "individual consciousness" learns discipline and is protected from moral corrosion and death ([1897] 1951: 381–83). The nearest things we have in America to compare to these 'corporations' are weak and corrupt professional associations, pressure groups, organized interests, and crumbling labor unions, which are not really comparable at all. The durability of the old "guild spirit" in the face of incredible external and internal opposition (something like a war on five or six fronts simultaneously) is worth further examination (Weber 1981: 136–61) but the decisive point, at this moment, is not that the old guild system or medieval corporations do not fit the bill but that we have the concept from which to generate a new fact.[26] Who knows what will become of us, but the main thing is that the affirmative resources for reconstruction, to the extent that capital and the state, i.e., the "mistress of capital" (Durkheim 1978: 99), have not completely destroyed them, are already here as extensions of prior social forms.[27] But even as the old forms have vanished or been forgotten, nothing logically or necessarily prevents their resurrection. Indeed, all our major classical theorists insist that not only can the dead walk again but that their reemergence is, in a way, *inevitable*. The old gods and impersonal forces rise again (Weber 1946: 149) because every society dies and is reborn and it is during these transitions that a new spiritual form relieves another of its charge and takes "over the empire of the world from its predecessor" (Hegel [1807] 1977: 492). Each 'fresh start' appears to do so without regard for the past, yet, the past is "recollected" and "preserved" within it (Ibid.). We may resist being dissolved under the weight of capital, that remains to be seen, but praxis will have to work out the concept in a more developed form. It would be nice if the collective consciousness of society (sociology) could lead the way, but unfortunately, it lost its way some time ago.

Before World War Two, science in general lost contact with society and, after the war, sociology decided to cash in on prevailing trends. The 'Frankfurt School' noted that, "In modern society, science is just another branch of the division of labor."

> In the same way that an automobile factory puts out trucks and passenger cars, and a farm produces grain and cattle, universities are supposed to provide new methods and techniques for industry and administration. The aims of production or administration are determined by economic needs or political agreements on which the scientific branch of the division of labor does not have any direct rational influence. The ends and aims of society are considered independent of reason and therefore irrational.
> Institute of Social Research 1944: 10

---

26 Weber too suggests a corporate or guild syllogism whereby the French and English forms were hobbled and dissolved earlier than the more durable German form precisely because the German "guild spirit" enjoyed the mediating particularity of urban political power in a way the other European forms did not (1981: 156–57).

27 Marx and Durkheim agree that capital seeks to decimate secondary groups and institutions leaving the state, under capital's control, to pick up the slack. And not only does the state do a terrible job in performing the functions that had been previously performed by secondary groups, to preserve the interests of capital and the allure of private enterprise, the state is actually required to do a bad job of it. In a capitalistic society, the state must necessarily be horrible, corrupt, and incompetent such that citizens look only to corporations to solve the big problems that cannot be solved by self-reliance. Of course, corporations are also the source of the big problems.

The only growth areas in the contemporary social sciences are criminal justice and criminology and the remnants incapable of self-immolation in the fires of corporate synergy have lost their way. Marx "dreamed of the economic being reabsorbed into a (transfigured) social; what is happening to us is the social being reabsorbed into a (banalized) political economy" (Baudrillard 1983b: 81).

I may have been too subtle in the previous volume but the key to the joint rejection of 'society' and the corollary 'authority' lies in the confusion of society (the universal) and community (particularity). As W.H. Auden says, society entails the subordination of individuals to a whole and, as such, the whole thing entails hierarchical systems of control. The modern sense of community, by contrast, is anti-coercive and the only authority on display is that which is freely chosen by each individual member (2002: 492). But community and society are not mutually exclusive, in fact, society as we think about it is only conceivable as filled out by a practically infinite number of communities. A universal makes little sense without the involvement of a plurality of mediating communities linking concrete individuals to a universal element and social life, reduced to a web of nothing more than free-choice communities devoid of shared substance and overarching duties, inevitably devolves into tribal identification and rancor. Lacking mediating institutions, the individual's relationship to the universal is futility itself — qualities remain deactivated (Marx [1867] 1976: 149) and personal devotion is reduced to the hurling of burnt sacrificial waste into a void hoping that it somehow registers with an invisible and forbearing god who will grant a miracle (cf. Smith 1927: 359–60).

Communities disconnected from a larger society are just a jumble of first names and puppy loves[28] waiting to be transformed into cash and corpses.[29] The function of critique is not to liquidate society and reduce life to a collection of one-sided individuals attempting to professionalize their identities, but to theorize and transpose alien forces and processes (reintegrate them into the symbolic order where they belong) such that consciousness can know its own dynamics and put them to rational use while still preserving a moral and aesthetic *residuum* that makes social life enjoyable. This is not a proposal for symptom enjoyment for members of the cult of immediacy. Hegel's deceptively simple idea of Spirit coming to know itself as Spirit is still the program and we could consider a great deal of progress to have been made if in the future

---

28   I hope fans of F. Scott Fitzgerald (1922: 6) will not be too disappointed.
29   The unattended individual is plagued by insatiable wants and desires — they want to *have* it all; communities represent the ground where desires are rectified with the basic needs for *being* a human; a society, as a unified constellation of communities, is a reconciliation of wanting and being in the sphere of *becoming*.

delusional fanatics could be made to understand that the command from on high to destroy their impure neighbors does not emanate from a cosmic being living behind the moon but from their own collective projections (Durkheim [1893] 1984: 56). Sociology's unique task in this endeavor is to explain collective action and institutional dynamics (the moment of particularity within the syllogism that links individuals to the dimension of the universal). Brains,[30] individuals, his-stories, and the cosmic unfolding are not our business[31] but everything in between is, or should be, our business.

Takeaways from the first volume include the weird nature of ritual energy strands (~) and the objectification of these filaments as durable aspects of social life as well as the crystallization of ceremonial energy yielding a 'parabolic allegory' of solidarity and regulation that can either disintegrate or hypertrophy depending upon the degree of eccentricity that it enjoys. We know, for example, that when innovations are taboo, a social system has closed into a tight and repressive circle and, conversely, when Barber's *Adagio* is transformed into an electronic dance remix, without so much as a criminal indictment, eccentricity has reached a linear extreme. Another advantage of this odd ribbon is that unlike the figure of the circle (Simmel, Durkheim, Wahl, etc.),[32] the Möbius accentuates dialectical *polarity* over the binary infinity of a closed system that leads only to identities or *diametric* oppositions. Biology is circular, but social history is not (Auden 2008: 476) and no form of social organization above the most basic is reducible to diametric antagonisms.[33] The dead end of hermeneutic subjectivism, with its interpretive circle, must be sublated. Hermeneutics "entails a sharp opposition to the sort of objectivity and non-implication which is supposed to characterise the scientific explanation of

---

30   Biological and psychological reductionism represent "intellectual nihilism" (Durkheim 1974: 9).
31   The psycho-physical, psychologies, and the merely subjective are dead ends (Weber 2000: 339).
32   "For too long have we wandered too far from things .... / For a true thing is a living soul.... / Yet the thing is there, dark radiance.... / Each thing is closed up in the manner of a circle" (Wahl 2017: 263). For Durkheim's image of the social circle see *The Sociogony*. With Marx we know that circulation itself does not make a thing a commodity yet, simultaneously, a thing cannot be a commodity outside of circulation. In the same way, a person does not rise to the level of a personality by virtue of belonging to a circle, yet, personality is impossible outside of the social circle. From Marx we also know that the circle of circulation is a syllogism ([1859] 1970: 94) and from Hegel and Durkheim we know that, as a peculiar subject, society is not only a conceptual being but one that works itself up syllogistically to higher forms of rational consciousness.
33   Unlike other creatures, the human being "cannot pass into any other organization upon Earth, without turning backwards, and wandering in a circle" (Herder 1966: 127).

things" (Ricoeur 1981: 165). The dialectic associated with the interpretive circle, itself opposed to the "enchanted circle of subjective idealism" (1991: 234) is sunk in antique dialectics (dialogue) whereas speculative dialectics are capable of reaching systematic objectivity. When two interpretations fail to resolve in the textual meringue of academic discourse the consequences are socially irrelevant; when one of *our* loops gets bent out of shape, i.e., brutal circularity or monstrous linearity (Worrell 2019: 215), we find a rise in mortality rates.[34]

In the previous volume I pulled on many threads that will be brought into systematic unity in the remaining volumes. In other words, I put myself in the awkward situation of writing a book I would have to negate in later books. Readers of *The Sociogony* may have been perplexed as I twisted Hegel, Marx, Durkheim, and Weber this way and that along a path through the arcane problems of the structure of the concept, syllogisms, and the defense of disobedience as the partners of freedom, reason, social facticity, and authority.[35] Social

---

34 The criticism aimed at pragmatism and phenomenology can be levelled at hermeneutics as well for failing to construct an ontology and method for raising explanations 'above' the scale of interaction networks (see Ricoeur 1981: 174) or even above the level of the abstract individual where ideological distortions are reduced to a problem of a "subject's self-misunderstanding" (Ibid: 260). Ricoeur does a fairly good job describing the shape and dynamics of Hegel's *Geist* up to a point (1991: 230) but where the reconstruction falls short is not grasping that a sociological phenomenology is neither *of* consciousness nor "spirit *in* the element of consciousness" but, rather, a phenomenology of Spirit as an external, coercive, and irreducible form of consciousness that is not 'in' consciousness at all. Per Marx, value is something that two commodities (alienated labor products masking a social exchange relation between owners) have in common yet neither one of them actually possess (cf. Hegel 1988: 455). "Production by a solitary individual outside society — a rare event, which might occur when a civilised person who has already absorbed the dynamic social forces is accidentally cast into the wilderness — is just as preposterous as the development of speech without individuals who live *together* and talk to one another" (CPE: 189). Surely, we align ourselves with the reconstructive agenda of hermeneutics, contra deconstructionism, but descriptions and intentions run toward infinite regression and sociology is supposed to be the defense against regression; rational explanations are limited and have defined limits (cf. Weber 2000: 332). Furthermore, the reduction of *Geist* to an ego-alter analogy as an analytically acceptable substitute is frankly absurd (Ricoeur 1991: 237). Ricoeur admits that Hegel has no real intellectual equal, but that Husserl has "the decisive advantage ... in his uncompromising refusal to hypostatize collective entities and in his tenacious will to reduce them in every instance to a network of interactions" (Ibid: 244). If this were an adequate criticism, and if interaction networks and the intersubjective bias were adequate to the task, Marx's analysis of the value forms, for example, would have pulled up short at the point where the universal equivalent "comes and goes" ([1867] 1976: 183) with each fleeting, accidental exchange (cf. Durkheim [1912] 1915: 228).

35 As we will see, continuously enacted disobedience produces life whereas obedience leads to authoritarianism and death (see Trueblood 1942).

facts are not necessarily indicators of an ontology gone awry, the failure of praxis, or of a world of individual subjugation in the way that critical theory normally apprehends them. Social facts are commanding and coercive, however, they also have pretensions toward being authoritative and, as such, should be capable of providing reasons in the face of challenges. A command is not directed to a thing but "implies that the person addressed is capable of obedience or disobedience" (Auden 2008: 202). If a commanding 'fact' cannot stand on reason then it can only rule on the basis of brute force[36] or terror and, in the final analysis, once a fact devolves to the point of an unloved, authoritarian beast, the public need do no more than let it fall through passive measures (avoidance) or active hyper-obedience (malice) that makes institutional processes come to a grinding halt. Critical sociology cannot imagine how capital and the commodity reign unchallenged except for assuming that the public is mesmerized or too terrified to disobey. But contrary to the beliefs of some Marxists, the commodity and money are as old as city life. These facts do not and cannot rule simply on the basis of reification, inertia, and terror for centuries or millennia so there must be some reason for their longevity and vitality (Durkheim [1912] 1995: 2).

Like other facts, the commodity is not an unalloyed object of love or hatred but a thing that inspires an ambivalence *"sui generis*, derived from respect more than fright, and where the dominating emotion is that which *la majesté* inspires in men"* (Durkheim [1912] 1915: 79). Even if we destroyed the capitalist regime of production tomorrow an equally awe-inspiring system of forced labor would probably ensnare the survivors. Capitalism is creepy, there's no doubt about it, and capitalism is not fulfilling the role of Spirit as Hegel envisioned it. If the capitalist free market was an actual universal moral system relating everyone then the *use* of human life as bits of variable capital would run up against a limit that prevents *abuse*, but empirically, we know that the abuse of life under capital knows no bounds, including mass murder. Nonetheless, even if it is weird and contradictory, capitalism is a spiritual form[37] and all forms of Spirit are surprising.

---

36   Submission to brute force suppresses reason and atrophies "intellectual and spiritual development" (Weber 2003: 92).

37   Value is a bizarre negative universal that manages to embody both modern individual and archaic particular autonomies while reducing almost all social relations to pure externality through exchange (cf. Durkheim [1912] 1915: 225). In the place of conceptual unity, we find only mechanical linkages and connections animated by some depraved force that leaves goods and dead bodies in its wake. It is likely not an exaggeration to suggest that, since time immemorial, when things fall apart society is plagued by monsters animated by evil forces. In a later volume we will explore the connection between social disorganization and the negativity (impurity) of universal force (cf. Durkheim [1912] 1915: 227) and

It has been imagined that if the proletariat cannot or will not dig the grave of capitalism as predicted by Marx, perhaps the owners of the shovels will do the work themselves. But if we wait around expecting capitalism to destroy itself I suspect we will wait a good long while. Revolution and authoritarian reaction cannot be our only options and before we slaughter one another, run billionaires through wood chippers, or ship rednecks off to reeducation camps we had better have a pretty good grasp of the shape and dynamics inside the house of the bad absolute and the prospects for a dialectical reformation.

> Where is the house of / any one dying?
> Thither I speed and / turn the knob of the door,
> Let the physician and the priest timidly withdraw,
> That I seize on the ghastly man / and raise him with / resistless will;
> O despairer! / I tell you, you / shall not go down ....
>   WHITMAN [1847] 1854

---

we will also have occasion to explore the retrograde particularization of grace in the evolution of Protestantism. As a preview, however, we can say that with Calvin's adherence to the doctrine of predestination we find an erosion of the universal positive reflected in Weber's phrase "even no god" ([1930] 2001: 61) and the consequent flourishing of the universal negative necessitating either the destruction of Satan and his realm, which was not pursued, because, after all, a bad universal is apparently better than none at all, or, alternatively, a mechanism that resolved the problem of the absconded positive devil (Jesus), which they did, in a new orientation toward labor within the confines of a calling. I think we would all agree that the sanctification of money, commodities, and capital was wide of the mark with respect to generating a new positive universal which makes one wonder why we would fight over Value and its forms rather than against Value and all its forms.

Acknowledgements

Thanks to Chris Altamura, Robert J. Antonio, David Arditi, Harry Dahms, David Fasenfest, Tony Feldmann, Dan Krier, David Norman Smith, Tony Smith, and all the participants of The Symposium for New Directions in Critical Social Theory at Iowa State University.

Figures

1. The odyssey of the concept 39
2. The external separation of the concept 54
3. Indeterminate regressions 55
4. Atomic disintegration 56
5. The dialectics of production 57
6. The social octahedron 223
7. The concealment of 'recourage' 225

Abbreviations

A number of sources have been referenced so frequently that abbreviations are relied upon for the sake of tidiness. I have also abbreviated some reference works such as encyclopedias and dictionaries the details of which are listed below.

AJ   *Ancient Judaism*, Max Weber (1952).
C   *Capital*, Karl Marx. *Vol. 1* ([1867] 1976); C, 2: *Vol. 2* ([1884] 1978); C, 3: *Vol. 3* ([1894] 1981). A reference to page 150 in volume 3, for example, would appear as: (C, 3: 150).
C, 2   see above.
C, 3   see above.
CPE   *A Contribution to the Critique of Political Economy*, Karl Marx ([1859] 1970).
DOL   *The Division of Labor in Society*, Emile Durkheim ([1893] 1984).
EFRL   *The Elementary Forms of Religious Life*, Emile Durkheim, translated by K. Fields ([1912] 1995).
EP   *Encyclopedia of Philosophy*, (1967). A reference to page 150 in volume 3, for example, would appear as: (EP, 3: 150).
ES   *Economy and Society*, volume 1, Max Weber, (1978); ES, 2: volume 2. A reference to page 150 in volume 2, for example, would appear as: (ES, 2: 150).
ESS   *Encyclopedia of the Social Sciences*, edited by Edwin R.A. Seligman ([1930–1934] 1933–1937). A reference to page 150 in volume 3, for example, would appear as: (ESS, 3: 150).
FMW   *From Max Weber*, edited by Hans H. Gerth and C. Wright Mills (1946).
G   *Grundrisse*, Karl Marx ([1857] 1973).
MECW   *Collected Works of Marx and Engels*, Karl Marx and Friedrich Engels ([1835–1895] 1975–2004). A reference to page 150 in volume 44, for example, would appear as: (MECW, 44: 150).
PESC   *The Protestant Ethic and the Spirit of Capitalism*, Max Weber (1930).
PM   *The Economic and Philosophical Manuscripts of 1844*, Karl Marx ([1844] 1964).
PR   *Elements of the Philosophy of Right*, G.W.F. Hegel ([1821] 1991).
PS   *Phenomenology of Spirit*, G.W.F. Hegel ([1807] 1977).
RC   *The Religion of China*, Max Weber (1951).
RSM   *The Rules of Sociological Method*, Emile Durkheim (1982).
S   *Suicide*, Emile Durkheim ([1897] 1951).
SGS   *The Sociology of Georg Simmel* (1950).
SL   *Science of Logic*, G.W.F. Hegel ([1812] 1969).

Introduction

> And so there come beggars in our streets and tramps on our roads; and poverty enslaves men who we boast are political sovereigns; and want breeds ignorance that our schools cannot enlighten; and citizens vote as their masters dictate; and the demagogue usurps the part of the statesman; and gold weighs in the scales of justice; and in high places sit those who do not pay to civic virtue even the complement of hypocrisy; and the pillars of the republic that we thought so strong already bend under the increasing strain.
>
> HENRY GEORGE [1879] 1956: 546

Social facts with universal world-historical significance include capitalism, of course, but also Greek philosophy, Roman law, the Catholic Church and the concept of office, medieval estates, and earth-shattering Protestantism. However, first on this list is ancient Judaism (AJ: 5). During the Babylonian exile, the priestly mediators of the literary arts managed to get the upper hand on, and, in the post-Exilic congregations, almost completely extinguished the charisma of ecstatic prophecy (AJ: 380). Prophecy and charisma were reduced to sectarian mysteries and relegated to the margins, whereas the center of (urban) religious life revolved around a new form of solidarity and control. Charismatic prophecy is one of the primary sources of social disintegration (Weber 1981: 45), collective *devaluation* (FMW: 329), and the rejection of ecstasy and prophecy is decisive for moving a people from fruitless alternations of anarchy and fatalism. Either the Jews would submit to a unified textual authority, "the first properly canonical book with binding authority on the national community" or they would be reduced to "'welter and waste'" (Alter 2019: xlv, xliii). Beyond the effects of previous legal codes, commandments, and lists of prohibitions and punishments, the Hebrew bible, if not eliminating magic entirely, by the time of Rabbinical Judaism, had eliminated positive magic (god coercion) and restricted its role to that of a negative demonology. The importance of the Hebrew bible, the rabbi, and the synagogue are impossible to overestimate with respect to the taming of superstition.

Miracles, religious predeterminism, and demonologies seem like delusions from the past (or the other side of the world)[1] yet, in contemporary America, the belief in a biblical god that runs the show, entirely or at least partially, is a

---

1 In Eastern and Central Europe, the belief in fate and miracles is a dominant position (Pew Research Center 2017).

dominant view among almost all people with a high school education or less and who vote Republican (Fahmy 2018) and nearly 80 percent of all Americans believe in miracles (Pew Research Center 2017). It is here that Durkheim says we moderns are still plagued by the primitive mindset (EFRL: 25). We have many of the same "habits and desires of previous ages, but … [have] found mechanical means of satisfying them" (Bernal 1949: 111). Because so few people are educated to grasp the existence of universal laws (i.e., necessary relations) of society, "true miracles are thought possible in society. There is, for example, the accepted notion that a legislator can create an institution out of nothing and transform one social system into another, by fiat" (EFRL: 25). Just make America great again. *Voilà*! Superstition combined with economic stress and political decadence is a condition ripe for "messianic fascism" (Bernal 1949: 345).

Yoga is definitely out, but miracles, faith healing, and speaking in tongues, are all compatible with most forms of Evangelicalism in the global north (Pew Research Center 2011). Belief in magic, however, is not as widespread except for Hispanics; the evil eye, magic, witchcraft, and sorcery are influential for roughly 44 percent of Latinos (Lipka 2014). But magic takes many forms beyond the belief in spirits. Critical theory has, of course, had a long history of dealing with *magical thinking* but, beyond the truism that virtually everyone is guilty of a little mental magic from time to time, it seems clear that old-fashioned magic has not been extinguished in modern America as much as it has been transposed to the spheres of economics and politics (both of which have their roots and substance in religion). In other words, in a social form lacking conceptual integration we can expect to find 'magic' everywhere, if not in name, nonetheless following the logical patterns of magic working behind the backs of individuals in unrecognizable forms.[2]

Between positive empiricism that insists that "two things cannot be in one and the same place" and the realm of the concept where "distinctions are not posited as exclusively of each other" (Hegel 1988: 423), i.e., all things can be in one place at the same time, there is the mystical middle ground of 'magic'

---

2 The educated and rational adult might find belief in magic to be an embarrassment, an insult to reason, but anything weird or absurd can be alluring so long as a prestige is attached to it. In Renaissance Europe, magic was "the property of the educated" (Bechtold 2019) and while the educated abandoned magic for science over time due to its superior control over nature, those frustrated classes blocked from the means of scientific culture always have some form of superstition at their disposal. And where science runs up against something that it cannot control or predict, the door is open to a regression into magic or the unconscious contamination of science with mysticism.

where, like money, things can be in two places simultaneously.³ Dialectical analysis always involves a 'magical' dissection of the social fact such that the observing consciousness raises itself from understanding to the point of the concept by way of a panoramic or stereoscopic view.⁴ In judgments, the moment of self-alienation can go 'sideways' (e.g., a practically infinite loop of self-negations) whereby consciousness gets lost along the circuit of reconciliation; a more powerful, external necessity penetrates the progression and hurls judgment toward an abyss of confusion and self-destruction. The domain of reactionary populist politics is just such a realm where vast sums of money and effort have been expended with the aim of legitimating mass suicide. The concept, by contrast, does not lead to death but to life and where we find life marching toward voluntary suicide we can expect to find some form of superstition⁵ leading the way toward the expectation of some miraculous intervention.

Trump is no magician, far from it, however if we keep in mind that one of the decisive aspects of magic resides in the pleasurable profanation and inversion of the sacred for utilitarian ends (EFRL: 39–40) and, if we view Washington as a 'swamp' of impurity and corruption, Trump's mandate seems clear and somewhat novel in high-echelon American politics: driven by a desire for revenge, the populist base has propelled a vulgar⁶ battering ram (cf. EFRL: 26, 306) espousing a magic-like formulation into a morally impure and dysfunctional system in order to at least humiliate it or reduce its power.⁷ Our problem

---

3 The senses tell us that things are in one place at one time; magic is the realm where a thing can be in two places at the same time; but the concept (where all determinations have a common third) is the realm where everything is in the same place at the same time.

4 See my forthcoming chapter, "Magical Marx," in *The Mirror of Capital* (SUNY Press). When consciousness lacks conceptual freedom (under the spell of magic, empiricism, etc.) perception is itself also lacking (Hegel 1956: 197) but dialectical analysis also begins at the moment of self-deception and a suspicion of foreground appearances.

5 Here, 'superstition' literally means survival by means of standing off to the side of the rational self-development of reason.

6 Trump's base might admire the man, they were certainly surprised by his campaign, and he might impress them, but none of these concepts pertain to the realm of the sacred (Durkheim [1912] 1915: 103). Trump's base is mostly the 'common people' (*vulgus*) and Trump is merely the uncommonly common as far as they are concerned, i.e., a vulgarity that happens to appear wealthy and powerful. Anyone who has lived in small-town America recognizes in Trump an exaggerated version of the local bosses and blowhards that fill the ranks of land development, retail, politics, banking, etc. Trump is able to occupy the mental space of the county kingpin transposed to the national scale.

7 Jonathan Sacks, the former Chief Rabbi of the United Hebrew Congregations of the Commonwealth, situates the problem of magical thinking within the context of worship. In the modern West, the thing most celebrated and treated as sacrosanct is the individual self. In

is capital but to comprehend the command of capital today we are necessarily led into the circuits of mysticism, magic, miracles, taboo, and religious ecstasies, i.e., the stubborn residues that reason has so far been unable to reconcile. Where the absolute, and its form of thought is lacking, people will fall for anything. The choice is that between reason and life or death by superstition, but reason cannot be willed into existence.

1 Marxheimianism and the Return of the Repressed

Prior to World War One it was an article of faith amongst orthodox Marxists that proletarian revolution was inevitable, that capitalism necessarily digs its own grave, and those freedom-loving workers would, simply by lifting up their putrid carcasses all at once, topple the bourgeois order, ushering in a communist utopia (Worrell 2008) where comrades would do things like "hunt in the morning, fish in the afternoon, rear cattle in the evening, criticise after dinner, just as I have a mind, without ever becoming hunter, fisherman, shepherd or critic" (MECW, 5: 47). The kind of reassuring certainty that comes with dogma melted into thin air during 1914 when the workers of the world, rather than throwing off their chains of oppression, began slaughtering one another on the

---

> other words, egoism is not only a symptom of social disorganization but also a force of further disintegration that generates anxiety and the desire for reconciliation that, lacking solidarity with others, can only assume irrational forms. Even when the holy ego is surrounded by others, these others are somewhat like carbon copies of ourselves, affirming what we affirm, and disaffirming what we disaffirm, creating a virtual tribal bubble of homogenous sentiments. Growth comes from oppositional encounters, working through disagreements, and, as we see in Durkheim's *Suicide*, the life of resistance. Sacks says that rather than living together in one, big, metaphorical house (a nation) people want the experience of living in an infinite series of hotel rooms where everybody minds their own business and the only obligation one has is to not disturb the people in the rooms on either side. A house has belongings, it belongs to people, but people and hotels do not converge at the concept of belonging. "Nobody belongs to a hotel." No common good can come from this. "Have you noticed how magical thinking has taken over our politics?.... All you [have to] do is elect this strong leader and he, or she, will solve all our problems for us. Believe me, that is magical thinking. And then we get the extremes: the far right and the far left, the extreme religious and the extreme anti-religious, the far right dreaming of a golden age that never was and the far left dreaming of a utopia that never will be. And the Religious and the anti-religious equally convinced that all it takes is God, or the absence of God, to save us from ourselves. That too is magical thinking because the only people that will save us from ourselves is 'We the People'—all of us together" (National Public Radio 2019).

battlefields of Europe.[8] Marx and Engels had insisted that "the proletariat alone is a really revolutionary class" and that all other classes were beyond "conservative"—they were "reactionary" ([1848] 1972: 344) but in the aftermath of the war, radical students and scholars looking to update socialist and communist political theory, began to question the psyches of their erstwhile saviors (the identical subject-object of history) and discovered that workers were not only unreliable but, to a great extent, even anti-radicals. For Marx, the deformed nature of the mass of workers was not an issue (the worse the better as far as he was concerned) but with Durkheim we know that the ability to think and act reasonably is anchored not in the brain but in social organization.

There have been many important currents of neo-Marxist thought over the decades including the Budapest school, Situationism, the Praxis group, etc., but the most important, from the standpoint of the social psychology of authority, is the work stemming from the Institute of Social Research, or 'Frankfurt School' as it later became known. From the 30s through 1950 (the year *The Authoritarian Personality* was published) a powerful and synthetic foundation for a modern psychology of authority was laid down by the Frankfurters and cultivated in later decades by former members as well as their students. I argued in *The Sociogony* that a synthesis of Marx and Durkheim was neglected by critical theory when it chose Freud and Weber to probe the riddle of worker reaction. However, the neglected affinity between Marx and Durkheim is self-evidently valuable. Of course, this affinity is not obvious to *academic* Marxists who see no need for anything beyond beating the old drum slowly. But in an imaginary world where the oppressed and their leaders read and comprehended Marx, the limitations of the traditional intellectual horizon, as vast as it is, would become apparent once the problems of class solidarity, voluntary sacrifice, and deference to authority presented themselves. Marxism does not, and never really did have, the resources beyond psychoanalytic theory (which grasps society in an inverted form) to account for why the oppressed would, like primitives, destroy their fellow comrades before forsaking their collective representations and divine imperatives.

Marx underestimated the power of the sacred.[9] Religion itself is not the sacred but only "the administration of the sacred" (Caillois 1959: 20). While

---

8 We should be careful of making history and empirical existence into the criterion of conceptual truth (SL: 112). If Marx's writings on communism are lacking, we need to find the crux of the problem in the contradictions of the philosophy itself. The deficiencies were addressed in *The Sociogony* as well as Worrell and Krier (2018).

9 It would be fairer to say that Marx's appreciation for ethnology and primitive religions is muted or latent in his critique of political economy and the commodity. To draw out the fetish character of the commodity is only the beginning and not the end of the problem. In

religion is good at numbing the mind and playing dirty tricks on the unsophisticated, the sacred itself is the horrifying and absolute power that bends the will of individuals and whole classes of people as it sees fit and demands human sacrifice in bulk. No theorist better grasped the sacred and the moral economy of sacred objects from a social-realistic point of view than Durkheim. For people trying to grasp the enigma of exchange-value it would seem that knowing its origins would be beneficial, however, critical theory is in about the same place it was generations ago. No progress has been made in grasping value or

---

fact, as Durkheim convincingly tells us, 'fetishism' corresponds to nothing definite ([1912] 1915: 186) and rests upon an unarticulated set of presuppositions. For example, in *Capital*, the 'fetishism' of the commodity blunts the critique somewhat by spreading out along myriad lines: "metaphysical subtleties and theological niceties"; transcendence; "grotesque ideas"; "mystical character"; "enigmatic character"; "mysterious character"; reflections; "substitution"; "suprasensible"; "social"; "fantastic form"; and finally, "In order ... to find an analogy we must take flight into the misty realm of religion. There the products of the human brain appear as autonomous figures endowed with a life of their own, which enter into relations both with each other and with the human race. So it is in the world of commodities.... I call this the fetishism which attaches itself to the products of labor as soon as they are produced as commodities..." ([1867] 1976: 163–65). It is perfectly sensible to draw the analogy between religion and commodification, but it would be more to the point to simply place alienated labor products and reified ritual products within the realm of the sacred. On the surface of things, that seems ridiculous since the ritual production of totems is about religion and the routine manufacturing of commodities deals with economics, but things are not as cut and dry below the surface—the reason Marx conjures the specter of religion to begin with. There is always an 'economic' dimension to the sacred just as there is a sacred dimension to production and exchange. Everything is enveloped in a moral economy; it is all born in the sacred and religion. The question is less about the sacred status of the commodity *per se* than why the sacred assumes the particular form that it does under the capitalist regime of accumulation. Marx takes another shot at it toward the end of *Capital* where he says that the old gods of Europe were suddenly overthrown by a new and strange god, profit ([1867] 1976: 918) but the drive for profits "as the ultimate and the sole purpose of mankind" is only one important dimension of the sacred and by no means exhausts the problem of the authority of capital. The "lust of gold" (Marx [1867] 1976: 229) has the power to transform anything, even objects normally beyond the commercial transactions, into money but the love of gold is by no means modern nor the decisive aspect of capitalism (Weber [1930] 2001: 21) and, to emphasize this point, Marx even mentions the Phoenicians transmuting everything into the shape of money. The 'sacred' comes off as little more than a lot of bourgeois claptrap ([1867] 1976: 477, 793, 874, 889, 939) in defense of private property and immutable economic 'laws' yet, setting aside owner flimflam and rationalizations, when we survey the individualization of the sacred for as long as we have written records we find private property as marks and means of personal success. Marx is not wrong *per se* in his inferences, but I would like to make the audacious claim that the most valuable preparation for reading *Capital* is Durkheim's *Elementary Forms*. The best way to grasp Hegel's *Logic* is by reading *Capital* and the missing framework in which to comprehend economic value is through Durkheim, who was kind enough to leave a hint ([1912] 1915: 466).

its sacred nature and, consequently, critical theory has been reduced to an assortment of harmless fringe rituals. This dilemma is not for a lack of reading Marx, no, the problem is more complicated.

The only way to get Durkheim wrong is by not reading him; a few careful passes through *Elementary Forms* and readers can more than likely grasp what mana is and convey that idea in a succinct and comprehensible manner. In contrast, the only way to get Marx wrong is to actually read him, i.e., read him through the 'lenses' provided by certified academic Marxologists. Even though Marx is clear his disciples constitute a complex of insulated cults that pay little attention to impure productions originating from outside the canon; synthesis of ideas is tantamount to contamination and sacrilege (cf. Durkheim [1912] 1915: 244). When we ask a self-contained Marxist to explain value they usually equivocate and perhaps dispense a negative definition. Value eats Marxists for breakfast because the concept is not merely a category of the understanding situated in the domain of political economy but is one manifestation in the universal history of the sacred, i.e., absolute power.

The bad news is that Radical Transformation™ will require, among other things, a radical form of collective consciousness determined by social organization. But the framework of socially determined thought is *sacred*. The only chance Marxism has against capital is if it profanes value or raises critique to the same level of sacredness as its nemesis. There might be some Radical Transformation™ on the horizon but, unfortunately, it will not be the kind that Marxism dreams of. If we see Marx as trying to solve the enigma of surplus value (rooted in the exploitation and liquidation of the proletariat for the enjoyment of the bourgeoisie) how could the founder of modern sociology be neglected when one of Durkheim's foundational texts deals with sacrifice and self-destruction? Indeed, a perfect subtitle for *Suicide* would be *Invitations for Self-Destruction* (see Durkheim 2006: 154–55).[10] The proletariat is not merely the passive object of destruction. Rather, the proletariat has proven time and again that, when push comes to shove, it actively prefers partial or total suicide and even mass murder to positive freedom and that the invitations are

---

10   What is money, after all, but the symbolic residue of collective sacrifice? Moreover, the master theorist of solidarity is neither Marx nor Engels but Durkheim. What defeats all but altruistic suicide is communal solidarity (2006: 178). If the victory over capitalism is not inevitable the only thing that can deliver freedom is collective solidarity. It is plain that capitalism succeeds best where solidarity is weakest, but the real mystery of anti-solidarity resides not in the power of corporations or states to bust unions wide open but in the anti-union sentiments of workers themselves.

somehow irresistible.[11] We can forget about actual revolution for now and if we cannot have all of Marx we must have some of Durkheim who envisioned the dialectical process of history transforming the person who chases value into the value of concrete personality (S: 336–37; cf. SL: 531). In this volume I will advocate for the return of the repressed and resume my case for the 'Marxheimian' perspective on authority and the hurricane of self-negations that constitute the world of class subjugation.[12]

When last we met, I made the claim that the 'progressive' and 'radical' war on authority *per se* is self-defeating because authority (everywhere perceived as essentially *authoritarian*) is also the foundation for class solidarity and when authority is negated in favor of the cult of immediacy, personal identities, Me-Me autonomy, and negative freedoms, a void opens that fills with monsters and the longing for miracles. Without authority we cannot have collective representations and, lacking our guiding stars, we find ourselves lured by narcissists into a tangerine dream of voluntary self-lacerations for the pleasure of inflicting revenge on people that we imagine are disloyal to us or making individuals and groups suffer for contaminating that which was once great and pure. Besides, anything authoritative is merely the appearance of truth as it comes to people *at first* (Hegel 1988: 477) and is certainly not the last word on things, which is merely restating the obvious fact that we are born into a world

---

11 My colleagues tend to maintain that every time the working class engages in some spectacular act of self-negation the "real workers" are not actually on display. We are assured they are not real workers. The "real worker" compared to empirically existing workers takes on a mythological existence. We are still waiting for the "real workers" to intervene on behalf of freedom. For Marx himself, the more mutilated, deformed, immoral and puny the empirical worker actually is, the better (Worrell 2008), but in reality, collective inferiority leads not to social democratic revolution but, in our case, to political nightmares (cf. Durkheim 2006: 190). And the Left knows this at some level because every year it scours the margins of society for some new, vanguard substitute. Last year it was the anarcho-afro-trans-sex worker that was expected to fill the revolutionary void. As if they were not already sufficiently burdened, this 'leading edge' of revolutionary progress has to also redeem history for Ivy League professors and activist hipsters.

12 Bottomore's superficial glance at the "mutual disregard" existing between the followers of Marx and Durkheim is plagued by a strawman reduction of Durkheim to "the movement of ideas" in contrast to the materialist superiority of Marxism (1981: 912). Bottomore concludes that Durkheim's sociology "seems to me not to embody any superior solutions" other than the suggestion that Marxism might have to "pay attention" to "social consciousness" going forward (Ibid: 914). In the intervening years it seems clear to me that Marxist sociology, with only a handful of exceptions, has offered no solution at all and, without exception, has left no impression at all on social conditions. This claim makes one automatically suspect for being a 'post-Marxist' but I would argue that if you think this is 'post-Marxism' you're probably a pre-Marxist hobbled by an archaic social ontology fit for running a bank or monastery.

of social facts that we are not free to ignore but are also not prohibited from changing (Ibid: 476–78). And let us not overlook the obvious fact that most, if not the vast and overwhelming majority of individuals, will never go beyond received authority and blind tradition and that this 'altruistic' adherence to norms or the discourse of the venerable dead (Cassano 2019) at least partially protects against the authoritarianism of the moral vacuum (the discourse of mortification) created by dramatic social changes. If nothing else, authority does inhibit the slide into "naïve egoism" and, even if it is defective, representational authority is a "preparatory and transitory" stage "to subordination under an objectively ethical law, which transcends the 'I' as much as the 'thou,'..." (SGS: 261). Still, we arrive at "subordination" and that does not sit very well with the modern person that equates subordination with humiliating submission or surrender, but we can be subordinated by our unconscious drives and the caprice of the tyrant or we can live according to our collective dictates.[13] But make no mistake, there are those that are subordinated and there are the remainders, i.e., the dead.[14] Because human thought is essentially social, hierarchy and subordination are inescapable. Without "subordination" we can neither reason nor even understand anything and the powers of the individual intellect are wholly different from reason and inadequate to the task of grasping reality (Durkheim [1912] 1915: 170–73).

The human being, says Rousseau, was and is "born free, and everywhere he is in chains.[15] One who believes himself the master of others is nonetheless a

---

13 If we wish to use the somewhat dramatic language of 'surrender' it is a fact that the social being has surrendered to something. But the nature of that surrender is decisive. When we surrender to anything less than the collective conscience, surrender "passes over into savagery, forgetful of all fixed bonds and trampling love itself under foot" (Hegel 1987: 122).

14 Before getting hysterical, keep in mind that the prefix 'sub-' does not just mean being *under* something but also *close to* and *towards* something. And *ordination* means having the sacred conferred upon oneself by virtue of an arrangement or ordering of things. What we like to think is that we are always, already holy by virtue of our mere existence as individuals, yet, that is a piece of superstition, and not really the case. Like all forms of authority, the sanctity of the individual is a conferred status and if we exclude the existence of a literal god beaming goodness from behind the veil of stars, that leaves other people and institutions to do the conferring. If subordination all by itself does not have what it takes to make one sacred (EFRL: 35), remember that if subordination gets one close, it also all by itself does not have what it takes to reduce a person to the status of a tool or a moral impurity. If you want to be special, you'll have to earn it by living up to external standards.

15 This "everywhere" is only a slight exaggeration. "As Adam Hochschild observed, as late as 1800 roughly three-quarters of the world's population could be said to be living in bondage" (Scott 2017: 155–56).

greater slave than they" ([1762] 1978: 46).[16] How this paradoxical condition of mutual enslavement comes into existence, Rousseau is unsure. However, one thing is clear: more than simple force or coercion is required to hold people in perpetual bondage. Simple coercion and the application of force creates grave limitations on those who wield it—at all levels, from personal psychology to foreign policy and international relations, brute force is virtually antithetical to stability and success. The fate of the Mycenaean empire is illustrative:

> [I]n the long run, wholesale resort to force undermined the high king's position. Every town sacked meant less wealth to support the apparatus of political centralization. An unsuccessful expedition, such as that sent against Egypt in the early twelfth century B.C., ... discouraged princes and sub-kings from answering any future summons to war. At such a juncture after a disastrous raid, when the high king's resources were strained, his disappointed followers and domestic rivals would be likely to revolt. Such civil disorder would make it relatively easy for rude outer barbarians—the Dorians of subsequent Greek history—to invade the land and destroy the Mycenaean power. Thus we may surmise that, once launched on a path of predation, the high kings of Mycenae strove mightily but in the end vainly against the disintegration of their power.
>
> MCNEILL 1963: 192–93

Subjugated people who feel themselves to be under the burden of tyranny frequently abandon their homes; knowing that their productivity and wealth will be heavily taxed, they work with less intensity; sycophants and followers actively undermine and betray their superiors; and fellow tyrants leave their former allies to wither on the vine of isolation. Domination and simple coercion alone lead inexorably to disintegration.

> The state which oversteps this divinely willed limit and allows or causes the punishment of innocent people, undermines its own authority and every regard for its sovereignty in the minds of the citizens.... If this call remains unheard, then the reign of Queen Justice will not be restored, then our German nation and country will go to pieces through inner putrefaction and rotting, in spite of the heroism of our soldiers and their glorious victories!
>
> GALEN 1941

---

16 "He is a tyrant; that is, the vilest of slaves, and at the same time the most miserable of beings" (Rousseau 1889: 49).

However, what seems illegitimate from one angle may actually be conceived of as legitimate by those who submit to power.[17] Contemporary social thought has done a poor job in keeping separate and distinct the problem of authority and authoritarianism. Our modern hostility to authority, our longing for individualism, and the cult of the immediate has undermined the bases of solidarity, which is the precondition for social democracy.[18]

Where *we* find authority, we are sure that it is in fact mindless and illegitimate authoritarianism (political sadism).[19] I made the case in the introduction to the previous volume that contemporary sociology operates under the paradoxical double spell of nominalism and money, that concepts are treated as worthless and reduced to lifeless variables, and that the very structure of reason is deformed and alienated from its social ground when the dialectic is sacrificed for hypotheses and measurements.[20] Subjectivism, Gestalt psychology,

---

17   It is almost pointless to remind readers that even in a state of legitimacy "no perfect state of legitimacy is to be found anywhere" (Luckmann 1987: 110). What is domination for one person is perfectly fine for another. Lovers endure a servitude that slaves would balk at (Kureishi 2017: 101).

18   Progressives expect solidarity, critical thinking, and justice to magically occur from an ethic of outsized autonomy and individualism that undermines at every turn the very foundations and principles of solidarity, organization, and reason. American pluralism was rooted in the seemingly paradoxical fusion of individualism and conformity (Bellah et al. 1985: 148). The "alchemy of assimilation" (Simon 1914: 180) has been replaced with hyper-individualism and pseudo-tribalism. Take for example, the neoliberal fetish for 'diversity' and 'tolerance.' We are not speaking about genuine pluralism but what Hegel might call *mere diversity* that worships difference by elevating accidental characteristics to the level of essentialities. 'Diversity' and 'diversion' have the same root *divertere*, to turn apart in separate ways. Haidt is wrong about a good many things but he is correct in saying that nothing kills solidarity like diversity (2012: 277). This is why privileged white men in positions of power are eager to propagate this bauble at universities and within plush corporate environs. It is a weapon for dividing a population, diverting attention away from white supremacy and patriarchy, by pushing the struggle down to the 'meso' level of institutional life and placing the burden of managing the resulting antagonisms onto the divided themselves.

19   Of course, the authoritarian always misconstrues what amounts to brutal domination for genuine authority. "'You are too lenient, too lenient by far...' asserted the Colonel. 'Authority, coercion are what is needed. Put your foot down good and hard; the only way to manage a wife. Take my word for it.' The Colonel was perhaps unaware that he had coerced his own wife into her grave" (Chopin 1899: 186).

20   "In the social world we must recognize the working hypothesis as the form into which all theories must be cast a completely as in the natural sciences.... What we have is a method and a control in application, not an ideal to work toward.... [F]oresight does not go beyond the testing of [the] hypothesis" (Mead 1899: 369–70). See Gillespie (2008) on the nominalist revolution and the ascendency of hypotheses and variables over concepts and dialectics. In the nominalist world, syllogism is nothing more than a weak form of

intersubjectivity, and the various currents stemming from phenomenological inquiry are largely irrelevant when it comes to the problem of authority because, in the final analysis, they cannot even distinguish between reasons and rationalizations (Rokeach 1961: 252–53).[21] One cannot even distinguish between authority and authoritarianism (cf. Freud [1921] 1959: 76), obedience and disobedience, conformity and nonconformity, etc., when individual rationalizations convert one fact into another in the act of grasping the meaningful understandings of atomized actors. What is objectively irrational behavior on the part of individuals is magically transformed into rational choice through interpretations that cannot even make a place for the notion of objectivity. Whatever Marx's own view on authority, orthodoxy does a bad job when it comes to comprehending the dynamics of submission.[22]

The further we delve into the social psychology of subject classes the more we find a longing for subjugation and that domination can be perceived as *legitimate* under some circumstances, and that "the wrong" can be viewed as simultaneously "valid" (Hegel [1821] 1991: 88). Herein lies the decisive difference between simple domination or *coercion* and legitimate domination or *authority*. It is undeniable that rule makes recourse to fear and force, but simple mechanisms are limited in what they can achieve. "In order to secure authority over its subjects, domination imposes, brutalizes, bribes; but it also seduces"

---

analogical induction that leads to absurdities. Rather, it is the work of social absurdities and monstrosities that reduces the syllogism to weak inductions.

21 Rationalism definitely has the potential to defeat reason (Maritain 1939: 4). I do, however, appreciate Luckmann's insistence that legitimation is not simply an automatic product of impersonal systems (1987). The language of systems is one of fatalism and futility even as we recognize the reality of social systems. With Durkheim, we must see that the active agents in the legitimation process are individuals and groups engaged in intersubjective life; 'systems' are not self-legitimating. It is completely justifiable to conceive of capital as a self-moving system but 'underneath' that impersonal shell of the 'system' are the practically infinite acts of creativity of workers and capitalists struggling to control the labor process (Clawson 1980: 266). The emphasis on subjects and relations does not reduce legitimation to the scale of intersubjectivity nor does it neglect 'reification' but merely expresses the truism that even though society is not made in our image it is nonetheless made by us. Sociology has to wrestle with the paradox of facticities such that money, for example, will die if we do not abide by the rules, however, just try not using money. The intellectual positions of Luckmann et al. are not 'wrong' so much as they are symptomatic of estrangement. For example, we find a nominalist tendency uniting phenomenology with old natural law philosophy that scoffs at the 'transcendental' as regressive (see Gierke 1934: 95–105). In modern terms, they cannot locate any kind of Other or, where there is a 'big Other' (à la Žižek) it is merely a fiction, a flimsy signifier linked to nothing substantial. In other words, the Other would be little more than some kind of prejudice that falls apart the moment it comes into contact with reality.

22 See Avineri (1976: 38) on Marxism and authority—every form of rule *per se* is dictatorial.

(Cassano 2019). "Only he who *wills* to be coerced" said Hegel, can be *coerced* into anything" ([1821] 1991: 120). It is true that people can become resigned to "enforced domination" but, in the final analysis, "they do not concur in it, and consequently such a state can provide no stable equilibrium" (DOL: xxxii). The irrational and exploitative ordering of social classes, like we find in modern capitalist societies, typically rests on a condition where we find at least "a minimum of voluntary compliance" on the part of the subjugated (Weber 1978: 212).

> Voluntary devotion, which is offered as a free gift of love, is something different than compelled subordination. The personality that is responsible for its own actions does not then end up in a contradiction with itself if it bends before another person's higher insight, more mature judgment, and greater completeness due to its own inner convictions, if it sacrifices for the higher aspirations of a greater person.
> WEBER 2003: 93[23]

For Marx, the mere stirring of the mass of workers could not happen "without the whole superincumbent strata of official society being sprung into the air" (Marx 1973: 78) but as it turns out, "wageworkers under mature capitalism *do* accept the system" (Mills 1962: 468–69). Why would wage-slaves willingly consent to their own exploitation? This is a problem of authority or loved domination and is the central question of critical social theory.

Durkheim says that if sociology could be reduced to only one question, it would be the nature of social authority and that we, i.e., sociologists, should "seek, throughout the various forms of external constraint, the correspondingly various kinds of moral authority and to discover what causes have given

---

23   "On the basis of such convictions, the autonomous woman can of course also make her husband's will her own, and place *her* wishes and interests behind *his*. But when that can occur may only be decided before the forum of her own conscience, and only from case to case. It may absolutely not be decided for all time at the very beginning of their relationship, as the principle of authority would require. In any case, where the wife knows that the husband is caught in a mistake—and the husband also 'errs, as long as he continues to try'—and where, for that reason, she cannot freely agree with him, then in the spirit of autonomy, her own inner voice must decide. Then she must, to express it religiously, claim the right: to obey God more than human beings. Only the free sacrifices of love for the aspirations of a greater person possess beauty and dignity. A husband's offer of these to the wife is also no disgrace. But if, instead of such free giving of one's self, the woman obliges his needs and everyday goals against her inner voice, simply because it is comfortable, for the sake of outward peace, or to please her husband, then she commits *blasphemy* against her own human dignity; then she devalues herself to a second-class being" (Weber 2003: 93).

rise to the latter" (EFRL: 210–11). Normative externality in itself does not signify a lack of essentiality or rational validity. "The laws of freedom always have a positive aspect, an aspect marked by reality, externality, contingency in their appearance" (Hegel 1988: 395). Echoing Rousseau, Durkheim indicates that where one confronts the appearance of simple coercion one should search for the deep, underlying moral dynamics that keep individuals and groups yoked. Many generations earlier, la Boétie noted that subjugation was the responsibility of the subjugated themselves, not, as it might seem, stemming from the qualities of unjust despots or tyrants reigning over them: "A people enslaves itself, cuts its own throat, when having a choice between being vassals and being free men, it deserts its liberties and takes on the yoke, gives consent to its own misery, or rather, apparently welcomes it" ([1552–53] 1975: 50).[24]

In *Elementary Forms*, Durkheim says "Society ... fosters in us the sense of perpetual dependence."

> Precisely because society has its own specific nature that is different from our nature as individuals, it pursues ends that are specifically its own; but because it can achieve those ends only by working through us, it categorically demands our cooperation. Society requires us to make ourselves its servants, forgetful of our own interests. And it subjects us to all sorts of restraints, privations, and sacrifices without which social life would be impossible. And so, at every instant, we must submit to rules of action and thought that we have neither made nor wanted and that sometimes are contrary to our inclinations and to our most basic instincts.
> EFRL: 209

Here, the problem of self-determination is sharply delineated: we are born into a society where norms are already established and enforced. Developed to the point of an advanced civilization or even global empire, society confronts the individual as a crushing Leviathan (EFRL: 226). Are we then just passive tools at the mercy of the absolute? Durkheim is usually presented as the champion of this kind of determinism and, in fact, one can make a fairly good case for it depending upon the interpretive spin. However,

> In 1898, Durkheim published an essay in which he wrote: 'The agent endowed with reason does not behave like a thing of which the activity can

---

24 Carlyle says "'our spiritual maladies are but of Opinion; we are but fettered by chains of our own forging, and which ourselves also can rend asunder...'" (in Barzun 1964: 294).

> be reduced to a system of reflexes. He hesitates, feels his way, deliberates, and by that distinguishing mark he is recognized.' In 1909, he stated categorically: 'Sociology in no way imposes upon man a passively conservative attitude.... It only turns us away from ill-conceived and sterile enterprises inspired by the belief that we are able to change the social order as we wish, without taking into account customs, traditions, and the mental constitution of men and societies'.
>
> SMITH 2014: 170

We are reminded of Marx who said that, with regard to our conduct and creativity, "Men make their own history, but they do not make it just as they please; they do not make it under circumstances chosen by themselves, but under circumstances directly encountered, given and transmitted from the past. The tradition of all the dead generations weighs like a nightmare on the brain of the living" ([1869] 1963: 15). Still, they make "their own history" even if their world has been reduced to a nightmare. Then again, one person's nightmare is another person's infantile wish-fulfillment.

Privileged members of bourgeois society seem to enjoy unlimited personal autonomy and that, far from the sentiments espoused by classical sociology regarding externalities[25] and coercions, life is, on the contrary, absolutely unrestrained. It is difficult to square the idea that the capitalist world is an "unalterable order of things" that "determine[s] the lives of all the individuals who are born into this mechanism, not only those directly concerned with economic acquisition, with irresistible force" (Weber [1930] 2001: 19, 123) with the obvious freedoms and enjoyments of the privileged and propertied classes. But things are not always as they appear. Freedom is not the homogeneous substance one possesses or lacks once and for all or the monopolization of enjoyment by one class at the expense of another. We should distinguish, at least, between two basic forms of freedom: the negative and the positive.

---

25 Externality of consciousness is both a symptom of malaise and part of the reconciliation process whereby individuals make their way back to solidarity. The individual who is alienated, i.e., does not enjoy the spiritual infinitude of collective consciousness and genuine individuality, feels externality as an oppression because *they do not have the concept* (DOL: 308). Where there is externality there is still, at least, teleological activity and a drive toward conceptualization. The simple and revolutionary abolition of externality *per se* is synonymous with the extermination of *understanding* simply because it has failed to produce *reason*. True, the understanding is not free, but understanding lies on the way to reason and simply jettisoning 'externality' (i.e., social facts as external things) is just a suicidal gesture.

2 Freedom and Anomie

Freedom means embracing the inevitability of unavoidable limits and reconciliation with the needs of others.

> Freedom is the key philosophical problem, the crown of all the efforts of theoretical thinking, the culminating moment of any mature philosophical system. There is nothing higher or more significant in any system of philosophical worldview or in the actual stream of human life.... Man is free not from nature, not from society and their laws, but within the framework provided by the operation of both the laws of nature and society.
> SPIRKIN 1983

'Reconciliation' comes from the Latin *reconciliatio* (reinstatement, restoration, renewal). It means a harmonization, compatibility with others, and the restoration of friendly relations. Marx's specific vision of post-capitalist utopia is likely impossible because it is predicated on faulty presuppositions regarding human nature and his early philosophical anthropology leads to what Hegel calls a paradise of "stupefied innocence devoid of consciousness and will" (1988: 217).[26] Plausible reconciliations fall on the side of Hegel, Weber, and Durkheim as theorists of the positive freedom of secularized vocations, callings, and professions.

Negative freedom is the freedom *from* material restraints and privations, such as hunger or the freedom *from* instinctual drives. We are also often free from necessary mental processes such as self-reflexivity and self-criticism (Reich 1974: 5). Positive freedom, on the other hand, means the freedom *to* do what we want. Given our impotence as solitary individuals, sublime creations and awesome achievements are possible only on the basis of collective life (Fromm 1941: 31–34). Here, with Simmel, we find that one of the basic requirements of positive freedom is "the right, at every moment and of our own free will, to remain dependent.... Freedom is not solipsistic existence but sociological action" (1950: 121). What appears to be the positively free condition of the privileged bourgeois class, the apparent autonomy to do whatever,

---

26 Our 'human nature' amounts to the becoming and form of our *relatedness* to one another (Hegel 1988: 362).

unrestrained by others, is in many respects an illusion masking a condition known, after Durkheim, as chronic anomie blended with pathological forms of egoism (narcissism, social autism, psychosis, etc.).

Anomie is a condition of social and personal deregulation (*dé-règlement*) or anarchy (S: 253). A regulated society is one that is settled and peaceful whereas one that has undergone a process of far-reaching deregulation (e.g., the US from the 1970s onward) is one characterized by traumatic malfunctions, disorders, and an unrelenting flow of crises. The domain of business is anomic to the point of being chronically afflicted, where anomie is not only the norm but is venerated as a sacred principle (S: 257). Here, a whole society driven by the principle of limitlessness strives toward the abstract infinite, something that it is not capable of achieving, and, as such, drives it headlong into one calamity after another (Worrell 2013). A nation that has embraced the principle of limitlessness has willed the abyss, sacrificed itself to the spirit of anomie, and abrogated the concept of society itself. All that is left is to pay the bill through installments (S: 324). It is little wonder that the 'revolutionary situation' appears to be always at hand. If we desire "moral regeneration" it will not happen in a social system devoid of "legal limitation and regulation" wrung out of the master class through a sustained powerful attack and in concert with sympathetic allies in the "social layers" not directly invested in the production process (C: 408–09).

Perhaps the most insatiable drive within the kingdom of anomie is the lust for unlimited accumulation. "Wealth" says Durkheim, "by the power it bestows, deceives us into believing that we depend on ourselves only. Reducing the resistance we encounter from objects, it suggests the possibility of unlimited success against them. The less limited one feels, the more intolerable all limitation appears" (S: 254). However, can money have a master? More likely, the rich mirror their hard-working slaves as co-inhabitants of the same realm between life and death and their mastery is a kind of pseudo-mastery (Kojeve [1947] 1969: 63–65). We find that the idle rich who seem to act freely are no less acted upon by impersonal forces than those at the bottom of the social order (see Lukács 1971: 133) and this over-exposure is reflected in higher rates of suicide for the affluent. Far from actual freedom, the limitlessness of the voluptuary or the aesthete is one where a mania for sensual pleasures, what Durkheim calls "morbid effervescence." (S: 368) leads to enslavement and self-destruction (cf. Sade 2006: 4, 19). Or, to put it simply, the aimless life of libertine debauchery is one synonymous with destiny (Baudelaire 2002: 43–44). Actual freedom, individuality, and the ebullience of life are the products of association and regulation.

3 Dynamism, Alienation and Reification

Human beings are unique among animals in that we relinquished our instincts in favor of symbolic culture. Even if we had instincts we could not use them in our present state. The benefits of the symbolic life include language, science, art, space travel, etc., but possessing nothing internal to ourselves to guide action and thought, we have to find our regulation in association with other people. This "biological weakness" vis-a-vis other animals guided by instincts "is the condition of human culture" (Fromm 1941: 32). What we lack, then, internally and subjectively, we replace externally and objectively in the form of others and society, our Absolute.[27] "Man is" therefore "always directed towards that which is other than himself" (Berger and Pullberg 1965: 201). As such, the human being is incomprehensible apart from its *heteron* (other). The paradox of the simultaneous deficiency and excess of human life led Pascal to exclaim: "What a chimera man is, what a strange monster, what a chaos, what a bundle of contradictions, what a prodigy! Judge of all things, and a miserable worm; a depository of truth, and a sink of uncertainty and error; at once the glory and the scum of the universe!" (in Levy-Bruhl 1899: 94; cf. PESC: 124).

Assemblage produces a surplus of exuberance that, once signified and projected, congeals into representations that reflect and refract in consciousness as reified things that seem to everyone involved 'as if' they had always already existed as autonomous and authoritative powers over and above the individual members of society. This process is transformative because while "society has no other active forces than individuals ... by combining [these individuals] form a psychical existence of a new species" (S: 310). Berger and Pullberg refer to this whole process as "objectivation" consisting of objectification, alienation, and reification (1965: 200). We can differentiate additional and important aspects; indeed, one can imagine a more convoluted sociogony, but the decisive thing for our purpose right now is that alienation results in a world that seems not at all like a spontaneous creation of our own activities: "alienation and sociation are de facto linked processes. In the course of sociation

---

27   If for no other reason this is why we must strenuously resist the misnomer 'capitalist society' that plagues even critical thought. One can have a society, or one can have capitalism, but one cannot have both in a unified and rational system. At the moment, capitalism and society are still at war with one another and the outcome is far from predetermined. It might be permissible to use the phrase 'capitalistic society' to denote the tension and pseudo-relation between the two concepts.

(simply understood here as the ongoing realization of social structure) horizons are narrowed and human possibilities become non-human or supra-human facticities. Founded on this process there *emerges* a world that is taken for granted and that is lived through as a necessary fate" (Berger and Pullberg 1965: 203, emphasis added). All the same, it *emerges*. Alienation is the central problem when it comes to deconstructing the facticity of collective creations that confront us not as spontaneous emergences but as domineering behemoths.

Within the capitalist system of commodity exchange and accumulation, we find employees who are alienated from their own means of subsistence and forced to sell their time and energy to others; alienated from the processes and products of labor; pushed around by bosses; subjected to quantifications and calculations; chasing after wages; kept at bay by the price barrier and private property laws from the consumption of the useful things surrounding them; alienated from others; alienated from a sense of the totality and meaningfulness of life; alienated from their desires and confusing alien desires for their own; and, ultimately, alienated from themselves in that life confronts workers as inhuman alterity (Marx [1844] 1964: 156). This is not merely alienation but compound alienation.

We can go beyond Marx with Durkheim and organize the various aspects of alienation into four types that encompass a variety of forms: *estrangement*; *possession*; *splitting* and *doubling*; and, finally, *bondage*. These forms will consume parts of this volume but for now these four types, these 'sociological monstrosities,' may combine into unique conglomerates or composite forms: e.g., *resignation* or the unity of estrangement and slavery, on the one hand, and *ecstasy* or the unity of splitting and possession on the other. The combinations are manifold. When we examine, for example, the internal structure of the exchange relation, we find all four of these moments of alienation operating simultaneously—the commodity under the reign of modern capital is, in a very real sense, the ultimate socio-historical monstrosity (Worrell 2014).[28]

More than a system of needs-satisfactions, capital is the divinity of the modern age (Marx 1976: 918; see Benjamin 1996: 288–91). There are no doubt residual gods still hanging on (particularities misrecognized as universalities)[29]

---

28   Compare the syllogism of the Father, Son, and the Holy Spirit (Hegel 1988: 473) with that of the Commodity, Money, and Capital. As we will see in volume four, both the general formula for capital (M–C–M') and the circulation of commodities (C–M–C) represent wrong syllogisms.

29   Santayana makes an excellent point: "I cannot help thinking that a consciousness of the relativity of values, if it became prevalent, would tend to render people more truly social than would a belief that things have intrinsic and unchangeable values, no matter what

but the only true, negative planetary god is capital and its diabolical energy, surplus value. And even though capital may seem all-powerful, ruling without consent, it still depends for its authority on the daily commitments and the active cooperation of billions of people doing what they are expected: producing, consuming, buying, selling, saving, investing, loaning, gambling, speculating, etc. And this negative god of the world does not rule uncontested. There is another that is not merely older but, in a way, eternal. Where Value seeks to reign absolutely it still must contend with a pantheon of human values that are far from extinguished. We can even go so far to say that even if values are repressed they are eternal and will always return. If a handful of us reject capital, we are exterminated mercilessly but if the majority of the disgruntled withdraw their consent to be ruled then it either topples or rules on the basis of pure coercion and, ultimately, that is no rule at all; just as all previous gods and social orders wither and die, capitalism, as a form of administering human time and energy, will *someday* pass. Keeping it going depends

---

the attitude of any one of them may be. If we said that goods, including the right distribution of goods, are relative to specific natures, moral warfare would continue, but not with poisoned arrows. Our private sense of justice itself would be acknowledged to have but a relative authority, and while we could not have a higher duty than to follow it, we should seek to meet those whose aims were incompatible with it as we meet things physically inconvenient, without insulting them as if they were morally vile or logically contemptible" (1913: 151). But what at first glance appears to be an appeal to relativism actually contains its own negation. The underlying condition for the relativism of personal and group (particular) values (a worthy goal) is the existence of a domain of absolute values, without which, warfare continues. And whether or not I am being shot with arrows or poisoned arrows, I'm still being shot at. The problem is not that an absolute dimension exists, but that individuals and groups mistake their singular interests and particular ethics for universalities. People who confuse their particular religion as a universal foundation for morality are on the road to fanaticism and conflict. Indeed, where we find prejudice and ethnocentrism (often masked as religious convictions) we can be sure we are in touch with a spirit of particularism in opposition to universalization, or, confusing itself with universality (see Bettelheim and Janowitz 1964: 54). Religion itself is not what is sacred (Caillois). "Rather than religion being the basis for morals, morals are ... the basis for religion. This is the inception of modernity" (Comte-Sponville 2007: 42). Most 'morality problems' are in fact not about morals but about religion. For example, "Homosexuality ... may be a theological issue.... It is not, at least not any longer, a moral issue—or rather, it is a moral issue only for those who insist on confusing morals and religion, particularly if they resort to a literal interpretation of the bible or the Koran to avoid having to think for themselves" (Comte-Sponville 2007: 43).

on many factors, not least of which is the willing self-enslavement of the working and consuming classes. It would be insufficient if workers and consumers were forced, by threat of punishment, to work and consume; class domination also depends on the lower classes of workers and servants *identifying* with their oppressors, aspiring to their alien but prestigious form of life. Actual revolution might entail a shift from identification to actual object choice and the cannibalistic absorption of the masters. As such, capital cannot eradicate other values without destroying itself; once one small group possesses all of the one and only value that is left, once they embody that surplus, they are easily disposed of by millions if not billions of people who no longer aspire to 'be like' the master but to simply 'be' the master. We are, I think, a long way from this kind of madness. The master-slave dialectic is so complicated because it too is entangled in a *sui generis* moral economy not of its own making. The nightmare of the past weighs on the master as much as it does on the slave. Perhaps the road to what we want is not in devouring the rich but to counter their abstract wealth with concrete riches derived from universal solidarity.

4   Masters and Slaves

We fear the strong man. Once some individual gains the upper hand over the weak, combining power into an 'imperium' (Green 1895: 54), they attempt to not only usurp but transform personal interests and subjective will into the recognized law of the land. However, in the relationship between the leader and their followers, Simmel says, "The seemingly wholly passive element [the group of followers] is in reality even more active in relationships such as obtain between a speaker and his audience or between a teacher and his class."

> Speaker and teacher appear to be nothing but leaders; nothing but, momentarily, superordinate. Yet whoever finds himself in such or a similar situation feels the determining and controlling re-action on the part of what seems to be a purely receptive and guided mass. This applies not only to situations where the two parties confront one another physically. All leaders are also led; in innumerable cases, the master is the slave of his slaves. Said one of the greatest German party leaders referring to his followers: "I am their leader, therefore I must follow them" (1950: 185).

The leader is, as Durkheim says, "the product of the crowd rather than its informing cause" (S: 126; see also Freud [1927] 1961: 16–17; Sartre 1976: 382).[30] In

---

30   When Elizabeth Warren said at her 18 March 2019 CNN 'town hall' appearance in Jackson, Mississippi, that "leadership starts at the top" she, like everyone else suffering from common sense, got the problem exactly backwards. The statement was, of course, a fitting swipe at the sitting president, however, one might argue that Trump, in all his narcissism, greed, arrogance, prejudice, incompetence, and moral rottenness is actually the perfect collective representation for a blighted contemporary America and his ability to link poor, dumb redneck populists (angry punishers) with affluent anti-populists (intolerant but dispassionate) cannot flow from any quality or skill he personally possesses (Smith 2019a). There are a couple of ways to think about Trump right now: on the one hand, Trump may actually save us from Trumpism in the long run; imagine if a celebrity oligarch was elected who could act like a competent adult—as it stands right now, the inevitable mini-Trumps of the future will be more easily discredited as "another clueless billionaire" as we saw with Howard Schultz who entered politics on a platform of (a) buy my book and (b) don't raise my taxes. Being saved from Trumpism only prolongs a dead-end status quo. On the other hand, if neoliberalism is bad, corporate politics and corporate media, etc., are bad, if capitalism is bad, if the state is bad, and so on, the status quo in all its parameters and dimensions are terrible and change will only come when this bad Thing is dismantled and rebuilt into something better. The odds of our society being rationally reorganized are far less likely than a dialectical diremption (a tearing apart)—in fact, we are well on our way to being ripped in half so the moment for sane reflection and reasoned action may have already passed. Some might say that Trump is the right horrible man for the job to exacerbate tensions, enflame emotions, make a mockery of the status quo, and accelerate the destruction of what will inevitably be destroyed anyways. After all, and if nothing else, Trump has exposed a truth much faster than anyone else could have: the state can no longer govern. However, these positions on Trumpism are probably lacking. David Norman Smith says that the contemporary situation is not Weberian, i.e., the authority typology we are familiar with does not apply (Trump is not charismatic, does not rule on the basis of tradition, and he revels in anarchy) and I agree. The moment is more comprehensible as Freudian (psychoanalytic) and Durkheimian (anthropological). Freud suggests that the situation in which conscience is exchanged for the leader object is temporary and carnivalesque ([1921] 1959: 81) and, in hindsight, I suspect Trump will be seen as a disposable puppet king that serves at the mercy of his base (cf. Harrison 1962: xxxvi). The moment is also Durkheimian insofar as genuine authority is incapable of setting itself up because in a state of chronic anomie (political and economic anarchy) the real value of morality and law is no longer capable of being judged. "The limits are unknown between the possible and the impossible, what is just and what is unjust, legitimate claims and hopes and those which are immoderate" (S: 253). The post-clown-show interregnum in which everyone is swindled will represent a back to business normalcy (it is unlikely another mini-Trump could provide a convincing sequel) with an extra dollop of repression heaped on top which means that the end is even closer than we might imagine, in fact, it is already upon us. This is the end. All empires die, of that there is no doubt, and this America will die. The questions that pertain to the end are: what will the body count be in the final tallying and how will the 'imperial republic' (Aron 1974: 259) be reorganized and under what form of control? Never has so much wealth (both fictional and real) been placed in the hands of so few people and once Americans transvalue the

short, followers create and raise up their own masters (Reich 1974). We are a long way off, however, from the seemingly identical sentiment expressed in Skinner's neo-behaviorism such that "The slave controls the master as completely as the master the slave" (in Fromm 1973: 39). Fromm's reaction is decisive in helping us see the difference between a dynamic grasp of authority and a static, mechanical ideology of reciprocal enslavement:

> I find this statement [of Skinner's] shocking; we are asked to believe that the relationship between master and slave is a reciprocal one, although, the notion of exploitation is not 'meaningless.' For Skinner the exploitation is *not* part of the social episode itself; only the techniques of control are.... One can explain Skinner's saying that the slave and slaveowner are in a reciprocal relationship only by the ambiguous use he makes of the word 'control.' In the sense in which the word is used in real life, there can be no question that the slave owner controls the slave, and that there is nothing 'reciprocal' about the control except that the slave may have a minimum of countercontrol—for instance, by the threat of rebellion. But this is not what Skinner is talking about.
> FROMM 1973: 39

Fromm is correct that the master holds the whip, has created a system in which to control all aspects of slave life, and extract as much obedience as they can from the human tools at their disposal, yet, at bottom, as Fromm indicates, control is only possible within a system in which slaves cooperate, for whatever reason, in their enslavement. If, as is the case of most slaves, it comes down to simple coercion, the answer is simple and is not sociologically interesting. However, in cases where the chains of servitude are imaginary, emotional, psychological, sociological, etc., we are looking not at mere coercion but at the willing consent of the subjugated to being reduced to a tool for the pleasure of another class. This phenomenon of constructing one's master and falling down in submission, even to the point of collective self-destruction, is one of the most difficult problems social psychology has to answer because every liberation movement and every revolutionary moment has, contained within it, these contradictory elements of self-defeat and downfall. Defenders of "the old world always benefit, at one point or another, from the complicity of revolutionaries" (Debord, Kotanyi, and Vaneigem [1962] 1981: 316). Hegel's

---

billionaire category from sacred pure to sacred impure, or simply place them at the center of a new sacrificial cult, the concentration of so much wealth in the hands of so few people will be seen in hindsight as an act of cunning genius.

well-known dialectic of lordship and bondage offers an interesting point of departure.

Hegel constructs a simple ideal-typical scenario in which two, self-conscious individuals encounter one another as adversaries; neither view the other as "an essential being, but in the other sees its own self" (PS: 111). This relation is one of self-duplication (alienation) where the other is reduced to the status of an empty mirror reflection of the self's desire for certainty, independence, and the utilization of the other as an instrument for its own satisfaction. But the interplay is reciprocal in that both selves make demands of the other that go unsatisfied, in other words, they can form no shared 'We' in which they recognize one another as free beings and cooperate spontaneously in shared projects. The lack of a 'transcendental' third term that unites them (Lefebvre [1968] 2009: 19–23) sets the agents up for a struggle in which the defeated person surrenders to avoid death, becoming the 'slave' or bondsman of the victor. The story does not end here but the decisive aspect that needs to be foregrounded is the nature of fear within the passage from slavery to freedom. The vanquished ego "has been fearful, not of this or that particular thing or just at odd moments, but its whole being has been seized with dread; for it has experienced the fear of death, the absolute Lord."

> In that experience it has been quite unmanned, has trembled in every fibre [sic] of its being, and everything solid and stable has been shaken to its foundations. But this pure universal movement, the absolute melting-away of everything stable, is the simple, essential nature of self-consciousness, absolute negativity, *pure being-for-self*, which consequently is *implicit* in this consciousness (PS: 117).

The slave or bondsman liberated from 'externality' and through their labor for the master "acquires" not only "a mind of his own" but also the feeling of "essential being" and makes a world for itself the master will be forced to recognize (PS: 119). Without fear, however, taken to the point of terror, the master-slave relation will not dissolve into spontaneous reciprocity and mutual recognition.

> If consciousness fashions the thing without that initial absolute fear, it is only an empty self-centered attitude; for its form or negativity is not negativity *per se*, and therefore its formative activity cannot give it a consciousness of itself as essential being. If it has not experienced absolute fear but only some lesser dread, the negative being has remained for it something external, its substance has not been infected by it through and

through. Since the entire contents of its natural consciousness have not been jeopardized, determinate being still in *principle* attaches to it; having a "mind of one's own" is self-will, a freedom which is still enmeshed in servitude (Ibid.).

We arrive, here, at our problem of a kind of freedom (negative) still encumbered by slavery. Classic studies have focused intensely on the role of work in this master-slave relation without giving due weight to the element of terror (e.g., Marcuse 1941) but Hegel makes it clear that labor combined with absolute fear represents the conditions under which the servitude relation is sublated.

Far from "cheerful robots" (Mills 1959: 171–76) or "automaton conformists" (Fromm 1941), workers have minds of their own, yet they are ambivalent. The aspect of fear in the master-slave relation has been read a certain way. Pinkard, for example, says, "The contingency that made the slave into a slave was his fear for his life and his willingness to submit to the other rather than die.... [H]e faced death and chose to live by submitting to the other..." (1996: 61). From this angle, fear is a precondition for being reduced to a servant and labor becomes the way out, and, I think this explains quite a bit: fear keeps the working class in its place. Yet, laboring was also supposed to be the way *out* of subjugation. Kojeve emphasizes another aspect: the "defeated and spared" individual that emerges from mortal combat is reduced to a member of the living-dead ([1947] 1969: 16). Again, however, the truth of the master is supposed to lie in the nature of the slave with an eventual inversion of the wrong into a right. Why are the laboring classes locked into eternal servitude of their own making? I think another reading of Hegel's dialectic of bondage offers a clue: in facing not just fear but the absolute terror and certainty of death and nevertheless surmounting this fear and plunging headlong into combat (positive or negative) and emerging from it alive but vanquished and being forced to labor in a milieu devoid of legitimacy is the proper reading whereby the slave turns the tables on the master.[31] Recognition is transposed to another register of transparency and works out its inner contradictions from which any pretense of validity melts into objective slavery. Anyone who has proclaimed, "Here I stand. I can do no other" or faced what appeared to be the certainty of a firing squad for their stubborn disobedience, and survived the ordeal, has pulled the curtain of authority back and exposed the master's tenuous grip. Because workers are unwilling to overcome fear and engage in mortal combat, they are, and will remain slaves. As compensation they follow demagogues

---

[31] Those that "will risk a wound but not life itself" face becoming "the slave of the other" (Hegel [1802–04] 1979: 240).

who play on their resentments and anxieties, seduce them, and absorb them "into the aims of ... stronger powers" (Frankfurt Institute of Social Research 1972: 81). Du Bois said that black Americans would never be free unless they took the fight to the absolute and bitter end.

> This the American black man knows: his fight here is a fight to the finish. Either he dies or wins. If he wins it will be by no subterfuge or evasion of amalgamation. He will enter modern civilization here in America as a black man on terms of perfect and unlimited equality with any white man, or he will enter not at all. Either extermination root and branch, or absolute equality. There can be no compromise. This is the last great battle of the West (1935: 703).

That battle that hinged on victory or death was not fought out to the bitter end. Generally speaking, it is difficult to imagine a critical mass of Americans willing to hurl themselves into the abyss of mortal combat for their freedom because, in a perverse way, it is emotionally more satisfying for most people to trade their freedom for resentment and the fantasy of revenge.

Demagogues like Father Coughlin during the Great Depression or contemporary right wing hate radio personalities today serve an ideological function by helping solidify command over subjects by displacing resentments and anxieties away from the root causes of social frustrations (lack of the means for self-subsistence, free market competition, wage stagnation, unemployment, etc.) and focus minds on things that cannot interfere with the accumulation of capital (homosexuality, abortion, skin color, etc.). "What the agitator does, then, is to activate the most primitive and immediate, the most inchoate and dispersed reactions of his followers to the general trends of contemporary society" (Lowenthal and Guterman 1949: 139) but, in so doing, does not diminish the sense of malaise on the part of their audience: "Malaise gives rise to agitation, and agitation battens on malaise" (Ibid: 138). Here I think we are on to the nut of the problem: the "general trends" of society and the "malaise" of the situation are essentially indicative of a universally anomic system. Above the level of psychology and the leader-follower dyad is simply lawlessness or deregulation that create the circumstances in which the people give away their freedoms.

> Only when the mass of the people has turned toward evil can such things happen. For a community cannot exist without law and justice; and only when the people turn away from them, will their administration pass into the hands of one man. The man would have to be made of iron who could

rob the law, the common advantage of all, from the multitude; since he is a being of flesh and blood, he can gain his rule only after he has debased the people into *anomia*.

in VOEGELIN 2000: 402–03

Once a social system has degenerated into chronic anomie the institutional supports and relations necessary for reason disintegrate and the masses turn to hatred, which, I might add, is a boon to capital. If a demagogue can get the rural working poor to turn against their fellow workers because of a different skin color, or whatever else, they can be delivered over to capital at a lower price—racism and sundry hatreds actually function as active forces within the organic composition of capital by destroying solidarity (Adorno et al. 1950; Worrell 2008) and increasing the volume of surplus labor. If the price of labor-power decreases, it increases the amount of unpaid labor time gifted to the employer on behalf of their employees. As such, if a demagogue can paint the unemployed as social parasites and get unsophisticated types to worry about cultural Marxism, queers, liberal elites, fake news, etc., their fury will be misdirected. One has to almost admire the feat of social engineering that went into the Post-Fordist 'conservative' project because they achieved everything they set out to do: defeat the USSR, destroy organized labor, increase the ranks of billionaires and millionaires, liquidate an entire civilizational complex from the bottom up, stagnate and reverse wage gains, choke social services, debase public education, transform universities into corporate asylums, stoke the fires of apocalyptic religion, promote cultural anarchy and cognitive relativism, transfer the resulting trillions of dollars to a handful of elites, and produce an enraged and irrational mass of millions of illiterate and semi-literate peons that can be whipped up through propaganda to take their revenge out on other poor people.

An important difference between the demagogues of today and those before the Second World War is the availability of 'The Jew' as the bête noire of history. Coughlin, for example, synthesized all his hatreds into the composite image of 'The Jew' that ruined life for both capital and labor. If it were not for 'The Jew' life would be a paradise because 'The Jew' is 'behind' finance capital, communism, and any form of social malaise. After the Holocaust, demagogues were compelled to tone down their antisemitism and construct more nebulous references to things like the New World Order, bankers, and machinate about United Nations plots to enslave the United States and concentrate all true American patriots in FEMA camps. The closest thing today's reactionary media have to 'The Jew' is their caricature of the transcendental 'Liberal' as the thing behind all problems, yet, anti-liberal demagoguery today pales in comparison to the antisemitism of the 30s because the imaginary Jew of Nazi propaganda possessed what were supposed to be supernatural powers of unlimited wealth and stealth. 'The Jew' ruled the world. In short, it was the negative charismatic (*otherworldly*) powers of 'The Jew' that transferred to the antisemitic demagogue his positively charismatic powers to expose and defeat the enemy. The agitator's fetish for "evil forces" (Adorno et al. 1950: 240) is the basis for his claim to be an emissary of The Good. Only the divine can defeat the diabolical.[32] Of course, the charisma of the leader is a conferred status. Dominance flows from the bottom to the top[33] and this bottom-up flow of power is true of all types of effervescent pleasures[34] and authority relations but especially important in our comprehension of charisma and social sadism.

5 Authoritarianism, Character, and Resonance

The authoritarian syndrome is rooted in a psychodynamic theory of sadomasochism. Sadism, named after the Marquis de Sade, is synonymous with deriving erotic pleasure in humiliating others, inflicting pain upon them, and treating people like tools.[35] Masochism, named after Leopold von Sacher-Masoch, represents the mirror opposite drive, namely, deriving erotic pleasure in being humiliated or punished by the other. The focus on sexual perversion took a turn with Freud's notion of "moral masochism" whereby frustrated sadists, lacking a satisfactory outlet in their interpersonal relations, turn their desire to humiliate and inflict pain upon others back upon their own selves, producing a kind of self-sadism or "secondary masochism" (1962: 48) which puts the terms of the debate on a more sociological footing (Worrell 1998). With the split

---

32 Antisemitism is practically indestructible but the old demonological forms from generations past are still fringe constructions in the US. This is one of the great victories in American culture: the real diminishment of demonology on the right and the consequent deprivation of its divine mandate for the punishment of evil forces.

33 "The despotism of social prejudice comes from below; this despotism reflects the opinion of the people, and the whole people are only a middle class of traders and businessmen who form their ideas according to their interests. The distinguished man submits to it with suffering and as a slave; the vast majority of Americans do not feel the constraint" (Boutmy 1902: 100, my translation).

34 "'A jest's prosperity lies in the ear / Of him that hears it, never in the tongue / Of him that makes it'" (Shakespeare 1963: 113, quoted in Freud 1960: 177).

35 With regards to life under capitalism, sadism is intimately connected to reification ('thingification') or the transformation of people into instruments. "The oppressed, as objects, as 'things,' have no purposes except those their oppressors prescribe for them" (Freire 1993: 42).

between sadism and masochism we can see the underlying thread of alienation: "Sadism and masochism, which are invariably linked together, are opposites in behavioristic terms, but they are actually two different facets of one fundamental situation: the sense of vital impotence. Both the sadist and the masochist need another being to 'complete' them, as it were. The sadist makes another being an extension of himself; the masochist makes himself the extension of another being.[36] Both seek a symbiotic relationship because neither has his center in himself" (Fromm 1973: 292).[37]

Using a survey instrument known as the "F-scale" (for measuring potential *fascist* dispositions) the authors of *The Authoritarian Personality* indicate that the various dimensions of the scale, taking into account "conventionality, authoritarian submissiveness and aggressiveness, projectivity, manipulativeness, etc., regularly go together" and that "all the clusters of which this scale is made up belong to one single, 'over-all' syndrome. It is one of the outstanding findings of the study that 'highness' is essentially one syndrome, distinguishable from a variety of 'low' syndromes. There exists something like 'the' potentially fascist character, which is by itself a 'structural unit'" (Adorno et al. 1950: 751). This is why anti-authoritarianism can take on a wide array of individual and particular forms while what we call authoritarianism is almost a world-historical fact. The very core of this toxic character is authoritarian aggression (sadism) and authoritarian submission (masochism). Boiled down to its essence, the authoritarian admires power and identifies with symbols that represent power and despise weakness and anything associated with weakness.[38] The conventional and traditional beliefs and ways of thinking of the majority have a kind of sway over individuals so authoritarians venerate it and want to punish deviants; authoritarians undergo excessive self-repression and project those leftovers onto others in what amounts to a kind of externalization of self-hatred; authoritarians see the malignant other as something to be dealt with in an instrumental manner and tend toward manipulative action and dealing impersonally with the problem of the weak but dangerous outsider or social impurity.

One of the key conceptual aspects of authoritarianism, from this psychoanalytic angle, is that character structure is the mediating point between the individual psyche and society at large—it is society individuated at one of its

---

36 The connection to the logic of magic whereby one controls a transfigured double is interesting and worth exploring.
37 Sadism inflicted on the weak is also a kind of authority "compensation" that the socially weak can exact form the physically weak or vulnerable (MECW, 4: 605).
38 "Now, in the eyes of the crowd weakness has no prestige; it turns always to force" (Le Bon 1913: 145).

single points of existence.[39] Authoritarian movements or parties rest not merely on an authoritarian ideological platform that manipulates atomized puppets but is founded on the durable set of dispositions (character, habitus, etc.) of those who throw their passive or active support behind authoritarian firebrands. This approach to the problem of authoritarianism takes individuals seriously but at the same time avoids some, but not all, of the problems associated with epistemological reductionism. *The Authoritarian Personality* created a firestorm of controversy because it discovered that many Americans, supposedly the bearers of democracy and personal liberty, were potentially the pallbearers of democracy and liberty; they were debilitated by the wish for an authoritarian solution to the contradictions that besiege a pluralist, liberal, and capitalistic society.[40] These insights into authoritarianism contrast greatly with mainstream, positivistic and behavioristic assumptions regarding authority, obedience and command. The two most important studies are, of course, the Milgram study and the Stanford prison experiment. There is no need to review these classics considering the breadth and depth of the secondary literature generated in their wake; we can focus briefly on their unitary grounds instead.

What the classic American studies into obedience all have in common is the belief that most people can be made to do anything under the right circumstances, that institutions turn people into mindless robots, and that most people would be executioners if placed into the role of an executioner; under certain circumstances we can count on anyone to play the role of executioner. However, what these studies all fail to demonstrate is a uniformity of effect and paper over the underlying characterological differences between individuals and groups. That 35 percent of participants in the Milgram experiment were disobedient in the face of Yale's scientific "mystique" (Milgram 1974: 143) is quite important and contradicts quite dramatically the statement that people

---

39 The obvious flaw in the theoretical positioning of character structure formulated thusly is that it treats character as a measurable substitute for institutions and social organization. Can we measure character in such a way that we infer the right kind of knowledge about social organization? In other words, if character is a middle term it probably falls within a syllogism that belongs to the domain of the abstract psyche rather than to social psychology *per se*.

40 Part of the authoritarian appeal is the promise of a pseudo-monism in the face of pluralistic chaos and relativism. Modernity is nearly synonymous with being adrift and bewildered. "The only possible strategy when facing a situation of total or near-total bewilderment is a monistic one.... Such attractive, foundation-worthy starting-points are those around which philosophies of merit are constructed. In the loss-of-orientation predicament, a monist strategy is really the only possible one.... [F]or us it is *unavoidable*" (Gellner 1974: 13).

obeyed with "numbing regularity" (Milgram 1974: 123). One of the most interesting insights into all these classic studies applies not to the participants or findings but to the studies themselves: they tend to simultaneously and sometimes unconsciously posit the existence of uniform bourgeois individuality and autonomy, on the one hand, while attempting to demonstrate that individuals are easily crushed by impersonal forces and reduced to nothing more complicated than animals following instincts or machines determined by programing. We arrive at the odd fusion of bourgeois autonomy and totalitarian heteronomy permeating the very designs and assumptions of the experiments themselves. If people were autonomous we would have no need for authority, everyone would simply regulate their lives; if people were purely heteronomous the problem of authority would never arise because it would never occur to anyone that there was anything to question. Logically, we must admit that most people, most of the time, are torn between a bewilderingly complicated complex of ideas, obligations, sentiments, and desires. However, let us assume that Milgram's study really does demonstrate a relative lack of ambivalence to obedience. Many participants did what they were told and delivered what they believed to be dangerous electrical shocks to their fellow human beings. Shiller has an interesting observation:

> people have learned that when experts tell them something is alright, it probably is, even if it does not seem so. (In fact, it is worth noting that in this case the experimenter was indeed correct: it was alright to continue giving the 'shocks'—even though most of the subjects did not suspect the reason). Thus, the results of Milgram's experiment can also be interpreted as springing from people's past learning about the reliability of authorities (2015: 177).

Few individuals are devils and fewer still are angels, but the Milgram study does not lend credibility to the ideas that humans are inherently bad, that 'human nature' is infinitely malleable, or that anybody can be converted into a sadistic torturer.

Many people are willing to defy authority even upon pain of punishment and death. If, as it seems clear, people are not robotic slaves to oppressors or natural-born killers, what is the way forward for a world of positive, spontaneous freedom and collective creativity, that takes into consideration the fact that they are still, nonetheless, actively participating in their own subjugation? For my entire professional career, I have worked on the problem of authoritarianism, yet, the concept may be so fraught with psychological baggage and methodological abstractions that it limits our capacity for sociological insight.

The classic studies on authoritarianism and the work being done today by psychologists and sociologists get to the bottom of attitudes by asking people what they think about X or what they would like to do to Y is not a sociological method. Sociology examines groups in action and asking individuals what they think about X, Y, and Z is not sociology. For most people, X, Y, and Z are not even concepts but vagaries they know little about. For example, a recent survey that percolated through the fringes of progressive media revealed that an astronomical percentage of Americans were opposed to the teaching of "Arabic numerals" in schools. What the survey purportedly demonstrated is the level of ignorance of the ordinary American (especially conservatives) and their prejudice toward things "Arabic." Leaving aside ignorance, it is obviously the case that had these dummies known that 'their' numbers are in fact "Arabic numerals" they would change their minds. Though, I have no doubt a hard kernel of remnants would insist on returning posthaste to Roman numerals, damn the consequences. We see that "Arabic" means next to nothing for these people; it is just a signifier filled in with nebulous animosities. A survey like this can crudely measure *prejudice* but sociology, or social psychology if you prefer, is not concerned with prejudice but with *judgments* and collective teleological activity. Surveys might reflect something about character and ignorance but not social character as it is found 'in the wild' engaged in actual social life and it never touches the essential, the teleological process as it unfolds.[41]

Character is a dynamic structure that *resonates* differently depending upon circumstances and authoritarians can be folded into functional anti-authoritarians under the right conditions. Marx thought the workers of the world would unite but the global unification of authoritarians seems much more plausible. Yet, time and again we see that authoritarians can be mobilized, placed into highly authoritarian institutions, and marched off to kill their authoritarian twins on the other side of the world for a multiplicity of reasons. Authoritarians are no less subject to a moral economy than anti-authoritarians, therefore it makes sense to have a better grasp of what a 'moral economy' means with respect to obedience and disobedience.

---

41   The foundation of sociology is the fact of two interacting oppositional groups. As such, the 'tribal' conflict between 'Red' and 'Blue' in the US is a perfect object of inquiry but neither survey research that relies on individual attitudes or studying voting patterns rise to the level of teleological activity. Voting in America is not a form of praxis but futility itself, which requires another kind of explanation. Whatever they were, American elections are now institutions that inhibit teleological activity.

6 Disobedience and Necessity

Disobedience runs in two sociological directions: rebellion and subversion. The rebel appears on the surface to oppose authority but, in reality, the rebel is "a lover of law and order" that has been rendered powerless within the existing normative order (Neill 1960: 313). "The psychic structure of a class" says Fromm "is an aspect of its objective situation" (1984: 209) and the rebel is plentiful in regions of advanced and rapid economic downward degeneration as well as localities where traditional norms are in the process of liquidation. An ideal-typical case of the rebel is the pseudo-individual that projects rebellious defiance toward, for example, the federal government while adopting a markedly submissive attitude during interpersonal relations where, for example, he is forced to play the bootlicking 'yes man' to his boss but then goes home and demands subservience from his family. This is why we often find rebelliousness combined with authoritarianism (Fromm 1984). The rebel wants to be an authority and tends to hate authority when it appears weak or impure—witness the howls of southern and rural protest against a federal regime (the Obama administration) that, ironically, delivers the same objective neoliberal policy set as the previous administration. And while Trump delivers next to nothing his followers never grow tired of losing because, if nothing else, Trump knows how to act like a strong winner even as he keeps right on losing. Right and wrong, true and false mean little in a moral economy that rotates on the principles of strength and weakness. Being strong means never losing.[42]

From the authoritarian standpoint Obama was the perfect physical carrier that signified weakness and difference, and nothing will satisfy the rebel or the rebel-authoritarian except another tough-talker because they only understand one thing: the world is divided up between the strong and the weak and the use of force and destructiveness is the best way to get what you want. Thus, it is completely valid to compare the psychology of the fanatical suicide bomber 'over there' with gun-toting religious fanatics in the US. One might venture the hypothesis that the speculative identity of rebelliousness, authoritarianism, and destructiveness is the concept of terror itself (Worrell 2013). The fearful want to be feared. The radical character or revolutionary, by contrast, is

---

42   For this reason, all American wars since Vietnam are of a form that cannot be lost. It is true that the war on terror or the war on whatever can never actually be won but they also can never be lost. There are no metrics either way. The only fact is the appearance of strength or weakness. One might say that the war on poverty or the war on fat, etc., were obvious failures but rather than admit defeat we just extend more credit or bar ultra-skinny models from fashion shows.

creative, loves life (is biophilic), and "has a passion for independence" (Fromm 1973: 346).[43] Destruction is sometimes necessary, even for genuine revolutionaries, but when forced to destroy an existing social order the revolutionary does so to erect a more inclusive, loving and sharing society (Fromm 1973: 278).

Actual freedom is impossible so long as people see their sorry lot in life as more or less legitimate (e.g., people get what they deserve).[44] We can have whatever we want but, first, we have to know what we want, how the prevailing social order frustrates and contradicts that desire, and how to go about getting things reconstructed. The last thing we can hope for is that some hero will come along and liberate us. Only the enslaved can deliver themselves from bondage. It cannot be done for them. We have to take them seriously rather than viewing them as helpless children. Reich put it well when he said:

> Under the influence of politicians, masses of people tend to ascribe the responsibility for wars to those who wield power at any given time. In World War I it was the munitions industrialists; in World War II it was the psychopathic generals who were said to be guilty. *This is passing the buck. The responsibility for wars falls solely upon the shoulders of these same masses of people, for they have all the necessary means to avert war in their own hands.* In part by their apathy, in part by their passivity, and in part actively, these same masses of people make possible the catastrophes under which they themselves suffer more than anyone else. *To stress this guilt on the part of masses of people, to hold them solely responsible, means to take them seriously* (1970: 345).

Just stop obeying. As I argued in the introduction to *The Sociogony*, genuine authority flows from the bottom up and is nourished by disobedience. Disobedience to law does not amount to impiety (Boutmy 1902: 136) and often the best way in which to honor law is through "boldly violating" the law itself (Freud 1950: 79). We must follow Whitman's injunction to resist much and obey little ([1892] 1992: 7). Disobedience is not a threat to rational authority because, when it is challenged, it can deliver reasons. Rational authority does not necessarily engage in harsh punishment when it suffers minor infractions

---

43 Fromm's critical social psychology is hobbled to a certain extent by egoism and an unrepentant mysticism. Why would a radical have a passion for *independence* when what is necessary is a passion for solidarity?

44 My kids attended a daycare in Overland Park, Kansas where the informal motto was "You get what you get, and you don't throw a fit!"

or criminal trespass, and, most importantly, the 'law' of necessity ensures that once one cuts all the way down to the bone of the absolute *and keeps going*, disobedience already contains its own punishment. Reason can only be bent out of shape so far, and for so long, before it reasserts itself.

Disobedience is not always possible or desirable, however, as William Penn says, obedience should only pertain to what is necessary because unthinking obedience in politics and religion leads to a loss of freedom (1905: 155). What is necessary, however, is tricky business. It is not simply the case that authoritarians obey, and free radicals always disobey. When it aims at infinity, disobedience results in nothing more than anarchy and the liquidation of social solidarity. Critical theory finds itself in an odd situation now. After Kant, social philosophy never again had to justify authority, but today, as society slips off its axis, the authority of reason and the concept of the absolute have to be justified.

In the recent film about the young Marx and Engels, the Wilhelm Weitling character tells 'Marx' that critique, when carried too far, devours everything and, in the end, devours even itself.[45] Critique and negations are our lifeblood but the goal is not to create a void lacking "all positive content" (S. 282) or to bleed our love object to death—even if that love is a negative one. Nelson says, "The good is the evil we choose to ignore" ([1917] 1957: 90; cf. DOL: 40). If this is true it confirms our idea, following Hegel, Marx, and Durkheim, that we do not obey a thing because it is authoritative but, on the contrary, it is authoritative because we obey it. Our recognition of its rightness and reason confers upon it the status of a good social fact. Disobedience does not make the thing vanish like a puff of smoke but does make visible the constraining elements resting on pure force and brute domination in opposition to the constraints resting on rational consent.[46] We must stop thinking in terms of diametric oppositions when it comes to obedience and disobedience; authority

---

45   In Büchner's play *Danton's Death* the protagonist declares, "The Revolution is like Saturn, it eats its own children.... No! They won't dare." But Lacroix despairs: "Danton, you're a saint of the people. But a dead saint and the Revolution doesn't deal in relics, it's thrown the bones of kings into the street and smashed all the images and statues in the churches. Do you think they'll let you be some kind of monument?" (2010: 18). Schwarz (2017) provides an interesting review of the young Marx film and quotes the section of dialogue I refer to. When I saw the film, I was immediately struck at how timely this line is. Marx's youthful war on 'abstractions' and crude materialist reductions are not the stuff that subversion can rest on; violent conflict, yes, but not subversion.

46   Authority not only puts constraints around people but actually lifts individuals (Scharf 1970: 152) to the sublime of individuality in solidarity with others.

is the realm of polarities (C: 140). Asch makes a good point: "Independence is not simply the weakening of conformity, nor is conformity the dilution of independence" (1961: 153). One does not simply obey or disobey in the abstract; "singing the praise of nonconformity apart from evaluation of the norm or value to which it is related may lead to an absurd dilemma" (Sherif 1961: 162).[47] Subversive disobedience and nonconformity are actually negative forms of obedience and conformity and, as such, are not reducible to infantile wishes to destroy but to reveal the obdurate framework of social necessity. The effort made to surmount necessity "is but a new exhibition of its necessity" (Green [1895] 1924: 3). Giving into physical or moral necessity or some overwhelming externality is not even a problem of obedience or disobedience since it does not involve the "power to obey" (Ibid: 4). If I cannot disobey I can also not obey, but merely comply or suffer the punishment.

As we will see in this volume, when a person commits suicide it may appear to be a simple act of a depressed rebel, however, each suicide is simultaneously obedience to one or more commands on top of disobedience to another constellation of imperatives. When society and the individual become alien to one another, when society loses its grip on the person, individuals are overexposed to the demands of forces that champion sacrificial estrangement, limitlessness, tyranny, and self-obliteration for the enjoyment of some transcendental other or collective goal that would render the individual a disposable tool.

We normally wonder what it will take, in positive terms, to change society toward more democracy and equality, etc., but what we *fail (or refuse) to do* as individuals and groups is at least as important, if not decidedly *more* important, than what we actively set out to accomplish. For example, it would be impossible to wage a war if nobody showed up for the war. Likewise, it would be impossible to extract surplus value from workers if they walk off the job. The problem is made more complex, however, when we see that simply freeing people from the spell of fetishism and ideologies is insufficient. As Žižek points out, today, people know too well what they are doing, that they are subjects of ideology, but they will cynically persist in their own enjoyable degradation (1989). Unfortunately, because he has no real theory of the big, Žižek's prescription is for more symptom enjoyment (cf. Freud [1927] 1961: 20) rather than

---

47 "The elevation of nonconformity alone to the level of a slogan has its roots in an untenable dichotomy between individual and group, in a preconceived inevitability of clash between the two" (Sherif 1961: 191).

risking the potential for a break from capital which provides our fantasmatic coordinates for life in bourgeois reality. There are no easy answers for this new chapter in the social psychology of authority but as we walk backwards into the future we will have to replenish our theoretical matrix from deeper wells and wider panoramas.

CHAPTER 1

Reflective Determinations

> To think with concepts is not merely to see the real in its most general characteristics but to turn upon sensation a beam that lights, penetrates, and transforms it.
>
> EFRL: 437

> But the beginning of things, of a world especially, is necessarily vague, tangled, chaotic, and exceedingly disturbing. How few of us ever emerge from such beginning! How many souls perish in its tumult!
>
> CHOPIN 1899: 34

The odyssey of the concept entails a continuous progression from the merely abstract or subjective concept (indistinct notion, vacuous name, or some kind of vague generality) to the fully actualized concept where reality is fully unified (the *Idea*). We may represent this dynamic by summarizing portions of Hegel's *Philosophical Propaedeutic* (1986: 97–104) while drawing upon other elements.

1 The Lifeless Universal

Working from the bottom[1] (of Figure 1) we find the abstract or "crudely formed" (EFRL: 434) *concept* in itself. At this embryonic stage (Hegel 1988: 407) the concept is a lifeless abstract universal (Durkheim 1961: 279–80) or a signifier lacking a rational structure hardly deserving the name 'concept'—it is "an empty word or some assumed, unjustified conception" (SL: 73) or is perhaps some isolated individual thing.[2] Stuck in this *undivided* condition, "theoretical

---

1 The distinction between a beginning and an end, or result, is not obvious. From the standpoint of science, the beginning is the result (the idea) whereas for ordinary experience the result (the idea) comes at the end. In this way, the end or the result, is already the beginning (Hegel 1988: 432–33).

2 Even the individual, abstracted and isolated, is a problem of conception, not perception (EFRL: 434). Contemporary neuropsychology is trying to catch up in an inverted and trailing manner with Hegel and Durkheim. Unfortunately, the way it is going, it will never break

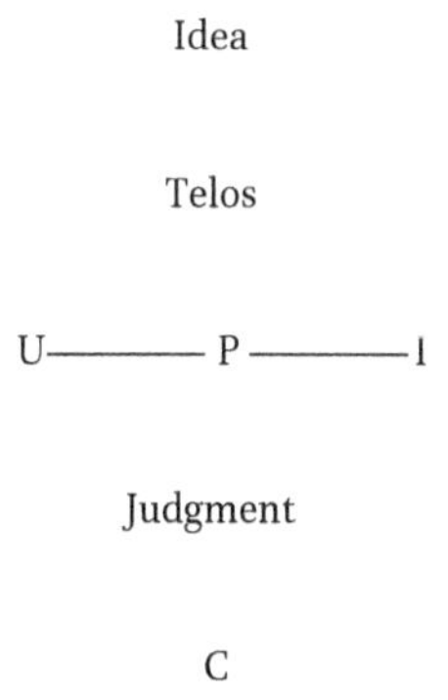

```
        Idea

        Telos

U ———— P ———— I

    Judgment
                        FIGURE 1
        C               The odyssey of the concept
                        SOURCE: CREATED BY AUTHOR
```

consciousness" (Hegel 1988: 416) has little to show for itself but figments of thought preferred by ignorant common sense (SL: 84–85). As impoverished as it is, the concept (a kind of lifeless or "undisturbed" universal or general mode of consciousness) nevertheless possesses the capacity for further development.[3] In order to keep living, this thinking (formless, lacking determinateness and being indifferent to its possible contradictions) will have to push itself forward through a series of self-negations, an inherent process of self-determination, and raise itself in thought from the abstract and the immediate to the concrete, mediated universal truth.[4] The concept might 'prefer' to stay at rest in an undeveloped state if possible (a kind of conceptual death drive) but its defects and imperfections eventually and necessarily require rectification (ERL: 435). This concept will *destroy itself* in the judgement.

---

through the subjectivist barrier. Barrett's (2017) conceptualist theory of the mind confirms some of the points raised in *The Sociogony* regarding color and perceptions, etc., but if we want to grasp the empire of the concept the *imperial* nature of some concepts has to be accounted for. To posit "ontological objectivity" or reification is not identical with the nature of the sacred. The problem with the latest trend is that it is based on an experiential or *a posteriori* foundation. It is truly amazing that every ten years, or so, a one-sided constructionism is reinvented all over again, in one discipline after another, in weaker and weaker forms, with little awareness of cross-disciplinary history.

3   "This progression is logical: it lies in the nature of the determining process itself to determine itself further in this way—this is logical necessity" (Hegel 1988: 407).
4   The truth is that which unites all people in the comprehension of their collective spiritual products as their own creations: Spirit knowing itself as Spirit. Capitalism has the power to connect the world in a *technically* rational totality of work and exchange relations, but capitalism cannot work itself beyond the moment of understanding which means that capitalism remains conceptually incomprehensible to Spirit (cf. Hegel 1956: 140).

2 The Judgement

The *judgement* is what we might call an initial or "primordial" or "primal division" (Hegel 1988: 196, 359) between subject and predicate resulting in a *relation* between, on the one hand, the initial *abstract* mode of consciousness and, on the other, a concrete, natural,[5] sensible, finite, external, alien other that it has created for itself (Hegel 1988: 416–17). This splitting or "falling away" (Hegel 1988: 417) is a self-creative and dynamic *experience*[6] because every something is only a something in relation to some other thing.[7] Human thought is essentially comparative and only through comparisons are any explanations possible (S: 41). We should, however, resist the temptation to characterize this splitting or division as a matter-of-fact process operating in a moral vacuum. We are at the scene where a prejudice (pre-judgment) is tearing itself apart and suffering distortions of the type we find in, say, dreamwork. These distortions entail the diremption, surface alterations, and dislocation of previous thoughts (Freud 1939: 52). This is a problem of the highest importance. Philosophy has the task of transforming representations into concepts (Hegel 1988: 145) but, as Durkheim reveals, not all representations are created equal.[8]

---

5   The Latin *natura* means the quality and essence of a thing.
6   "Spirit becomes object because it is just this movement of becoming an *other to itself*, i.e. becoming an *object to itself*, and of suspending this otherness. And experience is the name we give to just this movement, in which the immediate, the unexperienced, i.e. the abstract, whether it be of sensuous ... being, or only thought of as simple, becomes alienated from itself and then returns to itself from this alienation, and is only then revealed for the first time in its actuality and truly, just as it then has become a property of consciousness..." (PS: 21).
7   The generic or general exists only in relation with or "in" the specific or singular (EFRL: 434). The general is really just an alienated individual. For example, in Marx abstract labor or labor in general is just specific forms of concrete labor without regard for their unique qualities, reduced to the abstraction of *labor pure and simple* (C: 135; cf. EFRL: 434).
8   The profane representations of ordinary understanding are amenable to development with a natural and frictionless drift through time, but collective representations are akin to gods and demons, set aside or excluded, defended, permeated with projected mana, domineering, and therefore taboo. Even though ideas such as mana, grace, value, etc., all rest on different forms of social organization they nonetheless share the capacity of resisting determinations (Durkheim [1912] 1915: 221). The sacred as an absolute power can deflect, distort, or absorb signs except under unusual circumstances. Society's task is to periodically regenerate, defend, and preserve these representations. Sociology's task is the critique of collective (social) representations, separating the optional from the obligatory, unmasking the charlatans (e.g., Durkheim [1912] 1915: 103), and, like the protagonist in Nietzsche's *Zarathustra*, declaring an armistice in the face of iron necessity. After all, taken to extremes, critical disenchantment in the abstract really only disorganizes the ordinary understanding while leaving the sacred relatively unscathed and even more mysterious to individual consciousness. Critical negation is our calling, but we cannot lead consciousness from one bad ontology to an opposing

The judgment as relation does not create qualities or properties of a thing but the relation is what activates these properties (C: 149).[9] At first, consciousness might try to limit what is essential to the subject to a single predicate, but seldom do we find a quality that pertains to only one thing. Next, consciousness tries to relate more predicates to the subject (providing greater determination to the concept) but it faces numerous troubles when, for example, predicates seem to push the subject away from its concept (conceptual deformation); others do not recognize certain claims or assertions regarding the relationship between predicates and the subject; and, lacking objective ground upon which we might establish truth, we fall short of the subject's relation to the concept as merely probable (we wind up in the realm of probabilities rather than certainties). Moreover, simply adding more predicates to the subject[10] does not seem to accomplish what consciousness wants anyway;[11] while attaching things to the subject, consciousness thinks that it is arriving at some kind of positive universalization of the subject, thereby bringing it into closer actualization with its concept, but with every positive judgment the negations of those judgements seem also to adhere to it. Depending upon the point of view taken, the subject appears positively to be a universal but, from another negative angle, the subject appears to be a particularity that belongs to another universal. The realm of judgments is a labyrinth of confusions where things take on different qualities and valances depending upon how they are related.

The concept is undergoing some degree of development through its struggle and divisions and concretizing itself. It is on the road of *becoming* (SL: 115) but judgments are contradictory (the relationship between the subject and the

---

and equally defective ontology, e.g., from reified faith to bone-headed materialism. If theoretical negation could fully obliterate the sacred (a feat never accomplished in history as far as we know) it would leave the world devoid of 'jazz' and the enjoyment of moral supplements, guiding representations, and "objective signs," which makes no sense at all (EFRL: 9). Nothing is more difficult than working in opposition to society to expose the hidden dialectical processes that operate invisibly in the background (cf. C: 268).

9 "A second one comes, its caresses bestowing / And so by the changes of pleasure I'm blest" (Goethe 1983: 5).
10 When predication runs wild and the subject attempts to establish a universe of relations with itself we find ourselves in the position of the neurotic (cf. Freud [1921] 1959: 97).
11 Every social movement animated by the principle of inclusion faces the conundrum of adding predicates to its representations: sometimes the addition of new flag color generates backlash from the established colors and, in others, the addition of more acronym letters becomes controversial, cumbersome, and is simply terminated with a plus sign indicative of "many more."

predicate is ambiguous) and the concept so far lacks a ground in reason—i.e., the concept has not yet built for itself this rational ground and, as such, is enclosed within the sphere of the understanding which deals with sorting through the finite, prosaic aspects of its problem. In simple terms, consciousness is engaged in determining the essential qualities that correlate with its concept but finds that every determination is lacking or contradictory. However, in relation to something else it has the capacity for further self-particularization[12] (the generation of a *third thing* that can mediate and 'magnetize' the two extremes[13] of the judgement, because, now, with the separation[14] of the terms of the judgement we have a mirror whereby the parts are capable of reflecting off one another and finding something in common, i.e., that they are actually *related* to one another through another intermediary.

> I am the poet of slaves, and of the masters of slaves ... / And I will stand between the masters and the slaves, / entering into both, so that both shall understand me alike.
> WHITMAN 1847–1854

Instead of searching for all the predicates that might or might not belong to a subject, consciousness comes around to *the single quality that all subjects have in common*. It would be futile to limit any single subject to one predicate (the problem of essentialism), but it is quite another thing to find the one predicate that all subjects have in common. Finally, we have necessity and absolute self-ordering. To the extent that subjects are united by a common element, they are related to one another in a universal sphere while their excluded qualities dangle in another dimension, an infraliminal realm of ordinary understandings. This dualism is a progressive advance over the monism of older productive regimes, but that discussion will have to wait. One might be tempted to think that capitalism, with its absolute reign of Value, has achieved the desired goal of rational unification but exchange-value is an abstract subject that confuses itself for a substance. In economics, Spirit is reduced to something analogous

---

12   The immediate is everywhere already mediated (SL: 68) but the mediations (the things that made the present possible and determine their shapes) are lurking in the background of history or are sunk in unconsciousness. Education means bringing these invisible mediations into consciousness (Hegel [1840] 1995b: 422).

13   Going far afield into musical theory, "As soon as the third is added, the current is 'magnetized.' One of the tones ... definitely becomes generator, the other one being subordinated" (Levy 1985: 22).

14   Analytical separation opens the space for the emergence of a new concept (Kant 1991: 164).

to a pre-modern religious form (the reason modern economics eliminated 'value' from its technical lexicon and replaced it with *price*) and would therefore not satisfy the criteria of being Spirit's self-consciousness of consciousnesses.[15]

The reflective process[16] is the means by which we develop representations, judgments, and points of view (Hegel 1988: 260). The individual moments of this reflection are representations. No longer immediate, these things represent something for some other (Hegel 1988: 318). For example, in the commodity relation, iron 'knows' itself to be a value not in itself but in the physical shape of some other thing, e.g., corn, its equivalent in the exchange relation. The moment of active subjectivity is reflected in the representation of passive objectivity of the mirroring equivalent (the corn). Symbols, then, or representations, are the "ruling element" (Hegel 1988: 319) and hold sway, in part, due to their *enigmatic* nature (Ibid: 326). We may analytically separate representations, cut them out of context, but our dialectical method also includes the reunification of representations with their symbolic twins and determining their common concept.

Relating through splitting and mirror doubling is the reason Hegel's dialectic is called 'speculative' (rooted in the word *speculum* for 'mirror' and *specula* for 'watchtower' or 'lookout').[17] Reflections inherent in oppositional social interaction (S: 246) create "determinations of reflection" or reflective determinations. The authority relation, e.g., the king and his subjects, is one such *Reflexionsbestimmungen* (C: 149).[18]

---

15 By jettisoning the concept of value, economics has alienated itself from social reality and is not only useless as a force in teleological activity but functions as an ideological counterweight to conceptual progress. Negating value and substituting it with price is literally negating collective consciousness and replacing it with an empty sign, in effect, confusing reflections for mirrors and signs for things (cf. Goethe 1840: 302). Humanity might have been better off if, instead of the University of Chicago, it been afflicted with just another war or plague. But this kind of thing happens throughout academia: psychology no longer grasps the psyche; sociology no longer cares about society; anthropologists do field research in hotels, and so on. The university as we would like it to be is essentially dead and has been for decades.

16 Expectedly, the 'reflective' process involves distortions and inversions and operates mostly behind the backs of consciousness: "They do this without being aware of it" (C: 166–67). When we examine the reflective work of common sense we get the distinct impression that there is some kind of parallel with the processes we find in dreaming.

17 Dialectic (ultimately from *diá*, across + *légein*, to speak) is split reasoning (Worrell 2019: 159). 'I say' (*légō*) is related to 'speech' (*logos*) but the further we move back into the pre-Socratic world, *logos* is not merely 'word' or 'speech' but an impersonal and divine power.

18 'Functions' are "definite ways of acting that are repeated identically in given circumstances" so long as the conditions remain unchanged (DOL: 302). A 'moment' is anything that

3   The Syllogism

The *syllogism* (U–P–I) unites the two poles of the judgement together by way of a third concept that functions as a mediating ground. This self-generation of a third thing is "the fundamental process of … reason through every form of her varied work" (Sullivan 1871: 27–28). An example of the syllogism is found in Durkheim's *Suicide*.[19] Take, for example, the concept of individual autonomy as a half-baked or only partially articulated notion that whips us along the road of foolish endeavors: we are instructed from an early age that 'the sky's the limit' and that with enough willpower, and unrelenting effort, any goal is within reach. I should not let anything, or anyone hold me back. A person should do things their own way, go it alone, and on the road to personal success one should follow the code of conduct they find in their own heart. Yet, at every turn I find obstacles and, especially, the willpower of other individuals each striving to fulfill their personal goals. I also find that we are competing for the same prizes, trying to out-do one another, and that we cannot form positive relations with one another because those associations would hinder individual progress. We could combine our efforts but then I would be limited as an individual; our combination would not make me feel like I had augmented my power but that I had been diminished by allowing my energies to be dissipated

---

is reflected, i.e., entered into a speculative (oppositional) relation with something else. The word 'moment' comes from the domain of mechanics where "In the case of the lever, weight and distance from a point are called its mechanical moments on account of the sameness of their effect, in spite of the contrast otherwise between something real, such as a weight, and something ideal, such as a mere spatial determination, a line" (SL: 107).

[19]   In the first volume I briefly discussed the totemic syllogism found in *Elementary Forms of Religious Life* but another, short illustration of this kind of conceptual structure can be found in the discussion of the types of totems in the first chapter of the second book where we find that the totem is normally and primarily a universal or general object (e.g., the species kangaroo instead of this or that empirical, individual kangaroo) with abnormal or secondary types following later: the class-unique particularity as well as the individual ancestor. Further along the development of social organization, divisions, and effacements we find partial objects or bits and pieces of totems ([1912] 1915: 124–26). Also, with respect to the churinga, we find that in-themselves they are just individual rock or wood objects but their universal status as embodiments or carriers of mana are mediated by the particularity of the signification of the totemic mark upon their bodies (Ibid: 144). Once engraved with the mark, the object becomes a sign-thing of holy dread and must be treated and regarded separately from things not bearing the mark. How is the universal value status of an individual labor product signified to the world but through price-anointing? Critical theory is often quite glib when it comes to conflating prices and value but the two are as different as reflections and mirrors. There can be prices where there is no underlying value whatsoever just as there can be value without prices, after all, profits are priceless.

or expended in the affairs of others. If I want it all, I cannot partner with others who also want their share. One solution is to do violence to others,[20] enslave my competition, and make them extensions of my will, but I am outnumbered and surrounded on all sides, and, furthermore, my autonomy would thereby be contaminated by heteronomy because my quest for everything would be undermined by the material needs of my acquired dependents. Time and energy that should be devoted to the pursuit of the All would be squandered in management and supervision. Moreover, I want it all *right now* therefore getting involved with others would postpone the gratification of my insatiable desires. My feet may be on the ground, but my head is in the clouds and the journey finds me acting alone in the world, lacking the subjective and material resources to reach my goal of capturing the concrete infinite through trial and error (DOL: 278). In my impatience I might even resort to games of chance, lucky charms, and magical formulas.[21] "Have but contempt for reason and for science, / Man's noblest force spurn with defiance, / Subscribe to magic and illusion, / The Lord of Lies aids your confusion" (Goethe [1808] 1961: 195).

The bibelot of 'autonomy' has generated out of itself two contradictory moments: an ego that longs for the sensuously infinite on one side (that is incapable of actualizing the ideal of autonomy) opposed to the ideology of empirical limitlessness. So long as individuals battle in their own name toward the infinite they will experience only futility and premature death, either partial (Hegel 1988: 311) or total. We can judge that suicide is the natural outcome of this infinity problem—the infinity of my dreams or *egoism* and the infinity of my desires or *anomie* (S: 287)—unless some way forward out of this deadlock is found. A number of scenarios are likely, from the elaborate dance of self consciousnesses mirroring one another and recognizing themselves recognizing one another (PS: 112) to the mundane accident in which I get myself into trouble and somebody less self-absorbed comes to my rescue.

In my dealings with others I discover that assemblage produces physical and psychical effects that are found to be lacking in solitary existence and that mere linkages and connections (even if totalized) are no substitute for genuine, holistic association. I learn the hard way that truth and becoming are in positive *relations* with others in conjunction with the negative social calculus

---

20   When the striving and creative ego overcomes obstacles and others by means of violence and destructiveness we have made contact with the iconoclast, destructive hyper-individualism (Royce 1969: 303).
21   Magic involves a kind of half-baked, synthetic *a priori* judgment (Mauss 1972: 124). The magician and magical rites can, under some circumstances, serve as a "middle term" linking the collective with the individual (Durkheim [1912] 1915: 205).

of relativities and equivalencies (SL: 118–230).[22] Rather than continuing my path toward probable self-destruction following my subjective inclinations, hoping for a miracle to make things right, I accept that limitations and sacrifices are necessary,[23] not only for others but also for myself, and that competition and accumulation are not the only values in life worth pursuing. Indeed, in the absence of affirmative relations with others I discover that my previous values were in fact not even values to begin with but little more than one-sided rationalizations and reaction formations. I have learned the value of self-restraint as a necessary precondition for the education of Spirit from its enslavement to perceptions and magic to the freedom of reflection, concepts, and reasoning (Freud 1939: 144–45, 150). From now on, I treat and regard others not merely as obstacles and impediments (the competition) but as co-operators in some mutual project that has real and lasting value.[24] There is now something new in the world and my concept of self has grown to include others.[25] My conscience has also grown by leaps and bounds from internal strife, to an external compulsion, to finally, something objective and absolute that marks the return of the external as a new form of subjectivity: it is as if my regulatory life has been transformed "into a norm which must be satisfied for its own sake, not for my sake nor for yours" (SGS: 256). In other words, what was ideal has become autonomous, real, and concentrated.

Individuality is not actualized in running away from the objective but in working together toward shared, higher ideals. Sacrifices are made, that is true, but the compensation (infinite subjectivity, life, and personality) is greater than the losses (the spurious infinite and contingent impulses). I have been altered and have become something other. By acting with regard for people and accepting limits, a principle of altruism emerges and mediates the extremes

---

22   The work of *logos* includes not only ratiocination but also the formation of ratios. Teleological activity entails a *rationing* or portioning-out and self-limitation.

23   "For it is by the sacrifice, not survival, of the best that advance is made" (Younghusband 1915: 79). The infinite automatically accompanies the finite. 'Finite' and 'infinite' are philosophical re-castings of evil and good in the domain of religion (Hegel 1988: 301). For the infinite ego, the concept of finitude is foisted upon others, preserving for the one the freedom of the infinite. However, no one is free of doubt when action confronts insurmountable barriers or extraordinary difficulties. Reflection is the necessary outcome of the jostling of egos in a hard world and the infinity of one becomes shot through with the finite limits of the others (Cousin 1853, 1: 126–27).

24   See Freud's famous 'just-so' story of the sons of the primal horde father working out a compromise.

25   We also learn that 'our' concept was never our property to begin with but was the work and product of society (EFRL: 435) and to think and to be a human means to think and act in concert with others who share the same concept.

of egoism and anomie.²⁶ "The original content of morality is of an altruistic-social nature" (SGS: 260). This new spirit does not simply come and go with fleeting interactions. I will eventually come to desire the emersion in this way of acting, thinking, and feeling and even to desire obligations and duties (Durkheim 1974: 35–36). This permanent desire will crystallize into needs as well as a set of forceful representations that enable individuals to represent society within themselves (SGS: 255) and the resulting sanctity of society will be reflected into my increasingly integrated personality. Once I recognize my "limited autonomy" I have moved from a "dreamy and solitary" egoism to real "spirituality" and my "soul" is now "in the world" and entangled with others; my little spirit grows and merges with an objective Super-Spirit (Durkheim 1974: 28, 34) that covers the tracks of its sociohistorical genesis (SGS: 255; EFRL: 7).²⁷ The result of this syllogism (the sublation of the extremes in a negation of negations) is the leap from individualism (the value of the undivided *me*) to genuine individuality and personality (the value of the synthetic and organized *we*) that does not simply muddle along from one crisis to another but with an eye toward an objective goal.²⁸ The principle of altruism is not something 'in' me (I am not altruistic *per se*) but something we have in common and, once this new thing is objectified and reflected in some particular form, e.g., a constitution, guild organization, union, party, or state, etc., or we view it simply from the universal standpoint, it will function not merely as an abstract or separate representation but as a collective representation for all the individuals entangled in this common dialectic.²⁹ We have worked beyond the judgement and have arrived at a syllogism that promises life over death, however, we have gotten ahead of ourselves; the actualization of this syllogism lies ahead of us.³⁰

26   It would be equally accurate to indicate that action is itself, where the result is greater than the abstract ego, essentially altruistic (cf. S: 279). See the section on 'composite forces' in Chapter Three of this book for more on the dialectic of egoism and altruism and how society functions as the concrete universal mediator of opposing forces.
27   On the syllogisms of conscience and concrete objectivity see Simmel (SGS: 254–57).
28   Individuality separates the physical or biological entity from other entities whereas personality relates the individual to society. Personality is the "highest type of existence known to mankind ... [and] is distinctly, and it may be said solely, the product of the workings of what we know as society" (Cooke 1920: 19).
29   Laws are necessary but they exist to be broken. In the right kind of society, crime occasions the assemblage of society's members to reflect upon the core values of the collectivity. We need crimes and punishments because they require the solemn gathering of a jury for not only finding guilt of individuals who have run afoul of the law but also weighing the rationality and value of the laws themselves. We are accountable to the law, but the law is also subject to ceremonial accounting.
30   Crucially, we do not set out as individuals to create logic, rather, logic emerges from praxis and the construction of an organized society (EFRL: 433).

Two important points need to be made. First, to reiterate, the third thing is something that individuals have in common yet neither of them actually possess as empirical qualities[31] in themselves (e.g., the value of commodities is not 'in' the commodities except to say that 'commodity' already means an exchange *relation*). *The signifier of this thing might be held by the individual but the signified is not.* It is for this reason that when we examine a one-sided part of the whole it appears that is both *has* and *has not* the thing we are interested in (cf. SL: 824). Without the third thing we will never develop beyond abstract universality. "[T]his third must be present; for the two terms have no separate subsistence of their own but *are* only in becoming, in this third" (SL: 93).[32] Second, the syllogism as a relation actually involves a *doubling* that reintroduces

---

31 Two terms may attempt to find an empirical connection between one another but the empirical (contingent, finite, negative) is insufficient to hold them together and would also result in treating one pole as a passive mirror for the active other (this is the transition between the two poles of the expression) and vice versa. However, *transition* between the two "transient moments" (SL: 103) runs in both directions and what would constitute paralysis of a loop of changing from one thing into the other (SL: 106) is broken by the *becoming* through abstraction (SL: 93) or alienation—the negation of the negation, reducing the empirical to the generic, e.g., different forms of concrete labor to the unity of abstract labor. In Marx's accidental value form, we see this shift from transition and *change* to becoming and *exchange* as the dynamic between the relative and the equivalent poles of the relation. Two individuals come together and are alienated, reduced to a third, generic 'substance' in order to become commodities out of their prior existence as empirical labor products. Sublated (or cancelled upwards) they form an equilibrated ratio of values (X quantity of iron = Y quantity of linen).

32 "The unity whose moments ... are inseparable, is at the same time different from them and is thus a third to them; this third in its own most characteristic form is *becoming*. *Transition* is the same as becoming except that in the former one tends to think of the two terms, from one of which transition is made to the other, as at rest, apart from each other, the transition taking place *between* them" (SL: 93). Reflections are comparisons that bring together concepts and people into relations with one another. "When this reflection finds the same thing in two *different objects*, the resultant unity is such that there is presupposed the complete *indifference* to it of the objects themselves which are compared, so that this comparing and unity does not concern the objects themselves and is a procedure and a determining external to them" (SL: 91). The value of commodities pertains not to the objects themselves (they do not have value in them). They are reduced in thought to generic instances of abstract labor, labor pure and simple, without regard for anything else specifically. The absurdity of the capitalist syllogism is such that where two things like pizza and beer converge they find value (an abstract universal) is the thing they have in common. We cannot eat value and if we wish to eat pizza and guzzle beer we have to go through several bizarre contortions in order to arrive at consumables. 'Effective demand' means that *hunger* or *thirst* are never mediating aspects and, as such, when pizza and beer encounter one another in exchange their material shapes are haunted by ghostly doubles, taboo energies that keep them separated—one needs a special power, money, in order to exorcize the demons of value.

immediacy into the resulting, mediated structure—i.e., where the particular unifies and mediates the universal and the individual elements, it also now stands as an extreme in two separate judgments: (U–P) and (P–I). Examples of this double judgment include Marx's general formula for capital (M–C–M) dissected as separate analytic moments: (M–C) and (C–M) as well as the circulation of commodities (C–M–C) broken down into two separate judgements (C–M) and (M–C). Where there was previously one syllogism (the unity of two judgments) there now stands, as the result of analytic regression, two judgments necessitating further mediation and development. The immediate always presupposes mediation (the immediate is everywhere mediated whether we know it or not) and immediacy presupposes a drive to overcome isolation (abstraction). Once Spirit works itself up to the syllogism it has some ground to stand on, but it is not yet fully stable and is still in the process of creating or producing a more unified and absolute standpoint for itself; the subject and object, or the internal and external, are not yet synthesized or reconciled with one another.

4   Telos

Telos or the "teleological act" is another syllogism (this teleological act is mediating, practical activity or *praxis*, e.g., labor, political struggle, etc.) that brings together subject and object; the previous syllogism, in its most developed, disjunctive form, is the gateway to objectivity (as we see in Hegel's *Logic*) but telos is the actual synthesis, *Aufheben* (SL: 106–08), or violent innovation (EFRL: 435) of extremes in the objectification of Spirit.[33] What goes on in this syllogism is the working up of the real world in conformity with an ideal conception. The world will be bathed in the fire of conscious praxis (C: 289; Durkheim

---

33   *Aufheben* is usually translated as 'sublation' which means a kind of 'upward cancellation' whereby that which is negated or abolished is simultaneously preserved and transcended (cf. S: 388) or pushed to a higher point of conceptualization (elevated in thought). The word 'innovation' is also interesting in that it implies alteration, renewal, restoration, and return. Synthesis does not just happen but requires discipline and subjugation of the elemental: "However much we like, today, to sharply reject [the] demonization and rationalization of elementary vitality, one should not forget that precisely that Puritan breeding, which for long periods of time attained a never-before-achieved disciplining of the man, should be credited with a deepening of the spiritual and ethical relation between man and woman that since then has never been lost. Only then, when subjugation of the elementary was taken seriously, could the focus become the spiritual melting together of the partners, the intimacy of their spiritual relationship as the most important meaning of marriage" (Weber 2003: 88). D.H. Lawrence would be sceptical.

1974: 3). The concept is necessarily driven forward in relation to its efforts and the transformation of reality in relation to the determining power of the concept of what reality should be like—because, until we arrive at the standpoint of the absolute, nothing is as it should be. In Marxist mythology, the moment of telos is represented[34] by the proletariat as the identical subject-object of history that, as it performs exploited labor, simultaneously undermines capitalism by building, alongside surplus labor products, the actual ground for communist utopia regulated by the general intellect. "History loves such restorations, in which later fusions are redissolved and former separations become once more apparent" (Freud 1939: 44). Lest we imagine that synthetic unities are simply good productions, keep in mind that evil always rides side by side with the good.[35] If unities are greater than and different than their sublated elements, they may introduce unprecedented spectacles of horror and brutality, e.g., the sublation of beauty and the sublime into utilitarian purposiveness that produced "torrents of blood" (Hegel 1988: 375–86).

5   The Idea

The final syllogistic moment of the *Idea* (Hegel 2007: 276) is the actualized concept or identity of concept and reality. Here, reality is as it should be by virtue of consciousness working itself up to the level of science and by transforming itself and the world scientifically.[36] The Idea "releases its determinations freely and gives them a special existence" (Henrich 1971: 164). However, the Idea is not just a set of logical operations. Logic has no real existence apart from the service is extends to society. By attaining the actuality of the concept, Spirit has augmented itself with a *moral* or sacred quality. Spirit coming to know itself as Spirit is not a disenchanted condition even though the sacredness is known and expressed in rational and secular terms (Durkheim 1974: 69). In other words, the 'jazz' persists. The Idea cannot emerge

---

34   Here we see that the whole process of synthesis also involves various modalities or dimensions of consciousness such that the process of unification is open to mythology (see Cassirer 2013: 325) and the obfuscation of the rational, historical, and multiplicity with an irrational composite narrative.

35   "Nonidentity is the secret *telos* of identification.... but the ideal of identity must not simply be discarded. Living in the rebuke that the thing is not identical with the concept is the concept's longing to become identical with the thing" (Adorno 1973: 149).

36   Keep in mind that Hegel's *Wissenschaft* (holistic and systematic science) is far removed from the hyper-specialized and pinched empiricism of today's divided (alienated) scientific pursuits.

through the efforts of an abstract mind working out logical problems but is the product of the evolution of social organization. "We may say that what is moral is everything that is a source of solidarity, everything that forces man to take account of other people, to regulate his actions by something other than the promptings of his own egoism, and the more numerous and strong these ties are, the more solid is the morality" (DOL: 331). Where there is morality there is the Idea and where there is the Idea there is morality. We have arrived at concrete universality or, metaphorically, the worship not of "man in the abstract" (C: 172) but the concrete Personality (S: 336–37). Both Marx (revolution) and Durkheim (reformation) would be philosophically satisfied in the transition from The Person of Value to the Value of Personality (S: 336–37; cf. SL: 531). The full value of personality over abstract substances and other defective forms of thinking made possible from the abandonment of common sense and the working of thought up to the concept as Idea. Once Spirit can think conceptually it is empowered to fill itself out and strive toward a dictatorship of reason.

As Freud says, reason

> is among the powers which we may most expect to exercise a unifying influence on men—on men who are held together which such difficulty and whom it is therefore scarcely possible to rule. It may be imagined how impossible human society would be, merely if everyone had his own multiplication table and his own private units of length and weight. Our best hope for the future is that intellect—the scientific spirt, reason—may in process of time establish a dictatorship in the mental life of man. The nature of reason is a guarantee that afterwards it will not fail to give man's emotional impulses and what is determined by them the position they deserve. But the common compulsion exercised by such a dominance of reason will prove to be the strongest uniting bond among men and lead the way to further unions (1965: 212).

The extent to which the dictatorship of the intellect or reason is achieved is the extent to which the Idea has been realized and is also the extent to which the heart can feel and relate to others: "The heart can be no larger than the mind" (Durkheim 1978: 114). The Idea, in our sense, is collective conscience that knows itself for what it truly is; society possesses itself in its truth; it has its concept and through that concept grasps the whole (Durkheim 1961: 277). To the extent that it loses its concept via the intrusion of a powerful external necessity is the extent to which society degenerates and slides back into unconsciousness, conflict, and aimless self-destruction.

Throughout history Spirit has been stalked by an objective phantom and the appearance of sublime doubles that, ultimately, lack the power to remain concealed: Spirit uncovers the truth that these appearances are manifestations of its own activity (Hegel 2007: 276; EFRL).[37] Reason entails a moment of revelation.[38] Marx delivers one such revelation: the pursuit of surplus value is the disoriented and destructive pursuit of ourselves in an alien, transfigured form. Capital seeks life through death. When we arrive at the Idea, Spirit finally knows itself not as mana and totems or value and commodities but as Spirit. Consciousness is in possession of the truth. The Absolute Spirit is what Durkheim would call a "consciousness of consciousnesses" that, "as it sees from above, it sees far ahead; at every moment, it embraces all reality" (EFRL: 445). By raising itself up out of itself, the historical journey of the concept winds up

---

37 Ancient myths and philosophies may seem absurd or comical to the modern person yet, when we scratch beneath the surface, we find that people have been wrestling with most of the same basic problems that we deal with: material and cultural production, distribution, accumulation, inequality, servitude, ideology, exploitation, reproduction, death, identity, solidarity, regulation, individuality, destructiveness, just to name a handful. However, it is misleading to flatly assert that people in the past faced a lot of the same problems that we face—it is not that people everywhere all the time are doing and thinking the same things. We take the past seriously because our predecessors are "kindred beings" (Freyer [1928] 1998: 1) that had a hand in making a world that has been transmitted to us. We must take the past as our present because the person that examines "the historical only as past involuntarily makes it falsely similar to his own present" (Jaspers 1986: 480–81). We can generalize something that Adorno once said about the necessity of reading "earlier" sociology (i.e., stuff that is considered outdated by today's specialists): the scraps of the past, the outdated and obsolete, the dead, etc., continue to live on in our own world whether we realize it or not and we cannot know ourselves adequately if we do not know the past, our past, which confronts us as an alien past or those ghosts that lurk past the horizon of conscious awareness. The past must 'make sense' to us for us to 'make sense' of ourselves (2000: 98). As Freyer puts it, we are tasked with sinking ourselves into all the "expressions" of "alien life" if we are to comprehend the alien nature of our own existence. "In these expressions lived kindred beings: we read what they have written; we see what they have painted; we find what they have built. A piece of earth has been shaped through the activity of their mind. Because the course of the world has handed down to us the precipitate of this activity, even if in ruins, a mind now stands face to face, over time and space, with another mind. If both minds do not resemble one another in their fundamental structure, then no understanding would take place: the commonality of human nature in its essential composition, both present and past, is the prerequisite for the understanding of the human sciences" (Freyer [1928] 1998: 1).

38 With the arrival of Christianity (a religion of revelation) the way is finally open to the rational comprehension of the absolute whereas, in all prior religions, revelation is impossible and the sacred is indiscernible as what it truly is, the product of human teleological activity. Consult Westphal (1990: 196–201) on the more or less identical theories of god in Hegel and Durkheim.

sub specie aeternitatis (EFRL: 437) in Life. Liberated from contingency this Life is Beautiful.[39]

One can scoff at the image of consciousness working itself up to some absolute position, but I would argue that it is self-evidently true that, over the last two centuries, this is exactly what has happened on numerous occasions and is the underlying reason we will never get over Hegel, Marx, and Durkheim. Of course, Marxists insist that Durkheim's reduction of the absolute to a particular society does not affirm the universality of humanity (embodied in the united workers of the world) and followers of Durkheim write off the Marxist universal as an abstraction, or worse, a quasi-religious belief system that lacks concrete ground. When Marx and Engels wrote about the workers of the world in the *Communist Manifesto* it was an abstraction and now that there really is an interconnected global workforce all the individuals and units seem to prefer insular animosity over universal solidarity. Naturally, we look around and find that the world is not as it should be, it is not rationally united, or beautiful, and that where Marxism attempted to reorganize the world it led to horror. Even so, regression and nightmares are baked into this process Hegel soberly compared to a "slaughter-bench" of "enormous sacrifices" (1956: 21).

6   Necessity Versus Necessity

Conceptual evolution moves in the direction of truth and objectivity (EFRL: 438), and one can think of absolute sociology as the process whereby conflicting syllogisms or dialectics (Marxist and Durkheimian, for example) are sublated in a third dialectic, but the process could be represented in other ways that allows for the open-ended and 'fractal' nature of the journey of the concept across time and space that takes into consideration the failure of praxis in the moment of telos: dead ends, circuitous reversals (Hegel 1948: 79; cf. Žižek 2014b: 36), restarts, externalizations, inversions, etc.[40] It is true for Hegel that the dialectical process of the concept from mere notion to the Idea is internally *necessary* but necessity itself can be negated by powerful, external necessities. At one moment an entire people are drifting along self-contentedly when, all of a sudden, through conquest, or gradually, "through a slow and silent infiltration" (DOL: 279), they are "breathed upon by the spirit of foreign

---

39   The beautiful is "where all externality is completely characteristic and significant, is determined from within as from what is free" (1988: 324).

40   Cultural regression "happens regularly when a new mass of people of a lower cultural level effects an invasion or is admitted into an older culture" (Freud 1939: 112).

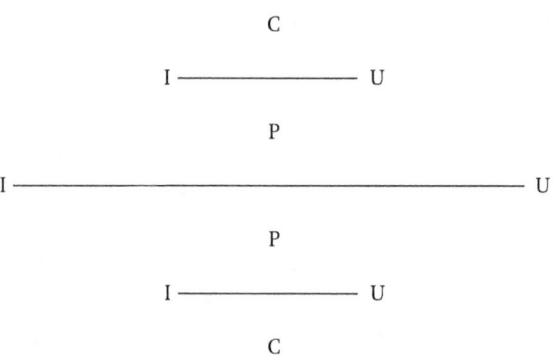

FIGURE 2   The external separation of the concept
SOURCE: CREATED BY AUTHOR

lands" and everything changes (Hegel [1840] 1995b: 403). An alien necessity alters the course of history and the "for itself" of one group becomes the "for us" of another (Hegel [1892] 1995: 155).[41] The end and the universal for one becomes a means and the particularity for another and the life of one is reduced to another's utility and function (cf. Nietzsche [1967] 1989: 77).

Here, (in Figure 2) praxis is disrupted by the intrusion of a 'larger' external form. At the center (bottom of the diagram above) we have the void or the abyss of the abstract concept (C) qua indeterminate notion attempting to work itself up to an Idea but suffering a division or separation not of its own making. The extremes are no longer internally necessary but rendered externally contingent. Praxis here falls into a kind of oscillation or Sisyphean repetition. After all, sometimes "Real extremes cannot be mediated precisely because they are real extremes. Nor do they require mediation, for they are opposed in essence. They have nothing in common; they do not need each other; they do not supplement each other. The one does not have in its own bosom the longing for, the need for, the anticipation of the other" (MECW, 3: 88). And let us not forget that things can be functionally *connected* or linked without having a proper *relation* (see Hegel 1988: 190) and continue to muddle along in spite of that deficiency (e.g., the march of the living dead under the rule of capital).

In reality, if the foundation of reason is the matrix of mediating institutions within the larger organization of society[42] these social forms will impinge upon

---

41   A group may claim to be politically decisive, and even believe that claim themselves, while, in actuality the true "political prerogatives" lie in the hands of others (AJ: 359).

42   Organized social life is the foundation of logical life (EFRL: 433).

one another in their own developments (see MECW, 25: 594). The novelty here is the subversion of telos that lacks the power to unify its tensions adequately to yield the emergence of the Idea and the promise of a beautiful life. Rather than mediating the relationship between reality and concept, praxis falls under the command of a stronger force, e.g., a master that cannot be defeated, undermining the emerging Idea through interminable struggle, resignation, or an act of ecstatic self-destruction. Where there should be a synthesis of the subjective and the objective or internal and external, the subjective is carried away and captured by an external process or spins off into indeterminacy (lifeless abstraction). Objectivity, likewise, degenerates into granular and disconnected individualism (atomization).[43] An example of this declination is represented by Freud's mass psychology syllogism whereby erotic love is subverted by the mechanisms of hypnosis and the subjection of the individual to a *leader* ([1921] 1959: 59). Note, this does not necessarily represent the end of the syllogistic teleological process but a lateralization or diversion of it along alternate routes. The result is a 'fractalization' or conglomeration (not web or network) of syllogisms each striving to complete the journey from the underworld of the indeterminate concept to the light of the Idea (rational unity of all parts).

And, of course, the disintegrating effect of external, meta-intrusions also means the reordering of the moments of the syllogism (i.e., altering the function of each moment): as we see (Figure 3) praxis falters and degenerates into lifelessness and becomes at odds with its individuality resulting in a return to the void of the indeterminate notion.

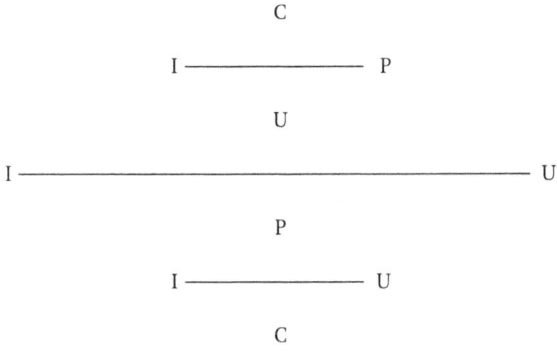

FIGURE 3 Indeterminate regressions
SOURCE: CREATED BY AUTHOR

---

43 Where the "social economy" devolves into tiny group identifications, the sentiment of unity is extinguished or fails to ever develop, and society remains unconscious to itself and incapable of grasping the elements that make it up (Durkheim [1912] 1915: 132).

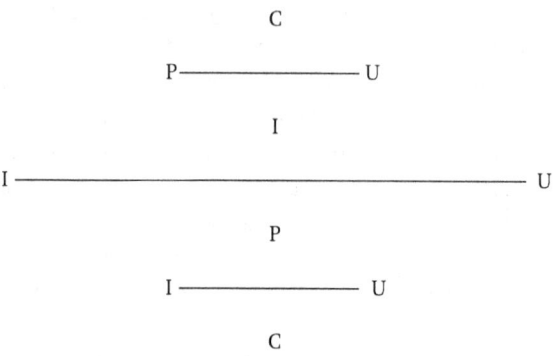

FIGURE 4   Atomic disintegration
SOURCE: CREATED BY AUTHOR

Or, (Figure 4) praxis is crushed and devolves into atoms and, lacking the power to mediate anything on its own, the notion persists undeveloped.

Commentators have pondered the syllogistic structure of capitalism as well as Marx's general formula. Tombazos ([1994] 2014: 140) maps the formula (Figure 5).[44] The capitalist world is comprehensible not merely as a matrix of intertwined premises and judgements but actually displays a structure of mediations. From another angle, Smith says that the M-C-M' system falls outside of the logic of the concept, and therefore syllogistic reasoning altogether, and locates the logic of capitalism in the doctrine of essences instead.

> In more Hegelian jargon, the Marxist critique is that the moments of universality, particularity, and individuality are not allowed to develop freely when all social life must submit to the drive for capital accumulation…. Marx is not content with a self-reproducing totality (even if capitalism could attain this in the long run, which it cannot). He too wants a totality that does not blot out the principle of subjectivity, individuality, personality…. Hegel's *Logic*, then, is not of importance to Marx's method because it shares the same perversions as Marx's object, the capitalist mode of production (1993b: 31).

But I think Hegel's *Logic* plays a decisive role in Marx's analysis of the commodity and we need to also bear in mind that Marx has a *theory of the commodity*

---

[44]   M = capital; P = production; C' = surplus commodities (a different and greater mass of commodities than were original purchased by the capitalist).

M – P – C' = U – S – P

P – C' – M = S – P – U

C' – M – P = P – U – S

FIGURE 5
The dialectics of production
SOURCE: CREATED BY AUTHOR

as his central problem rather than the abstract critique of capitalism. Indeed, I challenge anyone to find ten references to 'capitalism' from the pen of Karl Marx himself.[45]

7 The Commodity

Marx directly equates commodity circulation with a syllogism in the *Critique* (CPE: 94) and, in the *Grundrisse*, Marx tells us that, "production distribution, exchange and consumption form a regular syllogism" (G: 89).[46] One wonders, then, how Hegel's *Logic* is not important to Marx's method when he says: "I have completely demolished the theory of profit as hitherto propounded. What was of great use to me as regards *method* of treatment of Hegel's *Logic* at

---

[45] There are actually no references to *Kapitalismus* in the German edition of the first volume of *Capital*, and where it appears in English as 'capitalism' (and there are only a few), it is the product of the translators.

[46] The original German edition of *Capital* has the value form section (*Die Werthform*) squirreled away in an appendix (1867: 764) and offers a better 'read' (see Marx 1978) than the integrated section found in the Fowkes translation (Marx 1976). The general or universal is simultaneously a particular depending upon its function within a non-unified or protracted diachronic process where, for example, selling and buying are temporally separated (G: 150). For example, I labor for the first two weeks of November, get paid on the 15th (C-M) and buy my food later the next day (M-C). In the circulation of commodities, the particularity of money relative to the singularity of my labor power appears to be a universal particularity, at once a particular equivalent to my labor power and simultaneously the universal equivalent to all the commodities in the system of circulation. Here, money is at odds with itself; its universality as the *Gott der Waren* (Marx 1859: 103) contradicts its particularity. Being *a* thing contradicts its being *the* Thing. All buyers unavoidably profane the sacred (money). The capitalist has the ability to atone for this sin by magnifying the glory of god (accumulating surplus value, god + Δ god). Every expenditure of money by the laborer results in waste, but this sin can be atoned for by having their life energies extracted by the means of production qua the capitalist mode of human sacrifice. The difference between the capitalist and the laborer is analogous to the difference between the twin poles of the sacrificial relation (Hubert and Mauss 1964).

which I had taken another look by mere accident, Freiligrath having found and made me a present of several volumes of Hegel, originally the property of Bakunin" (MECW, 40: 249). Marx might be intellectually irrelevant today had he not made a return to Hegel and worked himself out of the dead end of ordinary materialism. Likewise, Hegel might have faded into obscurity had it not been for Marx declaring that he considered himself to be "the pupil of that mighty thinker" (C: 103). Not *a* pupil but *the* pupil. One need only make it to the "general division of being" (SL: 79) to see Hegel's three determinations reflected in Marx's analysis of the commodity: quality (use-value), quantity (exchange-value), and measure (socially necessary labor time). Actually, the chapter on the commodity in *Capital* is saturated in Hegel's doctrine of being. But Smith is correct overall, and I think this is the real point, that capitalism is not, in anyway, the fulfillment of the Hegelian project—capitalism does not represent the actualization of the Hegelian Absolute Spirit or Idea and does not appear to be working itself out following the necessity of the syllogism. The defect is not simply a logical feature of the capitalist syllogism, rather, the drive to actualize itself on a moral and substantively rational ground is criminalized. In other words, the theft of commodities is illegal and perhaps the greatest of taboos in bourgeois society. If capital were to live up to a rational standard we would find something quite different than a particular mass of capital, purchasing individual workers, machines, etc., to be instrumentalized and consumed within the labor process for the hopeful realization of a universal residue of surplus value (P–I–U). Rather, we would encounter a quantum of universal substance transformed into an ocean of particular utilities for the satisfaction of billions of individual needs (U–P–I). Under capitalist circumstances the actualization of this syllogism would require, on the one hand, either a revision of the law which would thereby destroy capitalism (holy crime) or, on the other, criminal conduct on the part of 'consumers' (diabolical crime).[47] But does this mean that capitalism is completely irrational and is there anything we can affirm in capitalism? In other words, is the capitalist syllogism as a social fact still 'inside' the teleological process, or, does capitalism represent a condition of historical arrest?

The capitalist system of production and accumulation is not *substantively* or morally rational. Capitalism is a *wrong* syllogism that has to undergo further negations to a higher form of rationality. From a critical-substantive perspective capitalism is just as insane and self-destructive as the poor creature who

---

47 The hatred of the criminal is not irrational since criminals are typically not revolutionaries. The revolutionary is a criminal that negates the abstract universal whereas the ordinary criminal is an enemy of revolution by harming fellow individuals.

just wants to love someone but ends up worshiping a narcissistic cult leader. Capitalism is a system of human sacrifice where people are reduced to virtual beasts and then transformed into money for the benefit of a ruling elite. However, from an *instrumental* or *technical* standpoint capitalism is highly rational, a characteristic found not only in factories but also in concentration camps and slaughterhouses. One might argue that it is hyper-rational. That the rational is contaminated with or is actually *identical with* the irrational is no surprise. I think Hegel's insistence on the necessity of the historical dialectic has led commentators astray on what exactly he means by necessity. Let us pause for a moment to consider the dialectic and how necessity can be diverted from its course.

8   The Dialectic

First, in the real, only individuals exist in an empirical sense and we find this commitment from the last of the Scholastics all the way through to Hegel, Marx, Weber, and Durkheim. But what is important is not the individual but relations and functions. Logical individuals may socially *function* as the individuals they are, or they may *function* as particularities or universals. Particularity (the social ground) is a product of institutional *relations*. Hegel sometimes makes it seem as if Spirit undertakes all of these moves and transpositions under its own, autonomous power but Marx and Durkheim demonstrate more clearly than Hegel that the self-development of Spirit is driven by class conflicts and changes in social organization. As a society changes, progressively or regressively, reason is affected (EFRL: 440). Hence, what seems like a valid syllogism at one point in time becomes absurd later on. Also, a proper syllogism may be simultaneously a syllogism and no longer a syllogism depending on the point of view; once a social ground loses its validity and slides off the supports of tradition or magic, etc., it disintegrates into a series of abstract judgments. Just as the rational can fall off its throne into absurdity, capital has the nearly unlimited power to transform absurdities into technical rationalities and specious justifications.

Second, the dialectic process is not always reducible to only three moments. Variations emerge, and these forms are important. Sometimes, the structure expands in various directions, e.g., the double middle term, the *quaternio terminorum* that appears to contain four terms, and at other times the mediating moment expands into infinity (e.g., all of the individuals must be included such that we have not simply U–I–P but U–i ... i–P), and in the disjunctive syllogism the mediating moment of universality contains itself again along with individuality and particularity (e.g., EFRL: 445). In Hegel's disjunctive syllogism the middle term (the ground) contains everything including itself. The middle term where the third thing unifies the extremes is always of decisive importance. When particularity, for example, mediates the individual's relation to the universal, we can say that 'P is the key.' We also find reversals of indifference here and there as well where extremes may flip positions because they amount to the same thing (e.g., Durkheim's critique of empiricism and classical rationalism in the introduction to *Elementary Forms*).

Third, sublation (*Aufheben*) leaves nothing behind—that which has been negated is negated upwards, carried forward, and contained in the 'higher' form of cognition—inclining toward the universal—not as empty generalizations or alienated individuals but concepts that enclose and self-relate all the vitality and richness that concrete reality has to offer. The old materials persist but their functions change, or, in the disintegrations of syllogisms, judgements are free to drift on the wind only to be captured by another process or function. Dialectical sublation is not a happy process where we take the good and leave the bad. The 'bad' is carried along as well but, hopefully, made to harmonize (relate) or function (connect) in new ways, and, if not, repressed in some kind of hellish but manageable sink. The repressed (negated) returns and totality is never free of contradictions and every "passing over" entails a simultaneous "withdrawal." We even see that the whole section on syllogisms in Hegel's grand logic does not start out with a cockeyed form and conclude with the perfected "general schema" but starts with the "general scheme" that makes sociological sense (my concrete universality is mediated by the quality and quantity of the groups I belong to) and terminates with the truly weird disjunctive syllogism where the mediating universality contains within itself everything as a result of its self-negation. The allusion to the sacrifice of a person for love and his resurrection as a good collective representation (universal equivalent of all universal equivalents) is not subtle.

Capitalism is in love with the bad, but every society is plagued by loves deserving and undeserving. As Durkheim says: "in the present day just as much as in the past, we see society constantly creating sacred things out of ordinary ones."

> If it happens to fall in love with a man and if it thinks it has found in him the principal aspirations that move it, as well as the means of satisfying them, this man will be raised above the others and, as it were, deified. Opinion will invest him with a majesty exactly analogous to that protecting the gods.... And the fact that it is society alone which is the author of these varieties of apotheosis, is evident since it frequently changes to

consecrate men thus who have no right to it from their own merit. The simple deference inspired by men invested with high social functions is not different in nature from religious respect ([1912] 1915: 244).

The truth is that nobody can predict whether or not the abstract universality of value under bourgeois management, going as it goes, will develop its potentially beyond itself in a rational form, or, whether, in a few years or decades, it will simply bring an end all conscious life on earth. The working class is in no mood for revolution and seems entertained with bad love and the anticipation of miracles as it watches as our institutions and secondary associations are liquidated. One is left wondering what exactly will occasion the necessary ferment of enlightenment. Durkheim clearly saw the role of education in sublating the abstract universality of French rationalism beyond its "geometric simplicity" into the concrete universality of science (1961: 279) but given the current state of corporate penetration into schools and universities one cannot help but feel pessimistic.

CHAPTER 2

Bad Love

> The great bulk of mankind are catching at things beyond their reach, which necessarily elude their grasp, and which become an interdiction to, and the bane of, social happiness.... And if I may be allowed the expression, I would observe, that it is become pretty evident that the people ... have blundered against the 'Universal Solvent' ... *which if not judiciously managed*, will dissolve every thing—even the bonds of society—the very empire itself.
>
> AMATOR PATRIAE 1829: 25

"Trust thyself" says Emerson: "every heart vibrates to that iron string. Accept the place the divine providence has found for you, the society of your contemporaries, the connection of events" (1950: 146). What happens, though, when the wire goes slack, and individuals are left to vibrate on their own frequencies? This free vibration of the great unraveling is not the kind of freedom we seek, though, it is nevertheless one species of freedom. The "positive evil" (S: 212) of collective existence devolves into particular evils and singular nightmares and, as Heraclitus might say, people live their deaths. The good is the product of a complex value system that engenders solidarity and regulates the members of a society (DOL: 331). When one power, for example personal autonomy, becomes outsized it creates a relative devaluation of other imperatives such as duty or loyalty and the system falls into anarchy and unlimited exploitation. Dostoevsky recognized this quality in the Western notion of autonomy whereby the individual demands to be the equivalent of the whole at the expense of the latter ([1863] 1955: 67).[1] If each abstracted individual is equivalent to infinity while holding fast to its difference (cf. SL: 531) there can be no underlying basis for brotherhood beyond utilitarianism and purposiveness

---

1 Again, we encounter the necessity of *Homo duplex* as providing the ground for an indifference toward difference. It seems like the most obvious thing, the surmounting of duality and the harmonization of the individual and the collective, but as we saw in *The Sociogony*, the way forward is not the merging of the two into one but the expansion of the duality into a 'triad.' The simple fusion of the ego and society is a romantic and reactionary impulse. It was Stalin who said: "There is no, nor should there be, irreconcilable contrast between the individual and the collective, between the interests of the individual person and the interests of the collective" (in Wells 1934). I think few would defend the Soviet Union's success when it comes to the satisfaction of personal interests.

and, consequently, actual social equality or authentic individuality perishes. Throughout this project we run into the problem of infinity divorced from its relation to the finite and, as such, the infinite is always abstract and "spurious" (Hegel 1988: 406). In modernity, "to be a person means to be an autonomous source of action" yet on the other hand our 'nature' as modern people means "to be a part of society" and to "play a part as one organ of society" (DOL: 335). The *autonomous organ* sounds more appalling than appealing.[2]

It seems at first glance that autonomy means being subjectively free of restraints imposed by others or the state, etc., or that autonomy might amalgamate with other ideals such as justice, diversity, and equality to produce some virtuous alloy, and that kind of outcome cannot be logically ruled out. However, rather than producing a 'higher' moral value, combinations are also capable of producing even more deleterious forces and monstrous entities of the kind we find in the political and cultural logic of neoliberalism (the miracle of success, market magic, austerity, severe inequality, populist anger, racism, demagoguery, etc.). Today, autonomy falls to the side of the categorical imperative of quantitative gain as an end in itself (PESC: 17). As we will see in volume four, once the drive to accumulate infinite surplus value becomes the supreme goal of social existence all other values that inhibit circulation and possessiveness are negated or relegated to the margins of social life.[3] The seeming paradox of neoliberalism is that the drive for infinite accumulation necessitates the liquidation of rules and laws which, in that resulting normative vacuum, yields inevitable self-destruction: success is commensurable with death. What would have been seen earlier as a "sign of madness" (Fanfani 1935: 192)—the maniacal

---

2 The solution to this contradiction is, of course, *Homo duplex*, and the matrix of reciprocal obligations worked out within the profession and the division of labor. Under the rules of the new economy, however, duality *which produces supplements* (Me, You, and the emergent Thing we have in common) collapses into a subjectivity of Me, Me, Me and the objective bleakness of a binge and grab free-for-all that leaves all but a few (and their retinue of toadies) in stagnation and overexposed to impersonal market forces. Of course, modern capitalism relies heavily on specialized laborers, many who love their careers, but increasingly careers have failed to materialize for millions trapped in contingent strings of dead-end jobs that provide little more than light paychecks and plenty of grief.
3 A little over 100 years ago Veblen argued that "extra-economic standards of value" were "dominant" and "weightier" than the pecuniary drive (1912: 294) but it seems apparent today that the state and the institutional "furniture" (as Veblen puts it) has been captured by the for-profit class and their sole interest in unlimited accumulation. The point is not whether or not we have lost our values, because every human value that has ever existed persists, but how long a society can function in such a one-sided and non-equilibrated form, what the re-equilibration process will be, the costs of re-equilibration, and how that cost will be distributed across society.

accumulation of wealth and a fanatical commitment to work—is a virtue once capitalism is in the saddle.

Anomie (limitlessness, etc.) and fatalism (inevitability, etc.) are not diametrically opposed but *polar* oppositions (cf. Marx 1867: 765).[4] The situation is never *either* one *or* the other, e.g., anomie or fatalism, but, like a dream, anomie *and* fatalism (cf. Freud [1901] 1952: 42).[5] The result of mono-valuation, the conversion of all things to prices, is a circular or hyperbolic[6] fatalism that liquidates social relations and, as disorganization runs its course, so too does the individual's ability to reason. Where there should be conceptualization we instead have mental anarchy. *Logos* (reason) is not an inherent personal quality but is conferred upon individuals through the work of institutional organization and education. Indeed, cut off from society the person becomes detached from *logos* and descends into *alogon*, animal brutishness (Sullivan 1871: 55). When collective consciousness inevitably loses power (DOL: 301) society and thought degenerate into chaos, the individual is liberated from the constraints of reason (from the laws that reason imposes upon itself) and, ultimately, freedom is "forfeited" (Kant 1998: 13). Freedom is extinguished in tyranny and the banner above the entrance to this negative heaven of autonomy and unregulated accumulation is *Wide is the gate and crooked is the way that leads to death.*

1   The House of the Absolute

'Society' may be a despised sociological leftover from a previous era[7] but our sociological absolute is neither dead nor vanishing in precisely the way we

---

4   One often wonders why Durkheim clings to Latin terms (e.g., *egoism*) or why translators turn Freud's "I" into *ego*, etc. "We shall often have occasion to notice that the technical language of philosophy employs Latin terms for reflected determinations" (SL: 107).

5   "The opposition between good and evil lacks the radical character ascribed to it by the popular conscience. Imperceptible gradations lead from one to the other and frontiers are often unclear" (S: 371).

6   Aron (1954: 19) credits Vilfredo Pareto with the notion of hyperbolic war (i.e., total war) but it was Guglielmo Ferrero that coined that phrase (Gaspar 2007: 291). My concept of eccentricity, which contains the moment of circular hyperbolism (*The Sociogony*) occurred to me while reading Karl Barth (1933), though, oddly, there was nothing in the text as far as I recall that actually suggested it. The idea of a parabolic curve to the fixed 'jelly' (Marx) of fluid ritual energy strands bears a strong resemblance to the 'parabolic allegory' in which the other's voice (allegory = *allos*, other + *agoria*, speaking) consists of an external shell of fictional images (the fable or the simile) veiling an inner and "remote" (but not inaccessible) truth arrived at by interpretation. In this respect we are all parables of the absolute (Fry 1811: 8–9).

7   In the wake of the disintegration of modernist 'grand narratives' the typical postmodernist move is to reject the concept of society (e.g., Mann 1986) in favor of a web of playful signifiers,

experience it. The denial of society on the part of independent individuals may in fact be all the proof we need that the absolute exists. Only an absolute idea determines itself in such a way that its certainty and freedom of itself resides specifically in dividing itself and letting the other exist as free and independent entities (Hegel 1988: 434). What appears as a unilateral disintegration may in fact mask a more complicated and dynamic sociogony. In the synthetic realm of moral dynamics, decomposition is not necessarily synonymous with death as it is in the realm of nature. As a matter of fact, religious practices often treat putrefaction and decay as sacred filth and as a carrier of special virtue (Durkheim [1912] 1915: 99; cf. Bataille 2004). Either way, life or death, decomposition also entails reconstruction (S: 375) and a social downfall is simultaneously a moment within a larger, historical unification process. Dewey says,

> The thing which concerns all of us as human beings is precisely the greatest attainable security of values in concrete existence. The thought that the values which are unstable and wavering in the world in which we live are eternally secure in a higher realm (which reason demonstrates but which we cannot experience), that all the goods which are defeated here are triumphant there, may give consolation to the depressed. But it does not change the existential situation in the least (1929: 35).

---

language games, and a conception of power that is essentially reductionist, i.e., power is not a moral substance but a name that is attributed to situations (Shad 1989). Negation is a substitution for repression (Freud [1925] 1959: 182). The thing negated is something the subject would rather keep repressed. To deny or negate the concept of society is tantamount to the wish for a world free of constraint. To negate the facticity of society or the idea of moral necessity is merely an infantile wish for a world where the ego is free to dissolve into nothing. When a person says that 'society' is an empty signifier or that it does not exist, or is merely a word, they are saying that they enjoy, at various levels and ways, the misery of unmediated subjectivity and that they 'get off' of the unceasing clashes of dyadic (intersubjective) combat. In Hegel's famous 'master-slave dialectic' the two individuals in the ideal-typical construct fail to recognize superiority (authority) in the other—one will not be subsumed within the other—and, as such, the ideal-type involves the conflict between two singularities wishing to subjugate the other and receive the recognition (authority) that comes from victory. Since the defeated chooses life over death, and submits only out of fear, the desired subsuming fails to materialize. The goal was for the emergence of a syllogism whereby the singular is reflected in the particular and both are enclosed by the emerging dimension of universality—creating a hierarchy of being and scale of existence. No such luck, however. The un-subsumed slave works to satisfy the needs and desires of everyone living off the slave's labor but, in so doing, the world comes to reflect not the master's spirit and will but that of the slave. One day, the master wakes up in an alien world built under their command but not by him and finds that they, not the slave, are the unnecessary supplement.

However, the existential situation is changed where there is still hope, and 'consolation' should not itself be devalued. Dewey's statement applies to those for whom valuation has been alienated (separated) from action. When we examine the turmoil of a divided society at odds with itself, engaged in self-lacerations and devolving into demonization and violence, agitation is proof that it is not values *per se* that are wavering but the image of reason. Strife can be (and will be) a sign of social decay and death spasms but it can also signal that society has some fight left in it (EFRL: 405; Inglehart 2018). In fact, we should not let what appears to be stupidity and violence lead us automatically to the belief that moral and intellectual progress is not being made. What is good in America also emerged from what is crazy, hectic, and savage (Smith 2019b).

Still, today there is a sense that some kind of valuable core of life has been vanquished, that a process of relational unification of individuals and groups has devolved into little more than coercive links and convulsive reactions (cf. C: 928). "Whether society be a spiritual vacuum or a battlefield of irreconcilable beliefs, it seems no longer to provide a shelter for the individual, or principles that would compel his integrity" (Kracauer 2003: 109). But make no mistake, society is always a decomposing and unloved surplus being challenged, overtaken, and forever being torn to shreds. The absolute is never separate from its own teleological activity. Disintegration is normal and integration is meaningless without its opposite. In the real world, "good rubs shoulders with evil, injustice is ever on the throne, and truth is continually darkened by error" (EFRL: 422; cf. Freud 1965: 207)[8] and all of these oppositions are preserved in the life of the whole (Hegel 1984: 499).[9] Part of our difficulty stems from the presuppositions of our discipline.

From the standpoint of classical sociology, society is the absolute, and that is true, society is the absolute, however, from the particular standpoint of sociology the absolute is synonymous with everything negative and defective. If, however, Simmel is correct, the syllogism can be constructed such that society is the contradiction that mediates the subject's relationship to a dimension of ideal and universal objectivity that resides "in an ideal realm above society and the individual" (SGS: 256). If this dimension is genuinely transcendental we run backwards toward Kantianism and if this dimension is only a word that corresponds to nothing real we regress to Renaissance nominalism, but if

---

8 Cf. Shakespeare in *Measure for Measure* where a portion of sinners ascend and some virtuous descend and where some are condemned for a single fault whereas the comprehensively vicious answer for nothing (1956: 21).
9 "Hegel is a thinker for whom the movement of falling is not a degeneration in the ordinary sense of the word, but a term of expiration—something which falls due" (Malabou [1996] 2005: 188).

Hegel, Marx, Durkheim (and Simmel) are correct this ideal dimension exists, "it is not abstract" (SGS: 257) but is an objective reality, and is under autonomous power to work itself up from the abstract notion (i.e., the concept lacking actualization) to its realization through the turmoil of social praxis. This Idea is a projection and a kind of surplus, if we want to use that language, but we have to see the concept of 'surplus' from a special angle. A surplus is not just a 'leftover' or a 'remainder' in an ordinary sense. If, for example, we want to know what Marx means by 'surplus labor' we have to see that it entails three moments, no less and no more: (a) ordinary, necessary, or obligatory labor that exists under both capitalist and communist modes of production; (b) *plus labor* (the ordinary Marxist sense of 'surplus labor') as excessive but variously regulated forms of exploited work that produce more labor products than are necessary, and therefore optional from our point of view, forming the basis for the creation of a reside of value (the sacred pure) that survives taxation, interest payments, rents, etc., (decomposition);[10] and finally (c) *super plus* labor where work devolves into the acute and anarchic exploitation of humans beyond what is normal under a liberal bourgeois regime, i.e., from exploitation to full-blown dehumanization (where the distinction between variable and constant capital collapses). Human life is, here, in this third moment, literally synonymous with brutalization and sacrifice in a virtual, twilight potlatch economy. We often forget that as a moral surplus the sacred (value) is simultaneously holy and diabolical, pure and impure, desirable and disgusting. Monstrous acts *en masse* are indices that society is not in conformity with its real form; it is not as it should be. If the Idea is not real, if the objective (Simmel) is really nothing but empirical subjectivity, then human life is doomed to perpetual anarchy and the best we can hope for is temporary lulls in the war of all against all and the enjoyment of egoistic delusions. Per Simmel, the absolute of sociology is society but the absolute of *absolute sociology* is the Idea of society (alloyed and allied with empirical society) and its reconciliation with this middle as well as the individuals that constitute its atomic substratum. This absolute or realm of objectivity is not a god or god substitute but is nonetheless sacred. It is, to use Simmel's term, "enthroned" (SGS: 256).

The Puritan god of loveless indifference promised nothing for most and life was reduced to endurance within a forced labor camp.[11] Notwithstanding the bleakness of this psychological position, a minority actually discovered what

---

10   Here, too, are the normal types of deformed personalities suffering neuroses of various kinds amenable to psychoanalytic treatment.
11   "A god relegated by his majesty outside of the universe and everything temporal, cannot serve as a goal for our temporal activity, which is thus left without an objective" (S: 376).

they believed to be true love and devotion within their callings and within the social division of labor. What those fanatics lacked in humanity they made up for in social organization and that love story continued through the liberal era in the form of the secularized professions.[12] We cannot overplay the successes of liberalism but there is a sense that the experiment was cut short due to gross passions. The ad campaign for neoliberalism promised immediate and universal access to a transcendental, transparent, rational mechanism that reserved a place for every individual, not merely those ensconced within a religiously-tinged vocation, at the trough of plenty. The result was, expectedly, quite different and deregulation, corporate hegemony, and the regulatory light-state opened the gates to lust, disorder, permanent war, and bondage.[13] When capital promises freedom through deregulation what it necessarily delivers is a concentration and centralization of control in the hands of fewer people and hyper-regulation of the subaltern classes. When law and regulations are dissolved at the universal level they are multiplied in bizarre and extreme forms at the level of particularity, e.g., dehumanizing corporate labor rules where there should be universal and humanizing standards (Anderson 2017).

When a leader promises to lift a social burden off the backs of individuals this should usually be translated as an invitation for voluntary suicide. And when million-dollar words fly out of the mouths of hundredaires, we should take that to mean that they are willing to make the attempt. There is, here, an obvious connection between narcissistic leaders who are loved but who cannot love their followers in return.[14] The Great Man setup is a commodity-like

---

[12] The duality of purity and impurity is reconciled in the vocation (Hegel 1988: 217).

[13] The state is always, at best, amoral and almost always immoral if not an embodiment of seemingly pure corruption. Just the same, it is better for citizens to strive for goodness together against a unified immorality as an object of resistance than for a government to promote individual evil in the name of goodness. Americans distrust the state but, as we will see, they are not inclined to see it destroyed or really even reduced. Capital dissolves secondary associations and even though the state, designed as it is to fail at everything, is no substitute for these institutions; a corrupt state it is still better than no state at all.

[14] On the first page of Robert Service's biography of Stalin we are reminded that, when the brutal despot died in 1953, he was mourned by millions of people "who had abundant reason to detest him and his politics" (2004; cf. Freud 1939: 103). To say that a thriving cult of Stalin exists in the former Soviet Union would be an understatement. According to a recent Levada poll, 51 percent of Russians ages 18 and over in 137 cities and towns "respect, like or admire Stalin" (BBC News 2019). "The current fascination with Stalin—now 60 years after his death—is not with the Communist dictator but the founder of the empire. The reasons behind it, surmises Vladimir Solovyov, a liberal TV journalist at the state channel Rossija ('Russia'), lies in the 'devastating present.' In light of broad corruption in government and administration, of abuse of power and social injustice, Solovyov says, many Russians feel a growing need to elevate Stalin. The dictator's personal belongings,

relation[15] between the symbol and the followers: the Great Man who has absorbed our love is what we have in common yet, upon inspection, we find nothing of that greatness dwelling within us.[16] Nothing is more absurd or necessary than love and what can be done for the commodity or the great man can be done for society.[17] "What is done out of love always occurs beyond good and evil" (Nietzsche 1982: 444).[18] And what is love but "the desire and pursuit of the

---

after all, were essentially limited to a handful of uniform jackets. Even his weekend homes belonged to the state" (Klussman 2013).

15   Compare the general value form (C: 159–60) with group psychology: "a psychological group is a collection of individuals who have introduced the same person into the superego and, on the basis of this common element, have identified themselves with one another in their ego" (Freud 1965: 84–85). Of course, the followers feel as if they possess the leader when, in fact, the common element necessarily stands apart.

16   The standard reading of the *Wizard of Oz* is backwards: "Their desires, as well as the Wizard's cleverness in answering them, are all self-delusions. Each of these characters carries within him the solution to his own problem, were he only to view himself objectively" (Littlefield 1964:57). The truth is that the qualities sought in the adventure emerge from the ensemble of characters and would otherwise 'evaporate' had it not been for the crystallization of those qualities in their symbolic forms and the preservation of their roles in the imagined future. More harrowing than the film was the screenwriting process and the many close calls that would have ruined what is a masterpiece. "The final script was the product of Yip Harburg's editing and blending of elements written by Florence Ryerson, Edgar Allan Woolf, and Noel Langley" (Harmetz 1977: 57). "'I liked a lot of things Langley had done and threw the other stuff out. I clarified the story. I edited the whole thing and brought back Langley's story, which was simpler. And I added my own.' The major thing Harburg added was the scene in which the Wizard gives the Scarecrow a diploma, the Tin Woodman a testimonial, and the Cowardly Lion a medal" (Ibid.). Importantly, in the pre-Harburg scripts, the characters lacking virtues were discovered to have always already possessed what they thought they were missing but "Harburg 'devised the satiric and cynical idea of the Wizard handing out symbols because I was so aware of our lives being the images of things rather than the things themselves'" (Harmetz 1977: 58). However, we should not read the symbolic substitutions cynically. Virtues are always best in moderation. Only puritans, fanatics, terrorists, etc., push virtue to the limits, arriving in the domain of vice and mass destruction.

17   No people have debased the word 'love' the way Americans have (cf. Freud [1921] 1959: 54). 'Love' derives from the Proto-Indo-European *lewb* for love, care, or desire, and the word might be 4000 years old, but the empire of money has reduced it to smut. "Our system does not bother itself much with ... love and vision. Our system makes money and destroys love. Makes money and destroys people" (Traubel 1910: 139).

18   The cult of Keanu has something endearing about it: "Like John Wayne, Keanu [Reeves] is spectacularly limited as an actor. Defined more by a guileless earnestness than any real ability to project a sense that inner emotional activity is taking place, Reeves has been cunning enough to snare roles in a handful of outstanding motion pictures.... In most of these movies, Keanu plays a character the audience views more with affection than with reverence or idolatry, like a kid brother who has bitten off more than he can chew and may need outside help to survive. Personally speaking, when I go to see a Keanu Reeves

whole" (Plato 1945, 3: 318). If our commanding representations are our stars, love is the power that can reorganize the stars themselves (Rolfe 1953: 282). But if we are waiting around for universal love to appear on its own accord, we will wait for eternity, though, we should wish Axel Honneth all the luck in the world (1995: 92–130). Still, there is another connection between love and our commanding stars for when the individual is surmounted by 'transcendental' logical representations or "type-ideas," there is a glimpse of the "intellectual world" and an "intuition of the realm of truth" (EFRL: 438). It is not love *per se* but the *love of truth* that guides our way.[19] "I mean to say that the love of truth has its reward in heaven, and already upon earth" (Nietzsche 1909: 64). And it is in the pursuit of truth and reflection that both love and hate weaken to a point beyond love and hate (Freud [1910] 1961: 21–23). Truth and reflection are difficult to sell in a world where ordinary Americans still cling to miracles (*miracula, dynamis*) and magical charms.[20] As Wallace says, "It is a total myth that man is by nature curious and truth-hungry and wants, above all things, *to know*" (2003: 12). To the extent that we are like 'primitives' in our speculative laziness, we have to be forced to think (EFRL: 54) but, sooner or later, we are forced to think. Knowing why things fall apart does not make the experience any better for the ordinary person sunk in mental confusions and conservative propaganda. Propaganda creates outrage and weak targets for punishment that preserve the taboo sanctity of the root cause. Conservatism is an attempt to block thinking and, while it sometimes wins, reaction is a sign that essential questions are being asked. Still, millions of people would rather die than think so we'll have to do the thinking for them.

Even under the best of circumstances, society is never a 'lovely' thing and it is tempting to dream of perfecting it, in making society lovable. But "the horrid and the nice are not two separate worlds, but parts of one whole; neither [can] exist without the other" (Auden 2008: 356). When we find tens of millions of Americans filled with hate we have to think of their hatred as another kind of

---

movie, I feel fiercely protective of the actor, wishing to see him shielded from the forces of darkness and the draconian rigors of the English language" (Queenan 2008). For whatever reason, Reeves is one of the few actors that fall outside the normal parameters of criticism.

19 "Love has *limits*, and a complete union of beings in our universe rarely or never takes place; the bonds of this union—desire and longing—necessarily subside precisely under the greatest strain, and unfortunately they often provide *ennui* and satiety instead of pleasure" (Herder 1993: 111).

20 It is interesting that the use of the word 'miracle' in English-language books declined steadily from 1870 onward, but when we get to 1980 (Morning in America) we find a steady rise in the usage rate.

love, a love for something that we hate. Red and Blue hate and love in their own ways. I hate Trump and believe that the GOP is a criminal conspiracy organized around the ideology of white supremacy[21] but is the hatred of, say, the Clintons or the Democratic National Committee, etc., not in some sense understandable and even a necessary corollary of my hatred? Trump and the new breed of Republicans may be traitors to America[22] but the Democrats also continuously sell American workers down the river at every opportunity. Žižek is wrong about Trump being a lesser evil (and was a fool to endorse him) but he is correct that another Clinton administration would have been the continuation of the normal catastrophe of the status quo.[23] No mainstream political party in the US[24] has any interest in addressing the central problem of American life (party strategies are oriented toward horizontal conflict rather than vertical welfare)[25] and, consequently, political theater spins on the axis of villains and victims, hate and love, and a mania for identity and criminality, punishment and surplus punishment, i.e., shame (DOL: 47) that eclipses other concerns.[26] When political institutions absorb the *pneuma* of criminality a special dialectic that liquidates both the external other and internal impurities is wound up.[27]

---

21 The Republican Party right now exists on an ideological continuum between the more extreme Alternative for Germany and the less extreme Freedom Party in Austria. See Chinoy (2019) reporting on findings from the "Manifesto Project."
22 We forget that 'Chinagate' (the 1996 campaign finance scandal involving the Clintons and the DNC) never progressed to the point of an independent counsel investigation due to partisan interference.
23 "Washington Consensus policy makers are committed to free market policies when they support the interests of big business, as, for example, with lowering regulations at the workplace. But these same policy makers become far less insistent on free market principles when invoking such principles damage big business interests. Federal Reserve and IMF interventions to bail out wealthy asset holders during the frequent global crises in the 1990s are obvious violations of free market precepts" (Pollin 2003: 8).
24 It is true that, from the standpoint of economic policy, America is a one-party political system, however, there are real and substantial differences between Democratic and Republican psychologies at the most basic levels.
25 "The modern party is a fighting organization in the political sense of the term, and must as such conform to the laws of tactics.... [and] the submission of the masses to the will of a few individuals comes to be considered one of the highest of democratic virtues" (Michels 2001: 31–32).
26 Both the American 'right' and the 'left' have converged at an inversion whereby political culture has devolved into a politics of culture (Rorty 1998: 13–15). This "retreat" is manipulated by the master class "just as it is equally ... seized upon by the dominated peoples in confusion" (Amin 2004: 20).
27 It is interesting that "winding up" is synonymous with the dissolution or liquidation of a (usually) bankrupt firm in British business lingo. A society of victims reduces the

Many people voted for the tangerine dream because they had reached a limit with both corporate political machines and we now view our neighbors and family members as immoral scum.[28] But it is also unreasonable to give people the choice between two bad things, insist that not choosing is bad, then denounce them as bad when they choose as only they could: badly. It is generally accepted that the American, winner-take-all political system (where capital chooses the candidates through contributions and where politicians choose their electorate through gerrymandering and dirty tricks) is one in which people vote for the candidate they hate the least. Holding one's nose while casting a ballot for Clinton is not voting for anything positive or concrete but against something perceived to be an even more terrifying monstrosity. In general the entire system of choosing political representation in the United States is not a moral duty pertaining to citizenship but an immoral and perverted institution where, as Engels might say, capital is made from discontent (MECW, 49: 328) and voters are left to affirm a lesser of two evils—the one that will destroy us with the least pain and the slowest velocity and, if we're lucky, punish our hate objects in the most entertaining manner possible.

It is tempting to read the current mood as one of growing anti-capitalist sentiment, however, in modern capitalistic society "voters behave like bourgeois and not like citizens: they organize themselves into associations to defend their incomes, wages, or profits, and into parties in order to seize the government or to exert a controlling influence upon it. In the strife between pressure groups, concern for the general good vanishes" (Aron 1954: 242). Death before communism! The problem of how economic antagonisms manifest themselves in the US is perplexing and is made more confusing by recent analytic regressions in the world of critical sociology.

My colleagues say we can forget economic distress and the financial aspects of Trump's base and, instead, focus on the racism or authoritarianism of Trumpsters, i.e., the duality of support for a strong man and the opposition to undeserving usurpers. I think these lines of inquiry are hobbled by positivist methods and, by dipping their sticks into prejudice, they make contact with the contingent, inessential (Hegel 1988: 401), and the "un-objective" (SGS:

---

remainder to active or passive criminals and life devolves into trials and punishments. Society becomes little better than a penal colony.

28 There is nothing remotely novel about a society absolutely divided as if each 'side' were not two parts of a whole but, rather, foreign countries existing along parallel lines. Indeed, this arrangement might be as old as social organization itself (see Durkheim [1912] 1915: 133).

259).[29] They forget that survey research is not even the beginning of sociological insight (S: 319)[30] and that rubbing variables together never produces music.[31] Are Trump's supporters generally prejudiced and hate-filled authoritarians? Of this, there is little doubt, but *sociology is not concerned with prejudging but with judgements.*[32] Probably half of Americans are, have been, and will continue to be prejudiced authoritarians to some degree or another and we

---

29   Surveys do not explain the "the complex" by way of "the complex" (Durkheim 1974: 29). Asking people if they would like to rid the world of evil and expecting an answer that reflects back into the earthly political domain is wide of the mark, in my opinion, because 'evil' is not even a political category. Asking people if they want to obey strong authority skirts the problem of what people understand to be 'authority.' If we ask Trumpsters what kind of authority their leader possesses, they couldn't say because Trump has no sociological 'authority' to begin with. Asking people questions about metaphorical "rotten apples" downshifts the problem from the synthetic domain to that of the profane. Surveys like this miss the mark twice by, first, voyaging into the transcendental and, again, by reducing social dominance to nothing more consequential than peeling apples. This approach would be appropriate if Trump supporters were vitally interested in making cider behind the moon.

30   It is true that society makes psyches for itself (DOL: 287) but it does not hold that we access society in probing individual attitudes. Sociology is interested in collective conduct and the preceding deliberations behind the actions but measuring attitudes after the deed is backwards and will always frustrate science (see Durkheim 1978: 95).

31   Durkheim states unequivocally that sociology amounts to *opinion* research (EFRL: 439) however our sense of 'opinion' as more or less subjective fancy is wholly inadequate to his concept. For example, egoism, anomie, and altruism are all "currents of opinion" (S: 321) but here 'opinion' is not a contingent attitude or situational preference but a power capable of mass murder. Public opinion is doom (Harrison 1962: 483). This sense of opinion is quite the opposite of Thoreau's where public opinion pales in comparison to the tyranny of self-opinion ([1854] 1960: 10). Sociologically, public opinion is an invisible but inescapable and dreaded power (Younghusband 1915: 13, 16). To reduce moral energies to our flimsy sense of 'opinion' would be like discounting the charisma of a god or the value of a commodity as whimsical daydreams lacking heft. Durkheim's 'public opinion' is closer to the meaning of a pronouncement that is to be feared as some kind of divine force (see Furedi 2013: 270). Indeed, if we think of opinions as beliefs we would have to say they are the kinds of beliefs that we find in religion where beliefs are drivers of action and provide moral reinforcement (see Jones 1998: 53).

32   The etymology of 'prejudice' means not only *prior to a judgment* but also "damage." Prejudice is a kind of broken and self-wounding pattern of thinking and feeling. Ironically, both prejudice and the academic methods used to *measure* prejudice result in the stultification of teleological praxis. Fitting with the multiculturalist trends in academia, once everyone is measured and classified they acquire taboo status as isolated untouchables. As an aside, many "Tabu" advertisements from the 30s through the 50s ("the forbidden perfume") feature a solitary female consumer backgrounded by an image of a couple in a romantic embrace. The ads speculate that the special evening "can" happen but the tension between background and foreground, guarded by the fragrant sentinel, seems to imply that

can count on about half the population to think the wrong way if they can think at all. It is true that racists and haters *mean what they say*: when they run down blacks, Mexicans, Jews, women, liberals, etc., they really do hate or greatly dislike all those groups. But people can mean what they say and still not know what they are saying or, indeed, say all that they mean.[33] Generally speaking, people do not even know what they know and say more than they know when they do not even know what they are saying. And, sunken as they are in the play of images, even angry and destructive children would be shocked if their fantasy constructs turned out to correspond to anything real (EFRL: 63). The essential is normally unspoken due to its overwhelming power and all-pervasiveness,[34] misapprehended due to ignorance, or, when dimly perceived, nonetheless occluded by substitutions, compressions, and inversions. It is a fact that a single representation can house a nebula of unarticulated symbols and meanings (cf. Cassirer 1955a: 251). What my colleagues actually demonstrate, in a negative sense, is that resorting to prejudice and speaking in the language of race and power is less taboo in America than attacking the sacred concepts of business (S: 255), profiteering, private property, and righteous inequality. After all, when people are suffocating or drowning, neither the deficiency of air nor the surfeit of water is held to blame.

Americans do not talk directly about capitalism. Lacking any kind of political economy, they *talk about fragmented aspects of capitalism in the enigmatic representations of race and authoritarianism* (Worrell 2008) and, as such, are easily plundered by demagogues (Willich 1973: 258). In other words, beyond good and evil, love and hate, Americans do not have the concept, and they lack the means to arrive at objectivity.

If we consider that economists[35] really know nothing about capitalism (Piketty 2014) we should expect ordinary people to know even *less than nothing* about it; it's as if consciousness has returned after a long journey to a position of spiritual immediacy and purposiveness one associates with archaic Roman

---

the liaison would be forever deferred. It is apparently better to desire than to have desire realized. But it would be best if moral ends become objects of desire (Durkheim 1974: 46).

33 Often, with Lacan, it is not people who are speaking but something alien speaking through them. The "group ... exercises tyrannical sway over" the individual and they lose their individuality "in the struggle, and his own talk becomes but the echo of that of others of the group" (Brinton 1902: 167).

34 For example, "As the unmarked category against which difference is constructed, whiteness never has to speak its name, never has to acknowledge its role as an organizing principle in social and cultural relations" (Lipsitz 1998: 1).

35 Economists do not have "a theory of the real world, of really-existing capitalism, but of an imaginary capitalism." Economics "is only para-science, closer in fact to sorcery than to the natural sciences which it pretends to imitate" (Amin 2004: 11).

religion. Americans do not even use the word 'capitalism' (and when they do, the word lacks any determination) and their political champions who have something to say about it, e.g., Sanders, reduce the contradictions to greedy bankers and thereby lead the duped into the cul-de-sac of capital fetishism, the splitting of capitalism into two species, pure and impure, e.g., productive and speculative (MECW, 37: 816).[36] Poorly educated people have few expressions at their disposal, and fewer concepts, and use the few that they have as musty boxes into which they throw a jumble of contradictory experiences—the "untrained ... fancies that in them it has something really well and truly determined" (SL: 115) when, in fact, they unintentionally lie to one another (EFRL: 437) and to themselves.

The bourgeoisie have blocked all the exits with arrant mental ineptitude so, when Billy Joe has a beef with the setup, his diatribe will assume the form of a starburst of hate that appears to have nothing at all to do with capitalism itself: Rothschild, Soros, the DNC, Sharia law, Islamification, gun control, abortions, the homosexual agenda, cultural Marxism, welfare queens, the Mexican invasion, Libtards, feminists, snowflakes, unicorns, entitlements, and the beat goes on. Are these types just confused *radicals*? Absolutely not, but while their feet may be on the ground, their minds drifts along in a parallel mythological universe. Knowing 'less than nothing' means relying on fantastical nonsense (distortions) that keeps the entire signifying process in a fractured state while lending the appearance of logical coherence. A big problem with our thought on 'economy' is how the concept has been narrowly defined; *economy* means less than it should when it is alienated from its enclosing, universal *moral economy* and, in a lower sphere, the amoral economy of the psychoanalytic 'It.'[37]

People are sick of alienation but what they desire is actually more alienation (the illness that cures the disease) or, really, more of the right kind of alienation and a generally valid (not necessarily *fair*) distribution of the sacrificial leftover, but definitely not the end of sacrifice itself. If one interprets America through the lens of Marxist class antagonisms, orthodox economic determinism, psychological variables, measuring prejudice, or admitting defeat and just downgrading Spirit to nothing more than the blind play of biological

---

36   Capital fetishism is also called "departmentalizing" and plays an important role in reactionary politics such as antisemitic propaganda (Massing 1949: 13; see also Herf 1984: 55; Lasswell 1933: 376; Wilson 1982: 623).

37   The present moment is too complicated to expect illumination by rubbing together a couple of variables. What is needed is a conceptual supernova that fills the conceptual universe with light. If we hope to someday penetrate the deepest crevasses of the underworld of the absolute, we will be hopefully lost if all we have are a few crumbs to drop along the way.

determinism, one will be perpetually frustrated. Of course, in the final analysis, it is all about the *economy* but not the Marxist or bourgeois definitions of economy—rather, what is decisive goes beyond material 'provisioning' and includes the moral or "symbolic economy" (Simpson 1937: 63). The οἰκονομία concerns dividing, dispensation, allocation, and the distribution of goods, both material and symbolic. Trump's base[38] consists of many who are both stupid and ignorant but many are simply foolish—and being foolish is definitely not a disqualification for democratic participation.[39] But whatever they may be, they intuitively know that the vertical integration of the previous setup (what we usually refer to as the Fordist system) has been fundamentally altered and that they are doing less-well than their predecessors but they cannot bring themselves to indict white capitalists because, at the end of the day, they wish they too were capitalists, and they cannot blame their own lack of effort, so that leaves the time-honored composite of conniving Jews, lazy blacks, and subhuman immigrants who, enabled by the Democrats and a liberal cultural permissiveness, have cut to the front of the line to steal from the traditionally privileged. It is the special capacities of the "symbolic economy" (Vincent 1879, 5: 15) that can turn even psychological anti-Trumps into supporters of dictatorial monstrosities and conspiracy theories once the normative structure slides off its foundation.[40] Symbolic economies are bound to go sideways when those who use the symbols know little of the underlying "reality symbolised" (Scott-Holland 1894: 64). If a better one-word starting point for the allure of Trumpism was being sought, I think narcissism, apparently the most powerful force in the known universe, would be a better place to begin.[41] Trumpism is not supported by a simple, homogenous psychological or material bloc but is an

---

38   Of course, if the 'base' consisted only of the dregs Trump would never have lasted. Beyond the social base, there are high-volume volatility traders making a killing every time Trump signals some impulse, triggering an erratic twist or turn in the markets.
39   "Democracy may indeed be only a euphemism for the rulership of fools" (Parrington 1958: 85).
40   In an essay from 1936, Dewey says "As if in substantiation of the old idea that nature abhors a vacuum, it might be contended that economic competitive individualism, free from social control, had created a moral and social vacuum which recourse to dictatorships is filling" (1946: 103–04).
41   Recall that collective consciousness is simultaneously and better grasped as *conscience* (literally a 'together knowing'). It is not strictly the case that Trump's base simply traded ego ideals for a leader symbol, rather, as social organization disintegrates, conscience goes with it and the ensuing void is filled by something, and here, we come back to Freud: the leader for this type is one that demonstrates a freedom of libido ([1921] 1959: 79), the perverse father of unlimited enjoyments. The "most primitive social states are often reproduced at the highest stages of evolution, but under different forms, forms almost the opposite of their original ones" (S: 385).

umbrella movement that is unified in some way that exhibits unexpected durability (Smith 2019a). The narcissistic economy might encapsulate fairly well the distribution of energy[42] we find in 'red' psychology as well as the drive to punish or seek revenge (cf. Bell 1976: 200). But we should leave the mentality of one mass to psychologists.[43] What concerns us is that where there is economy we also encounter nomos and nemeses. Nemesis is the personification of distribution and divine retribution (both as repayment and vengeance) but also of envious social leveling (Hegel 1988: 335; cf. Freud [1921] 1959: 66). The daybreak of the Reagan Era meant that the rotten apples of the world were on notice, but it also meant that the price to be paid by the faithful was suffering. Morning in America was synonymous with a *piacular* (self-destructive) form of mourning and we know that where there is suffering the desire for wrathful divine intervention is automatically produced (AJ: 259). With the ascendancy of megachurch payday religions entangled with "repressive populist" political revolt,[44] we find that it is also payback time, and the desire for revenge is

---

42 To refer back to the first volume, mental or moral energy is not to be confused with physical energy (Lipps 1903: 36) but it does have physical effects. Durkheim's descriptions of what we might call 'crowd psychology' (DOL: 55; S: 125; EFRL: 212) are useful for connecting the word and speech to the image and the ritual effervescence to the collective representation. Freud is clear that when it comes to consciousness, visual and tactile perceptions play a dominant role, but when it comes to the unconscious, it is speech that counts (1939: 124). Words, but by no means all of them, are our positive and negative gods (EFRL: 309–10). But words in themselves are fluid and must be 'mounted' or fixed to material supports for rites to crystallize around an emblem or image. Static representations (marks, images, symbols, etc.) "contain elements of a 'living' ... consciousness" (Hofstadter 2007: 231). However, we should not fall for the naive reading whereby meanings are literally 'contained' in a lifeless material object. The thing does not transmit a contained meaning but "it is a *pattern* imbued with fantastic triggering-power" (Ibid.) and "*where there's a pattern, there's a reason*" (Ibid: 127).

43 Psychoanalysis pertains to the psyche of individuals and can even cover mass or group psychology to a certain extent, i.e., the mental processes of Group A or Group B. However, social psychology (sociology) is primarily concerned not with isolated (abstracted or alienated groups) but with the form of consciousness and unconsciousness that emerges as a *sui generis* reality from the relation between two opposed groups.

44 Populism assumes myriad forms. What we have in the US presently is what Berlet and Lyons call a repressive movement "that combines antielite scapegoating ... with efforts to maintain or intensify systems of social privilege and power. Repressive populist movements are fueled in large part by people's grievances against their own oppression but they deflect popular discontent away from positive social change by targeting only small sections of the elite or groups falsely identified with the elite, and especially by channeling most anger against oppressed or marginalized groups that offer more vulnerable targets" (2000: 5). By attacking "small sections" of the elite (e.g., the banker abstraction) a fetish split is introduced that guarantees that the elite as a whole will retain power.

saturated in myriad hatreds. "O my father, what a fierce joy / flashes in your eyes!" (from *Rigoletto*).

Is it not the case, with Durkheim, that the other's hatred is merely an exaggerated expression of what we ourselves are already doing? The right fantasizes about walls, the deep state, and gunplay while revolutionaries might fantasize about mechanical wood chippers turning billionaires into fertilizer or building reeducation camps across Wyoming for millions of unredeemable rednecks. But purifications and purges have no internal restraints and, as Durkheim says, even in a community of saints,[45] deviants must be constructed to satisfy the need for punishment. Designating criminals in the absence of an actual crime is "a matter of social expediency or of social impulses" (SGS: 259). Our subjective loves and class hatreds are products of ancient folkways and shifts in social organization and the ideological narratives that are manufactured by elites turn what should be manageable sociological problems into ratings entertainment and tribal conflict. It is shocking to learn that those we hate might actually desire the same things we do. According to the Pew Research Center, there is very little public support for a reduced federal governmental (2019) and the vast and overwhelming majority of Americans on both 'sides' of the political divide want the state to increase spending on health care, education, climate change, Social Security, Medicare, Medicaid, reducing inequality, building and repairing infrastructure, as well as scientific research (Parker, Morin, and Horowitz 2019). It is as if the political processes and institutions in America work not only to turn people against one another but against their own selves. "Issues of common good pull to the right and then jump jarringly back to the center or left, only to pull rightward once again. Such is the nature of our current American atmosphere in which politics vacillate endlessly, exhaustingly, between ever-shifting poles" (Metzl 2019: 265). Where there is this much hysteria and energy expended in an elaborate, self-destructive mechanism, I think we would not be delusional in thinking that the conflict is a fabricated heat sink whereby surplus passion dies in futility. After all, as others have noted, once voting rights were extended beyond white male property owners, voting became more or less irrelevant;[46] when a black man can be the

---

45   "[T]he better is the enemy of the good" (Harrison 1962: liv).
46   For both subjective and objective reasons, most eligible citizens do not vote and, even if the average voter was not hobbled by crippling ignorance, their object choice is limited to a red or blue money shovel. The 2016 election witnessed a record turnout (137.5 million voters) or 61.4 percent of the electorate. Our natural inclination is to encourage and celebrate the mobilization of ever greater numbers of voters, however, one should not be surprised at the monsters netted from fishing deep and murky waters. The 1930 and 1932 Weimar elections were characterized by a "huge influx" of new voters (Brown 1987: 61)

president of the USA, the specific occupant of the office is no longer a pressing issue;[47] once women of color managed to battle their way into House of Representatives and the Senate, the real levers of power had obviously moved to new locations reserved for rich white men. The democratic process in America has been reduced to ineffectual rituals (Amin 2004: 74). This is the managed mismanagement of the deregulatory era where hate spreads across the land. To combat hate we do not need to preach love *per se* when regulation will solve a lot of our most pressing problems.[48] Love is regulated hatred, i.e., hatred within bounds or a limited hatred, and hatred is just the love we cannot get enough of. Alain says, "The god Limit [Terminus] is the strongest" ([1934] 1974: 88) but today Nemesis has the upper hand (cf. Paterson 1907: 252 ff.). Nonetheless, Terminus is the final and unavoidable destination without a new aesthetic and Idea of one society indivisible.[49] "History teaches us that peoples in which opinion is divided become incapable of any collective effort" (Durkheim 1978: 113–14).

The one thing the Soviet Union had going for it (at least during the Popular Front) was that everyone "strained toward the objective world, and not, like your own, sucked into the whirlpool of murky subjective puzzles. Even death in Moscow had more life…" (Freeman 1936: 524).[50] However, even in a world that appears to be nothing but a bunch of "subjective puzzles" objective forces lurk behind the isolated pieces[51] and linguistic abstractions. We are surrounded

---

that prefaced the rise of the Nazis. It appears that 2020 will be another banner year for mobilizing voters from the American political sidelines; how these voters slot into the old political model is unclear (Cohn 2019).

47 "Presidents come and presidents go, but we [capitalists] go on forever" (Stalin, in Wells 1934).

48 For example, gun control laws really do work to reduce the rate of suicide by firearms and the repeal of regulatory hurdles that stand in the way of obtaining guns increases the rate of firearm suicides. See Crifasi et al. (2015) and Rudolph et al. (2015) for the positive regulatory effects on suicide in Connecticut. For a compelling map of correlations between gun law and death see Kristof (2017). The percentage of Americans who support permits issued by law-enforcement agencies as a precondition for the purchase a firearm has never fallen below 70 percent between 1972 and 2014 (Carter 2017: 58). Americans, for the most part, are not anti-gun *per se* but they overwhelmingly want more regulation than we currently have in the US. Political leaders who opposed gun control are hirelings for the weapons industry.

49 We will have more to say regarding literature, poetry, and theory.

50 On Joe Freeman's connection to the Frankfurt School see my piece in *Rethinking Marxism* (Worrell 2009d).

51 "[D]own gravitation's / vortex into crashed / … dispersion … into mashed and shapeless debris…" (Hart Crane, in Kramer 2011: 80).

on all sides by 'evil' and Whitehead says the "ultimate evil in the temporal world is ... deeper than any specific evil."

> It lies in the fact that the past fades, that time is a 'perpetual perishing.' Objectification involves elimination. The present fact has not the past fact with it in any full immediacy. The process of time veils the past below distinctive feeling. There is a unison of becoming among things in the present. Why should there not be novelty without loss of this direct union of immediacy among things? In the temporal world, it is the empirical fact that process entails loss: the past is present under an abstraction. But there is no reason, of any ultimate metaphysical generality, why this should be the whole story. The nature of evil is that the characters of things are mutually obstructive. Thus the depths of life require a process of selection. But the selection is elimination as the first step towards another temporal order seeking to minimize obstructive modes. Selection is at once the measure of evil, and the process of its evasion (1978: 340).

The "struggle for existence" assumes many forms. One can, for instance, 'fit in' and 'play the game' (integration), adapt to circumstances and rely on tradition and magic to maintain an equilibrium (RC: 226–49), run away and go it alone (Horney 1945), become resigned and trudge along unhappily until the end, or simply take matters into one's own hands and depart prematurely (DOL: 228). Relatively few choose the latter but many try. In 2014 a little over one million Americans attempted suicide while a bit more than 42,000 succeeded (Drapeau and McIntosh 2015). Three years later there were 1.4 million attempts and more than 47,000 deaths (Rodrick 2019). As of 2017, overall deaths from suicide, drugs, and alcohol "hit the highest level since federal data collection started in 1999" (O'Donnell 2019).

Common sense chalks all this self-destruction up to psychological depression or mental illnesses but we know that personal psychology is only part the story. Sociology's focus is not the analytically isolated individual nor simple dyadic relations (I-deaths and Me-deaths) but in We-deaths or the dynamics and unique 'laws' of collective psychology (S: 312)[52] and, while depression accounts

---

52   Following from our first volume, *The Sociogony*, we know that what we are really talking about when it comes to "collective consciousness" is really *collective unconsciousnesses*. The 'laws' of the social sciences are not like the laws of nature; social laws are fixed constructs that result in a wide variety of outcomes when violated or ignored. 'Law' is derived from the Old Norse word *lag* for "something laid down." As such, the idea of a law as it is applied to the domain of nature, as we usually think of it, is filled with contradictions without recourse to an omnipotent being that lays down the law.

for much of our self-destructive conduct, depression is never pure nor is it necessarily personal the way we ordinarily assume.[53] A force that encourages and strengthens some class of people has the opposite effect of discouraging and weakening others (cf. Durkheim [1912] 1915: 142–43). Americans actually vote for suicide when they take the side of white privilege and libertarian deregulation (Metzl 2019: 274). Any concept of 'depression' would have to involve multiple scales of existence and substantial modalities and their inversions. Moreover, as we will see, depression harbors various transpositional mysteries whereby individuals experience devaluations and/or counter-valuations that result in transits from egoism to its polar opposite. But depression represents only one class of suicides among others and it is important to map the field of suicidogenic currents[54] because the classification of types and causes amounts to the classification of social defects (Peuchet, in MECW, 4: 610). As such, suicide is just one important manifestation of the larger problem of institutional and social morbidity.[55] Suicide rates are signs of social breakdown, the downfall of collective consciousness, and of an entire social system in crisis. Suicides are indices, that is, of social disorganization (Hodge and Kress 1988: 107–08).

---

53   We owe it to the Epicureans for the subjectivization of self-destruction: "Plato's 'objective' circumstances under which suicide was permissible [e.g., being commanded from on high by god] became subjective. Suicide was no longer an involuntary act dictated by outward [external] circumstances but a voluntary assertion of freedom" (Colt 1991: 146). From our perspective, however, voluntary death is a symbol of obedience to an external command whereas life is the daily rejection of the impersonal order to kill ourselves. The person who attempts this kind of self-liberation is still in submission to social force (S. 214). Life and reasons are grounded in disobedience. It therefore seems that life is the continual negation of authority (reducing all commands to tyranny) and the desublimation of society into a sand heap of individuals. But this would presuppose that no good reasons can be given for self-destruction. It also neglects the degree to which a well-developed social division of labor can mitigate the necessity for premature self-destruction. If the Bulgarians declare war on Milwaukee I can avoid conscription without shame or legal accountability due to my age. Likewise, if my local fire department is efficient and competent, I can let the professionals enter my burning house to save my cat, Henri Pester Nuisance. And if my professional life is reduced to shambles, can I not find a new calling in over-the-road freight hauling or perhaps the radio ministry? Where there is a twice-born there was a loser.
54   'Currents' and 'streams' are analogies still used and relevant in sociological theory. According to Unnithan, Whitt, Huff-Corzine, and Corzine (1994: 162) "the idea ... refuses to die because it corresponds to empirical reality." However, when one examines their empirico-volumetric use of the 'stream' analogy one realizes right away that they are far removed from Durkheim's theory of moral currents. Sociological 'currents' are not simply the volume of deaths but correspond to authoritative (positive or negative) representations driving social conduct.
55   Not to say that the morbid is not socially necessary (Mann 1948: 236).

From the reductionist standpoint of psychology and individual action, suicide appears to be the choice of a scattered few, but from the perspective of sociology, changes in the rates of voluntary death signal not just *choices* made by individuals but that something has chosen, that is, commanded people to throw themselves into the mouth of the volcano as human sacrifice, "as if in obedience to a command from on high" (C: 865).[56] We are not interested in the individual decisions but in the general invitation to self-destruction. Suicide is not random; invitations are sent (Durkheim 2006: 154–55) and there is a designation process (S: 322, 325).[57]

> Victims of suicide are in an infinite minority, which is widely dispersed; each one of them performs his act separately, without knowing that others are doing the same; and yet, so long as society remains unchanged the number of suicides remains the same. Therefore, all these individual manifestations, however independent of one another they seem, must surely actually result from a single cause or a single group of causes, which dominate individuals. Otherwise how could we explain that all these individual wills, ignorant of one another's existence, annually achieve the same end in the same numbers? At least for the most part they have no effect upon one another; they are in no way conjoined; yet everything takes place as if they were obeying a single order (S: 304–05).

We sometimes conceive of suicide as an act of "insubordination and revolt" (S: 329) but disobedience to one command is simultaneously obedience to another. We normally think of authority as the command of the sacred pure, but authority is equally the command of the sacred impure (S: 255). Both the holy (the positive devil) and diabolical (the negative god) are authoritative. In *The Sociogony* we focused on positive authority but in this volume a greater emphasis is placed on negative authority.

The self-destruction of the abstract, isolated, ego is never what it appears. The single and apparently disconnected individual acting in accordance with their conscience is, in reality, a member of impersonal groups.

---

56   To appropriate Hegel with respect to the satisfaction of personal choices, the "proliferation of arbitrariness generates universal determinations from within itself, and this apparently scattered and thoughtless activity is subject to necessity which arises of its own accord" (PR: 228).

57   Metaphorically, we can think of psychology as being trapped on the level of reflections whereas sociology is tasked with the unenviable task of working analysis back to not only the reflecting mirrors but also the reflected objects and things hidden from view in the hall of mirrors that is the social universe.

The phenomenon of cluster suicides, where there is knowledge and contact between victims, only illustrates this selection logic in a more spatially and temporally compressed manner. We might be tempted to think that in a society plagued by rugged individualism,[58] or one that is suffering the disease of egoism, that an absence of centralized mechanical control is the root of the problem. However, de Certeau insists, "Economic individualism is no less effective than totalitarianism in carrying out [the] articulation of the law by means of bodies. It just proceeds by different methods. Instead of crushing groups in order to mark them with the unique brand of a power, it atomizes them first and multiplies the constraining networks of exchange that shape individual units in conformity with the rules ... of socioeconomic and cultural contracts" (1984: 148).[59] Indeed, the individualism and hyper-subjectivity of late ('liquid') modernity appears to be knotted together precariously like a ratty fishing net by status consumption and commodity conspicuousness (Eco 2016: 2).[60]

Given that a selection process is active, and that suicide is an index of changes and disintegration, it is normal to conceive of self-destruction as something abnormal and purely pathological, and that is true to a certain extent; we should want to live in a world lacking suicide but we also know that self-destruction and contradiction are built into human reality and the line between normal and pathological is not clear and both rely more or less on the same basic mechanisms (Freud 1939: 160). Society "is at war with itself, and its very life-process is the process of its dissolution. In an absolute sense, it cannot be said *to be*, any more than *not to be*" (Caird 1893: 136). Progress is incomprehensible without regression just as life without death is meaningless. Degeneration obviously lacks an apparent attractiveness, but some forms come with compensations "favourable to the general economy" (Brinton 1902: 82). "Every death loosens a little the crust of habit, and is a step forward in life" (Santayana [1936] 1949: 22). If the winds of fortune blow favorably on one person, class, or nation, another person or class or nation endures misfortune; "indigence is the nursery to which the wealthy and powerful repair in quest of the objects their

---

58 "Since the two of us left Krotz Springs I'd been thinking occasionally in terms of 'we.' It irritated me; it smelled of softness, and I wanted none of it" (Chaze [1953] 2016: 22).
59 The granularization of dictatorship at the level of every boss and employer, etc., is also a central feature of bourgeois republicanism. America does not make absolute dictatorship a political necessity when a practically infinite matrix of particular dictatorships works just as well (Shaw 1933).
60 Veblen notes that conspicuous consumption entails a pressure for the creation of monstrosities (1912: 142) as objects of elite stylistic distinction.

lust or cruelty needs" (Sade 1966: 426).[61] Profits are made from poverty. The first landlord was a robber (PM: 91, 92). Money is dead people and the profit rate is rising.

In the domain of the infraliminal, things are alive or dead but in human societies one is always caught somewhere along a continuum between life and death.[62] Society formally commands its members to cling to one another and prohibits self-destruction (the fatal plunge into the profane)[63] but at the various points where society is compromised, the signal to self-destruct is received

---

61 Profits are "*deductions* suffered by wages" (PM: 71). Profits are an index of human brutalization and collective misery. The *labor process* under the capitalist regime of accumulation is brutalization itself, the *product* is brutality objectified, *value* is brutality considered from the point of view of its reified subjective-substantial form, and the *price* is the sign of the magnitude of that brutality expressed in dollars and also a claim that the vehicle (use-value) produced through brutality is a good that will satisfy the needs or wants of the consumer. When times are good, bodies are transformed or dissolved into goods but when the era of plenty devolves into debt and austerity the bodies also pile up, as with French Telecom workers where "executives resolved to make life so unbearable that the workers would leave, prosecutors say. Instead, at least 35 employees—workers' advocates say nearly double that number—committed suicide, feeling trapped, betrayed and despairing of ever finding new work in France's immobile labor market" (Nossiter 2019).

62 See *The Sociogony* on the distinction between the living of the living dead and the dead of the living dead.

63 As we saw in *The Sociogony*, the 'death drive' is actually the desire of the ego to return to profane, infraliminal existence—the negation of solidarity and collective effervescence—in favor of morbid satisfactions (e.g., shop 'til you drop) and privacy. According to Freud, libido inclines "living beings of the same kind" to combine more comprehensively ([1921] 1959: 64) but social forces can drive individuals into isolation and even devolve into a love of isolation and self-absorption. In Freud's view, "The individual feels incomplete if he is alone" (Ibid.) but sociologically we know that many individuals feel, instead, contaminated and diminished when in contact with others. They are "incomplete" in fact but they may not "feel" as though they are lacking. But the fact remains that being alone is not actual existence for the socialized human and when we set aside the profane necessities of keeping the body going, there is hardly any existence left—nothing more than what Byron called the "summer of a dormouse" (1982: 334). Likewise, those that would attempt to sacralize the individual body need to remember that "freedom and possibility do not apply to it" (Auden 2008: 151). As Schopenhauer rightly says, the body is unfree and our only freedom at this level is consciousness and the consciousness of necessity (cf. Auden 2008: 248). I don't know if sociology graduate students have changed much over the years but in the '90s we were treated to a continuous parade of self-debasing 'Copts' chanting *The Body* at every opportunity. Kant's thinking on the radical evil of the individual in his religious writings is based in this drive of the abstract ego to become animal. The contradiction is that our species can never return to animal status due to our constitutive lack of a self-regulating power—our lack in the real.

in less mitigated forms. In order to live we must disobey the command to die and adhere to norms that demand persistence or even just partial deaths.[64] Sacrifice is a normal and expected feature of life. Simply "to know one's limit is to know how to sacrifice oneself" (PS: 492). With some groups the notion of a prolonged life is abnormal and even unseemly (Strahan 1893). Total self-annihilation can be a great career move for some people and when it comes to prophets and entertainment personalities, suicide is not simply an occupational hazard but an act that can make all the difference.[65] Every celebrity has to respond to the suicidal imperative by either going 'all the way' at a young age or stringing it out for decades in a self-destructive spectacle worthy of continuous media attention. The spectacle, though, is only the visible crest of the wave of moral energy at work on everybody.

> [T]he transmission of facts such as suicide and, more broadly speaking, such as the various acts reported by moral statistics, has a very special nature not to be so readily accounted for.... The state of mind which causes men to kill themselves is not purely and simply transmitted, but—something much more remarkable—transmitted to an equal number of persons, all in such situations as to make the state of mind become an act. How can this be if only individuals are concerned? The number as such cannot be directly transmitted. Today's population has not learned from yesterday's the size of the *contribution it must make to suicide*; nevertheless, it will make one of identical size with that of the past, unless circumstances change (S: 308, emphasis added).

Suicide is not merely a thing someone does in the face of unbearable sadness, loss, or pain. Self-murder is a *contribution* and an act of submission to external forces.[66] The taboo against suicide, like all taboos, is both repulsive and attractive, both revolting and appealing, impure and pure (Freud [1913] 1950: 29). The

---

64 Cf. Freud's "anaesthetic men" ([1912] 1959: 209–10).
65 "Strange how a musician's very survival made him suspect. Pat had tried writing a song about this strange feeling—'So Sorry to Be Here,' he called it—but the song got bogged down in that junkie braggadocio and he never performed it" (Walter 2012: 155). And when the icon does manage to blow his head off there is the risk of seduction. Some poets, writers, and celebrities make death appealing (Proal 1905: 361).
66 A sociology that goes on and on about 'forces' needs to be careful and not treat them as some kind of transcendental substance emanating from a separate, prehistoric realm. "What appear as objective forces (such as globalization) are only the products of a logic specific to a given system..." (Amin 1997: 44).

holy and the accursed are but two dimensions of the same unity (Radcliffe-Brown 1952: 139).[67]

Organicism may no longer be the 'irresistible analogy' (Bourdieu) that it once was[68] but one thing is certain: suicides (partial and final) are not merely the desperate *psychological* acts of depressed loners but the willing obedience of a daily roster of self–*sacrifiers* (Hubert and Mauss 1964); the order to kill or maim the self is communicated to members of society who lack any other connection to one another other than exposure to these identical signals. Seemingly private acts of this type are actually social forces attempting to achieve through individuated means some negative goal that would otherwise be enacted by more obviously collective action (cf. Freud [1913] 1950: 92). Every one of us falls, unbeknownst to us, into cohorts of like–minded people who respond to commands issued from impersonal forces that we have "absorbed" in the course of our socialization (CPE: 189).[69] This holds true not only for suicides but mass murderers as well. The school spree shooter is not only a criminal at war with society but simultaneously obedient to impersonal, pathological ideals that demand action (Kimmel 2013: 81) and the slaughter of sacred victims. It is important to keep in mind that we are not merely pushed around by 'ideas' as if social problems were reducible to ideologies (MECW, 28: 101) but, rather, we are dominated, rightly or wrongly, by authoritative representations that occlude an entire economy of moral forces.

2   The New Economy and the Reign of Tyche

Since 1999 the US suicide rate has climbed 33 percent (Centers for Disease Control 2018b).[70] The self-murder paradise of America seems to be Montana where the rate increased 7.3 percent in 2014 until the state's rate of 'success'

---

67 To extrapolate from Radcliffe-Brown we can see that a suicide is not without its "ritual-value" and that suicide victims produce special effects (1952: 139–40).

68 If organicism was still a compelling analogy we would say that the body social was, through various processes such as military induction and incarceration, overdoses, etc., as disposing of something 'it' considers surplus.

69 This is far removed from Whitt where we find "suicides choose themselves as victims…" (1994: 28). "A man *called* to kill himself belongs only accidentally to this world…" (Cioran 1974: 49). And when it does not call a person to dispose of themselves it sometimes takes direct action: "Suicide, to her, was an invincible figure who rose up in front of you, like a praying mantis, and carried you off" (Roché [1953] 2006: 161).

70 Just the year before the rate was about 30 percent (Helmore 2018).

was double the national average (McGreal 2016).[71] Nationally, suicides among the specifically middle-aged (35–64) increased between 1999 and 2010 by almost 30 percent. For men the rate was 27.3 per 100,000 and for women, 8.1 per 100,000 (Parker-Pope 2013). The suicide rate among girls between the ages of 10 and 14 has tripled over the last 15 years (Bichell 2016) and the rate for their older teen counterparts doubled between 2007 and 2015 for a 40-year record high (Scutti 2017). Overall, between 2007 and 2014, suicides doubled for children and adolescents between the ages of 10 and 14 (Centers for Disease Control and Prevention 2016).[72] Additionally, more than half of US college students report having suicidal thoughts and suicide is the number two killer of undergraduates (Hecht 2013).[73]

Since 1998 the mortality rate for middle-aged white people has taken a dramatic upturn. Specifically, we are referring to those between the ages of 45–54, with a high-school degree or less, especially those living in the southern and western states. For those with the least education, the rate now stands at 134 per 100,000. "That means 'half a million people are dead who should not be dead'.... The reasons for the increased death rate are not the usual things that kill Americans, like diabetes and heart disease. Rather, it is suicide, alcohol and drug poisonings, and alcohol-related liver disease" (Khazan 2015).[74] Alcoholism increased 49 percent among American adults from 2001 to 2013.[75] The figure of 500,000 dead is nearly equivalent to the number of American deaths due to World War II, the Korean War, and the Vietnam War combined.

---

71   With the exception of Alaska, the highest suicide rates in the US fall within 'mountain time' (Rodrick 2019) or the states that make up what has been referred to as America's "suicide belt" (see Wray, Poladko, and Allen 2011): Arizona, Colorado, Idaho, Montana, Nevada, New Mexico, Oregon, Utah, and Wyoming. To put it blithely, *the concept* is dead in the American west and in its place is an abstract nexus of guns, addictions, and spurious infinities.

72   Suicides among those serving in the military have almost doubled since 2005 and the link between suicides and combat deployment is weak; merely being in the military correlates with a high rate of voluntary self-destruction (Philipps 2015). Suicides among female military veterans are nearly six times higher than for civilians (Zarembo 2015).

73   Data from 2003 indicate that, overall, roughly six percent of young people in the US attempt suicide by the age of 20 but that those with 'non-conventional' or 'minority' sexual orientations are at least four or five times higher (Suicide Prevention Resource Center 2008: 15).

74   "The number of 25- to 34-year-olds who died annually from alcohol-related liver disease nearly tripled between 1999 and 2016, from 259 in 1999 to 767 in 2016, an average annual increase of around 10 percent" (Chisholm 2018).

75   "Increases ... were greatest among women, older adults, racial/ethnic minorities, and individuals with lower educational level and family income" (Grant et al. 2017). On the rate at which English boomers are drinking themselves into the grave, see Siddique (2017).

Full-blown suicides are one thing but self-destructive acts, of the kind that fall into the category of embryonically suicidal conduct are another. Hospital emergency rooms today are "flooded" and overwhelmed with the mentally ill and substance abusers seeking help with no other place to turn (Scutti 2019).[76] In 2014 nearly eight percent of Americans used illicit drugs (other than marijuana) and nearly five percent of the population, over the age of 12, has used 'crystal meth' at least once in their lifetime.[77] Heroin use has increased 135 percent between 2002 and 2016 and the US now has nearly one million abusers of this drug (a half million are actually addicted) and heroin overdoses are up over 500 percent during the same timeframe (Kounang 2017).[78] The Governor of New Jersey, Chris Christie (who heads a commission to study the problem) "has compared opioid-overdose fatalities to terrorist attacks, saying, 'We have a 9/11-scale loss every three weeks'" (Kolhatkar 2017: 21).

From a more inclusive viewpoint, between 2006 and 2016 "deaths of despair" accounted for roughly one million people due to drugs, suicides, and alcohol and these deaths are occurring disproportionately in economically depressed counties that have become politically despondent (Monnat 2016). America is

---

76 From 2006 to 2014 saw a 44.1 percent increase in the number of the mentally ill and drug abusers seeking assistance at hospital emergency rooms (Moore et al. 2017: 6).

77 According to the Substance Abuse and Mental Health Services Administration's Center for Behavioral Health Statistics and Quality (2015).

78 Why do we love alcohol and hate junk? In Baudelaire's *On Wine and Hashish* we find the classic differentiation between profanation and sacralization: wine is social, engendering sublime effects, whereas hashish reduces the person to an enslaved beast lusting for the infinite through a substitute material substance that engulfs the ego (2002). What the alcoholic Baudelaire attributes to "hashish" (cannabis) are actually effects of opium lifted from De Quincey (see Grinspoon 1971). "Junk is surrounded by magic and taboos, curses and amulets" (Burroughs [1959] 2001: 6). This connection between drugs and taboo is not to be dismissed lightly. The junky is in some ways akin to a washed up negative wizard (cf. ES, 1: 401–02). See Durkheim's note on wine (2006: 63). The musical world has been overpopulated with chemical junkies, however, one can also detect an elective affinity between chemical addiction and certain educational strains in music. For example, Slonimsky's famous *Thesaurus of Scales and Melodic Patterns* is a portal into the "unbounded universe" of music. He says, with regard to practical infinity, "There are 479,001,600 possible combinations of the 12 tones of the chromatic scale. With rhythmic variety added to the unbounded universe of melodic patterns, there is no likelihood that the new music will die of internal starvation in the next 1000 years" ([1947] 1975: vi). The *Thesaurus* is one of those books that jazz musicians like to own but few actually use. The one most famous for really falling in love with it is John Coltrane, who kicked a nine-year heroin addiction in 1957, and who used the *Thesaurus* to help chart a unique form of mystical avant-garde jazz before dying at age 40 in 1967 (see Porter 1998: 149–50). On the correlations between the infinite and mental illness see Wallace (2003).

part of a larger 'genocidal' program[79] and at the heart of it, here, is an "epidemic of pain."[80] Despair and pain have contributed mightily to the creation of a new political base: the OxyCons.[81] When the Trump administration refused to declare the opioid epidemic a national emergency it revealed that there is some utility to ravaging the rural and suburban poor. As Marx says, the capitalist class has to figure out what proportion of the proletariat and reserve labor army must be weeded out through death "for the good of the rich and for their own welfare" (MECW, 4: 56–57).[82] In a "declining state of society" the "surplus" members of the working class "have to die." Marx calls this condition "misery with complications" (PM: 69). Of course, the opioid crisis is destroying more

---

79 According to Amin (2004: 34) the continued expansion of the global capitalist project will require the extermination of roughly 5 billion useless human beings, whole societies will have to be destroyed, and the near-total indifference to opioid deaths in the US can be seen within that larger framework. The state no longer wants to be in the welfare business (being whittled down to only technical administrative processes involved in the flow of money, goods, and labor power, as well as war and police functions). Whites constitute roughly 78 percent of opioid deaths and blacks about 12 percent. Hispanics, however, represent only about 8 percent of these deaths while constituting roughly 18 percent of the overall population of the United States. It is true that accidental opioid deaths are not just a white phenomenon (Shihipar 2019)—and these deaths are certainly *not* restricted to 'rednecks'—but whites are overrepresented by almost twenty percent. As we enter the 'third wave' of the opioid epidemic, however, where Fentanyl-related deaths replace Oxy-Contin and heroin, racial minorities are being hit harder (see Bebinger 2019).

80 "The epidemic of pain which the opioids were designed to treat is real enough, although the data here cannot establish whether the increase in opioid use or the increase in pain came first. Both increased rapidly after the mid-1990s. Pain prevalence might have been even higher without the drugs, although long-term opioid use may exacerbate pain for some, and consensus on the effectiveness and risks of long-term opioid use has been hampered by lack of research evidence. Pain is also a risk factor for suicide. Increased alcohol abuse and suicides are likely symptoms of the same underlying epidemic, and have increased alongside it, both temporally and spatially" (Case and Deaton 2015).

81 "Trump's 'oxy electorate' is swimming in a sea of correlations, not just to high rates of drug overdoses, but, as demographer Shannon Monnat has found, to suicide and deaths from alcohol as well, not to mention dramatic reductions in economic mobility. Not any single thread can be identified as 'causal,' but all help to form a picture of Trump's appeal — namely, a rhetoric and a campaign strategy that made these voters feel seen and heard, not just as measured against the Democratic Party, but within the power structures of the Republican Party as well. His rage matched their anguish; his gaze met their eyes" (Frydl 2016).

82 In times of war it is sometimes the case that a region of some arbitrary limit will determine whether or not a population is fit for sacrifice or salvation: "A day came when the decision was taken to declare all [French] cities of more than 20,000 inhabitants 'open.' That a village lived in by poor yokels should be bombed, smashed, and burned was, apparently, a matter of indifference to the noble apostles of humanity who upheld this view. But a city of solid tradesmen was quite another matter!" (Bloch 1968: 131).

than the 'dregs' of society—it is also consuming professionals, hall-of-famers, the rich and famous, the creative types, and virtuosos. Each epochal shift in American history has required a major war for the disposal of bodies by the tens of thousands or even hundreds of thousands but military conflict no longer has the same effect[83] (Worrell 2011) and the pharmacological death wave is indiscriminate and more terrifying in its apparent randomness.

In a nation that consumes 98 percent of the world's supply of OxyContin, West Virginia leads the way in fatal drug overdoses and opioid-dependent infants (Joseph 2016). Huntington, West Virginia, with a population of about 50,000 witnessed 26 heroin overdoses in just a few hours on 15 August 2016. Those 26 cases were non-fatal, but two fatalities arrived later in the day (Joseph 2016). PBS Newshour reports that Cabell County, where Huntington is situated, suffers from an addiction rate that is described as "incomprehensible." A full 10 percent of the county's residents are addicted to heroin or some heroin analog and 20 percent of the infants delivered are born with exposure to some illegal drug and exhibit serious neurological problems. In February 2017 there were 52 overdose calls within 32 hours in Louisville, Kentucky where the daily average is 22 calls (Ellis and Allen 2017). The coroner's office in Montgomery County, Ohio has so many corpses to manage that refrigerated trucks and temporary morgues are used to deal with the overload.[84] "In Ohio, fatal overdoses more than quadrupled in the past decade and by 2007 had surpassed car accidents as the leading cause of accidental death" (Freytas-Tamura 2017). What was a new reality in Ohio ten years previously is now a national fact: "For the first time in U.S. history, a leading cause of deaths—vehicle crashes—has been surpassed in likelihood by opioid overdoses, according to a new report on

---

83 This is why the 'one and done' conscription model has been replaced with a voluntary continuous redeployment strategy that keeps troops in a kind of perpetual suspended animation or simulated death on the imperial fringes. If a person survives a tour in Iraq they are sent to Afghanistan and if they make it out alive they might go back to Iraq or a flashpoint in Somalia, Syria, Niger, Yemen, etc. The military and war are basic to American foreign policy and industrial spending, but they no longer play into the popular imagination in a way comparable to WWII. In the '40s about 12 percent of Americans were members of the military and today not even one percent serve on active duty or the reserves (Crigger and Santhanam 2015). For several years I taught courses on war and terror at SUNY Cortland where I would ask students to locate Iraq and Afghanistan on a map and seldom did anyone know where they were located.

84 "The explosion in fentanyl deaths and the persistence of widespread opioid addiction has swamped local and state resources. Communities say their budgets are being strained by the additional needs—for increased police and medical care, for widespread naloxone distribution and for a stronger foster care system that can handle the swelling number of neglected or orphaned children" (Katz 2017).

preventable deaths from the National Safety Council. Americans now have a 1 in 96 probability of dying from an opioid overdose, according to the council's analysis of 2017 data.... The probability of dying in a motor vehicle crash is 1 in 103" (Stewart 2019).[85]

The number of accidental overdoses among white, middle-aged women has increased 400 percent from 1999 to 2014 (Kindy and Keating 2016) and deaths resulting from overdosing on fentanyl and its analogs increased 540 percent in the three years between 2013 and 2016 (Katz 2017). The most noticeable determinate in this die-off is the divide between urban dwellers and rural leftovers and it appears that the number of overdose deaths is increasing at an unimaginable speed. As of 2018, "Opioids are now on pace to kill as many Americans in a decade as HIV/AIDS has since it began, with leveling-off projections tenuously predicted in a nebulous, far-off future: sometime after 2020" (Macy 2018: 284).[86] We could pile up disquieting statistics on chemical degradation until pigs fly but the fact is that America is becoming the land of the walking dead. Drug deaths, like the homicide rate,[87] unemployment, incarceration, police executions,[88] etc., have to be grasped as indices of dysfunctional or altogether

---

85 The abolition of the 55-mph national speed limit has led to the death of approximately 37,000 additional motorists since 1995. "[R]esearchers from the Insurance Institute for Highway Safety found that for every 5 mph increase in a highway's speed limit, roadway fatalities rose 8.5 percent" (Barry 2019).

86 The overdose epidemic is terrible but Alkermes (the maker of Vivitrol) stands to make a killing off the crisis (Harper 2017).

87 The murder rate is so high in Chicago that we should probably think of it as an actual war zone. The number of civilians murdered in 'Chi-Raq' over the last few years is greater than the number of troops dying in combat overseas (LeDuff 2018: 172). The good news is that the homicide rate is on the decline in Chicago but the bad news is that it still represents a staggering 561 murders in 2018—down from 660 the year before and 770 in 2016. The *Chicago Tribune* reports that there are 25 fewer murders from 1 January through 3 February, 2019 than in the previous year (www.chicagotribune.com/news/local/breaking/ct-chicago-homicides-data-tracker-htmlstory.html). By contrast, the US has suffered three combat-related deaths in "Operation Enduring Freedom" (Afghanistan) from 1 January to 6 February, 2019. One should not overlook, however, that for every US combat-related death, Afghan troops take a real beating. From 2015 to 2018 the Afghans lost more than 28,000 soldiers and police officers (Nordland and Abed 2018). But as deadly as Chicago is, the murder and manslaughter rate per 100,000 (24) pales in comparison to St. Louis (66) and Baltimore (almost 56). In terms of overall 'violence' Chicago is not in the top five metropolitan areas. See Mirabile and Nass (2018) for metropolitan murder and violence statistics.

88 Fatal police shootings are up 250 percent from 2015 to 2016; consult the *Washington Post's* "Fatal Force" Project online: (www.washingtonpost.com/graphics/national/police-shootings-2016/).

missing social relations.[89] Auden's most famous poem, "September 1, 1939," contained a line (used in Johnson's famous 1964 'Daisy Girl' television spot) about the need to love one another or face mass extinction. Auden later renounced the work as "dishonest" and then tried to prohibit the entire poem from being republished in subsequent collections (Konnikova 2012). The opioid mass death event reveals something about the relationship between despair and love in America as well as Auden's conviction that he had been somehow less than honest. Killing oneself out of despair is to die for something—it is a final love letter inscribed into the symbolic order—a desperate and futile attempt to reach across the void to touch the absolute. The overdose is one of two poems: we must die if we are to avoid loving one another, or, we must die in order to finally be loved by something, to be absorbed by something greater than ourselves.

Capitalism involves the absorption or soaking up of bodies and personnel but this absolute is a bad one. The overdose and the "apathetic ecstasy" of drugs (RC: 232–33)[90] is one kind of a soaking—revealed in the etymology of the word (*socian*) for becoming saturated through immersion. It is related to *sucan* ('to suck'). But capitalism sucks up surplus bodies and personnel in a variety of ways apart from overdoses, most notably through confinement.

The US incarcerated more than two million people as of 2013 in what amounts to little more than warehouses for slave labor—"It may … work, it may be necessary for the sake of others, but only one's sadism can possibly approve" (Auden 2008: 387). Prison is the primary institution for soaking up the 'undeserving poor.' While the incarceration rate declined during the Obama administration, the apparent downturn veils what amounts to a granulizing of criminal justice where family members are transformed into unpaid jailkeepers to relatives wearing surveillance bracelets and paying exorbitant fees for the privilege of home-based imprisonment. On the side of the 'deserving poor,' the positive prison of military service soaks up roughly two million individuals (active and reserve troops combined) where they are kept in a state of suspension, many deployed outside the imperial core where they would otherwise cause trouble for the state. War and military institutions are important factors situated alongside other institutions for dealing with the oversupply

---

89 According to the *New York Times*, drug use among employees and job seekers is climbing from a high (no pun intended) of over 13% in the 80s. "All over the country, employers say they see a disturbing downside of tighter labor markets as they try to rebuild from the worst recession since the Depression: They are struggling to find workers who can pass a pre-employment drug test" (Calmes 2016). The surge in heroin abuse is also correlated with H.I.V. and hepatitis epidemics in some parts of the country (Seelye 2015).

90 "Drug-induced paranoia is just one degree away from euphoria" (LeDuff 2018: 15).

of human bodies and the contradictions of neoliberal accumulation. War can be credited with eliminating 1.19 million Americans between 1775 and 1991, excluding the thousands killed over the last generation as part of the war on terror (Department of Veteran Affairs 2015) that has cost taxpayers about $1.6 trillion dollars.[91]

The Belle Époque has been portrayed as an "age of self-destruction…. Social disintegration, the emancipation of the individual, poverty, and the influence of certain philosophers—including Schopenhauer and Kierkegaard—were among the factors blamed" (Edmonds and Eidinow 2001: 196) but there is more than enough fear and trembling in the shadow of the spectral empire[92] and contemporary America, the neoliberal colossus of inequality and mass destruction, seems hell-bent on playing second fiddle to no previous era.[93] As

---

91 The Congressional Research Service estimates the cost of the war on terror from 9/11 to FY2014 to be $1.6 trillion (Belasco 2014) but other academics estimate the 'true cost' to be more than twice that figure. Because much of what goes on in the Department of Defense is not audited we will probably never know the true costs involved in the war on terror.

92 There is a sense that America's position as a post-war imperial power and global equilibrator (cf. Aron 1974: 146 ff.) is coming to a close. Where we previously witnessed subsidiaries of American firms and banks spreading across the globe we now find ourselves as a nation, along with every other nation, serving as a subsidiary to transnational firms and banks. Where markets used to serve nations, nations now serve markets.

93 Inequality and polarizations are built into neoliberal deregulatory policies: "the real explanation for inequality lies primarily with an economic belief that, intentionally or not, serves to concentrate wealth at the top by extracting it from everywhere else. This belief system is called variously neoliberalism, Reaganomics, the Chicago School, and trickle-down economics. It is easily recognized by its signature ideas: deregulation; privatization; cut taxes on the rich; roll back environmental protections; eliminate unions; and impose austerity on the public" (Goerner 2016). You know inequality has reached an extremity approaching a revolutionary situation when billionaires publically beg the government to raise the tax rate on the wealthiest individuals (Helmore 2019). I suspect their pleas will go unheeded. But if a backlash erupts, from which segment of the working class can we expect unrest? The Federal Reserve data from 1989 to the first quarter of 2019 reveals an extreme divergence in the top half of society (the top one percent now own almost $32 trillion in assets and cash) and the nine percent below them are in possession of right at $40 trillion in total wealth. The 'middle class' has seen only modest gains for decades and the bottom half of society still has essentially nothing. In 2007 the bottom half of society owned what it did in the late 80s and never grabbed more than $1.5 trillion for itself. After the 2008 debacle, the bottom 50 percent were in the red (owned less than nothing), but as of 2019, the bottom of the heap is back to about where it was 30 years ago. Half of America could be renamed 'Algrenland' where the citizens are guilty of "owning nothing, nothing at all, in the one land where ownership and virtue are one" (Algren [1949] 1999: 19). If the proletariat were going to revolt it would have done so decades ago or after 2008 when it went upside down. The turmoil is not at the top or the bottom but the struggling 'middle' consisting of the 50 to 90 percenters outpaced by the top 10 percent (Board of Governors of the Federal Reserve System 2019).

conditions become more bleak and contradictory, the "Repressive State Apparatus" (Althusser 1970) ramps up the compression effect while market anarchy works the other side of the street. In short, chronic pain, addiction, isolation, hopelessness, the extinction of retirement,[94] the growing "financial abyss" and a gun-encrusted landscape of political and religious fanaticism have resulted in this social cataclysm (McGreal 2016). Sociology must dig for and signify powers that invite people to an early death. The obsessive type[95] believes in a fantasy that they rule themselves free from external constraint but in capitalistic society "the seeming freedom of the economic subject" who believes they are "acting according to personal determinations" is actually "exemplifying the working of an incalculable social mechanism" (Horkheimer 1972: 197). The prime "mechanism" of the last half century is deregulation (anomie) inclining in the direction of bourgeois egoism and anarchy.[96]

According to the United Nations Human Development Index[97] measuring *per capita* income, educational attainment, and life expectancy, in 2014 the United States, while still classified as a nation characterized by "very high human development" nonetheless ranks 28th globally and falls behind Hungary, Malta, and Greece when adjusted for income inequality.[98] Average annual HDI growth from 2010–2014 in the US (.018) falls well below the growth in development from 1990 to 2010 (.028). However, Americans do also report an overall life satisfaction that is barely different from populations enjoying higher HDI scores. There is no reason to suggest, at least from the standpoint of logical necessity, that immiseration and satisfaction cannot cohere.

Income inequality has reached historic and catastrophic proportions. According to Oxfam, "In 2015, just 62 individuals had the same wealth as 3.6 billion people—the bottom half of humanity. This figure is down from 388 individuals as recently as 2010…. Meanwhile, the wealth owned by the bottom half of humanity has fallen by a trillion dollars in the past five years. This is just the latest evidence that today we live in a world with levels of inequality we may

---

94 The demise of pensions and the move toward actively 'managed' retirement plans resulted in the transfer of roughly $12 trillion *in fees* over the last decade from the accounts of employees to Wall Street firms operating without fiduciary commitments.
95 Fink's discussion of obsessive neurotics (1997) dovetails particularly well with Durkheim's portrayal of the individual animated by the spirit of progressive anomie and infinity disease.
96 Bourgeois egoism easily devolves into what we might call, following Green, conflict modified detachment (1895: 55).
97 United Nations Development Programme "Human Development Report" (2015).
98 The difference between HDI and inequality-adjusted rank for the US is a staggering (negative 20) and, among other "very high" development nations compares only with Korea (negative 19).

not have seen for over a century" (2016: 2). Just one year later Oxfam revised its numbers and declared that a mere eight men held as much wealth as the bottom half of the global population (Hirschler 2017).[99] "Oxfam, which has for years been trying to focus attention on the issue ahead of the World Economic Forum, said in a report that billionaire fortunes increased by 12 percent last year—the equivalent of $2.5 billion a day—while the 3.8 billion people who make up the world's poorest half saw their wealth decline by 11 percent" (Pylas 2019). In the United States, the wealthiest 400 individuals "have tripled their share of the nation's wealth since the early 1980s…. Those 400 Americans own more of the country's riches than the 150 million adults in the bottom 60 percent of the wealth distribution" (Ingraham 2019). Piketty claims that, at the current rate of dispossession, the US will soon be exploring political-economic conditions reserved for nations embroiled in violent upheavals and civil wars (2014).

Wages for US workers have stagnated for decades. "After adjusting for inflation … today's average hourly wage has just about the same purchasing power it did in 1978, following a long slide in the 1980s and early 1990s and bumpy, inconsistent growth since then. In fact, in real terms average hourly earnings peaked more than 45 years ago: The $4.03-an-hour rate recorded in January 1973 had the same purchasing power that $23.68 would today" (DeSilver 2018).

Organized labor was never a genuine revolutionary force in the US; when the Frankfurt School set out to locate and analyze wartime American labor radicals they found not a single one (Worrell 2008). Still, even in its sociologically deficient form, the function of the American union is to produce some sense of class antagonism and at least raise the price of labor power. Today, union participation in the private sector is only 6.4 percent and overall union membership is half what it was in 1983.[100] It is interesting to note that just as worker shares of gross domestic product circa 1970 were approaching levels not seen since 1945 (the end of WWII)[101] the conflict in Vietnam was winding

---

99   For a breakdown on the global hyper-wealthy see Sullivan (2017).
100 "The union membership rate—the percent of wage and salary workers who were members of unions—was 10.5 percent in 2018, down by 0.2 percentage point from 2017…. The number of wage and salary workers belonging to unions, at 14.7 million in 2018, was little changed from 2017. In 1983, the first year for which comparable union data are available, the union membership rate was 20.1 percent and there were 17.7 million union workers" (Bureau of Labor Statistics 2019).
101 U.S. Bureau of Economic Analysis, Shares of gross domestic income: Compensation of employees, paid: Wage and salary accruals [A4102E1A156NBEA], retrieved from FRED, Federal Reserve Bank of St. Louis; https://fred.stlouisfed.org/series/A4102E1A156NBEA, April 10, 2019.

down and the final, full-scale assault on organized labor was beginning. The post-Fordist battle against organized labor has to be seen not only as an effort to suppress wages but also the subjugation of racial and ethnic minorities, especially women, who benefit the most from organization.

Unemployment in the US seems to be a weak force while rates of underemployment (roughly 14 percent) as well as the number of discouraged workers that have fallen out of the employment system altogether are relatively downplayed.[102] The opioid crisis in the US has contributed to an unemployability crisis and a loss of productivity estimated to be anywhere between roughly $50 billion and $80 billion annually with highest and most inclusive estimates around $150 billion, taking into consideration the insurance valuation of each lost life (Kolhatkar 2017: 21). Employers in the manufacturing sector can rely increasingly upon automation and robotics yet these forces lead to further crises in commodity devaluation, reflected in lower prices, and lost wages required for consumption resulting in a growing dependency upon consumer credit. But the larger problem behind the figures on unemployment, underemployment etc., is the falling share of the gross domestic product (GDP) for individual workers. From the early 70s to 2017 American workers have suffered a 16.6 percent loss in the share of GDP.[103] Americans do not have a problem working; they have a problem earning wages and going into debt bondage as a means to stay afloat.

Between consumer debt and home mortgages, Americans are about $5 trillion in the hole[104] with total outstanding debt in the US now in excess of $20 trillion (most of this is termed "national deficit") with students on the hook for

---

102 "In December [2018], 1.6 million persons were marginally attached to the labor force, little changed from a year earlier. (Data are not seasonally adjusted.) These individuals were not in the labor force, wanted and were available for work, and had looked for a job sometime in the prior 12 months. They were not counted as unemployed because they had not searched for work in the 4 weeks preceding the survey.... Among the marginally attached, there were 375,000 discouraged workers in December, down by 99,000 from a year earlier. (Data are not seasonally adjusted.) Discouraged workers are persons not currently looking for work because they believe no jobs are available for them. The remaining 1.2 million persons marginally attached to the labor force in December had not searched for work for reasons such as school attendance or family responsibilities", Bureau of Labor Statistics, USDL-19-0002, online: (www.bls.gov/news.release/pdf/empsit.pdf).

103 U.S. Bureau of Economic Analysis, Shares of gross domestic income: Compensation of employees, paid: Wage and salary accruals: Disbursements: To persons [W270RE1A156N-BEA], retrieved from FRED, Federal Reserve Bank of St. Louis: (https://fred.stlouisfed.org/series/W270RE1A156NBEA, April 10, 2019).

104 According to the Federal Reserve Bank of Philadelphia statistics, online: (www.philadelphiafed.org/consumer-finance-institute/statistics).

over $1.5 trillion in loans—an average of $37,000 per individual student (Berman 2018). In the bigger scheme of things, global debt has reached $66 trillion or roughly 80 percent of global GDP (Cox 2019). The two primary mechanisms for drawing down this debt will come in the form of austerity for workers and war, which is a mechanism for canceling or renegotiating debt obligations.

The new retirement model in the US is simply working until death.[105] Pensions were replaced by the 401(k) and other investment schemes and sold to workers as a way for them to take charge of their own financial futures and also as a way to enter the investment class. In neoliberal America, the belief is that we are all, or can be, little capitalists.[106] Experts advise Americans to have at least one million dollars stashed away for retirement (by age 65) yet the bold new investors have managed to put back a sliver of what is necessary.[107] 20 percent of Americans have literally nothing saved and another 10 percent have less than $5000 in their retirement accounts. Average retirement savings are less than $90,000. On top of this, faith in the future availability of social security is almost non-existent—only a quarter of Americans believe social security will be there for them (Northwestern Mutual 2018).

America leads the world in over-work (labor brutalization) and with labor union participation at an all-time low labor power is cheap and flexible. For those with full-time jobs or those cobbling together multiple part-time gigs the work week is in excess of 40 hours and for those that have sick days, vacation, and other forms of leave, there is a reluctance to utilize those entitlements for fear of retaliation. The result is a level of sleep deprivation (chronic in the

---

105 According to Transamerica about 60 percent of workers in their 50s expect to work past 65 or not retire at all (Transamerica Center for Retirement Studies 2015). This belief is delusional. Only 16 percent of retirees make it on the job past 65. Workers are out of the labor force at 62 on average and for half of them the departure is due to unforeseen circumstances such as health issues and disabilities, to care for family members, downsizing, and business closings, obsolete skills, and "other work-related reasons" (Brandon 2014).

106 Except for the fact that being a capitalist means not only accumulating profits but also actively striking down other capitalists (C: 929). Actually, we are not all little capitalists but little zero-interest bankers making temporary micro-loans through the over-charge and refund model. Just as being an employee means providing interest-free loans to the employer (Marx) being a modern consumer means providing deposits and overrun protections to providers of services.

107 The payoff for the individualization of retirement investment lies in the fees that companies charge unwise shoppers. According to the Securities and Exchange Commission (www.sec.gov/investor/alerts/ib_fees_expenses.pdf) if a saver does manage to live up to the suggested figure of $1,000,000 for retirement but pays a one percent annual fee over a 20-year period their portfolio will be reduced by nearly $300,000 in combined fees and lost investments (assuming modest four percent annual returns).

southeastern states)[108] that would astonish Increase Mather (Fischer 1989: 159) as well as an abundance of physical pain and suffering. As Fasenfest indicates, America is the only developed nation where the mere existence of health care is synonymous with access to health care in the same way that the existence of million-dollar homes signifies access to housing (2017: 815). And healthcare, where it is actually obtained, has become so expensive that the usual diseases that would have been treated in the past are now wiping out the most vulnerable members of society (Khazan 2016). The price of insulin is so high (roughly double what it was in 2012)[109] that 'Type 1' diabetics lacking quality medical insurance are rationing their doses and dying as a result (Sable-Smith 2018). It is little wonder that 'wellness' quackery and magic potions thrive in a land where actual healthcare is out of reach for millions. Anthropometric indicators suggest that Americans peaked in biological well-being at the apex of the Fordist era (the mid-50s) and have stagnated since; Americans are no longer the tallest and are among the fattest on the planet (Komlos and Baur 2003; see also Hacker and Pierson 2016). The war on obesity has been lost and Americans have surrendered. More than two thirds of Americans are now obese or overweight, fewer are attempting to lose weight, and fatter bodies are becoming the new 'normal' for individuals assessing their body compositions (Howard 2017). It is not simply a matter of people losing discipline and constantly 'pigging out' while parked in front of televisions but also the transformation of food into addictive junk. "The obesity epidemic is also a way of talking about the destruction of life, bodies, imaginaries, and environments by and under contemporary regimes of capital" (Berlant 2011: 104).[110] The success of agribusiness can be measured not only in profits but also by body mass index and the uptick in diabetes. "Claims for Type 2 diabetes—formerly known as adult-onset diabetes—among people younger than 23 years old more than doubled between 2011 and 2015, according to the analysis of a large national database

---

108   According to the Centers for Disease Control and Prevention (2014) sleep deprivation (defined as less than seven hours per day) plagues roughly 40 percent of the population (38–44 percent) in states like Alabama, Alaska, Georgia, Hawaii, Kentucky, Mississippi, West Virginia, and the old Rust Belt counties east of Chicago. Reservations (in Florida, Nevada, Oklahoma, etc.) are also especially hard hit. Basically, where there are the poorest whites in the backcountry, blacks, American Indians, and other minorities, there is a lack of sleep. There may also be a relationship between loneliness or living on the periphery of society that translates into less sleep, and lower quality sleep (Cacioppo, Capitanio, and Cacioppo 2016).

109   In 2016, type 1 diabetics paid about $5700 for insulin. The increase from 2012 to 2016 was nearly $3000 (Biniek and Johnson 2019).

110   Eating routines are also spatial-temporal mechanisms (episodic alterity) for coping with "the overwhelming feeling of 'sickening boundlessness' or endless absorbing interiority" (Berlant 2011: 135).

of health claims paid by about 60 insurers. At the same time, claims for prediabetes among children and youth rose 110 percent, while high blood pressure claims rose 67 percent" (Appleby 2017). We can look high and low and we find debilitating correlations of neoliberal deregulation in every domain of life.

According to the Pew Research Center, marriage rates in the US have declined nine percent over the last 25 years and the divorce rate has doubled for those aged 50 and older while it tripled among those 65 and older since 1990 (Geiger and Livingston 2018; see Wang and Parker 2014). Parenting is radically changing not only in style and structure[111] but in quantitative terms as well; the fertility rate has dropped to record lows for the last two years in the US and most factors point in one direction: economic insecurity and uncertainty (Miller 2018). The gig economy is mirrored in the free-market hook-up culture and sexually transmitted diseases are "raging at all time highs" in some parts of the US (Romo 2018). Americans are gun crazy. We now have about as many firearms in the nation as there are people and almost every month the Transportation Security Administration (2017) seizes a record number of firearms from passengers attempting to smuggle their weapons, many of which are loaded, onto airplanes and air-rage ("unruly passenger") incidents increased sharply in 2015.[112] Mainline religious institutions are crumbling and being replaced by charismatic cults and frenzied purveyors of wackadoodle and there have never been more hate groups in the US according to the Southern Poverty Law Center. During the Trump era the number of hate groups has grown 30 percent to 1020 identifiable organizations revolving, more or less, around the idea of white supremacy (2019).

We could keep going, piling up facts and figures on homelessness,[113] illiteracy,[114] the rising price of necessities, and so on, but the case has been

---

111   See the Pew Research Center's comprehensive study of American family life (2015).
112   The International Air Transport Association reports "Some 10,854 unruly passenger incidents were reported to IATA by airlines worldwide last year. This equates to one incident for every 1,205 flights, an increase from the 9,316 incidents reported in 2014 (or one incident for every 1,282 flights). The majority of incidents involved verbal abuse, failure to follow lawful crew instructions and other forms of anti-social behavior. A significant proportion (11 [percent]) of reports indicated physical aggression towards passengers or crew or damage to the aircraft. Alcohol or drug intoxication was identified as a factor in 23 [percent] of cases, though in the vast majority of instances these were consumed prior to boarding or from personal supply without knowledge of the crew" (2016).
113   "The National Law Center on Homelessness & Poverty currently estimates that each year at least 2.5 to 3.5 million Americans sleep in shelters, transitional housing, and public places not meant for human habitation. At least an additional 7.4 million have lost their own homes and are doubled-up with others due to economic necessity" (National Law Center 2015).
114   "Approximately 32 million adults in the United States can't read, according to the U.S. Department of Education and the National Institute of Literacy. The Organization for

made that Americans, in general, have been told to reject regulations and they are paying a high price for the privilege of pleasuring their corporate masters. The rules have changed for all, but the gains accrue to only one class.[115] At the level of the 'masses' the picture is wildly complicated but, overall, workaday Americans harbor bewilderingly contradictory opinions and are generally ambivalent about what they want and how to achieve their goals, if they even have any goals that can be articulated. As Berkeley stated, few people think whereas all have opinions (1843: 187). All of us, it seems, are at war with ourselves and filled with self-deception about our true motives and feelings (Auden 2008: 95). The political center appears to have evaporated but many Americans who are portrayed in the media as mindless sheep following demagogues and begging to serve oligarchs actually long for a return to a moderate political environment. That discourse on both the left and the right has devolved into nothing more than propaganda and perpetual spin suggests that authentic sentiments have been played out (see Aron 1954: 25). It is probably true that tens of millions of 'conservatives' in America are so dumb and mean that they are beyond redemption (they would rather die as to follow reason or be helped by or help others)[116] but America has always had its share of mean dummies. America is a land of permanent stupidity and hostility and it is wide of the mark to suggest that some people are just more reasonable than others or that some people cannot be reasoned with. We need to keep in mind Durkheim's remarkable achievement in *Elementary Forms*: reason is not something inherent in the species or reducible to individual psychology, rather, it emerges from, and is reflective of, social organizational circumstances. If society dissolves into chaos people will generally not reason their way out of trouble but regress to emotional infantilism and resort to violence.

This big, slow-motion, regression event combining voluntary and involuntary modes of self-annihilation, is the work of anomie elevated to the rank of a supreme spiritual power: anomie is sacred and any "restraint seems like a sort of sacrilege" (S: 255). Now that anomie is holy and inviolable it is left up to the social atoms to serve this god through acts of self-destruction. "Pills, addictions, and even guns … [are] modes of coping, ways of filling the void" of

---

Economic Cooperation and Development found that 50 percent of U.S. adults can't read a book written at an eighth-grade level" (Strauss 2016).
115 "The *rules* of a club are occasionally in favour of the poor member. The drift of a club is always in favour of the rich one" (Chesterton 1986: 346).
116 Metzl's (2019) work on the politics of resentment and the social costs on heartland Americans is highly relevant here.

anomie (Metzl 2019: 51).[117] But these are not just coping mechanisms. Guns are one trophy in the pool of consolation prizes available to losers in the free-for-all: war dogs, monster trucks, patriarchy, misogyny, homophobia, racism, nationalism, games of chance, spectator sports, McJesus, conspiracy fantasies, and so on.[118] The way most of the social sciences think of deregulation is merely the reduced role of the state and the decline of national sovereignty in the face of globalization. Where the state dilutes or slashes rules and regulations, corporate entities have either infiltrated the state's oversight function ("cozy" relations) or erected their own private "regulatory regimes and institutions for the governance of international economic relations" (Sassen 1996: 14–15). Corporate giants get new forms of arbitration and ratings agencies with their "private justice system" (Ibid: 16–17) but, of course, what sufferers is social justice, air, water, food, wages, housing, education, health, etc. The privatization of oversight in the banking industry, for example, means that an entire civilization can be brought to the brink of collapse by shady deals and reckless speculation and no one at 'the top' will ever be held accountable. Universal regulation and general interests have been replaced by particularized or contingent autonomic systems and singularized gains. The self-destructive spectacle of deregulation is analogous to the "dumb show" of "motivated ignorance" we find hysteria where "the patient, doctor, and family all participate" in an orchestrated manner to perpetuate, rather than eliminate, the problem (Simon 1979: 183). To conjure Marc Bloch's concluding pages of *Strange Defeat*, it appears that we too have found ourselves in an "appalling situation" where our fate longer depends upon our own efforts (1968: 174).

3   The Nightmare of Collective Unconsciousness

The present historical moment, says Žižek, is not Marxist but Hegelian: "not the moment of highest tension when the teleological (re)solution seems near, but the moment after, when the (re)solution is accomplished, but misses its goal and turns into a nightmare" (2014b: 37). Instead of the actualization of the concept, capitalism has delivered humanity to the doorstep of death and

---

117   It used to be that Americans could count on poverty and soul-crushing labor to check their horizons but now credit, lucky streaks and social media stoke the furnaces of unhinged dreams of wealth and fame.
118   We should not forget that progressives also have their prizes in the form of simulated hardships as well as cultivated ignorance that comes with life in purified, self-reflective enclaves (see Hochschild 2019 for the disconnect with reality among liberals).

absolute Spirit seems like a superstitious holdover, or perhaps, reduced to a skeleton of abstract links and connections that dances about like a thing possessed (C: 302). If the current neoliberal moment is a nightmare, and that would seem to be an apt metaphor, then there must be (if we cling to the metaphor) some dreamwork going on, the dreamwork of the hypertrophied bad absolute, an "automatic" and "dominant" god-like subject (C: 255–56) engaged in fantastic acts of self-laceration in pursuit of an "infinity of dreams" (S: 287) and a multitude of insatiable desires. We are not following Tarde who was famous for saying that "'social man is a somnambulist'" (in Smith 2014: 167) but merely stipulating that, first, teleological activity can regress under the weight of a more powerful external necessity, and, second, collective thought operates with dynamics comparable to those we find in Freud's theory of dreamwork.[119] At first glance, one might suppose that Durkheim would reject such a notion outright: the origins of religious thought (sacred consciousness and ritual conduct) cannot be traced back to the projective superimposition of distorting hallucinatory thoughts, generated in dream life, onto the things of sensual experience such that objective reality is obliterated by "mere figments of the imagination" (EFRL: 84). But this is not the argument. Social reality is not a dream, it is not modeled on dreams, and we will get nowhere if our argument starts with our current reality being nothing but the absolute's nightmare. One of Freud's brilliant contributions lies in the revelation that the processes of dreamwork form an unbroken continuum with neuroses, jokes, myths, legends, etc. The logic of dreamwork also has what we might call hermeneutic value beyond the dream itself (Roth 1987). Common sense, the mere understanding, and collective consciousness are characterized by compressions, splitting, displacement, substitutions, inversions, reversals, unexpected copulas, and dramatic compositions. It is unlikely that Freud's theory of dreams is accurate in supposing that everything comes down in the final analysis to the preservation of sleep, but these distortions do have the effect of guarding against disenchantment. Belief does not allow itself to be swept away by reasons alone and sub-scientific thinking guarantees that objective reality "does not accord with the testimony of the believers" (Jones 1998: 57). As Freud reminds us, "man never willingly abandons a libido-position, not even when a substitute is already beckoning to him" ([1917] 1959:

---

119   We need to avoid personifying collective consciousness as a mind that knows something, or, anything really. The 'social mind' is not a transcendental thinker that ponders or thinks about its own thinking.

154). Distortions (delusions, gods, genies, demons, psychological fictions, fetish objects, jokes, etc.) are symptoms of disintegration and the processes by which individuals attempt to reconsolidate the social real.[120] After all, delusions do possess a fragment of truth at their core (Freud 1939: 107) and social illusions "correspond to something in reality" (Durkheim [1912] 1915: 227). "The illusory ... is not *nothing*, but is a reflection, a *relation* to the absolute; or, it is illusory being in so far as *in it the absolute is reflected*" (Hegel [1812] 1969: 532). Do not confuse these 'illusions' for the fictions of empiricism and nominalism. With Marx and Durkheim, these illusions are real illusions, or, real abstractions (cf. Žižek 2000a: 15–16).

Both Durkheim and Marx comprehend that spirits are conjured, and that people mostly go through the motions "as if sleepwalkers, awakened from the dead, unconscious of what they are really doing" (Mazlish 1972: 335). Recall from the first volume, collective consciousness is mostly unconsciousness, and, from the side of psychoanalysis, consciousness is more of a capacity than the usual run of things; in society most consciousness is of a virtual kind (Freud 1939: 132).[121] In *Suicide*, Durkheim says that we are in a sense hypnotized[122] as group members and that our illusions and delusions form an unbroken continuum with hallucinations (2006: 44).[123] We do not mean the visual

---

120 Our classical paradigm (Hegel, Marx, and Durkheim) is exactly the opposite of Žižek's reductionist pose whereby the real of society is constructed when our cobweb of illusions and subjective fictions disintegrate and leave us incapable of continued enjoyment (2019). Anyone worried about society would be hysterical. Really, how devoid of substance is this line of thought? The percentage of individuals who kill themselves because they lose their psychological fiction must pale in comparison to the number of people who die because they have lost their *social relations*.
121 The unconscious is invisible but effective and surmounts the will of the individual even though they are unaware of its presence, lurking as it does, in a different region of the mind (Freud [1938] 1959: 380).
122 What is hypnosis—the "group of two" (Freud [1921] 1959: 76)—but the mind possessed by impersonal and 'supernatural' power? See Freud ([1921] 1959: 73). I think it is important to keep in mind that 'sleep' in this case simply means a *reduced state of consciousness*. If it is true that much of what we accomplish in daily life is done while unconscious of all that we do, then we might extend the concept of 'sleep' to waking life and of the normal person as one who occasionally sleepwalks through the day. The sleepwalker "has a mere inner intuition of the outer world and is altogether active *within itself* and proceeds to a whole series of external arrangements as one does in the waking state" (Hegel 1986: 154).
123 'Hypnosis' would merely consist of an extreme manifestation of social "suggestion" (Cooke 1920: 13). In society we are delusional, deluded, and are fooled and mocked by forces that treat us as their playthings. The inventor of the word 'hallucination' said of the masses that, in their ignorance, rhetoric supplants logic; the syllogism plays second fiddle to fables, that propositions are less compelling than parables, and "proverbs [are] more

and auditory blips suffered only by the isolated individual but, rather, the "objective phantom" (Hopkins 1884: 115) produced by the dynamics of collective consciousness. Bageant (2007) uses the metaphor of a hologram to describe this virtual reality or hallucination through which we Americans fumble and stumble to the bitter end. Of course, these are not the same hallucinations of archaic animism where minds float through a "fabric of illusion" disconnected from objective reality (EFRL: 65–66). The 'hypnotic' or delusional state of the normal person is a symptom of a regressive understanding of representational dynamics.[124] Both Hegel and Durkheim have as their mission the education of thought from the representation to the concept (Hegel 1988: 145; EFRL: 7) but normal society is only possible if people are capable of investing representations with energy such that they acquire an *external* quality vis-à-vis the individual psyche (see volume one for more on the externality of social facts).[125] In the interests of human freedom, externality should be overcome, sublated, and raised to a higher form of thought and freedom, however, in the teleological process of sublation, external and sacred representations are not merely obliterated as such but transformed from a totality of alien powers to a universality of related social forces raised to the level of the self-conscious thought. To negate 'externality' *tout court* is tantamount to condemning society to an abstract play of subjectivity devoid of conscience. For critical theory to run from externality prior to the negation of capitalism is merely capitulation and surrender to capitalism behind an empty rhetoric of "radical transformation." Teleological praxis has within it the moment of "triumph" when the internal and external unite (Freud [1921] 1959: 81) and consciousness moves from merely representational thinking to a more sublime form of thought. It is true that the Hegelian Idea does not require a symbol for itself, but the concept does make use of symbols and images in the work leading thought from

---

powerful than demonstrations" (Browne 1658: 9). 'Hallucinations' are in one sense just perceptions of physically non-existent objects (e.g., alcohol-induced paranoid psychosis) but the sociological concept means misapprehending and misperceiving things and is thusly connected to projections and fetishism. "The bad conscience racked by the torment of crime objectifies itself by ghostly shapes" (Hegel 1986: 154). Toward the end of my father's life, his daily consumption of alcohol was so great that he became convinced family members were plotting to murder him and, as a precaution, he took to wearing a sidearm around the house.

124 Importantly, for Durkheim hallucinations are not the cause of sacred thought but symptoms and reflections of sacred thought ([1912] 1915: 106–07). The 'engines' of collective effervescence, e.g., rites, spawn distorted and distorting representations that overwhelm (alienate) consciousness.

125 Hysterics suffer from a hyper-cathexis such that representations are over-invested with libido to the point of experiencing hallucinations (Fink 1997: 85).

the understanding to reason. A constitution is an inadequate representation of the Idea (Kant 1991: 176) but we might not want to live in a world lacking a constitution, at least until some better framework is created. Freud is famous for his 'just-so' story of the primal horde but he says that while it might be outlandish it nonetheless has value "if it proves able to bring coherence and understanding into more and more new regions" ([1921] 1959: 69). The Idea is an anti-mythical condition but going *through* myth, that "small treasure of human abstraction" (Herder 1993: 80), is nonetheless an inescapable leg of the odyssey. Any good teacher can relate to the plight of Nietzsche's character, Zarathustra, who, in attempting to raise the minds of the 'herd' to the heights of the sublime is forced to lower thought to the level of the herd (cf. Freud [1921] 1959: 88).

In *The Sociogony* we saw that our primordial psychology[126] and foundational "collective consciousness" is better thought of, per Durkheim, as mainly collective *unconsciousnesses*: for each particular circle of social or ethical immersion there is a corresponding consciousness or conscience (Hegel 1988: 335; Freud [1921] 1959: 78) that operates for the most part 'behind' the foreground dynamics of palpable signs.[127] It is not the case that the socialized are literally mesmerized but simply ignorant[128] and unequipped to break through the hard shell of reification.[129] However, let us not get off track. I want to take seriously the idea of the 'dream' or the 'nightmare' as more than just a metaphor when it comes to the subterranean energy that percolates under the visible aspects of the moral economy.

Displacements and other distortions are the work of what Freud, following Groddeck, called 'the It' ([1949] 1961) or what we know of as the Id. The alien economy of the Id is quantitative, amoral, and lacking categories, e.g., time and space, as well as ideas (Freud 1965: 90–94). The Id knows no contradictions

---

126 "We must conclude that the psychology of groups is the oldest human psychology; what we have isolated as individual psychology, by neglecting all traces of the group, has only since come into prominence out of the old group psychology, by a gradual process which may still, perhaps, be described as incomplete" (Freud [1921] 1959: 70–71). However, Freud's immediate correction of this statement is important because it sheds light on the narcissism of the leader who is loved but cannot love anything but himself.

127 Cf. Freud (1939: 170): "It is not easy to translate the concepts of individual psychology into mass psychology, and I do not think that much is to be gained by introducing the concept of a 'collective' unconscious—the content of the unconscious is collective anyhow, a general possession of mankind."

128 "[O]ne of the main lessons of the critique of ideology is that it is not only knowledge that is socially constructed but also ignorance" (Žižek 2014b: 209).

129 The "creative act" says Cassirer, "is not recognized as such; all the energy of that spiritual achievement is projected into the result of it, and seems bound up in that object from which it seems to emanate as by reflection" (1946: 61).

and negations are foreign to it. Dreamwork, of course, is intimately connected to the transformations of the "strong upward drive" (Ibid: 86) of immortal Id energy as the censoring function of the superego loosens its grip on the ego but this all seems far removed from the fate of social facts such as the commodity. Our epochal confrontation is with capital but if we shift our gaze to the labor product at a precise location in its journey from the grimy domain of production into the valorization process whereby a labor product (an ordinary object) becomes an enigmatic commodity, a thing, we find exactly what we are looking for: the alienation of the labor product and its transformation as a carrier of exchange-value is where quality is set aside.

In order to function as a carrier or bearer, a use-value must also simultaneously be a uselessness-value. The either/or of use or non-use is here replaced with the 'and' of use *and* non-use. It might seem that this all breaks down when it comes to time and space, however, we should not be deceived. The commodity is a thing of value, which means that it is a crystal of human labor in the abstract. At the end of the day, value is determined by the quantity of value embodied in the commodity, i.e., the amount of time that goes into production. However, let us recall with Marx that it is not time *per se* but socially necessary labor time that counts with respect to value; labor that exceeds that which is socially required is not rewarded and is synonymous with waste. Capital appears to be concerned chiefly with time; after all, time is money. However, this honored maxim actually distorts and masks the truth: first, there is the obvious inversion such that time is not actually money, rather, money is crystallized time or time in its symbolic form, at least from the standpoint of classical bourgeois thought. Second, the emphasis on the idea of socially necessary labor time should not be placed on *time* but, rather, on *necessity*. After all, as we already know, time beyond necessity is not time at all but waste and punishment. Necessity draws the line between crime and the possibility of redemption. However, it now seems that we have projected a moral paradox into what must be an amoral dimension if it is to hold true to our analysis. But necessity is a limit and the end of morality *per se*. As we will see in a later volume, necessity can be a short-circuiting of the entire moral economy and only necessity is strong enough to lift prohibitions (Durkheim [1912] 1915: 152) while preserving the chance for escaping prosecution and punishments.[130] Morality entails a choice of the free subject but when we act out of necessity we are no longer free but determined by fate. As Lacan might say, what is going to happen has already happened. Likewise, with an eye toward the polarity of things, if we

---

130 Where one violates the law through inevitability and unavoidability, chance without hate or malice, one should not be held liable for punishment (Bracton 1879: 277).

push necessity to the brink we arrive either in the land of anarchic passions and, again, we have eluded morality because the choices are made for us, or outside the moral economy altogether: the reduction of the human to brute physicality.[131] To emphasize time, in itself, amounts to being captivated by the capitalist point of view. Perhaps something else is really going on. When I am paid I am compensated not for the time I actually work but for the value of my labor power. It is then up to the capitalist to extract as much labor from me as they can. And when I perform labor it is not an abstraction but concretely which means that I worked not for such and such a quantity of time but that the labor process is subject to intensifications, hindrances, contractions, and prolongations that will appear later in the calculations of relative and absolute ratios of surplus labor that constitute the substance of surplus value. In other words, once we cross into the domain of necessity we are no longer dealing with 'time' but with brutal endurance[132] and the elasticity of effort in the labor process that will be reflected in the conscious abstraction of the organic composition of capital. Our conscious moral economy (the conflict between conscience and the ego) rises up out of this unconscious realm and depends upon it for its energy. The point is not simply that we are "sleepwalking through history" (even if we are) but that our hyper-rational, calculating, and objective mental capacities are inextricably linked to, and greatly determined by a whirlpool of chaos yet to be comprehended.

Common sense, half-baked understandings, rationalizations, propaganda, and ideologies rely on processes comparable to those in dreamwork because they are already extensions of this process. And if we are correct there is even a connection between what appears to be dream logic and production for exchange. Freud repeatedly says that waking thought is different than dream thought which consists of its own processes and structures, yet, the boundary between dreams and waking mental life consists of an unbroken continuum with hysterical symptoms, jokes, etc. In Freud's classic formulation, dreams represent the fulfillment of repressed or otherwise unsigned desires. In this sense, we can think of the fulfilling dream as a *negation of a negation*—the

---

131 A notion like "the freedom of necessity" is surely commensurate with Stalinism (and Bernal, the author of *The Freedom of Necessity* was an unrepentant communist) but collectivization and extreme privatization amount to the same thing, namely, putting the means of production and most of the wealth into the hands of a few.

132 'Endurance' and 'duration' share a common root in *hardening*. We are offered two ways out via suffering, i.e., making things hard for myself or making it hard on the other fellow. For the ascetic who is above suffering, everything is endurable for the sake of personal power but for the piacularist, in the grip of suffering, the pain is unendurable, too hard, and must be freighted upon a scapegoat (EFRL: 395).

return of the repressed.[133] However, the censoring of unacceptable wishes usually prevents the negation of the negation. "In most of the dreams of adults, where the dream appears on the surface to contain no evidence of any desire, the operative desire is one that is unacceptable to the subject's consciousness and has therefore been 'repressed.' This repressed desire can now be allowed to attain imaginary gratification only when it is not recognizable by the subject, so that it appears in another form by becoming distorted, perverted and disguised" (Jones 1931: 42). But the neoliberal epoch is one in which, if nothing else, it is a duty (Žižek *passim*) to somehow know what one desires and to fully enjoy gratifications without guilt, social circumstances notwithstanding.

Just as the difference between madness and sanity consists of a "seamless path" (Durkheim 2006: 45) there is also no unbridgeable gulf separating waking thought from the dream world—the two forms lie along the aforementioned continuum.[134] The products of the modern world do not confront individuals in a rational objective form but as mysterious and enigmatic things "abounding in metaphysical subtleties and theological niceties" (C: 163). The whole *filling* of the world appears to consist of pre-commodities, commodities, and post-commodities and the bad absolute of capital, with its detailed and forced divisions of labor, dissolves relations and merely reconnects atoms, preserving their abstract and external (alien) qualities. Disconnected (unrelated) individuals, either individual people or things, are abstractions in the Hegelian sense, they lack reality (Westphal 2018: 67)[135] and for the living unrealities of modernity, the world can only appear as some kind of mysterious and incomprehensible dream or fantasyland.[136] In the old liberal bourgeois world of neuroses, we could have our use-values but not enjoy them (utility was coupled

---

133   In dreams the unconscious can negate things such as the idea of "like" and metaphor collapses into identity. The example provided by Freud goes something like this: the conscious thought 'My daughter is *like* my wife' becomes 'My daughter *is* my wife' (1965: 46–47).

134   Importantly, there are a set of generic procedures and techniques underlying a wide variety of phenomena such as hypnosis, jokes, etc. (Freud [1921] 1959: 74–75). Recall that, with Durkheim, a single rite can be used for multiple ends; and, with Marx, the single machine can have more than one application within the labor process.

135   Westphal (2018: 67) says that unrelated individuals lack self-sufficiency and are therefore *ideal* in contrast to the reality of interconnected individuals. We can sense, then, how our absolute sociological project involves both an idealism (the analysis of the alienated) and a realism (the analysis of relations). Take care not to conflate 'ideal' with 'idea.' The philosophical 'idea' "is the concept that has an object, has determinate being, reality…" (Hegel 1988: 394).

136   Sometimes it is preferable to commit suicide in order to *preserve the fantasy* (Altamura 2019).

with guilt) but the neoliberal world is different and points us back to the world of dreamwork. In dreams, "No" is absent (Freud [1901] 1952: 42). In dreams "either/or" is replaced with "and" or "both" (Ibid.). This is the world of Lacanian perversion in a nutshell: the pervert wants their cake and to eat it too—i.e., without guilt (Fink 1997).[137] An advertisement for Infiniti automobiles ("The Rules of Luxury") encapsulates the formal shift from repression to regression well: in the previous social setup we could look but not touch; touch without use; use without enjoyment; and enjoyment without display. And now? "Luxury should be lived in." Of course, had the transition to a full-blown social perversion been actualized, the primacy of the pervert economy, we would not *need* Infiniti to drive us forward with its whips and lures. Buyers obviously have still to be persuaded to stop thinking practically and neurotically.

Our basic problem in this chapter might be formulated in an alternative syllogistic form: how do basically neurotic *individuals* satisfy the demands of a perverse *universal* god while embroiled in a disintegrating and psychotically structured matrix of *particular* (mediating) institutions that are "framed" for normal egos?[138] This is not a logic problem but one of voluntary and involuntary human sacrifice. If philosophy is learning how to die[139] sociology is learning how to draw lines, establish limits, and how to sacrifice (cf. PS: 492) with an eye toward personal longevity and the affirmation of collective life.[140] True limitation of the individual is not the condition of being checked by externalities but by lacking solidarity with others (S: 213) and the absence of the mediating current of altruism that emerges from association (S: 279). "It is true that something, in limiting the other, is subjected to being limited itself; but at the same time its limit is, as the ceasing of the other in it, itself only the being of the something; *through the limit something is what it is, and in the limit it has its quality*" (SL: 126). Only through the middle term of the limit is synthesis and

---

137 Perversion is also the forerunner and precondition for the development of excessive morality (Freud [1913] 1950: 199).
138 "All our social institutions are framed for people with a united and normal ego..." (Freud 1950: 57).
139 "For, truly, the man who does not know when to die, does not know how to live" (Ruskin 2015: 52). "Following Hegel, the existentialist philosophers have returned to the wisdom of Montaigne, that to learn philosophy is to learn how to die" (Brown 1959: 108). Montaigne says "He who has learned how to die has unlearned how to be a slave. Knowing how to die frees us from all subjection and constraint.... He who would teach men to die would teach them to live.... Let us gain this advantage, those of us who can; this is the true and sovereign liberty, which enables us to thumb our noses at force and injustice and to laugh at prisons and chains" (1842: 72, 75, 76).
140 Only with limitations established in the real can we provide a ground for unrestricted mental creativity (PS: 425).

harmonization possible (S: 248). Leaving aside those who have not learned how to make a gift of themselves (S: 271) it seems that the remainder sacrifice too much, too quickly even as they believe they sacrifice nothing for the gain of everything. One must moderate self-destruction, and aim in the right direction, in order to not only prolong the sojourn through the vortex of life but to also learn how to reach out and combine forces[141] in such a way that the maelstrom of moral energies[142] rising up from social assemblages take on reasonable shapes and that we are capable of participating in those forms in such a way that we satisfy our personal desires and also rise to meet the demands of the day. Lacking a rational and authoritative representational constellation we are left with nothing more than a blind selection process consistent with predestination (PESC: 20).[143] For the most part, ascetic Protestantism tamed the dilemma of fatalism but neoliberalism seems to have an affinity with Calvin more than it does with Calvinism.

The proto-liberal universe was characterized by a transcendent deity of variable degrees of approachability and friendliness that kept everything synchronized. The syllogism was God, Calling, Accumulation.[144] Still, the god of that world was not the transcendent being of the New Testament. By the 19th century the old god was reduced to a Sunday diversion from the real work of business and industry. Church was a weekly business awards ceremony that was good for credit and clients (FMW: 303). Consciously, the liberal syllogism was God, Profession, Accumulation, but the operating syllogism was Capital, Sacrifice, Salvation. This kind of bad syllogism residing behind a formal facade is common enough. When I was in the Marines the motivational syllogism was officially expressed in writing (crystallized) as God, Country, Corps but the

---

141 "Except by reaching outside himself, how could the individual add to the energies he possesses?" (EFRL: 427). The suicidal gesture can also be a desperate attempt to gain sympathy from others where sympathy or "fellow-feeling" is lacking (Douglas 1967: 304). 'Sympathy' is quite literally the quest for *pathos* and, for the egoist, a primary form of torment is *apathy*, the lack of pathos.

142 To refer to the previous volume, when we speak of energies or forces we are not pointing to physically real energies but the physical effects resulting from the symbolic mobilization, assemblage, fusion, and organization of collective representations within a ritual (fluid) or institutional (fixed) milieu. Durkheim's main books all contain 'crowd psychology' passages that illustrate this logic. Likewise, in Freud's mass psychology analysis we find that it is in "speech" that the energies of identification rest ([1921] 1959: 64). In Hegelian jargon, forces are phenomena that have been worked up to the point of conceptual interrelatedness (Westphal 2018: 68).

143 This 'blind' process is the reason behind the appearance of suicides lacking any "provocation" of any sort (Strahan 1893: 5). Of course, there is always a cause lurking somewhere.

144 Accumulated wealth was not a sign of grace and salvation but that one was expending energy within the calling set forth by god and not wasting god's time.

fluid (spoken) operational form was God, Corps, Country as if America itself was dependent upon the Marine rifleman for not only mere existence but also for its residual and undeserving sanctity. The grunts keep the whole thing connected to god whether it deserves it or not. Subsuming country under the Corps makes sense to the Marines because 'country' is a fractured object of scorn and derision, populated as it is with Civvies and Jodies. The unconscious syllogism of neoliberalism is Commodity, Credit, Attention, but, at the conscious level, neoliberalism cannot find the means to express itself in conceptual form without gauche contortions; when we get right down to it, it is just Me and my Money.

Post-realist theory suffers from the lack of an adequate and rational account of the Other. In Lacan, Fink, and Žižek we find there is "no big Other" or this 'Other' is merely a linguistic fiction. This way of conceptualizing the absolute leaves a gaping hole in our rational comprehension and departs from the revolutionary advances made by Hegel in sublating naïve realism and nominalist individualism. Marx has a theory of the capitalist Other but as a subject-substance value is abstract evil (it constructs mechanical links and connections while eradicating substantive moral relations) and his post-revolutionary 'society' amounts to the restoration of instinctual behavior backgrounded by automated hyper-production (unified in the notion of the general intellect). The capitalist world was created by neurotics who constructed institutions that, today, operate on the basis of a psychotic-like structuration, while depending upon the cultivation of mass perversion for the guarantee of continued accumulation. With psychoanalytic theory we find three principle mechanisms of negation resulting in three basic psychic structures: neuroticism (self-negation); perverse negation of the alter ego in the pursuit of direct enjoyments from the Other (postmodern consumerism); and the psychotic's negation of the Other. By returning to Hegel we are able to introduce the fourth basic negation: the Other's self-negation. Can the absolute kill itself? Essentially, though Hegel is nowhere to be found in Durkheim's classic text on self-destruction, *Suicide* is a mapping of the Other's self-negation. Hegel's *Logic* explores the mind of god before creation (SL: 50)[145] whereas Durkheim's *Suicide* helps to demonstrate the logic of self-alienation, the inevitable coup d'état, downfall, and the equally inevitable counterrevolution and regeneration of the absolute. This in no way a transcendentalism of collective conscience nor does it make a classical ontology out of the impersonal but places Spirit on an explicit social organizational foundation. Indeed, it is the will to

---

145 "Behold it aforetime / No eye ever did: / So soon it forever / From all eyes is hid" (Carlyle 1900: 475).

immediacy and the post-particularity of contemporary theory (subjectivism and dyadic and intersubjective webs) that projects the residue of the social absolute behind the moon.[146]

When I think I am doing what my little heart desires I am still doing the work of some Other and being guided by invisible but objectively real forces. And one never knows when these forces might rise up and suddenly sweep a person away.

> Thus I, a healthy and happy man, was brought to feel that I could live no longer, that an irresistible force was dragging me down into the grave. I do not mean that I had an intention of committing suicide. The force that drew me away from life was stronger, fuller, and concerned with far wider consequences than any mere wish; it was a force like that of my previous attachment to life, only in a contrary direction. The idea of suicide came as naturally to me as formerly that of bettering my life. It had so much attraction for me that I was compelled to practise a species of self-deception, in order to avoid carrying it out too hastily.
> TOLSTOY, in ALVAREZ 1972: 222

On any given day, a "half dozen people, strangers to one another, will take it into their heads to do one and the same strange deed,[147] whether it be a physical experiment, a crime, or an act of virtue" (Peirce [1892] 1992: 350).[148] These people "are in no way conjoined, yet everything takes place as if they were obeying a single order" (S: 305; see also Hesse 1963: 53).[149] The lack of physical

---

146 Žižek's "transcendental materialism" (Johnston 2008) presupposes the reduction of inquiry to the level of empirical idealism.
147 An example of the "same strange deed" performed by the physically disconnected are the 110 simultaneous lottery winners, who, in 2005 chose their winning numbers from identical fortune cookies bought at Chinese restaurants in six different states (Hechtkopf 2005). The cookies were manufactured by Wonton Food in Long Island City. "The same number combinations go out in thousands of cookies a day" (Lee 2005).
148 "Black: What about them other folks tryin [sic] to off theyselves [sic]? White: What about them? Black: Well, maybe them is the folks that you is like. Maybe them folks is your natural kin. Only you all just dont [sic] get together all that much" (McCarthy 2006: 81–82).
149 The members of this group will never come together except as a conceptual ensemble for us (see Freud [1901] 1952: 41). "We are all working together to one end, some with knowledge and design, others without knowing what they do; like men asleep, of whom Heraclitus I think it is says that they too are laborers and co-operators in what goes on in the universe. But men co-operate after different fashions…" (Marcus Aurelius 1945: 64). The negators also make their contributions. Negation is simultaneously production (CPE: 195). Reuters reports that "In [a] rambling, six-page manifesto… Harper-Mercer" [the Umpqua Community College shooter who killed his professor and other students before

contact between these individuals masks the reality of their "*anonymous social relations*" (Berger et al. 1973: 31 ff.). "Every morning, with six-wheeled precision, at the very same hour and the very same minute, we get up, millions of us, as though we were one. At the very same hour, millions of us as one, we start work. Later, millions as one, we stop. And then, like one body with a million hands, at one and the same second according to the Table, we lift the spoon to our lips" (Zamyatin [1924] 1993: 13). This invisible coordination of actions,[150] which appears on the surface to be the random acts of self-willing actors is "group process."

> Group process is the psychohistorian's term for actions in concert that run their course independently of individual volition, or again for people doing things together that have purposes and meanings for them collectively which are unknown to them as individuals.... Such collective, impersonal actions on a large scale pervade human history. Because historians feel just as self-propelled as anyone else, they tend like anyone else to mistake group process for a confluence or interplay of individual pursuits, for a combination or resultant of numberless personal doings.
> BINION 2005: 3

What Binion calls the work of history we would call the work of collective consciousness.[151] Of course, when it comes to total self-destruction, all but a tiny minority resist but, when we take into consideration not just cases of death

---

shooting himself in 2015] wrote of his social isolation which forced him to "align with demonic forces. 'I had no friends, no girlfriend, was all alone,' he wrote. 'I had no job, no life, no successes.' He also described the affinity he had with other serial and mass killers, including Ted Bundy and the school shooters at Columbine High School in Colorado and Sandy Hook Elementary in Connecticut. He urged others who have been rejected by society to 'give in to your darkest impulses'" (Coffman 2017).

150 "[T]he specific will seems to originate within the total and general will, even if an identity of action and will is assumed" (Tonnies 1988: 118). "Social action" includes dispersed and impersonal relations so long as the apparently unconnected individuals are part of the same impersonal mass exposed to similar operational influences. And it is important to note that these influences can be operating unconsciously (ES: 23).

151 Any time a debate oscillates between two extremes, e.g., homosexuality being, on the one hand, an individual choice and, on the other, that homosexuality is biologically determined, we know that two reductionist and erroneous judgements are seeking for their unifying middle term. Sociology could easily supply the mediation for these judgments but, having committed intellectual suicide long ago, sociology is no longer capable of providing the teleological activity that goes into sublating the moments of determinism and choice into a unified and impersonal or group selection process whereby the determinate sorting takes place separate from the consciousness of the immediate individual.

(and attempts) but, more importantly, the forms of "partial death" (Hegel 1988: 311)[152] and fractional self-negations that virtually everybody engages in every day, because they are normal and expected,[153] we arrive at a disconcerting portrait of society as a monster with an insatiable thirst for human sacrifice populated not with whole selves but decimated beings (Wesep 1920: 72). This is a commonplace among critical sociologists.

Military spending, war as an immensely profitable business, renders explicit this aspect, but it is more or less present at least implicitly in all parts of the capitalist system and manifests itself in different ways: through the unjust exploitation of labor by capital, through environmental devastation, through the international transfer of surplus value

---

152   "And here it must be said that to call suicides only those who actually destroy themselves is false" (Hesse 1963: 51). See George Simpson's editorial introduction to Durkheim's *Suicide* where the concept of "partial suicide" is connected to the sociological concept. Signing a contract is a form of partial annihilation as are, for groups, the formulations of treaties (Durkheim 1993: 85; see also DOL: 158–62;). "We reject everything having to do with contracts ... but in fact the world is only held together by a patchwork of contracts ... and in this network ... the trapped human beings are squirming. There's no way to get around contracts except by suicide. Contracts everywhere, they've already choked everything to death, a whole world choking to death on its contracts.... [A]nyone who thinks otherwise is a madman..." (Bernhard 1979: 153). "A man in debt is not free. A man who has made a contract is not free" (Sumner [1906] 1940: 161). In *Man's Fate* we find gambling characterized as "suicide without death" and the sacrifice of the other who depends upon the gambler (Malraux 1961: 205, 206); for a good analysis of gambling and the connections between luck, fate, and mana, see Lears (2003). It should come as no surprise that Las Vegas enjoys not only the highest suicide rate of any city in America but more than double the average. Another way to think of 'partial' suicides is to think in terms of symbolic or virtual suicides where one effaces their self within the social sphere in an attempt to expiate some sin or unconsciously discharge accumulated guilt. This is, more or less, a kind of debasement of one's precise coordinates within the domain of the symbolic, where the body and the self are plunged back into profane existence, a willed fall from grace. "Place in matter and in flesh the least of the values, for these are the things that hold death and must pass away" (Saroyan [1939] 2004: 10). Simpson references Fenichel ([1945] 1996) for "partial suicides" while Fenichel draws upon Brill and Menninger for this notion. The one-stop source for "partial suicides" is Menninger (1938). On a related but slightly oblique line of reasoning see Becker (1973: 182 ff.) on "partialization" as both fetishism and a creativity. Durkheim and Menninger demonstrate that the concepts of life and death are polar oppositions and that the Hegelian and Marxist concerns for the "living dead" or the "undead" (Žižek) are highly relevant for contemporary society. Are we fully living beings or are we all exiles located somewhere between life and death?

153   Individually, each person sacrifices a part of existence but classes, too, are made to lop off a certain mass of individuals. The working class "has always to sacrifice a part of itself in order not to be wholly destroyed" (PM: 67).

leading to poverty and death in the periphery, through marginalization of the poor, homeless, and unemployed, and through policies of torture, repression, and terror which increase and enhance such marginalization. The underlying logic of these various forms of death is a socio-economic system in which human beings are means to be exploited for the sake of profit, and the poor periphery is simply a means for the well-being of the center.

    MARSH 1999: 280–81

There is a lot of truth to this assertion. America is the place, after all, where Kürnberger said, "'They turn cattle into tallow, and people into money'" (in Weber [1905] 2002: 11; cf. C: 481) and where life is reduced to surviving a "forced labor camp from which the workers—perfectly innocent—are led forth by lottery, a few each day, to be executed" (McCarthy 2010: 122).[154] Is society a slaughterhouse, death camp,[155] or some kind of suicide machine? Is the modern world nothing more than a nightmarish existence ruled by an "earthbound Savage God" called self destruction that thrives on "blood sacrifice"? (Alvarez 1972: 225–26). Let us enter the *oîkos* of the bad absolute and investigate the economy of forces at work there.

4 Suicide

Suicide, says Durkheim, is "the term ... *applied to all cases of death resulting directly or indirectly from a positive or negative act of the victim himself, which he knows will produce this result*.[156] An attempt is an act thus defined but falling short of actual death" (S: 44). A trend among contemporary sociologists is to deny that socially honorable forms of sacrifice are actually suicides.[157] This

---

154 "*Ricardo* ... Nations are merely production shops; man is a machine for consuming and producing; human life is a kind of capital; economic laws blindly rule the world" (PM: 89). "The prison is an image of the bourgeois world of labor taken to its logical conclusion" (Horkheimer and Adorno [1944] 1972: 226).
155 Shades of Stirner (see Nielsen 2005: 21).
156 The victim knows they want to die but not why they want to die. Most people do not know the "real reasons" for what they do (EFRL: 340). They just do it.
157 "Today when a terrorist from a culture that is neither Christian nor individualist dies by blowing himself up, Westerners are apt to call it suicide. Such a phenomenon is not suicide but it does underline the close connections between a willingness to die in battle and altruistic suicide in the military that was emphasized by Durkheim.... Altruistic suicide is an end in itself.... Durkheim was wrong to blur the distinction between altruistic suicide and military sacrifice by adopting a peculiar definition of suicide..." (Davies and Neal

arbitrary exclusion (Durkheim 2006: 20) is nothing new; it is merely a return to the sentimentality of Esquirol, Falret, Bourdin (S: 66–67) and Faguet (see Besnard 2000: 102; Jankélévitch 2012: 37). "But we know that the nature of the motives immediately causing suicide cannot be used to define it, nor consequently to distinguish it from what it is not" (S: 67). Whatever the motives,[158] "they can only be species of a single genus" (S: 67). Softening Durkheim's analysis, basically taking what they view as the disturbing and critical edge off, renders the theory toothless and anti–sociological.[159] And nothing is more disturbing than the idea that altruistic sacrifice can be just another form of suicide. After all, was the death of Jesus a murder, execution, a case of self-sacrifice, or a premodern form of death by cop? If a charismatic leader is simply executed for being a criminal then they died for either breaking the law or for nothing, depending upon a person's point of view, but if that leader dies *for something*, then something else is implicated. Hegel gets us to Golgotha at the conclusion of the *Phenomenology* but in *Suicide* Durkheim reveals an absolute that is an insatiable entity that lives on human life.

Durkheim's classic has been dissected and criticized by many commentators over the decades so further discussion would seem beside the point.[160] Yet, as Taylor says, another look is worth the effort.

2000: 39; see also Strenski 2006: 274). What is peculiar is not Durkheim's definition of suicide but the peculiar death of sociology in the hands of those who take up Durkheim for examination from time to time. It is astonishing, really, how little was *done* with his classic work apart from sterile arguments over data and methods or the positivistic gutting of the theories by reducing everything down to variables. Many critics of Durkheim display a psychological and reductionist bent when they want to get down to the intentions of individuals who kill themselves. Anyway, altruistic suicide is not "an end in itself"—to argue this is to miss the entirely heterotelic nature of the altruistic act; each modality has a unique end in sight (e.g., the recovery or enhancement of prestige on the part of the *optional* suicides).

158 "How often we mistake the true reasons for our acts!" (S: 43). On "motives" see Goblot's comments (in Besnard 2000: 102). In the case of suicides "…deliberations … are only ever later justifications of resolutions taken for reasons inaccessible to consciousness" (Jankélévitch 2012: 32).

159 "Durkheim does provide his reasons as to why he considers acts of self-sacrifice and suicide to be fundamentally the same, but they do not add up to an argument that would convince someone who accepts the *conventional understanding* that they are two essentially different forms of renouncing existence" (Varty 2000: 59, emphasis added). Altruism is not the only domain of sacrifice anyway. Altamura (2019) demonstrates that we can find plenty of sacrifice in the fusions of egoism and anomie.

160 The literature built up around Durkheim's *Suicide* is quite voluminous and one is hard pressed to imagine that anything remains to be said regarding the concepts of egoism, altruism, anomie, and fatalism. Nevertheless, two interrelated features dominate the decades-long sociological commentary on Durkheim's famous 'four-cornered' typology

Although Durkheim's work had a major influence on subsequent sociological work on suicide, it is important to bear in mind the limits of this influence. Later generations of empiricist sociologists, while approving of Durkheim's pioneering work in defining the suicide rate as an object of enquiry and correlating suicide with a range of social variables, were more than sceptical of his attempt to explain them in terms of invisible moral forces of egoism, altruism, anomie, and fatalism. The majority of these later students adopted a positivist view of science. Positivism holds that science, and therefore good social science, proceeds by careful observation and description of factual phenomena and the relations between them. Only then can hypotheses and theories be constructed that are then tested by reference to the relevant established facts. There is, then, a rigid distinction between 'observational' and 'theoretical' categories..... From this point of view, Durkheim's notion of invisible but real collective moral forces 'acting upon' individuals and inclining them toward, or from, suicide was metaphysical and 'unscientific,' and Durkheim's general ambition for a science of morality an impossibility. Consequently, later sociological research into suicide rates, while bearing a superficial resemblance to Durkheim's work and often claiming to be developing or testing his ideas, has been confined to the relationships between suicide and observable, or concrete, social phenomena (1990).

We have been told that Durkheim is an organicist and that he falls back on thermodynamic and mechanistic metaphors and these are all true in that Durkheim is actually speaking in multiple 'voices' accentuating processes and forms from different angles for different readers. Murphy claims the existence of "two Emile Durkheims" (1971: 170) but truly there are (at least) three

---

(Besnard 2005) of self-destructiveness: first, these concepts are almost universally preserved in their ideal-typical purity in ways that Durkheim did not intend (as McCloskey noted as far back as 1976 and it is still generally the case more than thirty years later) resulting in a stultification of further theoretical insight; secondly, related to the previous point, not much attention has been paid to what Durkheim called the "composite varieties" of these concepts—the simultaneous "contradictory coexistence" of oppositional forces within one and the same society, institution, class, or self. In short, Durkheim's thought is littered with references toward these contradictory fusions of countervailing forces, i.e., in what we might refer to as the 'speculative identity' of contraries: the furtive relationship between empiricism and mysticism (RSM: 74); the masked egoism of the humble servant (RSM: 37) as well as the egoism of charitable giving; the Stoic desire to become enslaved to their own constructed false gods, and so on.

'Durkheims.'[161] Keep in mind that mechanism and organicism still had their adherents at the end of the nineteenth century and Durkheim was keen to attract minds to sociology rather than repulse them. I have argued that there is, in addition to these portraits, a 'dialectical Durkheim' that is most clearly evident when we learn that the self–sacrificing patriot or mother has, essentially, committed homicide of the self (S: 338) for the benefit of some concrete or abstract other such as the helpless child or honor or nation, etc., Eros objects.[162] We also see Durkheim's dialectical bent in phrases such as "the disease of the infinite" which is definitely something greater than, and different than, the sum of its parts (egoism and anomie) as well as in the idea of the "composite varieties" (S: 287) and, especially, in the manner in which "composite varieties" are presented along two planes: the mechanistic combinations and superimpositions and, along another, the negative unities that present greater complexities such as energetic melancholy where indifference fuses (cf. EFRL: 147) with ecstasy in the contradictory sentiments of the Stoic (S: 290). We see his dialectical imagination at work when we realize that sacred forces, both pure and impure, have common origins, are two varieties of the same genus, and that "it is not surprising that, even moving in opposite directions, they should have the same nature..." (EFRL: 416; see Radcliffe-Brown 1952).

I have no interest in surveying Durkheim's errors or the deficiencies of his data[163] as they refract through the uneven secondary literature on *Suicide*. The aim instead lies in engineering a theoretical constellation that offers us a better grasp of life within a disintegrating empire descending the spiral of

---

161   Not only was Murphy short one Durkheim but the other two were misidentified: "The first was the positivist ... and the second was the almost-dialectician who, like Marx, charted the relationship between society and the states of consciousness, between collectivity and the individual" (1971: 170). Durkheim was, despite the textbook claims, not a positivist and he developed an actual dialectic, not a close approximation, though obviously, Murphy is correct that both Durkheim and Marx mapped the dynamics between individual and the collective in a socially realistic fashion. Murphy's book is riddled with errors; yet, it often provides moments of negative education and is worth consulting. I am tempted to claim that there was one Hegel, two Marxs, and three Durkheims. As for Weber, maybe there are zero Webers or maybe four Webers. Consult Jameson (1973: 60–61) for Weber's philosophical repudiations. I would simply add that Weber's repudiations can make for great sociological insights, but they leave the ego overexposed to the unmitigated terrors of reality. The 'two Marxs' does not refer to a young Hegelian and a mature political economist (Samuelson 1986: 277) but the pre-1857 materialist and the neo-Hegelian of the 1859 *Critique* and of the first volume of *Capital*.
162   Sacrificial acts are also automatically inscribed within the symbolic order. Eros is, according to Freud, not only the power of human solidarity, but the glue that holds the world together ([1921] 1959: 31).
163   See Varty (2000) for some discussion of data and criticisms hurled at Durkheim's work.

death. In short, as far as Durkheim's *Suicide* goes, I do not want to wade into criticism of the work but to *do something with it* in this book and the one that follows. We are, as such, less interested in problems of definitions, rigged statistics, or even the fully realized suicides and more interested in those partial self-destroyers engaged as they are, every day, in direct and indirect, positive and negative practices that society demands because to have a society means to rely on voluntary self-negation. Recall, Durkheim says that suicides are only everyday forms of conduct pushed to the extreme or "exaggerated forms of common practices" (S: 45; cf. Durkheim 1974: 21)[164] and the self-destroyer has pushed virtue[165] to the point of viciousness.[166] Let that sink in: the people doing bad things are only doing more (or less) of what we ourselves are already doing.[167] They have taken to heart the American imperative that if a thing is

---

164   Pathological thought or action is an attempt to "supplement an otherwise deficient reality" (Levi-Strauss 1963: 181). Neuroses are distorted reflections of social institutions. Hysteria appears to be a "caricature" of art; obsession looks like a caricature of religion, and paranoid delusions are like caricatures of "a philosophical system" (Freud [1913] 1950: 92).
165   Virtue is synonymous with a preference for public life whereas vice is the ascendency of the private over the public. Without virtue there can be no democracy (Montesquieu 2002: 34).
166   Just as an excess or surplus of virtue can lead to perdition so can the insufficiency of vice (see Machiavelli [1532] 2005: 54). As Durkheim says we should not expect nor even desire a community of individual saints—the individual can raise him or herself up to only a moderate degree of virtue. Vice is not only to be expected but also more or less required or even implicitly demanded because fresh materials for atonement (sin, guilt, and repayment) must be readily at hand. "[T]ransgression affirms the very rules it intends to flout. Nothing supports the norm like deviation" (Kureishi 2017: 18). Durkheim says that even in a community of pure-hearts deviance would have to emerge in order to punish it. As Solovyov (1918) puts it, with a nod to Voltaire, the better is the enemy of the good. We are terrified by and fascinated by the terrorist, the gun nut, the psychopath, because "they caricature 'normal' behavior. Burning a cross on a lawn, raping a woman, shooting a stranger are but exaggerations of everyday acts of cruelty and thoughtlessness so normative as to be unacknowledged by their perpetrators" (Fellman 1998: 47). We apparently need victims, villains, punishment, and demonization. Sociality requires a continuous, ongoing process of atonement and sacrifice; sublimity (positive or negative, upright or inverted) is not a once-and-for-all attainment but a state that is floated on a rising current of continuous negation and violence. Besides, "The moralist cannot deny that, as a rule, well-bred though very wicked men are far more attractive and lovable than virtuous men; having crimes to atone for, they crave indulgence by anticipation, by being lenient to the shortcomings of those who judge them, and they are thought most kind…." (Balzac [1846] 1991: 51). The problem, then, is not vice *per se*, but the lack of mechanisms for the speculative transformation of vices. "Virtue flies from a house divided against itself—and a whole legion of devils take up their residence there" (Wollstonecraft [1792] 1983: 317).
167   "Human blessings and human ills commonly flow from the same source" (Longinus 1890: v).

worth doing it is worth overdoing. We now enter a moral economy or system of social forces (PESC: 65; EFRL: 206).

Moral forces and the social economy are not reducible to natural things; however, an analogy can be drawn between the two domains. From the antiquities forward, all complex phenomena have been conceived of as being the result of the interactions and combinations of four basic forces: "Everything is compounded from four elements or 'roots,' earth and air and fire and water. There are also two elemental powers, Love and Strife. The elements periodically unite into a divine and homogeneous Sphere. The Sphere then dissolves; various mixtures and unions take place, in the course of which our familiar world is formed…" (Plutarch, in Barnes 2001: 120).[168] Contemporary physicists, like their ancient counterparts, comprehend that "macroscopic phenomena [such] as friction, viscosity, translucency, pressure, and temperature [are] understood as highly predictable regularities determined by the statistics of astronomical numbers of invisible microscopic constituents careening about in spacetime and colliding with each other, with everything dictated by only the four basic forces of physics" (Hofstadter 2007: 33). Remember from our first volume that our mediating comprehension of nature is a distorted mirror of social organization and the models of natural forces are unconsciously derived from moral forces. Just as in the totemic system where there are as many forces as there are clans in the tribe (EFRL: 192) every group produces its own system of moral currents. These currents or social forces are "nonmaterial" but exhibit physical or material effects (EFRL: 192, 197). With the disintegration of society follows the disintegration of not only science but nature itself and as we lose our way nature will itself become more enigmatic. For example, we now have quark flavors and charm antiquarks, etc., that 'exist' because they fit into models and are necessary for theoretical coherence.

Spirit suffers a downfall or declination in time and experiences a decomposition (PS: 412–16) as a moment in a larger autopoetic process of revelation and reorganization. Life is negation and the spirit of negation drives humanity on to new depths and peaks. One of the principal features of modern life is the

---

168   This 'element' was "used to speak of water, air, earth, and fire, that is, in the sense of a *general thing,* midway between the spatio-temporal individual and the idea, a sort of incarnate principle that brings a style of being wherever there is a fragment of being. The flesh is in this sense an 'element' of Being. Not a fact or a sum of facts.… Much more: the inauguration of the *where* and the *when,* the possibility and exigency for the fact; in a word: facticity, what makes the fact be a fact" (Merleau-Ponty 1968: 139–40). The 'elements' represent a materialist regression of thought that projects morality into nature. "None of the four / Is this beast's core" (Goethe [1808] 1961: 157).

acceptance and exploration of the demonic for its creative capacity.[169] Experience is raised to the "supreme value" and everything, at least in thought, is permitted for the unfettered individual (Bell 1976: 19). A society in the process of disintegrating and changing forms suffers from an increase in the suicide rate and other measurable forms of self-destruction (S: 203). The main idea here is that normal and healthy social organization breaks down at decisive points. "The powers that had been united separated ... and confronted each other in their original purity" (Kroner 1961: 279). Some members of diseased society are "contaminated" by overwhelming suicidogenic currents and, thus, taken "possession of" (the current itself becomes incarnated or "individualized" in the form of the diseased person) and assigned a new mission, that of self-destruction (S: 321; cf. Kracht 2015: 56). Others are abandoned and wilt; the absence of an external demand to live leaves only the voice of the ego. Of course, no single person is predestined for autocide (only a few are destined to end prematurely as tribute) but the quantitative change in self-destruction that results from the loss of social equilibrium, the change in the rate, is predetermined and inevitable (S: 325).[170]

In *Suicide*, we find that society is characterized by three negative and pathological drivers or currents (egoism, altruism, and anomie) that operate independently or coalesce to form moral alloys.[171] As ideal-typical purities they would each amount to a complete "mental death" of the individual (Durkheim 1961: 224).[172] Their fusions may moderate or exacerbate the annihilation of social relations and consciousness, each depending upon their objectives, positive or negative. Further, we will see that the three currents are expandable to *four* when we take into account fatalism, a form that Durkheim thought to be anachronistic and of little analytical use for explaining modern problems. *Every moral sentiment, public opinion, collective passion, or ideal that a person or group holds is a particular fusion or combination of these three (for us, four) currents*.[173] There are

---

169 Let us recall that Freud explicitly connects dreamwork to the "'demonic'" ([1901] 1952: 63).
170 "A certain percentage, they tell us, must every year go ... that way ... to the devil, I suppose, so that the rest may remain chaste, and not be interfered with" (Dostoyevsky 1994: 45).
171 Sennett (2006: xvii) reduces the primary moral drivers or negative 'spirits' to "forms of social emotion" which obviously captures only a fraction of what is important.
172 Cf. Alcmaeon where the "monarchy" of one oppositional power (in contrast to an "egalitarianism among the powers") results in disease and destruction (reported by Plutarch, in Barnes 2001: 37).
173 The dynamism that generates moral currents is prehistoric but all our values date from the so-called axial age. 2600 years ago, humanity generated all "the great values that

no people among whom these three currents of opinion do not co-exist, bending men's inclinations in three different and even opposing directions. Where they offset one another, the moral agent is in a state of equilibrium which shelters him against any thought of suicide. But let one of them exceed a certain strength to the detriment of the others, and as it becomes individualized, it also becomes suicidogenetic... (S: 321).[174]

The hypothetical perfect 'balance' of these offsetting currents would produce something positively Good (the evil we choose to not only ignore but actually venerate).[175] Existence in this positive hell is regulated yet stimulating. Durkheim follows the basic outline of Comte's sense of religion as a fusion of submission and love that is necessary if egoism and resignation are to be sublated into a sustainable and creative form of life (see Caird 1885: 25–26). Perish the thought, however, of ridding evil from the world—we create it and recreate it with every action[176] and solidarity is absolutely no guarantee of goodness (Freud 2012: 47).

---

enable us to live together" (Comte-Sponville 2007: 27). Over the centuries we have not invented new values, nor do we need to invent more. "What we need to invent, or rather reinvent, is a new fidelity to the values that have been handed down to us" (Ibid.). Three or four-way reductions would seem to limit our complex emotional lives to only a handful of concepts. As individuals we imagine that our emotional depth is nearly bottomless, yet, our emotions are actually few and all capable of signification. If we do not have a name for it, it is not an emotion (MacCabe 1985: 2). At best, it would be an inchoate feeling but not a genuine emotion. Nonetheless, even if ideas, emotions, actions, etc., represent nothing more than various fusions of three or four moral currents, the number of discrete alloys would be sufficiently inexhaustible to escape the most scrupulously detailed analyses imaginable.

174   These "three forces or currents [for us, four] are all that is needed to account for the establishment of the social tie, its degeneration and the related individual actions" (Paoletti 2012: 71). These 'currents' of 'opinion' are not only positive but also negative; to develop a sociological theory of the 'death drive' we would make recourse to all four forms. The psychological theory of a death drive is centered within the domain of egoism and the withdrawal of the ego from collective effervescence, but the three other forms are also death drivers, if you will.

175   Anything can be made into a cult. "There's not a single failing without its advocate" (Gracián [1647] 2015: 19). Even murder can be raised to a fine art and criticized on the basis of its composition and sublime aesthetics. "People begin to see that something more goes to the composition of a fine murder than two blockheads to kill and be killed—a knife—a purse—and a dark lane. Design, gentlemen, grouping, light and shade, poetry, sentiment, are now deemed indispensable to attempts of this nature" (Quincey [1827] 2015: 5).

176   "Consciousness cannot divide its *données* into the true and the false, the good and the evil; it can only measure them along a scale of intensity" (Auden 2008: 141). If we desire the good, we have to see that it rises from evil (Goethe [1808] 1961: 159).

Where there is the stimulation of collective passions, suicide decreases, at least in its egoistic forms. War, "political upheavals," and "election crises"—so long as they involve an intensification and heightening of collective passions—lowers the suicide rate (S: 202–06).[177] The external shock, it is thought, pulls the ego out of itself and its subjective concerns and reorients itself to the collective ordeal. For minorities who feel discriminated against and harassed by mainstream society, already alienated to a great extent, the external shock may have the exact opposite effect, lowering the perceived value of life, driving them in the direction of self-destruction.[178] All other imperfect amalgamations may be values and goods that protect individuals from self-destruction but are contaminated to a certain degree. When the harmony of forces is thrown into gross asymmetry the currents seek adherents and engage in a multiform crusade of social annihilation, either passively or actively.

In his review of fruitless theories on self-destruction, Durkheim subjects the psychological work of Jousset and Moreau de Tours to criticism where four classes of "suicides of the insane" are drawn out (S: 63). The first class consists of maniacal suicides, the second melancholy suicides; the third obsessive suicides; and finally, impulsive or automatic suicides (S: 63–65). Durkheim argues that "Since the suicides of insane persons do not constitute the entire genus but only a variety of it, the psychopathic states constituting mental alienation can give no clue to the collective tendency to suicide in its generality" (S: 67). Still, the suicides of the insane are one variety of a larger genus to which all suicides belong. The varieties are connected not only to one another but also along a continuum that separates abnormal and normal acts of negation: "between mental alienation properly so-called and perfect equilibrium of intelligence, an entire series of intermediate stages exist" (S: 67). We might not to go as far as Brinton in suggesting almost no difference between the sane and the insane (1902: 84–85) but 'insanity' might rightly be considered an exaggeration of sanity or perhaps surplus sanity (cf. Herder 1966: 117). If Jousset and Moreau de Tours did not provide the answers they nonetheless provided a framework from which Durkheim builds a sociological version.[179] If one pays careful

---

177 "Passion individualizes and yet enslaves" (EFRL: 275).
178 Trump's unexpected and shocking defeat of Clinton during 2016 US election saw the volume of calls to suicide prevention hotlines more than double in the early hours of the morning as the new political reality came into focus (Mettler 2016).
179 It seems clear to me that this framework extends, in rough form, as far back as Galen of Pergamon and his theory of humors: the depressed melancholic (egoism); the warm-hearted and optimistic sanguine temperament corresponds in some aspects with the altruist; the anomie of the choleric temperament (dominated as it is by passions) is obviously; and the slow, methodical coolness of the phlegmatic is reminiscent of the one

attention to the substance of the four classes of "insane suicides" it is clear that they form reductions and inverted prototypes of the social forms deployed in *Suicide*.[180]

Maniacal suicide: "The most varied and even conflicting ideas and feelings succeed each other with intense rapidity in the maniac's consciousness. It is a constant whirlwind. One state of mind is instantly replaced by another ... [with] ... amazing speed.... The most trivial incident may cause these sudden transformations" (S: 63). This is a good description of *anomie*.

Melancholy suicide: "This is connected with a general state of extreme depression and exaggerated sadness, causing the patient no longer to realize sanely the bonds which connect him with people and things about him. Pleasures no longer attract.... Life seems boring or painful" and they seek "solitude" (S: 63–64). Here we have none other than *egoism*, or, insufficient attachment to others and the accompanying sadness.

---

resigned to their fate. This connection to Galen is introduced, but not analyzed, by Jankélévitch (2012: 38). The same can be said with regard to Choron (1972). We repeatedly find this system of countervailing polarities across the history of the moral sciences. Worth mentioning in particular is Eysenck's bio-reductionist personality model and the development of "superfactors" or "orthogonal dimensions" ([1967] 2006: 34) that provide a counter-arching organization of Galen's tempers. As an aside, it is also interesting to superimpose the characteristics of the four suicidal currents with the physical forces that science projects into nature: strong force (altruism), weak force (egoism), gravitational force (fatalism), and electromagnetic force (anomie) or with Platonic solids: tetrahedrons (sting like fire), icosahedrons (water), octahedrons (air), and cubes (earth). The point is that these analogies illustrate the fact that we project social processes and organization into the 'blank screen' of nature, the mirror of our social mind. "The model representations that underlie various cosmological and physical hypotheses, etc., are closely connected with, and co-determined by, the ontological conceptions of everyday life at the time, generally unconsciously so..." (Lukács 1978c: 19). Social organization is not modelled on the laws of physics but, rather, physics reflects society. As far as analogy goes, there is no point trying to work around it: even in the 'hard' world of natural science and physics "analogical transposition" (Pickering 1984: 407) is the norm and even the basis of continued developments.

180   "The word insane, of course, is not a medical term.... The qualities of the psychopath become manifest only when he is connected into the circuits of full social life" (Cleckley 1988: 3, 22). "Dix turned his glass in his hand. Cary Jepson was a clod. He wouldn't be married to a stupid little talking machine if he had any spirit. The obvious reach of his imagination was, 'He's insane, of course.' It would never occur to him that any reason other than insanity could make a man a killer. That's what all the dolts around town would be parroting: *he's insane of course he's insane of course*. It took imagination to think of a man, sane as you or I, who killed" (Hughes 1947: 48).

Obsessive suicide: results when a "fixed idea ... has taken complete *possession*"[181] of the person. "It is an instinctive need beyond the control of reflection and reasoning..." (S: 64). With the obsessive we are in the company of the *altruist*, the pure "automaton" (S: 65)[182] where the personality is either undeveloped or eclipsed by the collective consciousness.

Impulsive or automatic suicide: here, the impulses one might find in anomie are "irresistible" and "automatic." "In the twinkling of an eye, it appears in full force and excites the act..." (S: 65). Reason (or even irrationality) and will are negated (who knows what the "controlling idea" could have been?) and the person acts as if determined by some alien externality. *Fatalism* is here clearly articulated.

Durkheim's sociological explanation for suicide is not simply an elaboration on these four types but, rather, a sublation of the "insane" forms drawn from the psychological field.[183] He starts with a variety and proceeds to grasp the genus and universal ground that informs the domain of the psyche. These transpositions from one scale of human life to the other, up and down, if you will, are fascinating. It would no doubt come as a surprise to Karen Horney, for example, that her classic work on neurotic conflicts follows almost precisely the conceptual contours of Durkheim's work on suicide.[184] Where psychology,

---

181   Emphasis added here—the role of possession will be clearer in the later section on the modalities of alienation that correspond to the types of suicide.
182   Interestingly, for this "automaton," "when spoken to, the words sound to me as though echoing in a void" (S: 65). As we will see later, 'automatonism' (a theoretical and hyperbolic limit) is also characteristic of resignation and may even be considered one of the conduits connecting fatalism with altruism. However, another compelling way to grasp 'automatonism' is to view it as a result of the suspension of reason, the reduction of individual motion to physicalism (profanation) or pure externality, or the corruption of reason and its fall into irrationality (see Durkheim 1974: 3 for some indications).
183   Nye connects Durkheim's theory of self-destruction to French psychiatric models but bungles on interpreting Durkheim as confirming a biological and hereditary thesis regarding suicide rates (1984: 147). Durkheim was not a neo-Lamarckian.
184   Horney's mapping of the solutions, strategies, and consequences related to neurotic conflicts follows the basic outlines of Durkheim's work: "moving toward" = altruism; "moving against" = anomie; "moving away" = egoism; and various other strategies such as extreme overregulation and hopeless resignation belong to the category of fatalism. However, 'porting' this psychoanalytic work into the sociological matrix offers a chance to refine many concepts and lend them more precision. For example, Horney indicates that compulsive drives stem from feelings of "isolation, helplessness, and hostility" and that these drives lead to "neurotic cravings for affection and for power" (1945: 12–13). To put it mildly, this is a lot of lumping things together. But if we take Horney's insistence on a unity of oppositions seriously (1945: 29–31) we can map all these elements separately and sociologically without losing the dynamics and fusions that are found in empirical reality. How can hopelessness lead to its opposite? Is the answer simply that, well, that's the way some

though, places the mind of the individual at the center of analysis, sociology reorganizes experiences around the parameters of abstract and impersonal forces generated by individuals in association and thereafter guided or pushed around by their own alienated creations.[185] The kinds of experiences that Durkheim thinks are most important in the modern world revolve around the twin currents of egoism and anomie one finds in a "hypercivilization" (S: 323).[186]

> The hypercivilization which breeds the anomic tendency and the egoistic tendency also refines nervous systems, making them excessively delicate; through this very fact they are less capable of firm attachment to a definite object, more impatient of any sort of discipline, more accessible both to violent irritation and to exaggerated depression (S: 323).[187]

---

neurotics are, or, sociologically, that the currents of sentiments can synthesize at certain points to lure individuals and whole groups beyond hopelessness and into a completely opposite form of conduct? Horney reduces neurotics to zombie-like creatures—they move like the living "but there is no life in them" (1945: 74). It may well be that modern society, and the 'negative heaven' of the social octahedron is in fact a domain of the living dead, however, even the living dead are not mindless zombies or automatons simply pushed around by material forces (at least not all of them). Though the film was terrible, the excellent book *Serpent and the Rainbow* by Wade Davis was effective in demonstrating that actual 'zombies' are the product of a dialectic of culture and pharmacology; the existence of 'zombies' presupposes a belief in zombies. (1985). When we examine the extreme end of drug addiction we find individuals who, like elite mountain climbers, live at the extreme limit between life and death. The difference between a world-class climber and a dead climber is calculated in millimeters and professional climbing has progressed to such extremes that, with "so little margin for error," the old sacred rope-mate bond between climbers has been abandoned for an "every man for himself" ethos when disaster strikes (Krakauer [1990] 2009: 152). The best climbers personify the near-death existence. Likewise, for "some [drug] addicts, a near-death experience is not an error. It's the dream" (Achenbach 2017).

185 "[S]piritual forces through the agency of men catch sight of each other and battle each other without having any arbiter in the world besides individual men who feel themselves pledged to one or the other force" (Jaspers 1986: 510).

186 "Society suddenly finds itself put back into a state of momentary barbarism; it appears as if a famine, a universal war of devastation, had cut off the supply of every means of subsistence; industry and commerce seem to be destroyed; and why? Because there is too much civilisation, too much means of subsistence, too much industry, too much commerce" (MECW, 6: 490).

187 "Having broken all human restraints, the men of the [French] Revolution finally discovered that a society cannot live without them; but when they sought to create them anew they saw that even the strongest society, though supported by the fear of the guillotine, could not replace the discipline which the past had slowly built up in the minds of men" (LeBon 1913: 129).

In hyper-civilized society egoism is rampant and anomie is so bad that anarchy itself becomes the norm (S: 254; cf. C: 612).[188] To wholeheartedly identify as 'American' is to embrace the spectacle of "chronic restlessness, a constant hyperactive frenzy" that drives not only creativity and invention but self-destruction (Kimmel 2013: 19). 'America' is less a 'We' than a battlefield[189] where one ego surmounts opponents and losers take the hindmost. External regulation is felt to hinder the categorical imperative of competition and limitless striving (Halbwachs 1958: 44–47). The concept of the individual is held inviolably sacred and individualism has risen to the level of a cult where "man has become a god for men" (S: 334).[190] However, liberal autonomy,[191] deregulation, and detachment do not lead to the actual "exaltation of human

---

188   Obviously, rendering 'anomie' as 'normlessness' was a tremendous misstep. A system can suffer lawlessness (anarchy) while still making recourse to traditions, customs, folkways, taboos, mores, etc.

189   Halbwachs observes that one does not necessarily become a capitalist entrepreneur because one is an unhinged egoist but, rather, one must conform to and develop a weaponized egoism in order to compete within the capitalist system regardless of whether one is or is not personally an egoist (1958: 50). If a capitalist is not actually an egoist they will nonetheless have to act as if they are one or suffer defeat for their characterological weakness.

190   Pickering (2000: 72–73) sees a contradiction where there is none. Durkheim's conception of individuality is actualized and made concrete, in contrast to Christianity's abstract cult, through the mediating effect of secondary associations and vocational unity (see also Hess 1845 on the degeneration of the cult of humanity to the cult of the abstracted individual). As for humans becoming gods to themselves, see Jaynes (1990: 79). Sennett tells us that the Weberian notion of the calling is antithetical to anomie: "The psychology of a vocation is precisely opposite that of anomie, the latter a loss of faith that social rules provide much personal orientation. Whereas the point of a vocation is to stretch life out in time, the anomic suicide aborts his or her story" (2006: xxi). This would apply to the Protestant conception of a calling but Weber famously states that where the religious zealot "wanted to work in a calling" we moderns are "forced to do so"—i.e., we no longer have actual callings, for the most part, but over-specialized and dehumanizing jobs in the detailed or forced division of labor (we are now "specialists without spirit").

191   "The eighteenth century directed at worldly things the idea that every human being—precisely because he is a human being—is entitled to certain inalienable rights vis-a-vis all others and every earthly authority: against the state in the form of a demand for political participation and legal equality of its citizens, against the social community in the form of a moral demand on the part of the individual for a certain sphere of inner and outer freedom. These ideas achieved their deepest significance and their highest clarity in the ethical teachings of freedom of German idealism, through our great thinkers Kant and Fichte. That which in this context is of interest may be formulated in a few sentences: The human being is, as a bearer of reason, intended to govern himself—that is, to act not, for example, according to the arbitrariness of his instincts, but rather, in accordance with a conscience that has been subordinated to the moral law. As a bearer of this capacity for 'autonomy,' the individual possesses its specific dignity, which distinguishes it as a

personality" (S: 336) but to the degradation of the base of the "cult of man" (Ibid.). The bourgeois concept of the autonomous individual results in the individual being reduced to "virtually an enemy of civilization" (Freud [1927] 1961: 6). The Stoic notion of the spark of divinity within each person is good but the 'spark' is misplaced as originating from nature when, in fact, it is a social product. As we run from others we lose our spark and, lacking the energy to live, we run amok. "What is hard for modern man, and especially for the younger generation, is to measure up to *workaday* existence. The ubiquitous chase for 'experience' stems from this weakness; for it is weakness to be able to countenance the stern seriousness of our fateful times" (FMW: 149; see also Halbwachs 1958: 47–48). Here's the kicker: the resulting illusion of capitalist hypercivilization, rooted in the Protestant cult of abstract 'Man' consists in the belief that the individual enjoys a direct and unmediated relationship to a trans-social universal. The feeling is expressed thusly: I am a human being and I'll do whatever I want within my rights; and I might do a lot more than that if I can get away with it. I am set aside and therefore sacred. The act of suicide, placing destiny in the hands of the individual, elevates the individual to the point of a god or some transcendental power. The act of self-murder proclaims, in the case of egoism, not so much that 'there is no god' but, rather, 'I am god.' "He therefore becomes a god, not in any posing Nietzschean sense, but flatly, unflatteringly: there is nothing beyond him, or higher. Therefore the supreme assertion of this self-will is to assume God's function and allot to himself his own death" (Alvarez 1972: 220).[192] Missing from the ego's awareness is that they have only made a *claim* (while offering no *proof*) and the status of being a human (or a god) is bestowed not by the universal but by the mediating particularity that, in collaboration with the individual, and in *recognizing* his or her claim to humanity, constitutes the concrete, vibrant universality of social life.

Narcissists and egomaniacs, hyper-individuated Americans, believe that there is nothing 'above' them, atoms and dyads are misconstrued as being, somehow, already universalized (see Mészáros 2010: 71).[193] This is the good

---

'personality' before all other beings; it may, for that reason, raise the claim to be 'an end in itself'" (Weber 2003: 89).

192 "'I am a law unto myself'" (in Douglas 1967: 306).

193 "Vanity finds its fate within itself" (Adler 1954: 157). Recall that narcissism is not actually self-love so much as self-absorption. The socialized person loves their self because they love others (generated through solidarity) whereas the narcissist attempts self-aggrandizement through the manipulation of others through grand impressions. Egoism, if pursued universally, would be the end of society (Durkheim 1978: 107).

news proclaimed by pragmatists, symbolic interactionists, and the "happy go lucky" world of social entropy, mysticism, and monetary fiendishness.[194] Oblivious to hyper-individuals and the kind of sociology that measures atomic linkages, agreements, negotiations, and networks is the collective and substantial dimension that keeps this river of molecules running. Without commitments to society and the institutional "furniture" (Veblen) we arrive back at a quasi-premodern condition of "unstable flux" (S: 289) where the budding state grew people like a crop (Scott 2017). The absolute has indeed become disaggregated (S: 289) or sundered but it exists nonetheless in this altered, negative form.

> Indeed, the sort of transcendence we ascribe to human personality is not a quality peculiar to it. It is found elsewhere. It is nothing but the imprint of all really intense collective sentiments upon matters related to them. Just because these feelings derive from the collectivity, the aims to which they direct our actions can only be collective. Society has needs beyond its own. The acts inspired in us by its needs therefore do not depend on our individual inclinations; their aim is not our personal interest, but rather involves sacrifices and privations (S: 335).

The revolt of individuals is an act of obedience to a particular 'spirit' that presents itself erroneously as an absolute. The anti-god is still a god; the anti-capitalist is a capitalist; the anti-socialist is the highest contradictory expression of socialism; and the rebel without a cause is in service of The Cause. Society or some sector of it sets about destroying[195] itself or particular sectors to liberate more energy for exploitation (RSM: 115).[196] Even when society is granulated to the point of appearing to be nothing more than a "formless sand heap" (FMW: 310) the constellation of sentiments that arise from the contacts are not dissimilar in the minds of individuals (RSM: 131). This is the reason Durkheim paradoxically adopts a symbol from the French Revolution, the bee, to characterize modern life as a swarm. What looks like a bunch of indifferent

---

194   The mystic has a desire for static and fundamental (even primal) equilibrium where the endless and unendurable "tight-rope" of life is cast off (Fedden 1938: 319).
195   Keep in mind that suicide and self-destruction are creative acts.
196   It is routinely the case that many social 'functions' are completely irrational and self-destructive "because social phenomena generally do not exist for the usefulness of the results they produce" (RSM: 123). When one reads Toynbee a morass of absurdities are found on virtually every page but the idea that whole societies or even civilizations can commit suicide is plausible.

egos, dispersed by the incongruity of personal ambitions (S: 378) masks an underlying and unconscious alterity and collective logic.[197]

The problem is not that society has ceased to exist but that the postmodern superego injunction has shifted from an altruistic renunciation model to a narcissistic 'enjoyment' model where we are made to feel guilty if we do *not* indulge in our desires and pleasures (Žižek *passim*). As Žižek says in *Pervert's Guide to Ideology*, we do not live in a permissive, post-ideological world but, rather, we live in a system where each ego is whipped unmercifully to pursue aura and hidden treasures (the Platonic *agalma*),[198] where commodity fetishism is, in other words, pushed to the extreme. The denial of constraint, though, masks the essence. The post-Fordist, postmodern, neoliberal system needs low-cost (unorganized) producers of value-bearing objects; it craves isolated and materialistic consumers attached to *logos*; it can use people that can take on debt burdens and make loan payments, and it needs dregs to fill for–profit prison cells; it requires young men to populate the voluntary honor prisons run by the Department of Defense; our society churns out marketable spectacles[199] and mines personal data from streams of user-generated keystrokes; we love the entertainment provided by freaks and videogenic daredevils and so on, all of whom constitute the swarm of the living dead.[200] To the extent that a person does not fulfill these desires and cannot properly enjoy the delights of consumer capitalism they are unnecessary, a drag on the system, and encouraged to dispose of themselves. Each of us is bound for the abyss but our individual trajectories vary widely. Ultimately, Nemesis is omnipresent, and Themis has

---

197 "The bee was [also] the favorite insect of the English, a creature seen as chaste but, more important, highly productive" (Isenberg 2016: 13). The beehive-human society analogy does not revolve around leadership. The queen is "just the ovary" (Haidt 2012: 234). What connects bees and humans is the concept of "ultrasociality" whereby individualism is tamed and members "live in very large groups that have some internal structure, enabling them to reap the benefits of the division of labor" (Haidt 2012: 235).

198 See also Barthes (1982: 45–46) on the relation between the package and the contents.

199 As societies and the social division of labor develop into more elaborate forms a homogenization of mass culture develops as well. "One might almost say" according to Durkheim, "that a people is the more advanced the more superficial its character" (DOL: 136).

200 It is perhaps noteworthy that the 'King of Random' with an online following of 11 million died at age 38 in a paraglider accident. "One knows of people who continually do the wrong thing, as if with intention, and continue to live as though dead" (Fedden 1938: 29). "Round about California in that day were scattered a host of these living dead men—pride-smitten poor fellows, grizzled and old at forty, whose secret thoughts were made all of regrets and longings—regrets for their wasted lives, and longings to be out of the struggle and down with it all" (Twain 1872: 134).

the final word because, unlike money, that *"perpetuum mobile,"* we cannot for long maintain our "circular course" (MECW, 28: 136) without others.[201]

Fatalism is unfortunately reduced to a footnote in *Suicide* because for Durkheim it lacks contemporary relevance and, hence, it is "useless to dwell upon it" (S: 276). As such, Durkheim ends up working with a triadic model of forces where, as we saw in the preceding chapter, altruism plays a decisive role in the "teleological activity" or telos (Hegel 1986: 102–04) of the extremes of egoism and anomie.[202] Altruism emerges as a midpoint in this triad by mediating and sublating malaise, ennui, anarchy, etc.[203] Thankfully, contemporary sociology has seen fit to 'elevate' the problem of fatalism and place it on equal footing with the other forms[204] because the results are interesting if unwieldly.[205] Durkheim seems to have realized this at some level because even though he dumps the category off to the side he nonetheless recognizes its importance for groups attempting to maintain an equilibrium in a world of conflict and populated with enemies of symmetry.[206]

In his discussion of oppressed minorities, French Jews provide a model ready for sublation: arming themselves for the struggle against anti-Semites, Jews combine higher education (the "spirit of free inquiry") and high culture

---

201 "It might seem odd that in cities teetering at the edge of the abyss young people still go to class—in this case an evening class on corporate identity and product branding—but that is the way of things, with cities as with life, for one moment we are pottering about our errands as usual and the next we are dying, and our eternally impending ending does not put a stop to our transient beginnings and middles until the instant when it does" (Hamid 2017: 3–4).

202 With Hegel, telos is both a result (end) and an incomplete gateway to the absolute. "Teleological activity" or praxis is itself another syllogism beyond the syllogism whereby the mediating term attempts to synthesize (sublate) singular and universal extremes.

203 Ennui is "that terrible *taedium vitae*, that comes on those to whom life denies nothing" (Wilde [1890] 1995: 167).

204 It is not as if Durkheim never deploys the concept of fatalism outside the limited scope afforded in *Suicide*. Off the top of my head I can recall his characterization of Manchesterism as a form of economic fatalism that rankled German sensibilities (1993: 71). Often, fatalism is implied or couched in other terms in Durkheim's work. One good example is the role of the social division of labor in ending occupational fatalism (DOL: 270).

205 Arguably, no social setting is more overregulated than a prison or a concentration camp but what looks like external uniformity among inmates and prisoners masks psychological diversity (Kogon 1950: 301). Kogon's account of the three main survival strategies in Buchenwald lines up pretty well with Durkheim's classification: the lone wolf, the social group, and the partisan/political will-power party (Ibid: 308–14).

206 The "enemy of symmetry" is Maupassant's contribution ([1883] 1999: 26).

(characteristics associated with egoism and progressive anomie) with "unusual solidarity" and "strict union" (altruism) as well as "severe control" and "especially rigorous discipline" (S: 156–60). This type of mechanical equilibrium provided by the "superimposition" of currents, however, is *not* the ideal form that Durkheim's sociology aims; indeed, let us turn to the well-known bronze analogy: if the toxicity of egoism can be remedied by a dose of altruism we have achieved a balance that is true, but, this would be akin to reinforcing copper by laminating it with a disk of tin. To be sure, a laminate of tin and copper is stronger than either alone, but the resulting structure would lack the resilience and durability of bronze. The goal is not mechanical superimpositions (e.g., tin + copper or egoism + altruism) but actual synthesis. When copper and tin are melted down (vanish) and combined to form an alloy they are preserved in the new bronze form. We do not want egoism offset by a counterbalance of altruism; rather, we want organic solidarity, which is the 'upward cancellation' of both.[207] The way Durkheim constructs the case of French Jews results in a group of modern primitives:

> This is the reason for the complexity he presents. Primitive in certain respects, in others he is an intellectual and man of culture. He thus combines the advantages of the severe discipline characteristic of small and ancient groups with the benefits of the intense culture enjoyed by our great societies. He has all the intelligence of modern man without sharing his despair (S: 168; cf. S: 376).[208]

The example of Jewish solidarity is unsatisfactory but also points toward alternatives. Modern individuals need a dense network of intermediary commitments and identifications as connective tissue and organization between the state at the aggregate level and the individual and their family at the atomic level. The Jewish example did not exactly fit this requirement because the mechanical or laminated superimpositions of intellectualism, high culture, hyper-discipline, and hyper-cohesion resulted in an unacceptable degree of fatalism:

---

207   Dynamic equilibrium is not a functionalist concept but contains within it a dialectic and is in itself progressive rather than conservative.
208   On the notion of modern primitivism, anthropology has abandoned Levy-Bruhl and returned to what is essentially a Durkheimian position (Remmling 1967: 20; see also Boas 1916: 242). "One has the terrible suspicion that the Apostle Paul may have been one-up cognitively, after all" (Berger 1969: 46). Many institutions that are historically anachronistic or even regressive may still enjoy popularity and satisfy some essential functions in society—for example, the secret brotherhood that "satisfies the need for secrecy, influence, action, youth and often tradition" (Mauss, in Halevy 1965: 293).

"Judaism, in fact, like all early religions, consists basically of a body of practices minutely governing all the details of life and leaving little free room to individual judgment" (S: 160). This characterization fits precisely the nature of Calvinism that also sought a degree of hyper-control and regulation of daily life that would defy modern comprehension (PESC: 5).

Fatalism, in its active phases, seems to lead beyond itself in myriad directions: indifference, dispossession, poverty, lethargy and sloth, apathy, powerlessness, and so on (Voltaire 1962: 236–37). If we bring fatalism back into the theoretical fold we arrive at something new, a shift from a triadic model of forces to, at first glance, a quadratic model. Sociologists have noticed that the structure of Durkheim's analysis of suicide, with the inclusion of fatalism, involves "four categories" organized around "two oppositions" (Miller 1996: 112) and that this structure assumes the shape of a "square" or a "four-cornered" typology (Besnard 2005) or that it is organized around the axes of solidarity and regulation such that an X-shaped diagram is the appropriate form to represent the structure of his argument.[209] Nielsen posits a structure of quadrants

---

209 The repetition of squares in social theory, philosophy, logic and linguistics is fascinating. From the "four-cornered" typology of Durkheim's analysis of suicide, Bhaskar's "social cube" (2008: 160), the semiotic square, Lacan's L schema, Harman's four-pole ontographic model, and the various squares of opposition and contradictions in logic (2011: 124), to name just a handful. Literature, poetry, and myth are also fertile and interesting reflections on the nature of the square and the number four. Whitman's 'transcendental Walt,' a Kosmos, was also the fourth and final side of the "Square Deific." Perhaps this recurrence of the square originates in the allocentric intuitions and observations regarding the twin polarities of opposing forces that undergird all forms of social organization reflected in customs, tales, myths, theology, and philosophy. "The enigmatic axiom of Maria runs: '... from the third comes the one as the fourth' ... which presumably means, when the third produces the fourth it at once produces unity" (Jung 1969: 237). Kant organized a jumble of Aristotle's categories into a "fourfold" array that is found split into two in Hegel's logic (Jameson 2009: 77). Particularly interesting is the disjunctive syllogism in Hegel's big logic where the universal doubles itself to create a fourth moment out of a triadic configuration of individuality, particularity, and universality. Dyads produce triads and triads produce squares—totalities that 'contain' all. Far from a mania for triads commonly attributed to Hegel, his entire philosophy of history features a "quatriad" (i.e., tetradic) procession of freedom from the Oriental, Greek, Roman, and finally, the German (Croce 1915: 183; Croce 1917: 273). We find a parallel, again, in the L schema (Lacan) where the triadic expands *quadratus* (made square) through a redoubling process (Lacan 2002: 481) and the analyst's attempt at triangulation by taking a "tertiary position" (Lacan 2002: 481; Fink 1997: 106) via the imposition of a symbolic position juxtaposed to the dyadic imaginary relation between the analyst and analysand (ego-ego' or a-a') which produces a four-cornered structure (ego, ego', Subject, and Other) and, where there should be a subject that can respond to the Other of the symbolic order, we find instead a black hole (Fink 1997: 105). Dislodged, autocentric egos on the peripheries of society fail to perceive

produced by intersecting axes of forces incapable of crossing or interacting (2005) in such a manner that defeats any possibility of dialectical analysis. All these are suggestive but what I think Durkheim really provides is something more akin to an 'octahedron' of destructiveness or, really, a constellation of synthetic *a priori* judgments groping for conceptual unity. Let us briefly review the genetic process at work in moral life before investigating the singular forms of suicide.

To put it crudely, we concluded the previous volume with something like this: the *one* (energy, i.e., assemblage effervescence) has a *double* function of solidarity and control but appearing subjectively as a *triadic* complex of judgements pertaining to the ego, attachment, and control. Due to (a) the dynamic self-development of this dialectical 'triangle' of self-distinguishing unity (Rosenkranz [1844] 2002) and (b) from the objective observational standpoint of scientific *understanding*, this complex appears variously as a *square*, an 'X,' or something with four corners, etc.[210] The metaphor of the Möbius band (∞) represents this totality in a different way and from the point of view of the result of the absolute's disintegration that nonetheless preserves its earlier moments of genesis. But when we critically comprehend this totality as an absolute operating both consciously and unconsciously, and in simultaneously pure and impure modalities, its *octagonal* form (a matrix of judgments and faulty syllogisms) is revealed; here we can think of the lemniscate as the envelope of a rectangular hyperbola (imperfectly demonstrated at the end of the last chapter). It is not necessary to recount all the moments in the sociogony of moral energy; we will jump in at the present moment of decomposition where a void has opened in the place where the quest for moral individuality once reigned. In the next volume we will revisit the genesis and unfolding of the 'octahedron' since much will have changed by the time we work our way through the primary currents of self-destruction as they are presented here. Again, the current discussion is not result but a survey of a particular breakdown in teleological activity.

---

anything but a patternless and chaotic play of metaphor, and fluid hook-ups lacking durability. Verheggen (1996: 209–11) suggests that the structure of Durkheim's own thinking was shaped by the ten-point Sefirot diagram.

210 The shift from logical analysis to metaphysics is represented in the shift from a simple dichotomy to a four-way differentiation (Kant 1991: 164).

CHAPTER 3

The Four Horsemen of the Apocalypse

As Durkheim tells us, moral economies are self-containing and self-limited systems of forces and their corresponding representations. The inevitable consequence of system dynamism is that imbalances are integral, and the loss of equilibration is par for the course. Things fall apart, and once institutions lose their justifications for commanding, subjects retreat into their private spheres, think their own thoughts, develop their own feelings, and get weird. The being turned inward lacks universality (Hegel [1807] 2008: 723) and as people "sink deeper within themselves" they enter the ranks of the "departed" (Hegel 1988: 240). The 'individual' unencumbered by society is "in the strict sense of the word ... only a fiction" (Feuerbach, in Wartofsky 1977: 44)—i.e., a fictional person. The private-public or profane-sacred duality (*Homo duplex*) is here undeveloped or snuffed out.[1] Pushed to its conceivable limits, individualism actually transforms into its opposite. For example, according to Weber the genuine capitalist was dedicated not to an inflated sense of self-worth but to god and calling. Even when this purity of purpose 'de-sublimates' into utilitarian purposiveness or 'trans-sublimates' into a negativity of the iron cage of commodity fetishism, there is still some sense of devotion to a higher power. The transit into the domain of the Other is made through self-concern and the eventual alternation back into self-absorption is driven by that immoderate dedication of the self to something alien to itself. Likewise, to put it simply, the greatest anarchist is, eventually, destined to be an ideal-typical subject of hyper-regulation.

1 Egoism

We all seek to be individuals but what we normally think of as 'individuality' is the opposite of, and hostile toward, sociological individualism.[2] Being an

---

1 There is also the confusion of one or the other resulting in a dissolution of reality (Auden 2008: 248). In light of what has been said about the private-public divide, it should be noted that a 'private' life and 'private' property, etc., imply deprivation. My private property rests on depriving some other of its use. My private life is not a refuge from others but self-deprivation; 'Private' is derived from the Latin *privare*, 'to deprive' (Capra 1982: 195).
2 "A verbal similarity has permitted the belief that 'individualism' necessarily derived from 'individual' and therefore egoistic feelings" (Durkheim 1973: 54). Many commentators on Durkheim fail to distinguish between the individual, individualism, and individuality. An

individual literally means that one is not divisible, the ego is undivided, and this state of apparent personal unity represents the breakdown of *Homo duplex*. This sounds like a victory over alienation but this triumph of the ego is illusory. Egoism is a collapse back into the personal domain and a retreat from public life[3] whereas actual individuality is a sublation found only in society (CPE: 189).[4] When we think of egoists we typically think of self-absorbed elites and celebrities but, historically, Puritanism (with its liberalism, parliamentarianism, individualism, and free enterprise) was a revolutionary *middle-class* phenomenon. Once the middle is contaminated by a disintegrative force the extremes are no longer mediated and gross passions invert the means and the ends. Egoism or hyper-individualism is not merely a symptomatic attitude, mental problem, or social condition but, like anomie, an active force and prestigious ideal at work in the world that promotes further social liquidation. "Capitalist culture isolates us from the world and other human beings. We are forced into an interior enclave. A virtue is then made of necessity and we are counseled to prize our seclusiveness and a unique cultural achievement" (Lichtman 1982: 72). Where accumulation for its own sake gains the high ground, enterprise necessitates egoism and encourages the malignant growth of "self-pride" out of individualism (Parrington 1927: 7).[5] We see in *Capital* that egoism under the names of selfishness, self-interest, and so on, is a singular force that brings together buyers and sellers of labor power and "Each pays heed to himself only, and no one worries about the others" (C: 280).

The 19th Century placed a great deal of explanatory weight on the pathology of egoism. As Moses Hess put it, rather dramatically:

> Egoism or selfishness is the final source of all social oppression and exploitation. Cruelty, fraud and robbery, feudalism, chattel and wage slavery, pauperism and prostitution are possible only because men draw a circle around themselves and their nearest of kin, and focus attention so strongly upon the field of their immediate vision that they become

---

ideal-typical mangling of these different concepts can be found in Hearn (1985: 51). "The most enduring result of Hegelian logic is that the individual is not flatly for himself. In himself, he is his otherness and linked with others" (Adorno 1973: 161).

3 Egoism may, though, lead to the cultivation of perverse symbiotic relations, exploitative dependencies, and pseudo-community of "the clinging-vine type" (May 1977: 230). The egoist in society easily devolves into a fraudster or charlatan (MECW, 37: 601) that puts personal interests above class or general interests (MECW, 11: 160).

4 "[T]he movement of individuality is the reality of the universal" (PS: 235).

5 "Pride goes before destruction" (Proverbs 16:18).

indifferent, and ultimately blind, to the interests and the very existence of those who live beyond the line. Social institutions are such as to place a premium upon selfish behavior. And although this behavior is hedged in by rules of law imposed by the state, these rules themselves represent the organized selfishness of dominant groups. Capitalism or 'the system of free competition is the last word; of egoism.' It distorts and perverts every phase of culture—religion, art, education—by substituting for the ideals of the collectivity, private interest and private satisfaction as controlling factors.

in HOOK 1934

Sociological egoism is, negatively, insufficient solidarity and insufficient integration with others, and, positively, excessive individuation. The idea that everybody has a unique self and personal identity seems like the most natural thing in the world, yet, we know that it is of relatively recent origin.[6] As late as Roman antiquity, having a *name* was not a personal designation signifying individuality the way it is today, rather, it was a right to wear a mask and participate in clan rituals (Mauss 1979: 79).[7] It was not until Christianity that we find the tilt from person as a status linked to social roles to the "human person" *per se*, the personality elevated to a "metaphysical entity" (Mauss 1979: 85).[8]

After all, individualism ... extended is the glorification not of the self but of the individual in general.[9] It springs not from egoism but from sympathy for all that is human, a broader pity for all sufferings, for all human miseries, a more ardent need to combat them and mitigate them, a greater thirst for justice. Is there not herein what is needed to place all men of good will in communion?

DURKHEIM 1973: 49

---

6 Actual individuality is not crafted in isolation or in the withdrawal of the person from society but in the confrontation with impersonal social forces (see Lichtman 1982: 7).

7 Falling outside the sphere of citizenship and having no name or persona meant that the unfree, the slave for example, had no body of their own to control. The body was owned by somebody else. The startling contribution of Christianity was to provide a soul for those who had no body (Mauss 1979: 81).

8 "To consider Europe alone, the sense of the person remains embryonic throughout antiquity until the dawn of the Christian era" (Mounier 1952: xix).

9 Consider that 'individualism' in modernity is itself a collective representation (Duveen 2001: 7) whereas 'individuality' is the shape of being in which autonomy and heteronomy have been sublated.

This would be the actual meaning of a cult of personality. "Many gods have been done away with, but the individual himself stubbornly remains as a deity of considerable importance. He walks with some dignity and is the recipient of many little offerings" (Goffman 1967: 95). But when the atom becomes sacred (or considers itself as sacred) it is not necessarily the case that others retain their sacred quality as well.

Jaynes argues that the grand sweep of history inclines toward an actual "profaning of our species" (1990: 437) but what this means for sociology is that human history is one of growing individualism to the point where "individualism" is synonymous with hyper-individuation and estrangement from others and thereby the alienation of the self from itself. Self-aggrandizement and the notion of the sacred individual corresponds with the debasement of the species and the projection of any moral surplus into the inhuman. Taken to extremes, the egoist believes that only the self is real, the rest of the world takes on the appearance and texture of unreality, and the sole end of life resides in the individual's dreams and goals (autotelism).[10] For the egoist (Stendhal is a good model) enjoyment is a higher value than creation and self is paramount over action (Zweig [1929] 2012: 714).

Without others and action—which is a kind of othering or alteration of self—we lack the external regulators of our desires and we are swept away by contingent, overriding passions, if there are any real passions left. "Just as the person makes no definitive gift of himself, he has definitive title to nothing" (S: 271).[11] The two egoistic forms marked off by Durkheim are Stoics and Epicureans, both peaking in the twilight of the Roman Empire. The common thread unifying Stoics, Epicureans, and the Sceptics is the retreat[12] and the "tendency to pooh-pooh everything that the real world has to offer—riches, political power, worldly glory—and to substitute an ideal of living which makes the adherent absolutely indifferent to anything the outside world can do" (Singer 1983: 23).

Durkheim's ideal-types are constructed to accentuate a fairly distinct polar opposition between the materialism of the Epicureans and what we might call the idealism of the Stoics. It is true that both schools are formerly *materialistic* but, in the case of the Stoics, the *Pronoia* of Nature was not crude matter but

---

10   "The individual raised to an end, the species degraded to a means; that is the inversion of human and natural life in general…. The inverted conception of the world reigns rather in the condition of egoism because this condition is itself an inverted world" (Hess 1845). For more on autotelism and heterotelism see Baldwin (1902: 668).

11   "'Suicide is the absence of the others'" (Valery, in Choron 1972: 62).

12   Scepticism is always a preparation for mysticism (Pessoa 2012: 4) but, really, this applies to virtually all forms of egoism producing unique mystical objects of devotion.

the "finest material" —fire, and not "ordinary fire" but "intellectual fire ... which has consciousness and life, and is not subject to decay" (Murray 1915: 36; cf. EFRL: 47).[13] This imagined pure "fiery ether" (the "common light" of humanity) is distributed according to the law of nature as a fragment or spark of the divine in each individual that guides action through life and returns the individual, ultimately, to the essential fire (ESS, 14: 408). Stoics are presented by Durkheim as a rare form of egoism. They are idealists, reflective, and repulsed by the doings of others and the current state of society. Unhappy with the state of the world the Stoic attempts to find harmony in "abstract self-absorption" (Hegel 1988: 450). In contrast to Epicurean sensationalism, Stoics are above all intellectualists with a unique relationship to language and the luxuriousness of 'big words' that leave them over-exposed to boundlessness and an ever-expanding mental horizon;[14] bare reality pales in comparison to the creations of the Stoic mind (e.g. Mann 1936: 23–7).[15] Disillusioned with reality these egoists withdraw into themselves to the point of worshiping isolation (S: 279).[16] "'We have fallen out of nature and hang suspended in space'" they might say (Hesse 1963: 142).[17] Isolation means indifference in philosophy as well as in life. Whether we are referring to a concept or to a person, indifference means a lack

---

13   Stoic physics is indebted to Heraclitus where *logos* is a "creative fire" in the person and universe at large (EP, 8: 19). Stoicism has been classed as both a "quasi-idealism" and a "quasi-materialism" (Dewey 1946: 98; see also ESS, 14: 408) but I might call it a crypto-idealism. The Stoic form of egoism is averse to experience and tries to work everything out in the domain of ideas instead of action (see Becker 1973: 183). Stoics can easily develop a mania for symbols.
14   The physical horizon is actually insufficient to satiate the conceptual horizon: "The sea is vast, the sea is wide, my eyes roved far and wide and longed to be free. But there was the horizon. Why a horizon, when I wanted the infinite from life?" (Mann 1936: 26). All they are left with are the stars in the sky.
15   Stoics don't make very good sadists. Sadism is materialistic and relies on strong impressions and a highly developed fetishism (the fascination toward a singular, concrete object). Sadists are also hungry for bodily sensations and mechanical stimulations (Stekel 1929: 58–72). The realm of sadism is not one of laws and reciprocity but of protocol and revenge (Barthes 1976: 165–67). Where anomie reigns, sadism is not far behind (Packard 1959: 256). The place where Stoics and sadists converge is in their boundless capacity for fantasy, however, their fantastic fulfillments are of opposing tendencies.
16   Like the Cynics, Stoics were also outsiders to Greek society (ESS, 14: 407). Isolationism is the active rejection of existing society (SGS: 118–19). The "*social individual* who is both made of, and is the active co-maker of, a multiplicity of tangible social/interpersonal determinations—is radically incompatible with the standpoint of isolated individuality" (Mészáros 2010: 92).
17   Inattentiveness to life can result in the perception of life as having a dream-like quality. The individual is astonished to find themselves where they are, doing what they are doing, and the future seems predestined (Bergson 1920: 182).

of relation and, abstracted from others, it matters not whether it is or is not (SL: 87). Compare that indifference to the person still clinging to norms. As Hamlet says, "conscience does make cowards of us all" (Shakespeare 2001: 65).[18]

The desire to align life to natural law (the law projected and misplaced in nature) inevitably fails and devolves into sageism[19] and self-subjugation to a constructed "imaginary being" such as, for example, a mystic personification of pure, transcendental Reason (S: 289–90).[20] It might appear, on the surface, that Stoics, unlike Epicureans, have passions but both positions are "mere appearances, being sterile. They are dissipated in futile imagining, producing nothing external to themselves" (S: 279).[21] The Stoic is in love with the kind of dreamy sadness that romantics understand (cf. Freud [1921] 1959: 96).[22] Melancholy can be, as Burton says, "most pleasant at first ... a most delightful humour, to be alone, dwell alone, walk alone, meditate, lie in bed whole days, dreaming awake as it were, and frame a thousand phantastical imaginations unto themselves" ([1621–1628] 2001: 406).[23] Being alone is wonderful so long as

---

18   Subjective destitution of the kind we locate in the estranged ego means that, as far as it is concerned, death is irrelevant from any substantial point of view. Just as the death of a lama is inconsequential, because the sacred substance will simply inhabit another body, the death of the ego implies nothing so far as the autonomy and mobility of any substances are concerned (Hegel 1988: 313). There simply is nothing to consider, and, if there is, substance will immediately take up residence somewhere else or with someone else.

19   A 'sage' is one who knows how to properly divide and separate things.

20   'Sageism' might be a good way to conceptualize the polarity of the Stoic form of egoism with altruism (cf. S: 218). If more space were available we would explore the connection between the sage and prophecy (ES, 1: 445).

21   Compare this to Murray's claim for the religious nature of the Stoic's "exalted passion" (1915: 14). Nietzsche says that in the case of Epicurus, "Never before has voluptuousness been so modest" ([1887] 1974: 110).

22   In dreams, they are free (Schnitzler [1926] 1999). "Emma was privately pleased to feel that she had so very quickly attained this ideal of ethereal languor, inaccessible to mediocre spirits. So she let herself meander along Lamartinian paths, listening to the throbbing of harps on lakes, to all the songs of dying swans, to the falling of every leaf, to the flight of pure virgins ascending to heaven, and to the voice of the Eternal speaking in the valleys" (Flaubert 1957: 36–7).

23   We should not neglect actual dreaming: "Dreaming is thus one of our roads into the infinite. And it is interesting to observe how we attain it—by limitation. The circle of our conscious life is narrowed during sleep; it is even by a process of psychic dissociation broken up into fragments. From that narrowed and broken-up consciousness the outlook becomes vaster and more mysterious, full of strange and unsuspected fascination, and the possibilities of new experiences.... The infinite can only be that which stretches far beyond the boundaries of our own personality. It is the charm of dreams that they introduce us into a new infinity. Time and space are annihilated, gravity is suspended, and we are joyfully borne up in the air, as it were in the arms of angels.... In the waking moments

the person is not a loner. The enjoyment of being alone is predicated upon being part of a loving family, creative collaborator, enjoying a thriving career, etc. The Portuguese word *Saudade* captures some of the Stoic melancholy when Manuel de Melo defined it as "A pleasure you suffer, an ailment you enjoy."[24] More fleshed out in, say, the writings of Marcus Aurelius, Stoicism can be made to sound like an attractive form of life. We are even urged to not be anti-social. "We were born to labor together ..." not in opposition with one another so we had better be agreeable, moderate, friendly, generous, tolerant, have self-control and restrain ourselves from "frivolous enthusiasms" and, among other things, be reasonable above all (1983: 3–11). However, at bottom, the Stoic life is one of apathy (1983: 9)[25] and an avoidance of collective ebullience. "[T]he skepticism of the seventeenth century was tied to the Stoic notion of *ataraxia*, that is, imperturbability[26]—as a good to be strived for in life. Such a Stoic sentiment led one to distance oneself from wild passions and beliefs and assume a form of skeptical consciousness" (Seligman 2000: 135). The negation of effervescent life is of paramount importance because it separates the ego from the energies that underpin the sacred and the forms of consciousness, for good or bad, that marks the social person, i.e., a real personality.

The Stoic life, above all and under all circumstances, dictated by abstract universal Reason,[27] is one that inclines toward the sterility of disenchantment

---

of our complex civilised life we are ever in a state of suspense which makes all great conclusions impossible; the multiplicity of the facts of life, always present to consciousness, restrains the free play of logic (except for that happy dreamer, the mathematician), and surrounds most of our pains and nearly all our pleasures with infinite qualifications we are tied down to a sober tameness. In our dreams the fetters of civilisation are loosened, and we know the fearful joy of freedom" (Ellis 1911: 278–79).

24   "'Ah. Yes. Melancholy.' I nodded. 'Isn't here often a bright azure tinge of happiness to be found glinting away quietly inside the deep shadows of its murky-grey waters?'" (Barker 2017: 13).

25   "The goal of Stoicism was *apatheia*, not feeling, the goal of Epicureanism *ataraxia*, not being disturbed—both negative ideals" (Jenkyns 2007: x). As for "bourgeois *ataraxia*," says Adorno, "In attacking ecstasy it strikes at all human relations, at every attempt to go beyond a monadological existence" (1967: 103). As for the Stoics, Benjamin says that "Stoic equanimity is fundamentally distinguished from Christian resignation by the fact that it teaches only calm endurance and unruffled expectation of unalterably necessary evils, but Christianity teaches renunciation, the giving up of willing" ([1963] 1998: 112). However, as we will see, 'resignation' does not necessarily extinguish willing.

26   A better translation might be *tranquility*.

27   Especially important in this regard pertains to the 'coordinates' of *logos* within the sphere of fate, overregulation, and instrumentalization. The Stoic "assigns the individual a close dependence on universal reason and even reduces him to nothing more than the instrument through which this reason is realized" (S: 289–90). "The hypertrophy of reason

and the depression of endless self-reflection, and can devolve into an infinite loop of autology. Stoicism leaves one exposed to the twin infinities of the all and the nothing: "There is one motherland, stranger, in which we all dwell, and that is the Cosmos: there is one Father of whom we are all begotten, and He is the void" (ESS, 14: 408). Like existentialism[28] and other forms of thought that lose the universal thread, Stoicism has "one sacrament for the sinner—suicide" (Baudelaire, in Auden 2008: 173). The necessity of an unbounded imagination for intellectuals is both a gift and curse for science.

Descartes represents the disposition whereby doubt and uncertainty are pushed so far that simulated psychosis[29] becomes part of the scientific method and reality dissolves into incoherence: "I decided to feign that everything that had entered my mind hitherto was no more true than the illusions of dreams.... I noticed that while I was trying to think everything false, it must needs be that I, who was thinking this, was something. And observing that this truth 'I am thinking, therefore I exist' was so solid and secure that the most extravagant suppositions of the sceptics could not overthrow it, I judged that I need not scruple to accept it as the first principle of philosophy that I was seeking" (Descartes 1954: 31–2). This attitude is antithetical to solidarity. I see people but what if my visions are really just hats and coats covering automata? (Ibid: 73). Would I feel an obligation toward automata? For the Stoic, duty is praised but, in the final analysis, *indifference* creeps into and undermines ethics and the reference to amoral nature works at cross-purposes against collective life. Descartes was the father of modern philosophy, but that philosophy is also a reflection and symptom of social disintegration.

> Descartes is praised for having been a fearless doubter, for having invited us to seek the truth for ourselves. This is surely an imprudent exaltation of individual judgment. It is not self-evident that a society wherein each one was intoxicated with the Cartesian pride would soon be wholly lacking in the indispensable principles of cohesion? Where nothing is respected in common and everything is constantly called into question, the

---

entails a correspondent atrophy of the will. Thus, the critical spirit is a dissolvent for individual energy as well as for social synergy" (Bouglé [1926] 1970: 216).

28 Existentialist philosophy is a symptom of estrangement and hyper-reflection. Concrete solidarity with other people and life within the social division of labor are alien to this form of thought and, as such, infinity alternates with finitude and the inevitability of the 'meaninglessness' of existence drives the ego into the mist of the transcendental (cf. S: 210–12, 279–80). See Moyn's (2019) review of Martin Hägglund's *This Life*.

29 See the novella "A Chess Story" by Stefan Zweig ([1943] 2013) for "simulated schizophrenia."

unanimity which supports the social life crumbles into dust. To spontaneous communion succeeds mutual distrust or—still worse—egotistical indifference.

BOUGLÉ [1926] 1970: 215

Tönnies says, "In reality, the more perfectly egotistic one is, the more indifferent he is toward the weal and woe of other people. He is not immediately concerned with either their ill fortune or their well-being. But he can instigate ill fortune as well as he can further well-being if it seems to serve his ends" (1988: 130). But this instigation of ill will through indifference is even more antisocial than outright conflict. "Bad as they are, intolerance and persecution imply at least a partial recognition of the human rights and duties which belong to members of an intellectual community" (Creighton 1925: 69). Here we find an important link between egoism and utilitarianism, a point that will be expanded later. However, one decisive point is that indifference runs in myriad and seemingly contradictory directions. We might be lured by the prospects that the indifferent or disinterested egoist is capable of generating a more objective view of social conditions but in no way does indifference lead to an objectivity (Weber 1949: 60). What we find is the ego undergoing a positive process of self-inflation and sacralization of the ego such that it turns on itself and convinces itself that it is so far developed to be actual selflessness—the best altruist is the most fully developed egoist (MECW, 5: 253).[30] At best, as in the case of Hume, we find that utility can raise itself up to "generous and noble intercourse" but it does not have the energy to rise above "commerce" or the concurrence of mutual interests (1896: 521). Indifference to the collective state and an eye toward interests are pathological and a form of passive rebelliousness (Baudrillard 1983b) and has to be checked. For example, even if we are privately glad that another person is dead we are obligated to act the role of a mourner, going so far as to manufacture tears[31] because, if everyone were permitted to be indifferent or adopt a morally neutral stance (*adiaphora*) toward the health and

---

30 The negative process is one of self-laceration and self-wounding fractionalization (Meredith 1951: 500).

31 "By the rules of village life Elizabeth should now break down" (Greene 1929: 30). "She's trying her best to cry. Come, dear! Make another effort. That's better. Two tears, two little tears are twinkling under the black veil" (Sartre [1946] 1976: 11; see Durkheim on the facade of mourning in EFRL: 400–01). "Pascal says more or less: 'Kneel down, move your lips in prayer, and you will believe'" (Althusser 1970). Of course, the indifferent egoist may be found gathered with others due to formal obligations but display the exact opposite sentiment: my body is here but my spirit is elsewhere, gone away (Goffman 1963: 70).

well-being of others, society would sink (EFRL: 403).³² But let us not neglect the fact that Stoicism can also stretch out along other lines. Stoic pseudo-passion is also capable of ending in a kind of tyranny of self-government (i.e., fatalism and other exotic composite forms) combined with actions driven by "fits of anger" (Alain [1934] 1974: 56).

In Durkheim's construction, Epicureanism is the more common and simplified materialistic (minimalist) orientation to life.³³ To say that a philosophy is materialistic one must differentiate between positive and negative forms. What we normally think of as materialism is the attachment to, and the enjoyment of, external material objects. However, there is also a negative form of materialism that is much more interesting whereby the person who is dependent upon material life, their own body for example, as well as the material existence of others for their own survival, seeks to demonstrate that they are actually free from dependency on others who provide life's necessaries. This is a drive toward self-sufficiency or autarky. This drive toward self-sufficiency is contained in the lordship and bondage section of Hegel's *Phenomenology*. For example, I want to assert my freedom and thereby engage in mortal combat with some other self-asserting individual as a way to achieve not only acknowledgement of my supremacy through their suppression but also my factual liberty over nature and others. If I destroy the other, nobody will be left to recognize my superiority and, therefore, I spare the life of the one I fought with, who, for their part, prefers servitude to death. We arrive at a dependency relation based on the exploitation of a weaker other. Ironically, where one sought self-sufficiency, an opposite condition of dependency is achieved. The master grows to depend on the service and labor provided by the other (cf. Singer 1983).³⁴ One interesting outcome of the emergent 'lordship' relation is that the

---

32   "[T]o him [the others] had all withdrawn into the realm of ghosts. And although this made him shudder a little, there was also something soothing about this feeling, which seemed to release him from all responsibility, indeed from all connection with humanity" (Schnitzler [1926] 1999: 24). An interesting conflict here is the humanitarianism of many egoists with the disregard for humanity that we find in disinterestedness. I think it is the blending with anomie that negates the concern with others or reduces humanitarianism to the level of concern for abstractions, charitable tax write-offs, and utilitarian rationalizations. On Stoic indifference and insensitivity, compared to the Epicurean position, see Nietzsche ([1887] 1974: 245). Insensitivity of the egoist is also undoubtedly connected to asceticism which "deadens the senses" as do hedonistic indulgences (Wilde [1890] 1995: 153) where quantity swamps nuance and quality.

33   "You cannot imagine, if you haven't experienced it, the solace of an animal coming to keep you company when the gods have turned their backs" (Cioran 1974: 57).

34   One outcome of this, let's call it the revolutionary model, finds the slave constructing a world in their image that is alien to the will of the master who, no longer needed, is

ascendency of the master over the other that was not killed but merely subdued is that a fatalistic form of control encircles the vanquished who have nowhere to turn but inward, while progressive anomic freedom is apparently enjoyed by the victor.

The essential thing with this form of egoism is an avoidance of, or a freedom from, pain and suffering.[35] As such, any freedom at this coordinate of early retirement (Wundt 1897: 28–9) is of a negative variety. The minimization of needs-satisfactions, it is thought, resists the multiplication of desires because the Epicurean "can hope for nothing better" than what he or she already has and so demands nothing beyond what is in hand (S: 282). This dread of desire or what Marx calls the "*passion of possession*" whereby material property weighs on the mind as a "commanding *force*" (1974: 128) is shared by Stoics. Epictetus for example, equates wants and desires with servitude.[36] Perhaps, along with indifference, the common problem for egoists of all kinds is the foreboding over an explosion of desire.[37] Durkheim says that the pure Epicurean uses the

---

    deposed. In another model, let us call it the normal course of things, the servant is kept in a state of idiocy and never comes to the realization that with slight pressure applied at the right time to the right spot, they could liberate themselves from the tyranny of the lord. Where the capitalists outwitted the Marxists is in the detailed or hyper-specialized division of labor where the worker never objectifies their consciousness in the product of their labor. The industrial worker in fact puts next to nothing of themselves in the products. It is quite literally true that, in an automobile factory filled with employees, *nobody* makes the product. Workers are reduced to little more than units of energy to be exploited, used up as if they were so many lumps of coal. "Since his labor is abstract ... he behaves as an abstract I—according to the mode of thinghood—not as an all-encompassing Spirit, rich in content, ruling a broad range and being master of it" (Hegel 1983: Part Two, Actual Spirit, A. Recognition).

35 A life devoted to the avoidance of unpleasurable sensations is also one that is characterized by a diminution of "energetic cathexis" (Freud [1923] 1960: 12).

36 In the *Enchiridion*, Epictetus says that to release oneself from desire is to release oneself from slavery (2004: 32). The smallest of things easily at hand are within our power, Epictetus would say, and desiring those things do not necessarily lead us down the road to perdition. "And this is when the unlikeliest peace comes, and I smile. Because as fucked as the world is, as grim as the future surely seems to be, as grim as it revealed itself to be for my mother as she lay dying of the tumor that kills us all, there is a truth I cannot deny, a thing no creditor can take; even as my doomed boys stir in the cold unknowing of predawn sleep, even as the very life leaches out of me, soaks into the Berber, into the cracks of my arid grave, I must grudgingly admit—that was one great goddamn burrito" (Walter 2009: 15).

37 "We know that in a vacuum there can be hollows, plenums, masses of waves and anything else you like. But for Pascal, whether or not nature abhors a vacuum was essential, because this signified the abhorrence that all the learned men of his day had for desire" (Lacan 2014: 67–8). If Kant is correct that desire is a striving to be a cause (1991: 163) perhaps the real abhorrence of desire lies less in the matter of cause and more in the problem of unintended effects and the multiplication of uncontrollable effects.

life of the child or the animal as a conscious model (S: 282)[38] and we can detect a connection to the Cynics and Sceptics[39] at this point.

> In this case philosophic, dreamy melancholy is replaced by sceptical disillusioned matter-of-factness—which becomes especially prominent at the final hour. The sufferer deals himself the blow without hate or anger, but equally with none of the morbid satisfaction with which the intellectual relishes his suicide. He is even more passionless than the latter. He is not surprised at the end to which he has come; he has foreseen it as a more or less impending event (S: 282).

Cynicism is a "stern and bitter philosophy of a group of outsiders" and "nobodies" with a "social criticism aimed at shocking all conventions and prejudices of polite society" (ESS, 4: 680). Historically, cynicism cannot be thought of as a coherent 'school' of thought but "an erratic succession of individuals" (EP, 2: 284) who taught a similar path of personal happiness amidst the spectacle of social disintegration. The cynic[40] is a radical sceptic,[41] atavistic, asocial, and even anti-social (ESS, 4: 681; EP, 4: 284–85), opposed to money and custom, *nomisma* and *nomos* (Desmond 2008: 77, 99). Where the historical Stoics devalued money, their predecessors, the Cynics, sought to "deface" money[42] and strove for a virtuous life in purely natural values (EP, 2: 284). Cynicism has a trans-class and cosmopolitan appeal[43] that teaches that wealth is corruption and that poverty and asceticism are superior forms of existence over and against prevailing and laughable social norms.[44] Rather than the pursuit of the whole, with respect to possessions, the cynic agrees with Hesiod that, "'half is more than the whole'" (Desmond 2008: 14). Cynical freedom is purely negative

---

38 Children rank animals as their equals (Freud [1913] 1950: 157).
39 Although the distinction goes beyond the scope of this work, we would want to mark a difference between active and passive sceptics, the first falling in line with the frenzy of anomie and the second with the resignation and indifference of egoism.
40 The word 'cynic' comes from a Greek word for 'dog people.' For the double connection to dogs see ESS (4: 680–84).
41 The cynic is not a true political radical. Cynicism is the ideology of a declassed and disillusioned or "'parlor pink' revolutionary in thought but not in action" (ESS, 4: 684).
42 The motto of the Cynics was "'deface the coinage'" (Desmond 2008: 98).
43 We all want to be citizens of the world, but cosmopolitan apathy also embodies the defense against passions and indifference toward life and the plight of others (Wundt 1897: 25–8). On some relevant observations pertaining to universalism, cosmopolitanism, and national particularity see Galston (2018).
44 "[T]his is the cynics point: everything is laughable, there is nothing serious in mortality and one should not wrinkle one's brow with Aristotelian jargon ..." (Desmond 2008: 28).

in its orientation toward body, material life, work, the mind, and in social relations where *autarkeia* or the autonomy of the virtuous person is paramount (EP, 8: 19). We also find with cynicism "the earliest distinct expression of nominalism" with an eye for the singular and undefinable (ESS, 4: 682).[45] Cynical life is minimalistic and rejects idle speculations for practicality and the reduction of the person down to as few needs as possible, a trait shared with the Epicureans.

If we follow the logic of Epicurean materialism to its limits we find the shrinking of the person down to the level of an animal and subjugation to physics.[46] The small footprint of the life of the minimalist with easy needs-satisfaction does not, however, preclude, either logically or empirically, the spontaneous multiplication of wants and needs and the generation of new dreams because as soon as desires are met they have a tendency to stir up new wants.[47] In an archaic society it is possible to imagine a life of few needs and wants, the idea behind the affluence of 'stone age' societies (Sahlins 1972) but in a capitalist system new wants are created on almost a daily basis and once we satisfy those wants many of them are transformed into needs. Who twenty years ago wanted or needed a cellular telephone? According to Pew Research Center, as of 2013, 91 percent of adults in America own one of these devices making it "the most quickly adopted consumer technology in the history of the world" (Rainie 2013). Can we imagine life without one now? I walked the halls of my academic department and saw nearly everyone engrossed by what has been called their personal "dream machine," completely oblivious, it seems, to the world around them. But absorption by the device is just that, the attachment to the physical thing, rather than the actual ability to stimulate the imagination and generate new dreams; the content is too prosaic and mundane to dream the impossible dream. The attachment is to the physical object itself as a new kind of security blanket with real powers of capturing images and communicating instantly with friends and authorities. The capacity of the state security and surveillance apparatus pales in comparison to the all-pervasive surveillance powers of nearly the entire population, fractured as it is, into isolated, all-seeing eyes. Of course, these atoms are interacting with all the best

---

45 "'I have been in mad-houses full of tragic mopers, and seen there the end of suspicion: the cynic, in the moody madness, muttering in the corner; for years a barren fixture there; head lopped over, gnawing his own lip, vulture of himself; while, by fits and starts, from the corner opposite came the grimace of the idiot at him'" (Melville [1857] 1990: 22).

46 "For once human life has sunk into the merely creaturely, even the life of apparently dead objects secures power over it" (Benjamin [1963] 1998: 132).

47 We can find, at times, an inverse relation between the smallness of social and material surroundings and the gigantism of dreams (Hardy [1894–95] 2006: 11).

friends they've never met, which is an interesting aspect of egoism: both Epicurean and the Stoic philosophers value friendship but, as we all know, like charity,[48] when the going gets rough, the first thing to vanish are those so-called friends.[49] Petrarch, the father of modern individualism, discovered the ephemerality of the friend society: "in 1384 the Black Death arrived and 'all these friends ... in no time at all were destroyed in almost one stroke'" (Gillespie 2008: 46).

Friendship is free and good but also not identical with a dedicated, permanent moral community of shared values, destiny, and discourse—although, friendship and the common cause may combine. In the case of Calvin, friendship was highly valued as a source of stability otherwise lacking in his life but it was predicated on a "commitment to a common cause" and, as such, was somewhat volatile because Calvin believed that he had no intellectual equal and was often "fierce and intemperate" toward his friends; when contrite, he also failed to admit fault (Gordon 2009: 29–30). Even when egoism works itself up beyond a gaggle of friends to the level of an organization, being a member of the little group does not absolve it of its characteristic egoism (Hocking 1926: 259–60). Individual or small group egoism still leans in the direction of solitude, isolation, and loneliness—all pathological conditions. America is famous for being the land of the lonely crowd. "You have to live with others.... To live alone, you must be either very like God or a complete animal. But I would modify the aphorism and say: better sane with the majority than mad all alone" (Gracián [1647] 2015: 26). In America, however, we are alone together and, to modify the above, mad with the majority. America has also refined the various forms of being alone as few people have.

Isolation and loneliness constitute related but separate problems (see Arendt 1968: 474–78). "The most broadly accepted definition of loneliness is the distress people feel when reality fails to meet their ideal of social relationships.

---

48 For an historical peek at the crimes, self-serving cynicism, and failures of private charities in times of crisis, see Katz (1986: 58–84). A recent, high-profile failure is provided by the Red Cross intervention in Haiti where, after raising $500 million, managed to build only a half dozen houses (Elliott and Sullivan 2015). The systemic failure of Red Cross in dealing with floods in Mississippi and Louisiana (Kravitz 2016; S. Smith 2016) should dispel any notion that relief organizations driven wholly or in part by charitable donations, especially when it comes to natural disasters and climate-related events, represent rational and comprehensive solutions to regional and national crises. 'Altruistic' do-gooders and charities are not solutions to the ills and contradictions of capitalized association but merely make things worse (cf. Wilde [1891] 2003: 1174).

49 "'You will suffer in your friend's suffering,' says Epictetus. 'Of course you will suffer. I do not say that you must not even groan aloud. Yet in the centre of your being do not groan!'.... It is very like the Christian doctrine of resignation" (Murray 1915: 47).

Loneliness is not synonymous with being alone. Many people live solitary lives but are not lonely. Conversely, being surrounded by others is not a bulwark against loneliness. Loneliness is also not the same as depression, though the two often go hand in hand. The first, related to the drive to belong, is motivational. The other, a more general feeling of sadness or hopelessness, is not" (Nutt 2016).

Solitude means being alone.[50] We all need to be alone from time to time but the prolongation of solitude can be deadly. "The brilliant Costaguanero of the boulevards had died from solitude and want of faith in himself and others" (Conrad [1904] 1961: 331). So injurious is solitude as a means of producing loneliness that it is used as punishment.[51] We might say that the effect of isolation, pushed to its limit, becomes identical with fatalistic imprisonment.[52] "And thus far it was a life: in the void.... [they] went for walks in the park, and in the woods that joined the park, and enjoyed the solitude and the mystery, kicking the brown leaves of autumn, and picking the primroses of spring. But it was all a dream; or rather it was like the simulacrum of reality" (Lawrence 2001: 18). Deadlier than the prolongation of solitude are the more pathological forms of isolation and loneliness. Chronic loneliness is terrifying for humans and creates feelings of helplessness that have devastating effects on the brains and the minds of individuals (Cacioppo 2008: 51). Loneliness is also a growing and "serious public health hazard. Scientists who have identified significant links between loneliness and illness are pursuing the precise biological mechanisms that make it such a menace, digging down to the molecular level and finding that social isolation changes the human genome in profound, long-lasting ways" (Nutt 2016). The consequences of loneliness on health and vitality are comparable to smoking tobacco, obesity, and diabetes. "Today, social isolation is often an unavoidable lifestyle. But it puts the body, on the cellular level, on constant alert for a threat. That helps explain why lonely people are more likely to act negatively toward others, which makes it that much harder for them to forge relationships" (Ibid.).

---

50   For Halbwachs, the sickness of the 20th Century was solitude, "the sole cause of suicide" (Jankélévitch 2012: 40).
51   "'You have forfeited your right to a place among us. Creatures who are the slaves of passion, are, like beasts of prey, fit only for solitude'" (Catharine Maria Sedgwick, in Gay 1993: 494).
52   "My mother died last Tuesday. She had been suffering from a mysterious illness, and that morning she quietly slipped away. There was a simple funeral, and now I am totally alone. No mother. No pet starling. No sheep man. Nor girl. I lie here by myself in the dark at two o'clock in the morning and think about that cell in the library basement. About how it feels to be alone, and the depth of the darkness surrounding me. Darkness as pitch black as the night of the new moon" (Murakami 2014: 26).

Pushed to its extreme, capitalist social disorganization reduces individuals subjected to market forces to mere dots (G: 485) or, as Durkheim puts it, a flow of "liquid molecules" tumbling over one another due to a lack of a "central energy to retain, fix and organize them" (S: 389; cf. FMW: 310).[53] The 'connective tissue' between people breaks down and a negative freedom is achieved. As Royce says in his lectures on Hegel, "'My freedom from others is my doom, the most insufferable form of bondage'" (in Kaag 2016: 168).[54] Egoistic isolation is not good for people and leaves them susceptible to antisocial currents. "Solitude [taken to extremes] would ripen a plentiful crop of despots" (Emerson 1950: 442).

Setting aside for the moment the indissoluble relation between thinking and action (Vygotsky 1978: 23–6), solitude is a *necessary* phase of withdrawal from others, the retreat into reflection. As Durkheim says, we cannot think unless we stop acting and, separating ourselves from others momentarily, and engage in reflective contemplation, a point amplified by Arendt: "All thinking, strictly speaking, is done in solitude and is a dialogue between me and myself; but this dialogue of the two-in-one does not lose contact with the world of my fellow-men because they are represented in the self with whom I lead the dialogue of thought" (1968: 476).[55] One may object at this point that Durkheim and Arendt are in error here, a theory that appears to keep thought and action separate is futile or pathological, but this is not relevant and even misleading. One need only consult an improvisational or creative genius to know about the suspension of conscious thought. Virtuoso improvisers will agree that when it comes to practice and preparation, one thinks *intensely*, but during performance thought and reflection will destroy spontaneity and artistic expression. This point is fortified by Jaynes who observes that artistic performance is essentially unconscious—to become conscious of performance leads to sudden failure (1990: 26). Even in routine acts, for example, consciousness can be detrimental to health, e.g., one should not think about the act of walking down a

---

53 We are a long way from Enlightenment liberalism and the *republica noumenon* (Mills 1998: 133).

54 "*What kind of society is it, indeed, where one finds the profoundest solitude in the midst of millions; where one can be overwhelmed by an irrepressible desire to kill oneself without anybody being aware of it? This society is no society, it is as Rousseau says, a desert inhabited by wild animals*" (Puchet, in MECW, 4: 604).

55 "The real is what Marx called 'material productivity,' economic man as a producer of wealth. But the thinking and reasoning man is powerless to create; he can only understand or reflect the results, once they are given, of his material activity. By definition, the ideal is the reflection ... of the real" (Halevy 1965: 288).

flight of stairs while one *is* walking down a flight of stairs. I have also observed that while giving an address or speech to a professional audience or a lecture to students it is usually best to allow The Thing to do most of the talking while the conscious 'I' gets out of the way.[56]

Reflective thinking is essentially an egotistical moment whereas action is altruistic. Freeman illustrates the divide well:

> When I wrote economic or political articles, when I tried my hand at Marxist literary criticism, when my *mind* got busy, I was a communist. When I wrote poems and stories, when my emotions went into action, all the old feelings cropped up; the vanished village, the Brooklyn ghetto, the campus, the Renaissance, idealistic philosophy and romantic art crept out of their holes and spoke in my name. Fusion of intellect, emotion, and will around the communist idea hand not yet been achieved (1936: 657).

Solitude is necessary for life because reflective reason depends upon it.[57] However, when solitude and reflections become virtues unto themselves and the ego refuses to emerge from itself it swerves off into the despotic, or a thousand other directions, some of which we will explore further in the next volume.

Egoism is a symptom or effect of a breakdown of authority and social organization that, itself, engenders more collective disintegration (cf. Freud [1921] 1959: 95).[58] It is not just in the domain of religion that in all times and places "there exits groups of representations which allow or even invite incoherence, both because they are naturally fluid and are applied only to the invisible part of existence, and because they mix readily with foreign representations, which are themselves unstable" (Dumézil 1970: 356). The *symptoms* of disintegration become *causes* of further disorganization—here the desire to go it alone, antinomianism, the spirit of free inquiry (AJ: 206), or whatever it is, starts to "battle in its own name," acquiring a prestige and an example of anti-sociality for

---

56 I frequently have thoughts that only occur to me while talking to an audience and I often wonder where these things come from. As Jaynes says, "in speaking or writing we are not really conscious of what we are actually doing at the time. Consciousness functions in the decision as to what to say, how we are to say it, and when we can say it, but then the orderly and accomplished succession of phonemes or of written letters is somehow done for us" (1990: 27).
57 "Creative reflection is the lover of silence and solitude" (Bouglé [1926] 1970: 149).
58 Read Kant on the breakthrough of free thinking and its wayward course toward self-destruction (1998: 12–14).

others to follow (Schiller 1967: 27).[59] And 'intellectuality' itself may be considered nearly synonymous with 'infinity disease' though not identical. The former effect, antinomian independence, becomes now also a cause or function.[60] The solution to the plague of egoism is not a curtailment of education but more education—push the function to the extreme such that the ailment becomes its own medicine. "Once the social instinct is blunted, intelligence is the only guide left us and we have to reconstruct a conscience by its means" (S: 169). Contra Descartes, we cannot build a new reality ourselves but only in concert with others.

Thoreau is perplexed why anyone would seek congregation with people over nature and the friendship of the pine needle ([1854] 1960: 92–3). Even the relational vacuum would be preferable to being with others: "I love to be alone. I never found the companion that was so companionable as solitude." Society is "cheap" and people are "musty cheese" ([1854] 1960: 95). Musty cheese is an unpleasant companion but even that is preferable to the lack of the social mirror that isolation entails. Chateaubriand would certainly not approve:

> What do you do deep in the forests where you pass your solitary days neglecting your duties? … Presumptuous young man who thought that man can be self-sufficient! Solitude is bad for someone who does not

---

[59] "There is no denying that 'egoism' did in fact play a big part in the growth of bourgeois ideology; in this sense, then, it was not wholly inappropriate to relate the critique of the bourgeois class to this question. But it must be remembered that for the first great champions of this ideology (Hobbes, Mandeville, Bayle, et al.) the struggle to establish the new morality was a very real one. Not only was there a close connection between the war on feudal morality (and that of the Puritans when the bourgeois class was just emerging) and the elaboration of the theoretical cornerstone of the whole bourgeois ideology, classical economics, but this ideology also provided very important weapons for the bourgeoisie's actual class struggle" (Lukács 1926). Protestant subjectivism champions 'free inquiry' to a degree that is alien to medieval Catholicism but make no mistake the "fanatics among the Protestants are by no means friends of liberty and free inquiry" (Carus [1900] 1996: 449). New England Calvinism (updated oriental despotism) brutally repressed free inquiry (Parrington 1927: 15; cf. Amin 2004: 62). With respect to 'free inquiry' both Durkheim and Weber see it as a development arising out of social disintegration, estrangement (AJ: 206), and "the capacity to be astonished about the course of events" (AJ: 207).

[60] Wundt used the term "heterogony" to capture the dynamic relationship whereby "means are transformed into ends, but one sees the same means serve several ends successively" (Bouglé [1926] 1970: 80). In RSM "Durkheim claims that in seeking to understand the functions of a social fact, sociology complements causal explanation, given that 'cause' and 'effect' are related through reciprocity (*réciprocité*), which Durkheim formulates as 'energy' (*énergie*)" (Gangas 2007: 324). See also Marx (C: 949) on how the commodity is both a precondition and result of the capitalist mode of production. Somehow it got into the heads of some Marxists that capitalism invented the commodity.

share it with God; it redoubles the soul's powers while depriving them of any subject on which they can be exercises.

in JANKÉLÉVITCH 2012: 41

The lack of a social mirror sets the person on a quest for doubling, duplication, replication, and myriad inhuman substitutions. With Thoreau, we find nature serving as mystical compensation for the loss of society and the projection of "society" into nature: "Yet I experienced sometimes that the most sweet and tender, the most innocent and encouraging society may be found in any natural object, even for the poor misanthrope and most melancholy man" ([1854] 1960: 92). Durkheim's polarity of egoism and altruism (1961: 215) is interesting given that the egoist suffers precisely from their estrangement from collective life while being simultaneously free from possession by any 'transcendent' other providing regulatory commands—if we examine the rich literature of aristocratic egoism, we find the lack of the other as a source of torment.[61] The self can become such a burden that it has to be alienated and gifted to an other who can put it under control and restrain its over-nourishment.[62] In other cases, the lone ego is not free of the other but the exact opposite, the tool or servant of the other for the benefit of the group that is helplessly sunk in corruption—e.g., the hardboiled detective (see Bellah et al. 1985: 146). It is little wonder, then, why Engels could imagine a thorough-going egoism leading to communism (MECW, 38: 11). The status of the ego's social mirror, the other, is worth considering further.

Fichte's solution to the unsatisfying theory of freedom laid out by Kant hinged on the idea of self-determination where "self-determination means that the self acts according to its own concept of itself, that it becomes only what it conceives itself to be, so that its essence or nature conforms entirely to its own rational choice" (Beiser 2002: 277). The doubling of the self is essential

---

61 See Kaag (2017) on Thoreau's desire to be possessed by nature. As we will see, possession 'belongs' to altruism but the estranged egoist can long for possession and search for it. Interestingly, with Thoreau, the search does not lead to other people and not to inanimate things either but to nature (the fetishization of the profane). "No one lives in the woods. Animals only go there to hide.... Man cannot live there.... Life in the woods is a fiction; the man of the woods is a fugitive" (Alain [1934] 1974: 73).

62 "An elder was one who took your soul, your will, into his soul and his will. When you choose an elder, you renounce your own will and yield it to him in complete submission, complete self-abnegation. This novitiate, this terrible school of abnegation, is undertaken voluntarily, in the hope of self-conquest, of self-mastery, in order, after a life of obedience, to attain perfect freedom, that is, from self; to escape the lot of those who have lived their whole life without finding their true selves in themselves" (Dostoyevsky 1912: 27).

for the self's ability to have itself as an object, but it also sets up the paradox of disunity and the unfreedom and alienation of self. The commodity world has transformed the self and its other into a problem. "In a certain sense, a man is in the same situation as a commodity. As he neither enters into the world in possession of a mirror, nor as a Fichtean philosopher who can say 'I am I' ..." (C: 144). Once mirror relations progress beyond the accidental dyadic moment the logic of recognition and universality become inverted and fetishized. "The entire dialectic which I have given ... the name of the *mirror stage* is based on the relation between, on the one hand, a certain point in life—as disconnected, discordant, in pieces—and there's always something of that that remains—and on the other hand, a unity with which it is merged and paired. It is this unity that the subject for the first time knows himself as a unity, but as an alienated, virtual unity" (Lacan 1988: 50). With Durkheim, though, we must situate alienated unity within the context of larger social life processes in which dyads multiply. In a striking passage, Buber relies on the Peter-Paul dyad to suggest then when these two meet there is not simply an I and Thou but a 2 + 6 formation where the two "living beings" are accompanied by "six ghostly appearances" (1965: 77). If society is a "whole lacking unity" (DOL: 304) then it will produce selves that remain incapable of attaining full integration and persist at best as ghostly remainders that haunt the living. Anomic social disorganization is the master architect of the disintegrated psyche and this disintegration is reflected in critique.

This core feature of social life, reflective doubling and duality, extends back to our earliest written documents, myths, and oral traditions. In Genesis, being a 'god' meant not merely knowledge of good and evil, i.e., participation in the domain of the sacred, but the capacity for individual judgment, personal decision-making, and accountability.

> The woman said to the serpent, 'We may eat fruit from the trees in the garden, but God did say, "You must not eat fruit from the tree that is in the middle of the garden, and you must not touch it, or you will die."'
>
> 'You will not surely die,' the serpent said to the woman. 'For God knows that when you eat of it your eyes will be opened, and you will be like God, knowing good and evil.'
>
> When the woman saw that the fruit of the tree was good for food and pleasing to the eye, and also desirable for gaining wisdom, she took some and ate it. She also gave some to her husband, who was with her, and he ate it. Then the eyes of both of them were opened, and they realized they were naked; so they sewed fig leaves together and made coverings for themselves (3: 2–6).

Much of what sociology revolves around is here in these few passages from the Hebrew bible: authority and disobedience, the possibility of freedom, alienation, self-consciousness, identity and identification, and, of course, for those that read further, punishment, pain, and a life of ceaseless toil and exploitation. The actual development of human self-reflexivity is due to a long and complicated process of biological evolution and dramatic changes in social organization, occurring thousands of years before even our most ancient documents begin to record the doings of people. The mythological representation of this transition is interesting, and every culture or civilizational complex has concerned itself with this rupture of self-consciousness. For the ancient Greeks, e.g., "The god Kronos first ruled over the lives of men, and his rule signified a Golden Age during which men lived in immediate unity among themselves and with nature."

> But Kronos was the god of time, and time devoured its own children. Everything that man had accomplished was destroyed; nothing remained. Then, Kronos himself was devoured by Zeus, a power greater than time. Zeus was the god who brought forth reason and promoted the arts; he was the 'political god' who created the state and made it the world of self-conscious and moral individuals.
>
> MARCUSE 1941: 239–40

Note the halo of nostalgia on the reign of Kronos: the period before self-consciousness was conceived of as a "Golden Age."[63] The transition forward was, in essence, a tumble or an open wound contaminated with guilt and a 'perversion' of nature (literally, a 'wrong turn'). Anaximander, among the first of the ancient Greek philosophers, equated being with virtual crime where "the secular process of birth and perishing is described in *moral* language. The passing away of things into the elements is called 'making reparation,' 'paying the penalty of injustice.' The words imply that injustice was committed in the very fact of their birth into separate existence. The manifold world, in Anaximander's view, can arise only by robbery and misappropriation.... Birth is a crime, and growth an aggravated robbery" (Cornford [1912] 2004: 10).[64] We find sin of origins carried over in Judeo-Christian myth as well where the

---

63 "Nostalgia is suicidal" (Lilla 2017: 23)
64 "All the Elements are our Enemies" (Mandeville [1732] 1924, 1: 344). Cornford says that for Anaximander, "the general scheme of the growth of the world is this: the one primary stuff, called 'Nature,' [*physis*] is segregated into provinces, each the domain of one element [earth, air, water, and fire]. And this is a *moral* order, in the sense that transgression of its boundaries, the plundering of one element by another to make an individual thing,

development of human faculties, the dramatic 'leap' forward, was really a descent into sin. The result of eating from the 'tree of life' ('The Fall') was that humans made a transition *not* from simple animalism to human being but from the point where human beings graduated from knowing themselves as some inhuman other (the mythological point of departure for the Old Testament is the point where humans see themselves *as* human from a moral point of view).[65] This breach in the mindless flow of nature, material organisms moving around in the real, has been represented in morbid and even violent terms:

> The young Hegel proposed as a possible definition of man a formula that today in the midst of the ecological crisis, acquires a new dimension: 'nature sick unto death.' All attempts to regain a new balance between man and nature, to eliminate from human activity its excessive character and to include it in the regular circuit of life, are nothing but a series of subsequent endeavors to suture an original and irredeemable gap. It is in this sense that the classic Freudian thesis on the ultimate discord between reality and the drive potential of man is to be conceived. Freud's claim is that this original, constitutive discord cannot be accounted for by biology, that it results from the fact that the 'drive potential of man' consists of drives that are already radically denaturalized, derailed by their traumatic attachment to a Thing, to an empty place that excludes man forever from the circular movement of life and thus opens the immanent possibility of radical catastrophe, the 'second death'.
>
> ŽIŽEK 1991: 37

---

is injustice, unrighteousness. The penalty is death and dissolution. No single thing can begin to exist without an infraction of this destined order" ([1912] 2004: 10).

65 "This is the hallmark of the sublime and absolute destiny of man—that he knows what good and evil are, and that it is his will which chooses either the one or the other. In short, he can be held responsible, for good as well as for evil, and not just for this or that particular circumstance and for everything around him and within in, but also for the good and evil which are inherent in his individual freedom. Only the animal can truly be described as totally innocent" (Hegel 1975: 90–1). Hegel makes a brilliant point: we are far from wholly responsible for the state of our society let alone even what is in our thoughts and feelings (reflect on how many thoughts we have that we have no idea how we arrived at them, where they came from, and how many thoughts we wish would simply go away—I once overheard a person say "I don't even *want* to know half the things I know"). Ethical conduct is made possible because we are not simple animals but must choose how to act and every choice burdens us with unintended consequences and responsibilities. In short, Hegel is saying that the difference between the 'World Historical Individual' and the 'everyday' person who acts ethically is only quantitative, not qualitative. I think we can see an echo of Heraclitus here: gods are immortal men whereas men are mortal gods ([1892] 1995, Chapter 5).

This becoming and having life (as contrasted with simply 'being' life in the case of simple animals)[66] revolves around the ability to take oneself as other[67] and to seek out the self in the form of other human beings. Milton has given us an insightful glimpse into what we would today call the 'mirror stage'[68] of mental development:

> I [Eve] first awaked, and found myself reposed
> Under a shade of flow'rs, much wond'ring where
> And what I was, whence thither brought, and how.
> Not distant far from thence a murmuring sound
> Of waters issued from a cave and spread
> Into a liquid plain, then stood unmoved
> Pure as th' expanse of heav'n; I thither went
> With unexperienced thought, and laid me down
> On the green bank, to look into the clear
> Smooth lake, that to me seemed another sky.
> As I bent down to look, just opposite,
> A shape within the wat'ry gleam appeared
> Bending to look on me: I started back,
> It started back, but pleased I soon returned,
> Pleased it returned as soon with answering looks
> Of sympathy and love; there I had fixed
> Mine eyes till now, and pined with vain desire,
> Had not a voice thus warned me, What thou seest,
> What there thou seest fair creature is thyself, ([1667] 2000: 85–6).

Prior to catching a glimpse of herself in the pool (cf. Michener 1965: 88) Eve's capacity to imagine herself was limited to the functions of the cerebral cortex, namely, its production of sensory 'homunculi' maps of grotesque proportions (mostly lips and hands). Seeing her reflection in the pool is a dramatic alteration of her self-image. Yet, her image is fragmented, limited to her face (she cannot see her whole body). Since Eve can never imagine herself as a totality by falling back upon her own sensory capacities, to 'know' herself wholly she must find herself in the body of another person and in this myth her 'other' is

---

66 We occupy, says Augustine, a middle point between immortal and rational angels, on one hand, and the mortal and irrational animals on the other—we are mortal but also rational (1972: 359).
67 To "take oneself as other" does not quite go far enough, actually. The Ego or 'I' *is* other—there is no self or ego apart from or apart from others (Lacan 2002: 24).
68 The connection between Milton and the Lacanian theory of the 'mirror stage' has not gone unnoticed (Kerrigan 1983; Champagne 1991; Mintz 2003).

Adam. Of course, Eve's relation with Adam is her relationship with herself in her external, transfigured form. She finds not only her consciousness in the form of the other but her existence as a human being in the form of another human being.

> Than that smooth wat'ry image; back I turned,
> Thou following cried'st aloud, Return, fair Eve;
> Whom fli'st thou? Whom thou fli'st, of him thou art,
> His flesh, his bone; to give thee being I lent
> Out of my side to thee, nearest my heart
> Substantial life, to have thee by my side
> Henceforth an individual solace dear;
> Part of my soul I seek thee, and thee claim
> My other half: with that thy gentle hand
> Seized mine, I yielded, and from that time see
> How beauty is excelled by manly grace
> And wisdom, which alone is truly fair.
>
> MILTON [1667] 2000: 85–6

The Lacanian theory of the "mirror stage" of psychic development goes some way in comprehending the dialectical process of identification central to any social psychology amenable to the tradition of classical sociology. Lacan holds that humans are born incomplete or premature. Compared to instinct-driven animals like chimpanzees, humans do not have it all together, so to speak. With chimps, god only knows what's going on behind those brooding faces (Park 1950: 238). Nevertheless, unlike the chimpanzee, the infant human is capable of recognizing the image of their self in a mirror—we see, above, how Eve is captivated by their reflection.[69]

As terrible as egoism is, it has benefits. For example, humanitarianism belongs not to the side of altruism but egoism.[70] The egoist does not tolerate the

---

69 Even though she is biologically mature Milton plays out the genesis of the mind from 'infancy' and, importantly, Eve does not leap forward from a state of animality, but is 'created' with a human brain.

70 "For the first time in my life a feeling of overpowering stinging melancholy seized me. Before, I had never experienced aught but a not-unpleasing sadness. The bond of a common humanity now drew me irresistibly to gloom. A fraternal melancholy!" (Melville [1856] 2009: 20). Of course, humanitarianism is often partial or a mere rationalization. Many egoists take as their motto: I love humanity, it's the goddamned people I can't stand! "It is easy to work for some 'ism' that we hope will blossom out in some far-off time, but it is hard to get on with one's neighbor" (Wesep 1920: 74).

degradation of selves well or, if nothing else, the egoist is "too busy taking care of his own good to have time to cause misfortune to others" (Žižek 2008b: 92). The humanitarianism of the egoist applies especially to sceptical subjectivists (e.g., the Sophists) who obliterated the distinction between human and savage and who inspired Cicero to coin the term *humanitas* (Koepping 1983: 84). The altruist places no value on selves (theirs or others) whereas the self is for the egoist a spark of the divine, a sacred thing, a status projectable onto others (S: 360). In short, the pathology of egoism is a signal that real individuality has gone astray because the social order has allowed the individual to escape through punishment or disintegration. Egoists may fall into resignation, as we will see, but genuine reconciliation is impossible.

Taking the ego to be the highest authority, the individual (the undividable) loses contact with the universal social dimension (collective consciousness is diminished) and withers on the vine or runs into the arms of a theology or some dogma that promises eternal life or certainties. Both Hegel and Durkheim agree that, for the person properly installed within the social and symbolic order, problems of eternity and narcissistic entrapment, etc., are negated.

> It could never or hardly ever have struck him [the Greek and Roman] to ask or beg for persistence or eternal life for his own individuality. Only in moments of inactivity or lethargy could he feel the growing strength of a purely self-regarding wish. Cato turned to Plato's *Phaedo* only when his world, his republic, hitherto the highest order of things in his eyes, had been destroyed; at that point only did he take flight to a higher order still.
>
> HEGEL 1948: 154–55; see HARDIMON 1994: 33

This position was amplified by Durkheim when he said it is "untrue that life is only possible by its possessing its rationale outside of itself" (S: 211). Immortality is irrelevant to the person who clings to society (S: 212). Where the egoist is unreconciled to the world, the altruist is unreconciled with their self.

2 Altruism

On the surface of it altruism seems like a social good. After all, Durkheim frequently recommends a dose of altruistic self-renunciation as a cure for egoism but while 'altruism' in the modern sense may be nothing more than a sympathy towards others or ego-gratifications by way of charity, etc., the artificial purity of premodern altruism is more theoretically useful; where egoism is the domain of self-absorption, altruism is the sphere of the absorbed self and "a living death" (Hegel 1956: 221). Fustel de Coulanges draws out perfectly the altruism of the ancient Greeks in their relation to the city and cult.[71] It would be a mistake to see the ancients as lacking a private sphere but duty and obligations to the city were "absolute."[72]

> The city had been founded upon a religion, and constituted like a church. Hence its strength; hence, also, its omnipotence and the absolute empire which it exercised over its members. In a society established on such principles, individual liberty could not exist. The citizen was subordinate in everything, and without any reserve, to the city; he belonged to it body and soul ([1873] 1956: 219–20).

Altruism, in its pure form, where it is raised to the level of the *acute* form, is pure otherness; the self is either absent or reduced to pure heteron, a total eclipse by some larger social organ. Here we encounter the "multitude actuated by a common impulse" (Gilman [1915] 1998: 36). The acute altruist seems to be the one with the least personal development but, perhaps, we find in it that not only is there some individuation but that the emerging ego is experienced as an unbearably alien or hostile 'thing' to be abolished. The narcissist, the fanatic or martyr's speculative double, definitely has a problem with the ego (it is inflated and overvalued constantly in search of external supports) whereas the coordinates where we least expect to find individuation (the acute moment in altruistic life) may in fact be one of relatively inflated ego and the desire not to strengthen it and cultivate it further but to destroy it and anything that would even recognize it's right to existence. The boundaries between narcissism and the fanatic, sectarian, and martyr are fuzzy and imprecise. But they have a common unity in 'thingification.' Ultimately, the ego will become a thing disposed of for something other than itself—the martyr aims at mass and number (Auden 2008: 248).

Capitalism may seem like a garden of hedonistic opportunism but, for the bottom rungs populated by the working poor, it is a world of heteronomous subjugation and forced altruism. As Wilde says, "The majority of people spoil their lives by an unhealthy and exaggerated altruism—are forced, indeed, so to

---

71 Recall, however, that egoism alloyed with altruism would result in something different than either of the two currents.
72 "The ideal for the Greek artist and citizen was not the formation of individual character or personality but assimilation to an ideal model" (Gillispie 2008: 31).

spoil them" ([1891] 2003: 1174). The hallmark of altruism is the devaluation of self and the parallel devaluation of the other, or, the trans-valuation of the other into an impurity requiring annihilation. In the case of simple devaluation (the other as a cardboard cutout) Mead would say that, here, there is no projection of a self into the other qua blank screen but a co-emergence of objective selves in conjuring the other's attitude in a conversation of gestures ([1932] 1977). But the problem is that, ideal-typically anyways, the entire social field is populated by a homogeneity of action, thought, and emotions; self is reduced to the that status of an automaton or one of Le Bon's zombies (see Freud [1921] 1959: 10–1). Political and religious fanatics[73] come close to the pure form (S: 212; Voltaire 1962: 267–69).[74]

Fanatics are "filled with enthusiasm" and "once and for all" dogmatists with the holy truth[75] on their side.[76] "They are the janissaries of the absolute, which they reduce to the narrow dimensions of their own good conscience and perceive as their private property.... Spinoza summed them up admirably when he said, 'They fight for their servitude as if it were their salvation'" (Comte Sponville 2007: 25). A temporary convert to Isis reported that when she had become totally radicalized by her new associates in Brussels (a group of disaffected teens) she "was not thinking my thoughts. I was not who I am" (in Burke 2015). Taken to the extreme, we would say the pure altruist is "inhuman." The Kantian

> indefinite judgement opens up a third domain that undermines the distinction between dead and non-dead (alive): the 'undead' are neither alive nor dead, they are precisely the monstrous 'living dead.' And the same goes for 'inhuman': 'he is not human' is not the same as 'he is inhuman.' 'He is not human' means simply that he is external to humanity, animal or divine, while 'he is inhuman' means something thoroughly different, namely the fact that he is neither human nor inhuman, but marked

---

73 "The greatest fanatic is the greatest doubter. Without knowing it" (Tranströmer 2006: 196).
74 In my little book on terror (Worrell 2013) I make the case that the terrorist blends all three subtypes of altruism with other currents in a unique manner. Voltaire's comments on fanaticism are rewarding because he rightly connects fanaticism to ecstasy and enthusiasm as well as points in the direction divine inspiration being elevated above all laws and connecting fanaticism to mania. In our own terminology, we would unify anarchy (extreme anomie) and acute altruism in the concept of 'sociological heterarchy.'
75 The enthusiastic truth is, of course, not one generated by individual thought (Kant 1998: 6) but the desire of the absolute working through singular vessels.
76 "Fanaticism is mistaking one's faith for knowledge or attempting to impose it through force. The two almost invariably go hand in hand: Dogmatism and terrorism are mutually reinforcing" (Comte-Sponville 2007: 132).

> by a terrifying excess which, although it negates what we understand as humanity, is inherent to being human.
>
> ŽIŽEK 2006a: 47[77]

Let us refer back to the end of the sociogony chapter in volume one where we encountered zombies and the living dead. The theoretically pure, ideal-typical case of the inhuman zombie, the hypnotized tool we find in Le Bon, is not found in reality. The key to the 'zombie' is not that the mind is totally enslaved to the other or its envoy, rather, it is the reduction of life to external necessity.[78] In zombie stories the monsters are neither living nor dead, but merely material manifestations of pure drive. The living dead are actually the pursued survivors who are caught between life and death,[79] reduced by external necessity to suspend everything not directly related to the maintenance of bare minimal existence. I am not certain how monsters are distributed throughout the disintegrating social field, though I have some ideas:

> Egoism: transformation of the individual into a monster; regression to some hybrid of human and animal (*The Fly*, *Metamorphosis*, etc.); autistic monsters, estranged, seeking avoidance. Our bungling, anomic misadventures turn us into these monsters or lead to inadvertent contact with monsters that want to have no contact with us:
>
> Anomie: making the double; Frankenstein's creature (regressive) or Dorian's image (progressive); schizoid monsters;
>
> Infinity disease (egoism + anomie): alternation (*Dr. Jekyll and Mr. Hyde*, etc.); bipolar monsters;[80]

---

[77] It could be argued that the basic underpinning of the Christian life is that of being simultaneously alive and dead. In Paul we see "'I have been crucified with Christ; it is no longer I who live, but Christ who lives in me.' In other words, the life Paul lives is already a kind of postmortem existence" (Droge and Tabor 1992: 120).

[78] Ancient Chinese rituals of devotion, where the self is pledged wholly to an other, "'one gives oneself *entirely*: henceforth one would be incapable of serving a second master.... To reveal a double (soul) ... is a crime'" (Granet 1951: 227).

[79] In the aftermath of the American Civil War "The machines won; and the war kept on. Its casualties were not always buried at Antietam or Gettysburg; they moldered, too, in libraries, studies, offices. The justifiable ante-bellum optimism of Emerson turned into a waxen smile. Whitman lost his full powers in what should have been his prime. Among the young men, many a corpse was left, to go through the routine of living" (Mumford 1973: 50).

[80] In the *Strange Case of Dr. Jekyll and Mr. Hyde* Robert Louis Stevenson provides a remarkable portrayal of human duality and the 'identity' of the sacred pure and the sacred impure, good and evil ([1886] 1992: 61–71). Many important specifications are provided for in his classic short: the human being is double; the two parts (twins) are bound together in

Fatalism: zombies; mindless shells driven by necessity; pure drive without desire or consciousness;

Revenge monsters; irradiated, giant, fire-breathing lizard (the return of the Real);

Warning monsters; ghosts and evil spirits of various types; guilt projections.

The primary type of altruism that all other forms are based on, obligatory altruistic suicide, is a negative stance in that the death is sought in order to avoid the stigma of existence (S: 222; e.g., Augustine 1976: 30). Cioran makes the case for obligatory suicide:

> The age-old conspiracy against suicide is responsible for the congestion and the sclerosis of societies. We must learn to destroy ourselves *at the right moment*, to run joyously toward our ghost. So long as we do not determine to do so, we deserve our humiliations. When a man has exhausted his raison d'être, it is odious to persist.... To last is to lessen: existence is loss of being. Since no one dies when he should, we ought to call to order anyone who survives himself, encourage and if need be assist him to abbreviate his days (1974: 52–3).

As Nietzsche says in *Twilight of the Idols*, "Man is finished when he becomes altruistic" (1982: 536). The *devaluation* of the individual, he says, is poisonous and contagious. We find a link here to anomie (negative or regressive) whereby real or perceived loss in conjunction with the disconnection with the Other (including loss or devaluation of symbolic status) contributes to an energetic self-eradication. Let us return to Montana and note that the once unquestioned social supremacy of the white male has in recently become less secure (McGreal 2016).

Unlike the negativity of obligatory altruism, the positive, obligatory form of self-destruction seeks not the avoidance of something but gain or conversion:

---

the same physical envelope (the body); the good or pure self is essentially self-denying and the impure or evil self is an excess or leftover, selfish and so on; and there exists an unending conflict between these polar oppositions that leads, ultimately, to self-destruction. The person cannot, apparently, live as a singularity. It is, admittedly, a stretch but I also find it interesting that the potion used to transform the person is described as an "ebullition"—as if Stevenson knew, and expressed it metaphorically in the form of a 'potion,' that it takes an energetic reaction, the boiling and smoking so to speak, to divide and change the person.

Court-martialed for an illicit liaison he was conducting with a married woman in Calais, where his regiment was stationed, Baron Philippou, colonel of the Legion of the Somme, shot himself rather than face the punishment his behavior merited. Before doing so, he wrote a note in which he pardoned his rival, whom he had earlier challenged to a duel, and described the act he was about to commit as motivated by his sense of honor: 'Victim this day of the cruelest injustice, at least I have courage enough to exercise the only option that still remains, that of ending my days, my heart beating in joy to have finished my career in an honorable fashion ...' Philippou undertook to sacrifice himself rather than engage in a duel because he could not, in good conscience, 'deprive a young woman of her husband and a child of his father,' he wrote. His decision shows evidence of cunning as well, for in the sentimental realm in which he would ultimately be judged, the coolly calculated suicide of honor counted more than the duel, which was of passionate inspiration. And in fact, though Philippou's fellow officers had roundly condemned his immoral liaison, he received a military funeral.... Romantic formulas were adopted, with great success, to lend nobility to the act of suicide ....
LIEBERMAN 2003: 108–09

Pushed to the extreme, altruism, at its "highest pitch" becomes *acute* and is the door through which one passes to its polar opposite, egoism in its infantile narcissist form. As we saw, Durkheim characterizes egoism as the "infinity of dreams" (S: 287) but this 'dream state' is just one side of the infinity problem inseparable from the "infinity of desires" linked to deregulation.

3   Anomie

According to Delta airlines "It's okay to want it all." Luckily, for those that fear limitlessness Delta delivers only a fraction of the promised totality.[81] Genesis automobiles informs us that "There are two things we don't believe in: limits and limits." Perhaps the Korean manufacturer of horseless carriages will soon enter the market for suicide machines. Lexus has named its LF-1

---

81   "Harry told me about a certain philanthropist who spent twenty years of his life in trying to get some grievance redressed, or some unjust law altered—I forget exactly what it was. Finally he succeeded, and nothing could exceed his disappointment. He had absolutely nothing to do, almost died of *ennui*, and became a confirmed misanthrope" (Wilde [1890] 1995: 129).

concept car the "Limitless" and this is "because the future will always be human." However, the future of humanity is in doubt precisely because of our mania for the infinite.[82] We are powerless against the infinite to the extent to which we reject mediating restraints. In syllogistic or dialectical terms, we only care for fluid and abstract middle terms lacking the power to pin us to the universal. But, really, we prefer no middle terms at all unless they are magical and filled with the wonderful.

As undergraduates we learned that anomie is synonymous with "normlessness" (e.g., Merton 1957: 161)[83] but, thankfully, that misnomer has started to come undone in recent years.[84] In its simplest terms, anomie refers to a process or condition of "deregulation" (S: 253) or an absence of regulation (DOL: 304) that produces anarchy or lawlessness.

> The term 'anomie' was introduced into the French language by Jean-Marie Guyau, who ... employs it with a positive connotation to designate the absence of fixed law, the disappearance of the categorical imperative and absolutes in future morality. For Guyau, anomie registers the individual's originality and emancipation from group conformity. Durkheim, on the other hand, uses the term in a clearly pejorative sense[85] to designate a state of anarchy, demoralization and deregulation. Durkheimian anomie

---

82   "The Lexus LF-1 Limitless concept. Beyond autonomous driving. Beyond artificial intelligence. Beyond limitations." To infinity and beyond! Beyond autonomy (heteronomy) is precisely where we do not want to go.

83   Early references to anomie as 'normlessness' can be found in Kingsley Davis (1936: 243) as well as Barnes and Becker (1938). Sennett renders anomie as "ruleless-ness" (2006: xix) which is equally inadequate.

84   As Hilbert (1986) indicates, 'norms' are an important aspect of Durkheim's sociology but the theory of anomie is not rooted in 'norms' *per se* but 'social facts'—the bedrock of Durkheim's entire sociology. Some writers claim that there is no real distinction between anomie and egoism, that the two are inseparable, yet, if we regard anomie as a kind of limitlessness we can see that suicidal philosophies such as Stoicism, Epicureanism, and Cynicism which all promoted self-destruction have built within them the preservation of "the right of man to limit the length of his life ..." (Dublin and Bunzel 1933: 184). The impulse behind collapsing anomie into an attachment and integration problem (e.g., Sainsbury 1955; Gibbs and Martin 1964; this was Whitney Pope's stance as well in his well-known analysis of *Suicide*) is a positivistic drive for reducing concepts down to variables. Witness the wreckage in Maris (1981: 156–69) as this, that, and some other thing are used as 'indicators' of anomie (which gets mangled in a number of ways). If the concept is the "sunrise of existence" (Hegel [1807] 2008: 731) the variable is the twilight of critical social reason.

85   One is reminded of Weber's deployment of 'charisma' in a way that departed radically from the religious meaning provided by Rudolph Sohm.

is the disorder which results from the rules no longer exerting any moderating action on collective life, especially in the economic sphere. A sort of permanent war is generated by the passion[86] for gain and the pursuit of individual interest which encounter no limits, as if in the absence of a moral force capable of curbing rivalries and appetites, men were returning to something like the Hobbesian state of nature, governed solely by the law of the strongest.

JANKÉLÉVITCH 2012: 33

Aron also provides good insight: "No society in history has lent itself to a complete assimilation of all its members. But modern societies increase the causes of anomy, if one may define anomy in the most general sense as *the absence of a system of values or of behavior patterns which would at once impose itself with self-evident authority*" (Aron 1968: 157). The lack of self-evident authority opens one of the worst features of deregulation: limitlessness or *apeiron*.[87] The anomic world is one that is devoid of taboo, characterized instead by *noa*— things are 'untied,' limitless, and over-free (Steiner 1956: 36, 41, 48). The spirit of limitlessness[88] is all-pervasive in a chronically anomic society.[89] The "monstrous urge" (Hegel 1988: 326) of the subject to break free of constrains is visible all around us in signs of decay. The anomic world is one where freedom is backwards: the anomic current attempts to fetter thought and liberate the will, but in reality, will and praxis are very much limited and freedom, if we were to be true to ourselves, is acting within the limits established by reality (Hegel 1988: 190). Of course, negative limits are no substitutes for the concept and concrete freedom, but limits are also a precondition for the working up of the concept (Hegel [1821] 1991: 58–9). Anomic society (if that phrase even makes any sense)

---

86   "There is internal war in man between reason and the passions.... [H]aving both, he cannot be without strife, being unable to be at peace with the one without being at war with the other. Thus he is always divided against, and opposed to himself" (Pascal 1941: 130). God "has confin'd Reason to a narrow corner of the brain, and left all the rest of the body to our Passions; as also set up, against this one, two as it were, masterless Tyrants Anger, that possesseth the region of the heart, and consequently the very Fountain of life, the Heart itself; and Lust, that stretcheth its Empire everywhere" (Erasmus [1509] 1913: 31).

87   Freedom is the product of limit, *peras*. "The term *to apeiron* apparently originated in Greek tragedy, where it referred to garments or binds 'in which one is entangled past escape'" (Wallace 2003: 44).

88   Where reason prevails there is a constant "limitation of infinity" (Zamyatin [1924] 1993: 64).

89   See the Aristotelian distinction between economics and chrematistics that "strives for ... the unlimited" (C: 253). In short, chrematistics are inherently anomic in the sense of lacking bounds and limits.

loses its sense of proportion, craves distortions and myths, and its reality principle succumbs to a misguided will to power (Worrell 2013).[90] Having some money is never enough, "'you've got to have drifts of it, lumps of it, and little piles of it only make you sick and petty'" (Chaze [1953] 2016: 16). Mere directions are the equivalents of actual destinations "and the Way is completed from the moment it is trodden" (Schiller 1967: 59). In other words, everyone is going nowhere fast and the roads are congested with fetish-wielding perverts using magical charms to repel authorities, inflate the self, and pave the way for unlimited enjoyment (Chasseguet-Smirgel 1985: 78–80). Somewhere Hegel uses the phrase "pure axial rotation" with a wink and a nod to describe this loss of traction and the futile spinning of wheels.

No society is free from anomic influences. Anomie is the experience of an unreality (Holzner 1968: 12). Even in a well-regulated, 'normal' social situation there is an "irreducible residue" of uncertainty leftover (Ibid: 13) that functions as a kind of fermenting agent and accelerant for breakdowns in the symbolic network—a kind of built-in potential that is both activated and helps to liberate language from reification.[91] Underlying the spirit of limitlessness is the loss of the anthropomorphic doctrine: where aims and desires have become unmoored from the "truly human" (Wesep 1920: 74) and spin off into the inhuman and monstrous.[92] At its purest, capitalist ideology pines for absolute deregulation. Milton Friedman goes so far as to admonish the "liberal" restriction of medicine to those with licenses. "I agree that the case for licensure is stronger for medicine than for most other fields. Yet the conclusions I shall reach are that liberal principles do not justify licensure even in medicine and

---

90 "I am not among those who consider Homer's Archaean type, the indomitable hero confident in his strength and putting himself above rules, as necessarily disappearing in the future. If it has often been believed that the type was bound to disappear, that was because the Homeric values were imagined to be irreconcilable with the other values which spring from an entirely different principle.... It is quite evident that liberty would be seriously compromised if men came to regard the Homeric values ... as suitable only to barbaric peoples" (Sorel 1950: 232). I think it is safe to say that the consensus position among classical sociologists is the opposite of that expressed by Sorel. A society animated by "Homeric values" is basically one that has descended into barbarism.

91 Anomie is necessary to limit overregulation: "a tendency does not limit itself, it can never be restrained except by another tendency" (S: 366)

92 "We cannot be gods, for we are not gods; we cannot be animals for we are not animals. What we can be is human being and that is sufficient, for in so doing we shall be avoiding on the one hand the Charybdis of trying to be more than we can be, which is destruction; and on the other hand the Scylla of being content with less than we can be which is stagnation—between which there is no more difference than between chopping a tree down, or letting it starve for want of water; for both mean death" (Wesep 1920: 74).

that in practice the results of state licensure in medicine have been undesirable" (1962: 138).

The so-called Reagan Revolution (which actually began well before Reagan took office) was a plan to use "deregulation" as a formula to depoliticize capitalism, inequality, and class stratification as well as "reduce the social base of Democratic Party political strength, break down institutions that had been built from the 1930s on, and reduce the need to mobilize consent politically" (O'Connor 1984: 234). Another goal was to increase "the variability of labor-power and the invariability of traditional authority" (Ibid: 235). When we consider the regulation and deregulation of capital it is important to keep in mind that the political regulation of capitalism as a whole has only ever applied to the advanced, core, or central capitalist states. The more regulation applied to the core (impeding the uninhibited accumulation of surplus value) the more chaos and deregulation can be found on the periphery. Likewise, as the core devolves into anarchy we find fatalism along the periphery. When the central states undergo deregulation the resulting consequence for the entire global order is the descent into imperial chaos. The "empire of chaos" is "One of maximum instability beset with violent contradictions: renewed rivalry between the centers and explosions in the periphery of the South and East" (Amin 1994: 202).

Anomie is characterized by what Durkheim calls a "will mania" or a "hypertrophy of the will" (1915) or what Hegel refers to as a "wildness of will" (1988: 225).

> It is permissible to consider the [French] Revolution as being partly a necessity, but it was above all—which is what the fatalistic writers already cited do not show us—a permanent struggle between theorists who were imbued with a new ideal, and the economic, social, and political laws which ruled mankind, and which they did not understand. Not understanding them, they sought in vain to direct the course of events, were exasperated at their failure, and finally committed every species of violence. *They decreed that the paper money known as assignats should be accepted as the equivalent of gold, and all their threats could not prevent the fictitious value of such money falling almost to nothing* [emphasis added]. They decreed the law of the maximum, and it merely increased the evils it was intended to remedy. Robespierre declared before the Convention 'that all the sans-culottes will be paid at the expense of the public treasury, which will be fed by the rich,' and in spite of requisitions and the guillotine the treasury remained empty.
>
> LE BON 1913: 129

Sorel connects the Achaean spirit of Homer's epic poetry with that of the New England Yankee and the cowboy frontier (1950: 231).[93] There are many objections that can be raised about this comparison; however, the individual's pursuit of a symbolic premium through the medium of large-scale violence in the face of an inexorable fate is one fruitful point of contact.

The "conquest" of the American "frontier was based on individual performance ... and produced individualistic ideologies in all strata of American society. But this individual pioneering also at all times as based on teamwork."

> Exploration of new areas, migration, assimilation of new territories, conquest of new riches—all this would have been impossible without close cooperation of individuals in innumerable small teams.
>
> Individualism of pioneering teams, though sometimes conflicting with the trend towards uniformization, did not fundamentally contradict the patterns of work imposed by industrial civilization.
>
> American settlers, pioneers of American individualism, lived in open communities founded on individual action but held together through the participating individual's public affiliation with recognized religious units. Individualism did not preclude organized forms of collectivity. Considerable efforts were made to preserve and develop them. Teamwork was the foundation of social and cultural life. Used to living and working in teams, these individualists were adapted to accept teamwork on a larger scale, in giant industrial plants.
>
> The American pioneer dream certainly did imply that it was not impossible for the individual worker to become a millionaire. Yet, the worker, as long as he stayed a worker, was expected, and did expect, to fit into the frame of a team as the basic operating unit of industrial life.
>
> Institute of Social Research 1945, 2: 413–14

The overriding spirit of destiny and inevitability paves the way for anarchy. When one pushes fatalism to the extreme, in the form of inevitability or predestination, one is already in the domain of anarchy and luck. Chance is the alias of predeterminism (MECW, 37: 895). If what is going to happen has already happened, ambivalence may not be totally eliminated but the way is open to conduct that is whimsical while appearing to be fated (i.e., relying on the sheer contingency of augury or cartomancy). Suicide is not always a positive embrace of death but also the half-hearted embrace of life, e.g., riding one's motorbike in the rain. Destiny (depression or negative elation) opens the

---

93 Achilles chooses glory on the battlefield over the prospect of long life at home.

way for a diminution of self-control and poor decision-making. Once the tension of destiny becomes extreme the "leap" (see Rosenkranz [1844] 2002) into its polar opposite is inevitable.

We may think of the classic 'Yankee' as the middle point between the English aristocratic strand of Puritans and the full-blown, rugged American frontier individualist (Parrington 1927) and the 'Man' of daring deeds.[94] The correspondences of Marx and Engels are littered with references to Yankees as humbugs and swindlers, but I think this applies mainly to the desublimated offspring of puritanical New England culture. But limitlessness is not only inevitable but actually a social necessity[95] just like any other virtue which has been pushed to its vicious extreme: "If these people didn't live intense and rather disordered lies, if their emotions didn't ride them too hard—well, they wouldn't be able to catch those emotions in flight and imprint them on a few feet of celluloid or project them across the footlights" (Chandler 1995: 300). Where would art be if it were not for the spirit of anarchy? Durkheim is correct when he says that society actually needs anomic monstrosities and moral athletes, daredevils, extreme artists, etc., to demarcate limits and push the horizon of social achievement. Voluntary self-destruction, like crime, is a part of social progress, which is itself inconceivable, apart from regressions.

Some groups adapt somewhat easily to sudden life changes whereas the hyper-developed do so with less aplomb. "[A]s a person who has known success the problem for [the] ego is not the sudden opening of unlimited possibilities

---

94   In his fictional account of the fascist takeover of the American government during the Great Depression, Roth deftly captures the power of the individualist ethos. When Charles Lindbergh lands his *Spirit of St. Louis* (taken out of mothballs as a prop to support his run for the White house) he is greeted by adoring crowds: "And wherever he landed in California that day, it was as though the country hadn't known the stock market crash and the miseries of the Depression (or the triumphs of FDR, for that matter), as though even the war he was there to prevent us from entering hadn't so much as crossed anyone's mind. Lindy flew down out of the sky in his famous plane, and it was 1927 all over again. It was Lindy all over again, straight-talking Lindy, who had never to look or to sound superior, who simply *was* superior—fearless Lindy, at once youthful and gravely mature, the rugged individualist, the legendary American man's man who gets the impossible done by relying solely on himself" (2004: 30).

95   "In Hegel evil is the form in which the motive force of historical development presents itself. Herein lies the twofold meaning that, on the one hand, each new advance necessarily appears as a heinous deed against what is sacred, as a rebellion against conditions, though old and moribund, yet sanctified by custom; and that, on the other hand, it is precisely the wicked passions of man—greed and lust for power—which, since the emergence of class antagonisms, have become levers of historical development—of which the history of feudalism and of the bourgeoisie, for example, constitutes singular continual proof" (MECW, 26: 378).

to one who has hitherto only known a single fate, but the transition, for all but the few internationally famous, from being of considerable consequence to being of little consequence" (Auden 2008: 183). Negative or regressive anomie is a world of hate, not love.[96] "Hate tends to destroy all restraints and duties that we have formerly acknowledged on behalf of its object, and any others which stand in the way of its ends. As soon as we begin to hate anyone the sense of these duties begins to decline, until one after another such protections against our enmity are abolished, and the man has no longer a right to his own life" (Shand 1914: 118).

> And when workmen hate their employer they feel themselves justified in the wanton destruction of his property; and when the socialist hates, instead of merely opposing, governments that have a capitalist basis, revolution, calumny of those in authority, the appropriation of property without compensation, and the destruction of human life are no longer felt to be crimes. Let us then enunciate tentatively this law of hate: Hate, so far from developing, like love, a relative ethics of its own, tends to destroy all virtues, ideals, and duties that restrain it from its ends (Ibid.).

What worker does not possess at least one particle of hatred for their employer? Being struck down by gainful employment is almost synonymous with antagonisms between workers and bosses. The whole system of selling labor-power involves the devaluation of the human being and the reduction of life to that of a 'talking tool' to be used up in the production process. And just as the profit rate is an index of human exploitation, so too is deregulation an indicator of disintegration.

The dismantling of the Glass-Steagall Act during the 80s and 90s led to massive deregulation of finance and, in combination with other pressures such as wage stagnation, debt explosions, deindustrialization, ignominious wars, and so forth, this reversal has set the US on an interesting course that, if dialectical theory offers any insight at all, may swerve in a completely unforeseen direction when least expected. Deregulation was supposed to spur competition, innovation, and lower prices, yet, all through the 80s and beyond, deregulation did nothing to inhibit monopolization (Harvey 1990: 158). Deregulation was

---

96 "Love doth approach disguised" (Shakespeare 1963: 79). What is hate but negative love? "I rather look upon Love altogether as a sort of hostile transaction ..." (Byron 1982: 330–31). "But love, when you get fear in it, it's not love any more. It's hate" (Cain [1934] 1997: 88). For an especially good example of this flash of love-hate self-destruction see Paul's drowning in Maupassant ([2004] 2015).

supposed to bolster economic independence for individuals, but we know that to achieve this independence individual freedom is merely nominal in the absence of a complex and necessary set of rules (DOL: xxxiii). Empire and ego, macrocosm and microcosm, may at any moment appear to be a lost cause, tumbling headlong into a cataclysm, but every constellation and social pathology contains the germs of their own transformation. Intervention, not even on a grand scale, but only mild intercession with an eye toward 'facts' may be all that is required to effect a dramatic and sudden reversal or inversion. Or, if virtue carried to excess is a vice,[97] then perhaps vice, pushed even further into unreality, is an underground tunnel into another polar reality.[98] Either way, Huysmans has crafted the line for our epoch as well: "May you crumble into dust, Society; old world, may you expire!" We have to leave open the possibility that the regressive is inextricably and necessarily linked to the progressive—in a sense, then, it is true that the negative is positive and that the good really is evil.

Imagine if one were to discover a diamond as big as the Hotel Ritz: "There was no valuing it by any regular computation ... and if it were offered for sale not only would the bottom fall out of the market, but also, if the value should vary with its size in the usual arithmetic progression, there would not be enough gold in the world to buy a tenth part of it.... He was, in one sense, the richest man that ever lived—and yet was he worth anything at all?" (Fitzgerald 1922: 157). Attainment of *the All* is the realization of nothing. All that diamond, and it would be useless as well as worthless. Today's accumulators face no such problem: "Let me lay to rest the bugaboo of what is called devaluation" (Richard Nixon, in King 2017: 50).[99] However, the problem is still the same: the more you get, the more you want (S: 248; Durkheim 1960: 81; Eco 1983: 180; Hocking 1926: 303)[100] and once that course has been set it can lead only, and ironically, to ruin. We might say, with Wollstonecraft, that sentimentalism has struck

---

97 "The provocation to vice proceeding from the sacrosanct ..." (Mann 1948: 100).
98 Perhaps vices are merely "virtues gone mad" (Chesterton 1986: 233).
99 The bugaboo of devaluation line from Nixon was part of the famous 1971 address now known as the "Nixon Shock" that led to the abandonment of the Bretton Woods agreement and the gold standard for a free-floating currency.
100 "The surest way to make a child unhappy is to accustom him to obtain everything he wants to have. For, since his wishes multiply in proportion to the ease with which they are gratified, your inability to fulfil them will sooner or later oblige you to refuse in spite of yourself, and this unwonted refusal will pain him more than withholding from him what he demands. At first he will want the cane you hold; soon he will want your watch; afterward he will want the bird he sees flying, or the star he sees shining. He will want everything he sees, and without being God himself how can you content him?" (Rousseau 1889: 48).

down the citizen. Educational underdevelopment combined with an incomprehensible flood of material goods has completely thrown the mind off kilter. Desire is unleashed (S: 258, 255)[101] and the capitalist mode of overproduction delivers the goods like nothing else has. In the process, deliverance generates a continuous hurricane of wants, desires, and the multiplication of needs. "However immense empires may be, they never satiate the appetite of the Caesars" (Aron 1954: 97). Much like the stone age economic thesis whereby our prehistoric ancestors were relatively more affluent than we, and, by extension, our pre-scientific ancestors were more knowledgeable than we can ever hope to be,[102] we moderns, surrounded by every conceivable splendor, are the dumbest and most impoverished in history (cf. Boutmy 1902: 64). But just as sudden regression disturbs equilibrium so does sudden progress.[103]

Modern life is one where sudden changes in fortune (*metabasis*)[104] lurk behind every corner but we cannot have it any other way, really, if it is true that the present moment in the odyssey of America is some kind of midpoint in a dialectical process. Telos is regressing into a geometry of disjointed and unmediated judgments colliding with one another. The spirit of the age is one of aiming for the infinite. Capitalists, for example, are not satisfied with relative wealth but, on the contrary, dream of "absolute wealth" (C: 252). By virtue of its competitive logic capital is forced to aim for all, the infinite, (G: 538) but through finite means (the not-all). The paradox and contradiction of the pursuit of the infinite is that it reduces everything to the finite. The more energy that is expended in pursuit of the infinite (the good) the more evil (the finite, the "lesser good") is produced.[105] Our only hope for touching the 'infinite' is to have the concept and exist as integrated members of society but the more we pursue the pseudo-infinite opened up by capitalism, the more we recede into nothing.

---

101 "One never pines for what he has never known" (la Boétie [1552–53] 1975: 64).

102 One need regress only two or three full lifespans to arrive at a point when a university graduate was expected to have a fairly good grasp on the full range of European knowledge.

103 "Today an individual person can still acquire money fortuitously, and its possession can therefore have just as destructive an effect on him as it had on the ancient communities. But the very destruction of this individual in modern society is only the enrichment of the productive part of society. The owner of money in the ancient sense is destroyed by the industrial process which he serves willy-nilly" (MECW, 28: 156).

104 This *metabasis* or change of winds also entails a corresponding deficiency or breakdown of reasoning (see Rinofner-Kreidl: 2004: 44).

105 See Harrison (1962: liv). The antithesis of finite and infinite is only the modern, "meager and delicate" (i.e., Kantian) form of the ancient religious struggle between good and evil (Hegel 1988: 301).

The capitalist class as a whole suffers from a "boundless drive for enrichment, this passionate chase after value, is common to the capitalist and the miser; but while the miser is merely a capitalist gone mad, the capitalist is a rational miser" (C: 254). It is a well-known fact that, in contemporary capitalism, the wealthy, aiming for the possession of all and everything, give relatively less to charity than do members of the working class who are left to fight over the leftovers that escape the grasp of elites.[106] The rich and the famous provide a glimpse into at least one side of what Durkheim calls the "morbid effervescence" (S: 368) of modern life. The overflow of wealth and access to cheap credit leads to a binge and grab frenzy of material consumption and 'mindless' activities. But the laboring classes are also lured into the dreams of consumption frenzy.[107] Capitalist markets for labor power and the relations of overproduction, exchange, and accumulation dissolve organic social structures leaving in their wake what H.G. Wells described as "a dull useless boiling-up of human activities, an immense clustering of futilities" (in Mayo 1945: 3). Says Bacevich, "For the majority of contemporary Americans, the essence of life, liberty, and the pursuit of happiness centers on a relentless personal quest to acquire, to consume, to indulge, and to shed whatever constraints might interfere with those endeavors" (2009: 16).[108] Miserable is the one who pursues happiness (Byron 1982: 355).[109]

What is this if not Durkheim's concept of progressive anomie? Failure to abide by the striving imperative can even engender animosity toward those that fail to live up to the standards of achievement and acquisition. Dramatic mobility (upward or downward)[110] correlates with feelings of rootlessness,

---

106 If workers hope to receive dignity and respect they have to extend it to themselves rather than wait for the bourgeoisie to genuflect to the honor of labor. "Today, disrespect is baked into working-class jobs in a capitalistic worldview that considers workers as merely costs to be minimized. And that cost-minimization plays out in the form of low pay, miserly benefits, unstable schedules and an overall withholding of dignity by society for their hard and important work" (Draut 2018).
107 "They call themselves 'jitter-bugs,' bugs which carry out reflex movements, performers of their own ecstasy. Merely to be carried away by anything at all, to have something of their own, compensates for their impoverished and barren existence" (Adorno 1967: 128).
108 The "present age" says Nietzsche, offers the spectacle of "delight in all the *coarser* eruptions and gestures of passion" ([1887] 1974: 112).
109 "[E]ver thinking he shall never have enough, he's the poorest of all men" (Erasmus [1509] 1913: 52).
110 Growth economies (both the over-controlled and under-controlled) combine gains with misery: "Last year, the U.S. economy grew by nearly 3 percent, China's by 6.5 percent, and India's almost 7.5 percent. Between them, they added roughly $1.8 trillion of GDP at market prices, but almost twice that when adjusted for purchasing power. An extra $3 trillion—even when divvied up among three billion people—ought to buy some

isolation, and lack of sincerity and impatience toward others[111] as well as prejudice against people who do not mobilize their strivings in the prescribed manner (Packard 1959: 256–60). When infinity is the object, rage and futility and ruin are sure to follow because progress to the infinite is not only impossible[112] for the individual but will necessarily entail setbacks and insurmountable obstacles that hurl the unsupported and unmediated[113] individual back down.[114] Gods may do as they please (Homer) and *abstract* Reason recognizes no limitations (Feuerbach) but mortals must be anchored to terra firma.[115] As Cassirer indicates, animals rooted in instincts know nothing about possibilities but humans, on their own, do not recognize the boundary between reality and possibility (1944: 79; cf. S: 246). 'Impossibility' blurs into the possible because the act of thought produces the thing (Ibid.). As Hegel makes clear, the personal enjoyment of 'infinity' is possible only to the socially enclosed person. The enclosure of selves necessitates limits that protect members of society from sudden shocks of either a positive or negative nature (S: 246). People who feel as though limits do not apply to them are overexposed to contingencies. So long as the affluent remain affluent, life is an easy flow of wish-fulfillments, however, when forced suddenly to live on a reduced scale

---

    happiness. But you wouldn't have found it on the faces of people or in the conversations in Washington, Beijing, and Delhi. Instead, what was striking was the joylessness.... My hypothesis is that all three economies are superficially healthy but deeply stressed. In China it is the strain of suppression, in India that of inefficiency, and in the U.S. of partisanship. The strains are showing up not in headline statistics but in the moods of people. Beijing was clean and censored, Delhi sick and polluted, and Washington prosperous but depressed" (Gill 2019).

111 Anomic impatience is a hallmark of romantic poetry: "They must make a world of their own, and in a day, too. At the same time they are without any definite faith. In fact, definite faith would endanger for them the freshness of their emotions. They fear any creed but one self-made. And they can more easily tear down than build up" (Royce 1969: 256).

112 Durkheim stands in marked contrast to Chateaubriand on the connection between the infinite and progress: "The infinite ... is part of our very nature; if you forbid our intelligence, or even our passions, to dream of unbounded prosperity, you reduce a man to the level of a snail and you metamorphose him into a machine. For make no mistake, if we cannot hope to penetrate the ultimate, if we do not believe in eternal life, there is annihilation everywhere" (1962: 105).

113 Mediation puts a halt to the "progress of infinity" (SL: 673).

114 The German *Unendlichkeit* conveys much of what interests us in the concept of infinity: endlessness and boundlessness.

115 "As she spoke he pulled the herb out of the ground and showed me what it was like. The root was black, while the flower was as white as milk; the gods call it Moly, and mortal men cannot uproot it, but the gods can do whatever they like" (Homer 1944: 124). "'God is the infinite being, the being without any limitation.' But that which is not a boundary or a limit for God is also not a limit for reason" (Feuerbach 1986: 6).

(S: 252–54) life becomes painful and less desirable—*renunciation* is a word absent from the vocabulary of luxuriousness (Wharton 1924: 117).

When the goal is infinity no progress can be made (S: 248). "Points of a journey do not matter when the journey has no destination, only an end" (Amis 1984: 194). The spirit of limitlessness results in chaos and the "unfettered freedom" of individuals reduces them to caricatures of gods, "elemental beings raging madly against one another in a frenzy of destructive activity" (PS: 292). "The sense of the unlimited has its grandeur, but it is painful and there is something morbid about it" (Durkheim 1993: 121). Indeed, the 'unlimited' belongs to the category of *nothing* (SL: 113). As Mill states, the most favorable condition is one where poverty is limited by blocking the infinite horizon of riches. "Most fitting, indeed, is it, that while riches are power, and to grow as rich as possible the universal object of ambition, the path to its attainment should be open to all, without favour or partiality. But the best state for human nature is that in which, while no one is poor, no one desires to be richer, nor has any reason to fear being thrust back by the efforts of others to push themselves forward." (1881: 453).

Unregulated accumulation, consumption, and possession are incapable of establishing the ground for the saturation and total penetration of objects by the individual's consciousness—'everything' cannot be 'mine' and the open-ended 'everything' is 'unrecognizable' to not only myself but also to the society in which I live. My pursuit of things results in an "empty proprietorship which might be called a madness of personality" (PR: 91). The headlong, anomic accumulation of multiform wealth means the opposite: the things survive, and the individual perishes.[116] As Goethe put it in *Elective Affinities*, "He who wants to rid himself of an evil always knows what he wants, but he who wants something better than he already has is night-blind…. He will catch something, perhaps,—but what?" ([1809] 1971: 34).

Goethe was also attuned to the effervescent aspects of modern commercial cacophony. Money and greed bring together a motley conglomeration of people in a frenzy of buying and selling. It is interesting that Marx turned to Hegel to unravel the mystery of exchange and that Hegel was, in turn, indebted to Goethe's "Walpurgis Night" section of *Faust* for insights into the logic of phantom relations.[117] In conjunction with Goethe, we might also think of anomie as

---

116 The serial infinity and irrationality of possession emerges in an ethical vacuum where the drive to accumulate is not "subordinated to the higher spheres of right" (PR: 77).

117 "At the historical dawn of the capitalist mode of production—and every capitalist upstart has to go through this historical stage individually—avarice, and the drive for self-enrichment, are the passions which are entirely predominant. But the progress of

the 'disease of care' when conjoined with material possession: "Once I [Care, i.e., anxious concern or sorrow] make a man my own, nothing in this world can help him; everlasting darkness falls, suns no longer rise or set—though no outward sense has failed, all is darkness in his heart, and however great his treasures, there's no joy in their possession. Good and bad luck both depress him, he is starving though there's plenty; source of joy or spot of trouble, it's postponed until the morrow—caring only for the future, he gets nothing done at all" (Goethe 1984: 289).[118]

The anomic individual suffers impatience,[119] loss of compassion, the desire to multiply their powers, and loses a grip on reality (Schnitzler [1926] 1999: 82). The anomic character finds the familiar uninteresting and longs for the formless and the nameless, the enigmatic and mysterious.[120] *Faust* provides a good example of the necessity of liberty vis-à-vis the instrumentalization of others in the impatient pursuit of the infinite.

> Faust attempts to establish that he is indeed independent, that he, as Faust the individual, is capable of doing as he pleases in that world…. For Faust, independence is thus simply unimpeded freedom to do 'as he pleases' unconstrained by past convention or mores. Faust desires to see himself affirmed as free in the sense of being unimpeded in his doing what he wants. In this way, Faust stands for the darkly self-realizational romantic side of modern self-understanding, the desire to cast away the past and push all limits simply in order to have it affirmed for himself that he *can* do so, that there is nothing in the past or in current mores that *could* count as a reason against his doing anything.
>
> PINKARD 1996: 93–94

If we had more space, we could multiply classic examples from Werther, "enamoured of infinity" (S: 286) who kills himself due to unrequited love or Don Juan who pursues infinite sexual conquests and embodies the spirit of quantification negating qualities (Camus 1955: 62–72), *ad infinitum*. In the pursuit of having and doing everything, having only a single and solitary self is insufferable; one needs more than just one self to keep pace with the windfall of

---

capitalist production not only creates a world of delights; it lays open, in the form of speculation and the credit system, a thousand sources of sudden enrichment" (C: 741).
118   "*Calamitosus est animus futuri anxius*" (Montaigne 1842: 5).
119   "Impatience demands the impossible, to wit, the attainment of the end without the means" (PS: 17).
120   "Nothing can slake my thirst / for the nameless and the obscure" (Baudelaire 1993: 122). Interestingly, these two lines are from the poem "Sympathetic Horror."

possible pleasures, necessitating some means to double and multiply effects via masks and magic.[121]

The boundary between the progressive and the regressive is blurred.[122] Others long for death as a moment of gain (e.g., Paul, Antigone, Socrates, etc., where "death is a gain because it brings an end to life's hardships" (Droge and Tabor 1992: 121). Here, a person can decide to die on the basis of not what has happened but what might happen. Mark Twain made a contribution to the problem of what we might call 'imaginary' anomie of the progressive form in *The $30,000 Bequest* where the fantasy of suddenly and unexpectedly acquiring wealth, where there had previously been only poverty, utterly unravels marriage, life, and psyche: "It seemed to her husband that a ton of chains fell from his limbs. He did not say a word; he was happy beyond the power of speech.... Vast wealth, to the person unaccustomed to it, is a bane; it eats into the flesh and bone of his morals. When the Fosters were poor, they could have been trusted .... How easy it is to go from bad to worse, when once we have started upon a downward course!" (1872: 21). What Durkheim calls the "crisis of prosperity"[123] is here played out perfectly and with "fatal resolve." "During three days the couple walked upon air, with their heads in the clouds. They were but vaguely conscious of their surroundings; they saw all things dimly, as through a veil; they were steeped in dreams, often they did not hear when they were spoken to; they often did not understand when they heard; they answered confusedly or at random" (1872: 28).[124]

> They lived yet two years, in mental night, always brooding, steeped in vague regrets and melancholy dreams, never speaking; then release came to both on the same day.
> Towards the end the darkness lifted from Sally's ruined mind for a moment.... 'Vast wealth, acquired by sudden and unwholesome means, is a

---

121 "How could the Church have failed to condemn such a practice on the part of the actor? She repudiated in that art the heretical multiplication of souls, the emotional debauch, the scandalous presumption of a mind that objects to living but one life and hurls itself into all forms of excess" (Camus 1955: 82).

122 For an illustration of the dyadic interplay of anomic polarities, progressive in the ego and regressive reaction in the alter ego, see Maupassant ([1883] 1999: 91–3).

123 For Marx's part, capitalist prosperity always and necessarily leads to mass unhappiness (PM: 69). Unhappiness is simply horror unappeased (Alain [1934] 1974: 109).

124 That the rich seem clueless about social reality is little wonder. Indeed, it would be exceptional for those struck down by wealth, the living abstractions, to have more than a tenuous grasp on the concrete. Confiscating all those trillions of dollars would be an act of mercy.

snare. It did us no good, transient were its feverish pleasures; yet for its sake we threw away our sweet and simple and happy life ...' (1872: 32).

What makes Twain's short story so delicious is that there was never really any increase in wealth at all—an inheritance hoax led them to play at investing their imagined wealth and accumulating imagined gains by the millions. It was all a dream, yet, the eventual nightmare of a return to modesty, which they never actually left, destroyed the couple. The hysterical world of what might be or could have been, where we are tormented by the unbearable prospects of gain and loss, drive people to despair. In *Macbeth* we find this interesting dynamic illustrated by the anecdote of the "farmer that hanged himself on th' expectation of plenty" (Shakespeare 2000: 30). The world-renowned three-star chef, Benoit Violier killed himself with a shotgun hours *before* the release of a new Michelin guide in which he feared he would lose one of his stars (Willsher 2016).[125] Negatively or positively, a crisis is a crisis whether or not it is imagined or real—the mental processes are not dissimilar (Cavan [1928] 1965: 122) and we see here, too, the polarity of doom and anarchy.

Deviating from Durkheim slightly, we will reserve the term *anarchy* for the extreme limit or embarkation point of anomie, which is more or less synonymous with chronic anomie. As Durkheim says, capitalism is essentially anarchic and even chronically so (S: 254 ff.). Business anarchy colors our version of the democratic process, which is flooded with graft and special interests.

> American democracy comes from a society of adventurers and businessmen, that is to say, speculators and gamblers, and the temperament which corresponds to this origin is that which is deployed in politics. What penetrates it, colors it and gives it its physiognomy, it is a frantic sport, broad, noisy, rude, optimistic, without animosity or resentment, of very bad tone and very beautiful mood. Every game won in this sport provides some positive benefits that we do not disdain; but one yields first of all, by indulging in it, to a passion of the kind of those which meet on the stock exchange or around a bookmaker shop.
> BOUTMY 1902: 143–44

---

125 For the first time a French three-star chef, Sebastien Bras, asked to not be included in the Michelin guide due to the overwhelming pressure attendant with "upholding that honor" and a desire "to feel free, without asking myself whether my creations would please the Michelin inspectors ..." (Wamsley 2017).

Capitalism pushes desire to new heights with a drive toward infinite horizontal expansion (C, 2: 252).[126] Capitalist industry, says Charles Loudon, is war combined with gambling in the economic sphere (in PM: 76). But 'anarchy' is not automatically and absolutely a dirty word. We are all anarchists in some respects. Nothing cultivates anarchism like the stench of personal interest paraded as a public good or patriotism as a rationalization for mass murder and corporate greed.[127] One thing is for certain, however, with regards to anarchy: freedom here is illusory and veils massive and frantic dependency (Brecht, in Willett 1992: 223).

One of the worst features of anarchy is the proliferation of prophecies and charismatic prophets bent not on collective well-being but on individual fate. For the prophet, "Life itself is individual, and the most significant things in the world—perhaps in the end the only significant things—are individual souls" (Hocking 1926: 97). This fits with the notion that virtually every culturally significant religious leader suffers from intense and malignant narcissism (see Krakauer 2004: 309). As Durkheim says, all moral innovators and religious prophets basically fall into the ranks of the mentally ill (2006: 57).[128] These narcissists "fuel the cultural, spiritual, and economic engines of Western society" (Krakauer 2004: 307).

In the negative or regressive form, anomie is associated with rage and destruction.[129] Nietzsche puts it well:

> The desire for *destruction*, change, and becoming can be an expression of an overflowing energy that is pregnant with future ... but it can also be the hatred of the ill-constituted, disinherited, and underprivileged, who destroy, *must* destroy, because what exists, indeed all existence, all being,

---

126 William Bridges Adams: "'The whole structure should be set out on the principle which governs the beehive—capacity for indefinite extension ...'" (in C, 2: 252).

127 There is no need to fear genuine patriotism. With Augustine, a nation is just a common love object and if we want internationalism there must be a relation of nations. As Royce says, in the progressive direction, "The modern national spirit itself sometimes appears to be a sort of preparation for some larger enthusiasm which, as we often hope, may, in a far-off future age, make the community of mankind its main object of fraternal devotion, and the whole earth its country" (1914: 4–5).

128 "I have heard ... that one Protestant denomination puts all its candidates through a series of psychological tests to eliminate the 'maladjusted.' One cannot help wondering how St Paul or St Augustine or St Francis would have scored on such a test" (Auden 2008: 206).

129 The negative form pertains to contractions and failures and lacks what Shakespeare (2000: 21) called the "vaulting ambition" we associate with the limitlessness of positive anomie. If one needs credentials, Drexel University is now the school where "Ambition can't wait."

outrages, and provokes them. To understand this feeling, consider our anarchists closely.

NIETZSCHE ([1887] 1974: 329)

We can leave the destructive madness of negative or regressive anomie for the next volume. For now, let us merely state that individuals and classes can become so enamored of liberty that it can tolerate nothing impeding its will, and, pushed to the extreme of anarchy and chaos,[130] we approach the exact opposite, slavery (Camus 1955: 58; see also Kant 1998: 13) and where there is slavery there is anarchy (Auden 2008: 371).[131] Of course, just because the world seems to fall apart into disorder and depression, does not mean that everyone loses hope and ceases to dream. "Journalist James Rorty took a trip across America in the midthirties and encountered little to show that the Depression had dampened the power of what he called the 'dream culture.' If anything, he wrote, both economic misery and the profit motive had 'augmented the demand for dreams'" (Leach 1993: 382).

4   Fatalism

The opposite of deregulation or anomie is over–regulation or fatalism. According to Durkheim, fatalism has little contemporary relevance, limited, as it is, to the lives of young husbands, slaves, and childless women (S: 276).[132] The modern world seems too fluid to ever have an iron grip on individuals and,

---

130   "Lured by the love of chaos, / an Angel, unwary pilgrim / caught in Nightmare's current, / struggling like a swimmer / pitted in deadly panic / against the howling vortex, / whirling and faster whirled / down, down and under ..." (Baudelaire 1993: 125).

131   The liberated slave offers insight into the paradox of hyper-regulation and anarchy and lawlessness: the "emancipated slave ... knows no law at all. The law whose yoke he bore was not given by himself, by his reason, since he could not regard his reason as free, as a master, but only as a servant ..." (Hegel 1948: 80).

132   The Marine Corps recruit and the prisoner languishing in solitary confinement represent two contrasting pure types of *collective voluntary* and *individuated involuntary* incarceration. Sometimes the two cross, when, for example, the youngster is offered the choice between jail or the Marines, as was the situation with one of my comrades while serving in the Corps. From what I was told, a high school prank led to the accidental death of one of his friends and the presiding judge offered him a choice between juvenile incarceration or, specifically, six years in the Marines—the 'chance' for a new start. Interestingly, in the blended type Nietzsche says that they are incapable of blending smoothly into society, are criminalized, and that they experience the world "fatalistically" (1982: 549). Indeed, despite being offered a fresh start via a stint in the Marines, my comrade died at the age of 36.

regardless of "however precise the regulatory system may be, it will always leave room for much dispute" (DOL: 302). But the domain of fatalism also includes forces such as predetermination that prevents backsliding into merely pragmatic equilibrium on the basis of accidental "trial and error" (DOL: 301) whereby external standards[133] come and go with each fleeting contact (C: 183; cf. DOL: 302). Fatalism is also a current of opinion that drives the criminal and the king (Freud [1913] 1950: 56–8; cf. Harrison 1962: xxxvi). Whereas *sinners* are those that have run afoul of religious injunctions and not met the obligations associated with altruistic currents, *criminals* have either broken an existing law or been reconstructed as vehicles for the establishment of a new law. Leaving aside mass-incarcerated slave laborers, the 'criminal' fulfills a role of genuflecting to higher powers, expressing sincere remorse, and receiving forgiveness in return. This process is a kind of 'engine' of the absolute whereby the hardened and bad are reconciled with the universal—a return from merely external existence into something essential for society (PS: 407). Society has a need for punishment (DOL: 40) if only to establish "guilt" which is "accountability" for doing what is right (Hegel 1988: 214).

Fatalism is, as Weber points out, a world of finality, of the "once and for all" where rites and ethics are powerless against a resolute god (AJ: 214). This finality is an undeniable experience for many individuals, but the capitalist setup seems like a world where what is going to happen has never before happened. Durkheim worked around his devaluation of fatalism by building into his analyses of the other suicidogenic currents the attending problems, futilities, and *aporia* that each engender. As such, Durkheim could very well have soldiered on through the teleological activity reflected in the egoism-anomie-altruism triad without formal recourse to the category of fatalism. However, the inclusion of fatalism does add value and analytical coherence to the study of self-destruction by expanding the matrix of synthetic triads.

We can extrapolate many distinct subtypes of fatalism for our purposes: inevitability, determinism, predestinationism, and so on. Fatalism puts us in contact with primary historical concepts. "The invariable laws under which Humanity is placed have received various names at different periods. Destiny, Fate, Necessity, the Heaven, Providence, all are so many names of one and the same conception: the laws which man feels himself under … and … without

---

133 In the absence of an absolute standard (or an objective constellation of standards applicable to all) we have not double standards but capriciousness and, where there are different standards for each individual, class, and situation, there are no standards at all.

the power of escaping from them" (Congreve 1874: 289).[134] For Congreve and the positivists, the perfection of this fate is the submission under one necessity, the love of humanity. But as an imperfection, fate is simply the confrontation with power (cf. Hegel 1987: 123).

Modern secular thinkers have rightly taken a dim view of 'necessity' as brute externality. "The external authority is necessary as a transitory stage, but it must not be preserved [forever] and regarded as an abiding and final norm" (Solovyov 1918: xxi). External necessity is merely mechanical or material force applied to the individual; internal necessity seems to arise from the psyche of the individual—it is nothing more than "freedom from mechanical necessity" (Solovyov 1918: 19) and the demand for personal rights. Keep in mind we are nowhere near the domain of rational, positive freedom. Necessity or external compulsion simply means that one must act, think, or feel a certain way, and there appears to be no choice in the matter. Once necessity holds the reins, humans can be made to do almost anything including mass ruin on a national and civilizational scale.[135] But the other name for external necessity, surprisingly, is *chance*. "Chance is the same as external necessity, that is a necessity which relates to causes which are themselves merely superficial circumstances. We must seek a general purpose in history, the ultimate purpose of the world" (Hegel, in Koselleck 1985: 128). Either what seems to be chance is actually necessity or what appears to be necessary is actually a matter of chance.[136] "Her marriage ... was purely an accident, in this respect resembling many other marriages which masquerade as the decrees of Fate" (Chopin 1899: 46).

For Marx, historical necessity refers to a necessity of nature, not of morality. In the *Paris Manuscripts* history is natural history—mirrored in much neo-Marxism, e.g., Debord's *Society of the Spectacle* (Chapter 5). The domination of capital strips the proletariat of any genuine moral necessity and reduces the laboring classes to brutal toiling. Necessity in the domain of the moral is, if anything, a fetish (Engels, in Marx and Engels 2008: 147) to be eradicated, through revolution. Communism represents a restoration of natural necessity

---

134 Providence is "the myth that allows power relations as the sole determinate of social relations" (Bechtold 2019).

135 "Human beings—the Germans proved this during the war—can become accustomed to almost anything if they are led to believe its necessity" (Mann 1938: 36).

136 "Chance and necessity are dialectically connected and cannot be considered apart from one another and apart from the whole scheme of the universe; what is chance on one level ... is necessity on another ..." (Bernal 1949: 363).

over unnatural necessity (capitalist, religious, ideological, etc.). But "The past predetermines the future. In other words, there exists a certain allocation of rights and duties that is established by usage and that ends up by becoming obligatory" (DOL: 302). If we limit ourselves to the domain of the understanding, the profane, the individual, and the linear then, by rights, we are free in a sense to do as we please. In the moral domain, however, our rights give way to necessity and disobedience reduces our humanity (EFRL: 12–3). As an individual, having rights is necessary but as a personality, a social person, necessity is what is right. And if necessity is abandoned for one-sided rights then rights are also lost in nothingness, which means that the reality of 'rights' appearing external to necessity is illusory and rightly belongs to the domain of necessity. Right is another name for *internalized* necessity as opposed to external necessity and leaves open the possibility that necessity can be experienced as a sort of freedom so long as it is subjectively internalized—this is the basis of, e.g., Quaker optimistic fatalism (Fischer 1989: 517 ff.) as we all as compatibilism, the idea that freedom and necessity are compatible with one another. "In suicide there is not the full union of self and not-self. We do not unity with necessity but borrow its form to clothe our self-will" (Bosanquet 1912: 28).

'Rights' in our negative heaven are *abstract* rights rather than the sacred rights of the "absolute concept, of self-conscious freedom" and puts us in proximity with things, slaves, contracts (partial slavery), and deception, etc., (Hegel [1821] 1991: 59). In other words, in bourgeois society it would take a miracle to unify rights and necessity. *Recht* is both law and right and the function of external and objective law is to produce internal and subjective rights (see Wilson 2008: 210; cf. DOL: 73). Rights are incomprehensible without law so when the spirit of anarchy descends upon a society, rights expand to the heights of the transcendental. Our 'rights' are our rights—individual rights (Lilla 2017: 29). Right as it is worked out in bourgeois ideology is necessarily individualized and, pushed to an extreme where it is lopped off from collective obligation, devolves into "narcissistic solipsism, a competitive me-firstism that can only take without giving anything back" (Kimmel 2013: 134). The best proof that 'rights' belong in the domain of fatalism is that the wealth-accumulation rights of three white men are more sacrosanct and inviolable than the general welfare of 200 million Americans. The most that can be hoped for with respect to rights and necessity is an oscillation that leaves an enclave for the individual, but this is no better than admitting that autonomy is always conditioned by heteronomy and is therefore an illusion. Genuine freedom would entail the sublation of these moments into a higher calling and concept.

In the capitalist necroverse we tend to feel most passionately that our personal rights are absolutely inviolable and feel outraged when they are infringed upon[137]—my rights as a human being are sacrosanct and necessary whereas the rights of others are, it is true, nominally obligatory and necessary, yet, in practice, so long as my rights are being respected I treat the rights of others as practically optional. It is for the best when others are treated and regarded in the right way but so long as things are right in my world I can ignore the plight of others. What is in principle necessary as far as I am concerned is practically optional with regard to others, and, of course what is optional for me should be obligatory for the remainder. The opposing, totalitarian conception liquidates rights altogether: "It's clear, isn't it?—to assert that 'I' has certain 'rights' with respect to the State is exactly the same as asserting that a gram weighs the same as a ton.... To the ton goes the rights, to the gram the duties.... Forget that you're a gram and feel yourself a millionth part of a ton" (Zamyatin [1924] 1933: 111). But, in truth, equilibrated 'rights' exist not 'in between' the egoistic-anomic and the altruistic-fatalistic conceptions but in a sublated individuality. "No one ... can have a right except (1) as a member of a society, and (2) of a society in which some common good is recognised by the members of the society as their own ideal good, as that which should be for each of them" (Green 1895: 43).

Instead of a must, right imposes the idea that one *should* do something or another. Rather than being obligatory, a right is optional. One could always waive or otherwise relinquish a right whereas one is powerless in the face of destiny. However, the two, right and necessity, may be combined as we see when Nietzsche characterizes the categorical imperative as saying that one should because one must — *amor fati*, love what is necessary (Nietzsche 1967: 258).[138] Or, with Žižek (*passim*), we find that the autonomous choice is always undergirded by a hidden heteronomy[139] that can run in multiple directions,

---

137 "Our dignity as moral beings is therefore no longer the property of the city-state; but it has not for that reason become our property, and we have not acquired the right to do what we wish with it" (S: 337).

138 Heidegger transformed this Stoic alignment of will and fate into a kind antinomian will-mania whereby fate has justified all willing that could be hitched to any program, such as Nazi conquest (see Löwith 1995: 217).

139 "The heteronomy of the will is its submission to the impulse of pleasure-seeking, as that of which man is not in respect of his reason the author, but which belongs to him as a merely natural being" (Green [1895] 1924: 4). Tension in the US between intense individualism and the ideology of 'adaptation' to prevailing conditions and changes paradoxically glorifies heteronomy (Adorno, in Adorno and Becker 1983: 106). The deification of autonomy leads inexorably to its opposite, the sacralization of fate. If we wish for anarchy in some domain of society then we must be prepared to accept the appearance of the iron fist in that same domain or as a reflection in an adjacent compartment. The modern horror of heteronomy is overblown. It is the height of arrogance and hubris to believe that

the two most important for us at the moment, are, on the one hand, the transit to some Other that runs the show (see Freire 1993: 43–4) or, on the other hand, to predestination where you are free to choose (autonomy) so long as you make the right choice.[140]

The secret of autonomy is that it 'belongs' not to the dimension of the concrete singular (the ego) or the abstract universal but to the particularity of one's coordinates in society: the group, the social circles, the profession, etc. It is "at the point of intersection of a certain number of groupings, the individual feels himself ... inclined and prepared for autonomy. He is no longer shut in by life with all his tendencies canalized, as it were, in advance. He can seek out his path, create for himself his own proper synthesis, retouch, in his fashion, the table of values" (Bouglé [1926] 1970: 256). It is from within the mediating function of the social division of labor and self-development that one avoids egoism, anarchy, automatonism, and fatalism. When one is incapable of ruling the self or being ruled by others one is reduced to being ruled by things and "superstition—the fettering of the mind to a sensuous object" (Hegel 1956: 413; cf. Aquinas 2000: 10). Superstition (from *super* + *sto*) unites infinity and the finite (taboo) by cutting directly across the intersection of mysticism and magic as an immobilization; rather than progressing the 'I' is at a standstill.

> Mankind so far has been ruled by things and by words, not by thought, for till the last few moments of history, humanity has not been in possession of the conditions of secure and effective thinking.... Unless we master things, we shall continue to be mastered by them; the magic that words cast upon things may indeed disguise our subjection or render us less dissatisfied with it, but after all science, not words, casts the only compelling spell upon things.
> DEWEY 1978: 78

---

one's "rigor" is tight enough to reduce humanity to the laws of nature (see Bataille [1962] 1991: 160).

140 "[O]ne can be an autonomous agent without being magically free of determinations. Autonomy is rather a question of relating to such determinations in a peculiar way. To be self-determining does not mean ceasing to be dependent on the world around us. In fact, it is only through dependence (on those who nurture us, for example) that we can achieve a degree of independence in the first place. The autonomous subject set up by most postmodern thought is a straw man. To be free of all determinations would not be freedom at all" (Eagleton 2016: 13–4). "One great virtue of a determinist approach is that it sensitizes us to the external forces at work in our thinking, helps us to focus on them, and, therefore, by a reflexive process, deepens whatever obscure 'autonomy' may in fact be there" (Berger 1995: 71).

This is where the rule of things leads back to authoritarian bondage, barbarism, the lust for power, debauchery, "vulgar corruptions, hypocrisy, and deception" (Ibid.).[141] Freud makes a good case for the connection between superstition and authoritarianism when he says that "superstition originates from repressed hostile and cruel impulses" and the desire on the part of the superstitious to heap misfortune upon others (1951: 146). Fundamentalist Christianity is so rife with the premonition of evil and impending doom (every disaster is god's punishment for our sins) that it is less a religious form and more of a demonology.[142] Where there is superstition or "the rule of demons" (Farrar 1912: 143) and the rule of things over human life we have pure determinism and the inevitable flow back into anarchy.[143] We can very clearly see this in the section on the "law of the heart" in Hegel's *Phenomenology* where hedonism and something akin to Durkheimian "will mania"[144] are internalized as following a natural law that is valid for everyone else, not just the subject—the idea of a natural law that does not apply to everyone is strange and implies some kind of exceptionalism and the intervention of charismatic gifts from on high, which in itself also deviates from natural law theory that conceives of god as only an occasional agent of *retribution* (Gierke 1934: 95–101). Of course, determinism is, for us, closely related to one of its religious forms, predestinationism[145] and we can see, in the writings of Calvin, one of the social forces driving the development of an idea like predestinationism: the problem of unregulated (anomic) conduct and institutional corruption.[146] Calvin notes that the idea of predestinationism is perplexing to those plagued by "human curiosity, which cannot be restrained from wandering into forbidden paths, and climbing to

---

141 The superstitious person makes use of things to stir unseen forces but in the using the superstitious are themselves used. "Man the savage is ruled by things .... And on the other hand, man the citizen, man civilized, rules things, makes of them what he pleases" (Brooks 1893: 27).

142 'Premonition' (from *praemonere*, *prae* 'before' and *monere* 'warn') shares an etymological connection with 'monster' (*monstrum*, also from *monere*).

143 Assuredly, we are all shackled by a baseline predeterminism by virtue of our past and history (DOL: 302) so anything like a pure freedom is a logical extremity.

144 Will mania (Durkheim 1915) is the catastrophic point where a person has nothing left to wish for. In the ego's futile strivings for everything (the more it gets the more it wants) it ends up longing for a condition of non-willing (Schelling [1813] 1997: 134).

145 Weber explicitly renders "predestination" equivalent to or identical with "determinism" (ES, 1: 522).

146 Where Calvinism did embrace *limitlessness* was in the arena of laboring within a calling (see Grossman [1934] 2006). Labor *per se* may or may not be waste but within the boundaries of a calling the sky is the limit.

the clouds, determined if it can that none of the secret things of God shall remain unexplored" ([1559] 1981: 203).[147]

In the preface to the *Phenomenology*, Hegel cryptically mentions that the problem of what appears to be external necessity is one that is always retroactively comprehended from the standpoint of time and a sequential demonstration (PS: 3–4).[148] Inevitability really only follows revelation (Chandler 1995: 1007). All the same, even if it is a retroactive construct one cannot go back in time to choose another course, so, practically it might as well belong to the future; from the standpoint of fate, the past is the future. Time belongs to the problem of infinity whereas taboo is a matter of space. Pushed beyond the limit established by 'inevitability' we find life reduced to mechanical determination (the trap from which there is no escape)[149] and a violent panic reaction is possible that may hurl the individual around the bend into the speculatively opposite quadrant of regressive anomie and pure anarchy (cf. DOL: 305).

5 Composite Forces

The four, principle suicidogenic currents are not encountered as ideal-typical purities in reality and, like parapraxes, "composite structures" are irreducible to their elements and must be accounted for "on their own account" (Freud [1917] 1966: 51). Durkheim provides a diagrammatic summary of the "basic" and "mixed" types of suicide in his "Aetiological and Morphological Classification of the Social Types of Suicide" where we find the combination of egoism

---

147   On the connection between fatalism and predestinationism see Adams (1983).
148   Cf. Royce (1969: 252–53): "Hope says that even if our unhappy experiences exceed in number and intensity our happy experiences, still the future will arbitrarily turn the scale by regarding the whole series of experiences as essentially good."
149   "Evils which are patiently endured when they seem inevitable, become intolerable when once the idea of escape from them is suggested" (Tocqueville 1856: 214). Some conditions and circumstances are inevitable, as Freud says, such as death, pain, suffering, and the unhappiness caused by other people ([1930] 1961: 26). The pain caused by others is a kind of surplus unhappiness above and beyond the pain of the body and that delivered by nature. Even if we run toward solitude to avoid the pain of others, what Freud calls "the happiness of quietness" (Ibid: 27) we encounter more pain because we are social beings and cannot thrive in isolation. "The rows of cells in a modern prison are monads in the true sense of the word defined by Leibniz.... Absolute solitude, the violent turning inward on the self, whose whole being consists in the mastery of material and in the monotonous rhythm of work, is the specter which outlines the existence of man in the modern world. Radical isolation and radical reduction to the same hopeless nothingness are identical" (Horkheimer and Adorno [1944] 1972: 226).

and anomie as "Ego-anomic suicide"; the combination of anomie and altruism is rendered "Anomic-altruistic"; and, expectedly, egoism and altruism combine to form "Ego-altruistic suicide" (S: 293). Here we find an example of the 'mechanistic' Durkheim where combinations appear to be summations of constituent parts mutually reinforcing one another.[150] This mode of presentation should not prevent us from seeing the 'organic' Durkheim in addition to the more exotic 'dialectical' Durkheim at work in the pages of *Suicide*. Keep in mind that Durkheim never adheres to his own injunction to forsake the popular front for cult esotericism (RSM: 163). Instead, he operates along multiple lines of argument providing formulations that will appeal to mechanists, organicists, and synthesizers alike. Durkheim is, at heart, a unifier rather than a divider.[151] Let us back up and take for example the juxtaposition of egoism and anomie. When we arrive at the composite forms or compound alienations we have to grasp these dynamics as polar oppositions rather than diametrically opposed.[152] They are opposed to one another and are contradictory, but they are nonetheless polar contradictions, which means that they are capable of combinations and fusions. It is obviously true that the world is contradictory but rather than being stuck in permanent material opposition, moral currents can harmonize and produce something better than pure evil.

From the standpoint of the limited everyday experiences of the individual it seems that pure currents of egoism and altruism, or anomie and fatalism, are impossible—ideal-types that are not to be encountered in reality. But reality is, despite appearances, "infinite in every direction" and "infinitely complex" (Pickering [2000] 2006b: 105). "At the extreme depth of his inwardness [the

---

150 There is no ego-anomic-altruistic suicide type for the same reason there is no three-way combination of libidinal types in Freud's erotic, obsessional, and narcissistic typology: "such a type would no longer be a type at all, but the absolute norm, the ideal harmony. We thereupon realize that the phenomenon of different *types* arises just in so far as one or two of the three main modes of expending the libido in the mental economy have been favoured at the cost of the others" ([1931] 1959: 250). Drawing on Freud ([1913] 1950: 92) one has to wonder if science is not the sublime culmination of an historical procession from hysteria (art), obsession (religion), and paranoia (philosophy).

151 "I consider truth to have a single reason for and a single mode of existing: that is to be known. The more it is known, the more it will be. Therefore, to wish for it only the restricted cult of a few initiates is to diminish it, just as the sun would appear less magnificent to us if it illuminated only a small portion of the globe" (Durkheim 1973: 28).

152 "In the language of physics, sanctity is a *polar* force, it both attracts and repels" (Smith 1927: 370). This polarity applies to all moral forces. Remember, the concept of polarity in physics was borrowed from the polarities of religions.

egoist] ... joins an infinite outside" (Hocking 1956: 22). Reminiscent of Hegel's 'speculative method' Durkheim locates the obscured common source behind appearances.[153] Observe the structural imagery of the following passage and note that if negations or alienations are symptoms of social disintegration they are also solutions, i.e., negations of negations:

> We can only attach ourselves to [others] by getting out of ourselves, by alienating ourselves, by disinteresting ourselves in things narrowly or essentially personal. It is proper, therefore, to reserve the designation of altruistic for these inclinations. Thus, what differentiates altruism and egotism is not the nature of the pleasure that accompanies these two sorts of our observable behavior. It is the different direction that this activity follows in the two cases. When it is egotistical, it does not go beyond the acting subject; it is centripetal. When it is altruistic, it overflows from its subject. The centers around which it gravitates are outside of him; it is centrifugal.
>
> Once we admit this distinction, the unbridgeable gulf that at first seemed to separate selfish tendencies from altruistic ones disappears. These tendencies seemed at first to be so unlike that it appeared impossible to trace them to one and the same origin. Indeed, my pleasure is entirely within me. Someone else's pleasure is entirely within him. Consequently, between the two forms of activity whose objects are so distant there could not be anything in common; one was even justified in asking how they could ever come together in one and the same being. But this is no longer the case if the difference separating these two sorts of inclinations is reduced to that which is between the notion of an object outside the individual and the notion of an object that is immanent.... We have altruism ... when we are attached to something outside ourselves. But we cannot become attached to an external thing, whatever its nature, without representing it to ourselves.... By virtue of this fact alone—that we do represent an external object to ourselves—it becomes in certain respects internal. It exists in us in the form of the representation.... In this sense, we have become attached to ourselves. If we suffer because of the death of someone close to us, it is because our image of the ... person ... as well as the representations of all sorts of associations linked with him cease to

---

153 Durkheim's conception of the relationship between, say, egoism and altruism, is dialectical in that the concepts are opposites yet are also unintelligible apart from one another (see Lichtman 1982: 43). Bert is hate personified without Ernie; peanut butter is absurd without jelly; pizza is an orphan in a land without beer.

function.... We suddenly feel a painful void in our consciousness. We are vitally hurt by everything that diminishes the vitality of the beings to whom we are attached; being attached to them is to be a part of ourselves that we are attached.

Thus, we have egotism embedded in altruism, conversely, there is altruism in egoism. Indeed, our individuality is not an empty form. It consists of elements that come to us from the outside (1961: 214–15).

Egoism is not limited to blending with altruism in a dialectical reconciliation but can also alternate with altruism or remain externally connected to it in *mysticism* or form other mystical sublations (S: 290). In what follows we will examine how egoism combines with anomie in the form of what we have been calling *infinity disease*, chart the relationship between egoism and fatalism as a form of *resignation*, posit ecstasy as a unity of anomie and altruism, and envision how taboo is connected to infinity through superstition.

The sublation of egoism and anomie constitute what Durkheim calls the "disease of the infinite" (S: 287).[154] "The Stoics say, 'Retire within yourselves; it is there you will find your rest.' And it is not true. Others say, 'Go out of yourselves; seek happiness in amusement.' And this is not true. Illness comes" (Pascal 1941: 154). For Pascal, genuine happiness could be found only in god, or, sociologically, within society. The composite (*syntheton*) of these two currents is not simply "ego-anomic suicide" (S: 293) rather, as we saw earlier, the negative unity or *transdescendance* of the two (Jean Wahl, in Sartre 1950: 38–9) is a unique product that is greater than and different than the sum of its parts: "the disease of the infinite" (S: 287) or "infinity disease" (Worrell 2015).[155] We can see here that negations of negations do not exclude the negation of mathematical affirmation; the collision of one bad and another bad results in something even worse. The convergence of multiple forces, the points of intersection, creates a multiplier effect (DOL: 41).

Modernity is the age of monstrosities and what Chateaubriand called universal corruption whereby the individual overtakes society in moral importance, conscience contracts, and moral authority crumbles (1962: 100). If we are to strive for actual 'spiritual' relations with others, have actual concrete determinateness of being, and stand in a necessary relation with the world, we

---

154 "Here all boundaries fade away and the world reveals itself for the mad slaughterhouse that it is. The treadmill stretches away to infinitude, the hatches are closed down tight, logic runs rampant, with bloody cleaver flashing" (Miller 1961: 182).
155 "I balk at sleep as if it were a hole / filled up with horrors, leading God knows where; / my windows open on Infinity / and haunted by its vertigo my mind / envies the indifference of the void ..." (Baudelaire 1993: 228).

must embrace finitude and limitation (SL: 86). But "The stir of modern life ... has awakened sensibility, quickened desire, aroused the passion for freedom, disturbed old traditions" (Royce 1969: 255). 'Infinity disease' is an expression of this historical arc.[156] Egoism is characterized as the "infinity of dreams" whereas anomie is characterized by the "infinity of desires" (S: 287).[157] Together they constitute a new 'spirit' of boundless energy expenditures.[158] A milder form of this malady can be found in the spirit of Renaissance Humanism where the ideal typical humanist is restless, adventurous, independent, unreliable, unstable, thirsty for variety, and "indifferent to all other obligations usually incumbent upon men" (Simmel 1955: 137). Hocking also provides a good description of this malady:

> Social development brings with it a sharpening of individual self-consciousness, increased awareness of wants and cravings, an enhanced uneasiness in view of any repressed or incompletely satisfied wish. As wealth is got by ministering to desires, a premium is set on making men conscious of hitherto subliminal discomforts. The mentality of civilization is expert in its attentiveness to residual cravings .... Social unrest is due in part to radical abuses, maladjustments, wrongs. It is due in part to material progress itself, the states of mind it engenders, and the philosophies which abet those states of mind (1926: 303).

A worthy candidate for the official slogan for infinity disease might be "Passion will have all now" from *Pilgrim's Progress*. I (egoism) want (desire) all (unlimited) now (impatience).[159] In his remarks on "The High Repute of the Progress

---

156   Actually, the difference between disease or sickness and monstrosity is one of degrees. Durkheim distinguishes between sickness and monstrosity by saying that monstrosity "is an exception only in space; it is not met with in the average member of the species, but it lasts the whole lifetime of the individuals in which it is to be found. Yet it is clear that these two orders of facts ... are of the same nature. The boundaries drawn between them are very imprecise, for sickness can also have a lasting character and abnormality can evolve" (RSM: 105).

157   These conceptions of the 'infinite' are substantively close to the Kantian twin infinities of the inner and the outer (see SL: 230).

158   The first tiny seed of what we are calling 'infinity disease' emerges faintly with the Neolithic revolution, the shift from hunting and gathering to settled farming. Hunting and gathering societies were generally at ease with scarcity and did not suffer from want—they were, in a sense, highly affluent in their scarcity (Suzman 2017: 16).

159   I tend to locate narcissism at the extreme edge of egoism, yet, it could be replaced by sociological autism, leaving us with some wiggle room to shift narcissism over to the coordinates of infinity disease where much of the qualities of the narcissist overlap with the fantasy drives we find in anomie, especially its progressive or positive forms.

to Infinity" Hegel tells us much of what we want to know about infinity disease: the modern propensity for continuously striving beyond reasonable limits, taken to be a kind of sacred duty, leads to futility, "wearisome repetition," and the *"impotence"* of the subject and inability to break through to the domain of objectivity. A fixation on quantity (a "terrifying journey" of "heaping and piling up") and a "hollowness of ... exaltation" dooms this ego to a dreamlike experience where "one goes on and on down a corridor which stretches away endlessly out of sight ..." (SL: 228–30). The circulation of capital (M – C – M') in the pursuit of surplus value, is a perfect example of a mad circle that can lead nowhere but frustration and pathology.[160] The one thing that can prevent a slide into the infinite, the *absolute*, seems to be missing (Kant 1951: 89)[161] from those afflicted with infinity disease and, with capital, (the modern bad or abstract absolute, the miracle of miracles) we find a merciless slave-driver whipping us toward the cliff.

The drive for the infinite is connected to not only anomie and social dissolution but also to self-denial of the ascetic form:

> The quest for pleasure in its general form and avarice are two particular forms of greed for money. The abstract quest for pleasure implies an object that can embody the possibility of all pleasures. The abstract quest for pleasure is realised by money in the determination in which it is the *material representative of wealth;* avarice is realised in so far as money is merely the general form of wealth as against commodities as its particular substances. To hoard money as such, the individual must sacrifice all relation to the objects that satisfy particular needs, he must abstain, in order to satisfy his need or greed for money as such. The greed for money or quest for enrichment is necessarily the downfall of the ancient communities. Hence the opposition to it. It itself is the *community*, and cannot

---

160 "'Things possess an infinite quality when moving in a circle which they lack when advancing in a straight line'" (Galiani, in C: 255). It is also interesting to note the connection between the geometry of the circle and formalistic reduction. Durkheim says that European education for 1000 years was trapped within a circle of abstraction, reductionism, and pure formalism because it was turned inward upon itself, the alienated mind of man in the abstract, and indifferent to the external world of nature as an independent object of inquiry (1977: 280).

161 From Lacan's standpoint, what used to be labeled as 'paranoia' fits pretty well in the coordinates of infinity disease where the subject "was a nasty person, an intolerant one, a bad-humored type, proud, mistrustful, irritable, and who overestimated himself (1993: 4; Fink 1997: 244). Paranoia literally means having two minds side by side.

tolerate any other standing above it. But this implies the full development of exchange value, hence of a social organisation corresponding to it.

MECW, 28: 155

Capital constantly encounters real barriers and concrete frustrations but imagines that it can ideally surmount everything that stands in its way, and that it has ideally overcome every limitation, however, "it does not by any means follow that it has *really* overcome" those limits (G: 410). One is reminded of Karl Rove, the imperial reality-maker. We can see that the unfettered imagination, fueled by unregulated desires and the drive for the infinite, is at odds with existence in concrete reality. In a sense, capital is a purely otherworldly orientation because the finite can never satisfy its aim. While capitalism in no way gave birth to the infinite it certainly played a powerful role in amplifying and ennobling this spirit—it is virtually taboo to reject the idea of limitlessness and the questing ethos. As far as commodification, marketing, and popular culture go, we are an odd form of "animal governed by an infinity of desires."[162] This concept of humanity argues that what is most 'human' about people is their quest after the new, their willingness to violate boundaries, their hatred of the old and the habitual ... and their need to incorporate 'more and more'—goods, money, experience, everything" (Leach 1993: 385).

The alloy of isolation and deregulation, depression combined with mania, the disease of the infinite, can assume many forms. For example, with regard to the acquisitive or hedonistic individual we find an adequate expression in *Dead Souls*: "Solitary life gave ample nourishment to his avarice, which, as is known, has a wolf's appetite and grows more insatiable the more it devours; human feelings, never very deep in him anyway, became shallower every moment, and each day something more was lost in this worn-out-ruin" (Gogol [1842] 1996: 134). The desire to consume everything and devour others is not only encouraged in Western society but a kind of duty. The negative freedom[163]

---

162 "Where he became a being,—whose desire / Was to be glorious; 't was a foolish quest, / The which to gain and keep, he sacrificed / all rest" (Byron 1880: 311).

163 Negative freedom is the ambiguous and contradictory freedom *from* "the sweet bondage of [natural] paradise, but [this negatively free person] is not free to govern himself, to realize his individuality. 'Freedom from' is not identical with positive freedom, with 'freedom to.' The emergence of man from nature is a long drawn-out process; to a large extent he remains tied to the world from which he emerged; he remains part of nature—the soil he lives on, the sun and moon and stars, the trees and flowers, the animals, and the group of people with whom he is connected by the ties of blood" (Fromm 1941: 35). Freedom *from* hunger, for example, is not identical with the freedom *to* feed oneself on the basis of possession and control over the means of producing the material means of survival. Under capitalism most people are *formally* free (Weber's terminology) to dispose of their time and energy in exchange for a wage but at the substantive level, they remain unfree.

of the individual from obligations toward society[164] resulting from the breakdown of traditional institutions and authority, combined with Protestant theology, market expansion, and political liberalism creates a pathological form of individualism that finds it difficult or impossible to cooperate with others and certainly difficult to subordinate the self to the dictates (or rational needs) of others.[165] This classic American pathology is the central message in Arthur Miller's *Death of a Salesman*: "I never got anywhere because you blew me so full of hot air I could never stand taking orders from anybody.... I am not a leader of men, Willy, and neither are you. You were never anything but a hard-working drummer who landed in the ash can like all the rest of them! I'm one dollar an hour, Willy!" (1950: 131–32). Egoistic detachment combines with the spirit of limitlessness and will-mania (anomie) to drag individuals to their misery and doom.[166] Egoism and anomie, however, do not always form a synthetic compound; sometimes they alternate or oscillate (akin to the outdated 'manic-depressive' terminology).

> The alternating moods of determination and discouragement suggested a familiar Protestant oscillation between manic engagement and depressive withdrawal. The same pattern characterized gamblers, stock speculators, and enthusiastic Christians in the throes of conversion (at least according to their critics). From the evangelical-rational view, the calm acceptance of Providence was the antidote to manic depressive excitability and the precondition for a life of disciplined achievement. Submission to Providential order and assertion of personal independence paradoxically coalesced."
>
>   LEARS 2003: 147

---

164 "The assumptions which comprise possessive individualism" are encapsulated in the "freedom from dependence on the wills of others.... Freedom from any relations with others except those relations which the individual enters voluntarily with a view to his own interest. The individual ... owes nothing to society.... Human society consists of a series of market relations.... Since freedom from the wills of others is what makes a man human, each individual's freedom can rightfully be limited only by such obligations and rules as are necessary to secure the same freedom for others" (MacPherson 1962: 263–64).

165 With regard to negative freedom, Durkheim says that, "we cannot limit ourselves to this negative ideal" (1973: 55).

166 "In indifference to myself / (I watch) / what surrounds me / calm empty void / which is nothing / the absence of limits / escapes me in every direction" (Bataille 2004: 50). The will-maniac considers everything he or she is in contact with under his or her dominion and incapable of independent existence—see the cases of murder-suicides examined in Cavan ([1928] 1965: 254 ff.).

Beyond compounds, oscillations, and alternations,[167] we can also find laminated superimpositions and balancing acts: the Deist coupling of "the most extreme relativism" with "the most rigorous and uncompromising absolutism" (Kaye 1924: xli) or modern primitivism (EFRL: 25)[168] that superimposes "severe discipline characteristic of small and ancient groups" (fatalism or overregulation) with Stoic intellectualism and an affinity for high culture.[169] "He has all the intelligence of modern man without sharing his despair" (S: 168; cf. Freud 1939: 116).[170] This form of equilibrium, however, is of a *static* or mechanical

---

167 Alternations are interesting in that polar opposites, for example egoism and altruism or terror and relaxation, wear the mask of the exact opposite (Merleau-Ponty 1973: 93). The symbol for egoism is altruism just as the manifestation of value for the relative pole of the exchange relation is the body of the particular equivalent. Weber describes emotionally intense Pietistic alternations between "ecstasy" or possession and "abandonment" or estrangement (PESC: 82). For seemingly incomprehensible alternations between feverish cult rituals interjected with the purely prosaic and mundane affairs, see Douglas Smith (2016) on Russian sectarianism.

168 "[T]he most primitive religions are not the only ones that have ascribed to sacredness such an ability to propagate. Even the most modern cults have a set of rites based on this principle" of contagion (EFRL: 326). The 'primitive' is not relegated to history but right next door (Freud [1913] 1950: 3; DOL: 204) and in the unconscious (Certeau 1984: 64). And by 'primitive' or 'savage' we have in mind more of an epistemological and ontological primordiality (see the editorial comment in Hegel 1988: 130, fn. 41). It is too long to quote but on the fear of contagion see Santayana ([1936] 1949: 24–5). "Here ... we have a clear case of the re-emergence into the light of day of a cult of the most primitive totem type, which had been banished for centuries from public religion, but must have been kept alive in obscure circles of private or local superstition, and sprang up again on the ruins of the national faith, like some noxious weed in the courts of a deserted temple" (Smith 1927: 357). Events "from the beginning of time" extend into our present. "You come back, wavering shapes, out of the past / In which you first appeared to clouded eyes" (Goethe, in Kaufmann 1965a). In short, there is a "solidarity of the ages" (Bloch 1953: 41, 43). "Even if the conception of reality in contemporary everyday life is not wholly a continuation of the primitive experience of the world, it is nevertheless so closely related to it in structure that in our everyday spontaneous experience of the world—notwithstanding our superior theoretical knowledge derived from natural science—the sun is still seen by us as a disk and, notwithstanding our knowledge of causality, magical ideas still govern our horizon of expectations. And we [also] control our fears through secret charms. Things have faces, and a lingering animism still leads us to see the objects and growths of a place not as bare but as charged with a mood (sometimes malevolent—a raging stream; sometimes joyful—a spring landscape)" (Mannheim 1982: 207).

169 Because the Jews had the concept of themselves, i.e., worshiped a spiritual abstraction, they achieved unparalleled durability (Freud 1939: 116).

170 Freud's personal obsessive compulsiveness is interesting here. "What kind of personality is able to achieve so much within the span of only half a lifetime? [24 volumes of work beginning at age 39] Most people of outstanding intellectual achievement exhibit traits of personality which psychiatrists label obsessional.... Freud himself recognized that his

superimposition rather than the dynamic equilibrium of a rationally integrated, synthetic society (DOL: lii).[171] Fear not, equilibrium is not a conservative concept but part of the continuous becoming of society—the coming-to-be and the ceasing-to-be of its moments (SL: 106).

We also have to be wary of deceptive forms of pseudo-alternation. The 'beauty' of having a one-party political system with two personalities is that one can prance about as a friend of public welfare while the other can portray itself as a partner in business and security (Miliband 1969: 184). Once the party of welfare has run its course, it is time for the 'other' party to take the reins and 'rebalance' the excess generosity lavished by Team Blue. Of course, all this is sheer nonsense. For example, when the Bush regime set out to destroy as much labor regulation as it could in the aftermath of two Clinton terms, business types explained that they were necessary and "only aiming to restore balance after Clinton had, in their views, advocated too ardently on behalf of workers. The only problem with this business view was that Clinton never consistently supported workers' interests, either in terms of labor laws and regulations, or, more generally, through the overall impact of his policies on working people and the poor" (Pollin 2003: 120).

By now, it should be apparent that the dialectical oppositions and polarities in Durkheim's model, e.g., egoism and altruism, etc., point to the weird, speculative identities of what appear to ordinary consciousness as absolutely diametric oppositions that can never combine or interact.[172] But we can discern in Durkheim's evolved rationalism a bond with the romantic sacralization of the individual. It has been claimed that Durkheim's god is society but

---

personality was obsessional.... His intellectual precocity, and his dedication to work, which remained compulsive from boyhood onwards, are characteristic" (Storr 1989: 8–9). Additionally, what I find of great interest is the "peculiar oscillation between scepticism and credulity" probably necessary for creative intellectual leaps (Storr 1989: 9).

171 "We do not sustain ourselves in virtue by our own strength, but by the balancing of two opposed vices, just as we remain upright amidst two contrary gales. Remove one of the vices, and we fall into the other" (Pascal 1941: 118). See also Gramsci's interesting theory of progressive and reactionary Caesarism whereby countervailing forces equilibrate "in a catastrophic manner ... [and] reciprocal destruction" (1971: 219).

172 Freud says that altruism can be a reaction-formation of an identical egoistic drive where observation can be deceived into perceiving a change of content where none is present. The form changes but the content is identical. Drives (improperly translated as 'instincts' in English-language texts) are ambivalent, literally two-sided values (*ambi*, is Latin for 'of both sides' and 'valent' is derived from *valere*, Latin for worth) that form oppositional pairs, such as egoism and altruism or love and hatred—but underneath the polarities we will find a single drive ([1915] 1959: 296). Where there is anything 'ambi' there is not only two sides but, as with *ambition* (*ambi-re*), a circle—a going around, eager for honor.

the "masterpiece" of civilization is actually the individual personality.[173] This identity between rationalism and romanticism, between rationalism and anti-rationalism, is well established. "In this quest for spontaneity, immediacy and the plenitude of life Romanticism represents an extreme extension of the rationalist view of man as good, of the individual as supremely important, indeed sacred" (Talmon 1967: 145).[174]

Just as virtue pushed to an extreme is vicious, the rational pushed to the extreme becomes its opposite, but another way to look at, e.g., the vicious, is to see it as surplus virtue, not merely as a lack; likewise, virtue is merely vice that has failed to live up to its potential. The immoderate rationalism of romanticism led it to seek out the unmediated just as Freud's rationalist quest led him, like the romantics, into the "bottomless abyss of the unconscious" (Talmon 1967: 145). The romantic, then, in their longing for the sublime is engaged in a suicidal calling; the disenchanted life is not worth living (Binion 2005: 67). Pushed to the extreme, the altruistic fanatic reveals their narcissism, an extreme form of egoism; the two moments form a speculative identity. The isolated loner, in a bid to escape isolation, seeks the other in some form, some double in which to establish moorings for existence (S: 289–90).[175] Again, we circle back to the problem of the social mirror and our attempts to erect some alter-existence for ourselves. We all need others to live but the egoist is not content with co-existence, reciprocity, or cooperation but self-magnification within the sphere of the double. Take for example the traditional role of women as supporters of men:

> Women have served all these centuries as looking-glasses possessing the magic and delicious power of reflecting the figure of man at twice its natural size. Without that power probably the earth would still be swamp and jungle. The glories of all our wars would be unknown. We should still be scratching the outlines of deer on the remains of mutton bones and bartering flints for sheep skins or whatever simple ornament took our unsophisticated taste. Supermen and Fingers of Destiny would never have existed. The Czar and the Kaiser would never have worn crowns or lost them. Whatever may be their use in civilized societies, mirrors are essential to all violent and heroic action. That is why Napoleon and

---

173   "Humanity is the third god which puts an end to all gods, to the tyrants of the skies and of the earth" (Mauss [1920/1950] 2006: 48).

174   In *Magic Mountain* (Mann [1927] 1955) the deified man is presented as the balance point between communal mysticism and individualism.

175   This traversal of the narcissist-fanatic identity is separate from the sageism of the Stoic, though there are points of contact, intersections and overlapping currents.

> Mussolini both insist so emphatically upon the inferiority of women, for if they were not inferior, they would cease to enlarge. That serves to explain in part the necessity that women so often are to men. And it serves to explain how restless they are under her criticism; how impossible it is for her to say to them this book is bad, this picture is feeble, or whatever it may be, without giving far more pain and rousing far more anger than a man would do who gave the same criticism. For if she begins to tell the truth, the figure in the looking-glass shrinks; his fitness for life is diminished. How is he to go on giving judgement, civilizing natives, making laws, writing books, dressing up and speechifying at banquets, unless he can see himself at breakfast and at dinner at least twice the size he really is?
> WOOLF [1929] 2001: 43–4

Positive hedonism (really *sybaritism* since the historical hedonists were themselves minimalists when it came to the pursuit of material pleasures) is one route to self-destruction. "'Listening to his friend, Balzac's character is persuaded to destroy himself aristocratically, by overindulging in pleasures.[176] 'Intemperance, my boy, is the most royal of deaths. It has lightning apoplexy at its command. Apoplexy is the pistol-shot that does not miss....' In contrast to 'the swollen bellies and the decomposing green and blue flesh' of the morgue, the two can enjoy orgies and gambling, prostitutes and wine ..." (in Lieberman 2003: 97). Chasing physical pleasures leads to bondage through fear and excites "a wish for obedience to itself which other desires ... prevent from being accomplished" (Green [1895] 1924: 4). Anomic hedonism offers us an obvious example of cannibalism when, pushed to the extreme, we find people who desire to consume the whole world (Freud's object-choice over identification). The connection between Durkheim's formulation of anomie and psychoanalytic cannibalism is striking: "Intake and expulsion proceeded at a rapid rate. This was shown in the manic's flight and distractibility. The associations showed that words were equated to feces, and perceiving to eating; it was as if the manic gobbled up perceptions in his overalertness to expel them immediately in his logorrhea" (Lewin 1961: 32).[177] The egoist, too, is a cannibal: "By introjecting and incorporating the object, the [person] identifies himself with it, and the

---

[176] "The great object of life is Sensation—to feel that we exist—even though in pain—it is this 'craving void' which drives us to Gaming—to Battle—to Travel—to intemperate but keenly felt pursuits of every description whose principal attraction is the agitation inseparable from their accomplishment" (Byron 1982: 356).

[177] Is it not the case that, as they approach the end, people often engage in hyper-consumption of food or drink before swinging around to an opposite hypo-consumption?

taking in is conceived in the [person's] fantasies as a devouring, a necrophagia" (Lewin 1961: 27).

Altruism and egoism, together, "are two concurrent and intimately intertwining aspects of all conscious life" (Durkheim 1961: 217).[178] The optimal fusion of egoism and altruism seems difficult to achieve but decisive since "The humanity of man is only conceivable within the human aggregation and, in one sense at least, as existing through it" (Davy 1957: xlvi). Without the aggregate there is no individual because the isolated ego is an "untenable void" (SL: 231). If the ego fails to reach 'escape velocity' from its own pit of fascination with abstract selfhood, the beyond (beyond society) will become the fatal "ultimate" (SL: 231).[179] We find many attempts to connect the ego to its other in the form of desperate transpositions, alternations,[180] faulty bridgework and scaffolding, and myriad structural absurdities at the rim of the abyss.[181] Magic is one such egoistic regression (Bloch 1966: 63) whereby the properly religious forces (terminating in this case in the precise coordinates of *optional* altruism[182] where concerns for prestige are found circulating) are subverted by egoists for personal ends.[183] Magic is certainly egotistical but we will reserve that concept for the fusion of anomie and fatalism and focus, instead, on the utilitarian and mystical aspects of egoism and altruism.

On the purely subjective side, the ego may attempt, in a process known through Freud as 'introversion' to latch onto purely imaginary or fantasy objects. Fantasy may be thought of as a general feature of any coordinate within the overall moral geometry, but one can find its purest expression within the alloy known as infinity disease. Fantasy space, regardless of its form, can lure a person away from reality with its seductions of being someone else or something else or can merely function to provide a fantasmatic support that enables one to endure reality. A fantasy can become, in a sense, "fully operational"

---

178 Egoism is *ego*-morphism; altruism is *alter*-ation (Nietzsche 1968: 167).
179 "The void seems to beckon us down, but really it is our own freedom that beckons us down, the very fact that we can always choose to go down the quick way" (Cox 2012: 50).
180 The pendulum life is an unbearable source of anxiety (Ivimey 1946: 67) and cannot be considered a viable or rational solution to turbulence.
181 This abyss is linked to modern transformations of mana and taboo—it is horrifying yet attractive; we cannot avert our gaze. The conceptual tie is that of the sublime; "the imagination works harder in darkness than it does in bright light" (Kant 1998: 195).
182 On magic and optionality, compared to religion and obligatory acts, see Radcliffe-Brown where we find that magic is a means to an end whereas religion is always felt to be an end in itself (1952: 136–37).
183 "[F]rom the purely moral point of view, being deprived of life is not necessarily a loss, and may even be a gain for the victim" (Solovyov 1918: 12).

(Bechdel 2006: 61) where it begins to eclipse reality. The fantastic or representational is a problem because it disallows Spirit to move from the finite (evil) to infinite subjectivity, i.e., scientific and conceptual thought (Hegel 1988: 344–45). When reality is eclipsed by fantasy or merely unknown due to ignorance[184] we can expect dreams and desires to carry a person away on a wave of enthusiasm that overflows in all directions. Here, we find this surplus energizing the transit between the ego and altruism. On the intersubjective side the ego may attempt to replicate itself in purely inverted forms.[185] Along the frontier of matter, the ego can attempt to prop itself up with goods and fetish objects. *Utilitarianism* is also relevant for our construct.[186] Rather than delivering the promised benefits for the majority, "the great idol" of self-serving Utility[187] swerves off into progressive anomie and sybaritism, or, perhaps, all the way into anarchy which is only the inverse of its speculative opposite, namely, the extreme limit of fatalism, all the while patting itself on the back for being such a benefactor to humanity.[188] At the core of utilitarianism is a Lockean ontological individualism whereby the pre-constituted subject precedes voluntary contractual association for the satisfaction of self-interests through intercourse with others (Bellah et al. 1985: 143).[189]

---

184 "For the vulgar, the infinite proceeds from the indefinite.... When man begins to see no more clearly, he imagines, he dreams, he admires, he believes" (Boutmy 1902: 85, my translation).

185 A pristine example is provided by former Rutgers philosophy professor Anna Stubblefield (white, married, privileged, intellectual, female) who attempted to 'possess' herself in the form of her inverted social mirror, a black, unmarried, subaltern, diaper-wearing male with the "mental capacity of a toddler." Stubblefield was convicted on two counts of first-degree sexual assault (Engber 2015) and was sentenced to 12 years in prison. Basically, through 'facilitated communication' Stubblefield transformed her alter ego into a human Ouija board.

186 "[A]s soon as the neighbor (or society) recommends altruism *for the sake of its utility*, it applies the contradictory principle. 'You shall seek your advantage even at the expense of everything else'—and thus one preaches, in the same breath, a 'Thou shalt' and 'Thou shalt not'" (Nietzsche [1887] 1974: 94, emphasis in the original). On utilitarianism as a counter to Comte's altruism, see Irwin (2009: 414).

187 "Utility is the great idol of our age, to which all powers are in thrall and to which all talent must pay homage. Weighed in this crude balance, the insubstantial merits of Art scarce tip the scale, and, bereft of all encouragement, she shuns the noisy market-place of our century" (Schiller 1967: 7).

188 "We quite agree that nothing is more deserved than that such doctrines [as utilitarianism] be considered anarchical" (Durkheim 1973: 44).

189 "Throw in constant innovation and you arrive at the economic promised land of infinite appetite and endless growth, i.e., limitless production, consumption, and accumulation. But as with any psychic disorder that exhibits neither a mean nor moderation, advanced economies based on the social ideal of the *popolo grasso* [well-fed urban professionals]

It is not only the utilitarian that advocates progressive anomie but utopians and libertarians of various stripes as well.[190] My Robot Marxist colleagues (automation is salvation under the rule of the general intellect) are also fond of dreaming of never-ending days of spontaneous fishing trips, casual herding, and campfire philosophizing.

> In postcivilized society this standard of life [universalized leisure] is extended to all men, and the very poorest and meanest has the capability of living like a Roman emperor. The Roman emperors, however, while they all may have lived luxuriously, rarely lived virtuously. It is all too easy to visualize a postcivilized world of besotted hedonists with wires running into the pleasure centers of the brain, enjoying enormous but meaningless sensations of rapture in a totally stable and unchallenging mechanical environment. Such a world would lose its adaptability to the point where a very slight worsening of the overall environment might destroy it. The most successful leisure classes and the ones which have maintained their vigor the longest seem to have done so by practicing a set of artificial miseries and discomforts such as fox-hunting, dressing for dinner, opera, court ceremonial, and athletic games. Therefore if the human race is to prevent itself from disintegrating through sheer boredom or lasciviousness in a postcivilized society, it may be necessary to introduce artificial discomforts and it may be hard to do this when comfort is so easily attainable. The ideal is of course to find a way in which comfort and virtue can go hand in hand, but so far we do not seem to have been too successful in finding this happy combination.
> BOULDING 1964: 149; see also WORRELL and KRIER 2018

The Stoics represent another crucial form where a sage is constructed and then becomes an object of slavish devotion; Durkheim simply used the term 'Stoicism' to represent this idolatrous aporia (S: 280).[191] The image of the sage, however, also figures in altruism.

---

suffer consequences such as credit fever, environmental degradation, collapse of fertility rates, loss of solidarity, and axiological confusion, to name a few" (Munkelt 2017: 146).

190 The legacy of Scottish common-sense realism that took root in America toward the end of the 18th Century provides a justification for anarchic-libertarian deregulation with ideas that individuals instinctively know through a "moral sense" the difference between right and wrong. This "moral sense" provides "'a broad rationale for individual self-determination in every aspect of human activity'" (Herbert Hovenkamp, in McCall 2017: 182–83).

191 Along with the pantheism of Stoic materialism (which, at the end of the day is an idealism) sageism is another point where the Stoic philosophy flips into irrational religion. As

For the pure egoist, there is no authority beyond the self; yet, the ego must find external supports and some indices of the attainment of subjective power. The altruist, too, though they find no authority that is not purely outside of themselves, cannot locate it within the dense spread of inert matter and the altruist becomes thirsty for rapture. Here the sage satisfies the requirements of both currents. "To the neo-Platonic philosopher ... matter—namely, the material and real world in general—is no longer an authority and a reality. Fatherland, family, worldly ties, and goods in general, which the ancient peripatetic philosophy still counted as man's bliss—all these are nothing for the neo-Platonic sage. He even considers death better than corporeal life" (Feuerbach 1986: 45). Sageism is one form along with several others such as acedia, mysticism and utilitarianism, providing distinct, negative unities of egoism and altruism.

Mystification "derives from powerlessness, and powerlessness is itself an expression of alienation" (Lichtman 1982: 26). This notion of powerlessness, however, needs clarification. We can see how the egoist, isolated and disenchanted, is powerless and sets out to emulate the sage or perfection personified (e.g., the aura of Socrates) but the altruist, the opposite pole of mysticism, clearly resides in an 'empowered' dimension of life. Is the altruist (e.g., fanatic, maniac, martyr, and so on) actually powerless? These types are energized, of that there is no doubt, they circulate around the coordinates of ecstasy but, ultimately, yes, they are also powerless in that their bursts of energy are in the end merely destructive. Terrorists are effective however they build nothing; they want attention but achieve nothing beyond a momentary and negative attention. They feel harmed and wish to harm others in return.

Mysticism is "the tomb of freedom" (Vacherot 1870: 174) and mystics who flee from reality fail to live up to their own measure (FMW: 128). But not all forms of mysticism are necessarily pathological. We often find, with musicians and other artists, for example, a productive and life-affirming fetishizing of nature and things. For example:

> Take the time to give the note your full attention by just listening as deeply as you can and recognizing, on those subtle levels, how that note makes you feel. Merge your being with the name of the note, along with the

---

Murray says, when it comes to Stoicism, it is entirely appropriate to view it as both philosophy and religion (1915: 14).

personality, emotion, and color of the note. See how the notes differ in hue from one to another. In doing this, you are essentially creating an intimate relationship with each individual note.... This is a meditation of sorts, and the more you focus on the resonance of each note, the deeper your personal relationship with that note will be. By the way, the notes love it when you do this with them. They will start singing to you.
>
> VAI 2019: 9–10

Poetry and music are the ego's refuge from itself and conduits to the realm of the "wholly other"—the portal to the world of ecstasy and action (see Jaynes 1990: 370–77). In *O Pioneers!* we find the buffeted ego raising itself up:

> As he listened ... he seemed to emerge from the conflicting emotions which had been whirling him about and sucking him under. He felt as if a clear light broke upon his mind, and with it a conviction that good was, after all, stronger than evil, and that good was possible to men. He seemed to discover that there was a kind of rapture in which he could love forever without faltering and without sin.... That rapture was for those that could feel it.... The spirit he had met in music was his own.
>
> CATHER [1913] 2000: 213–14

We know of many biophilic mystics in history that blend altruism with egoism into a positive formation but the negative type of mysticism combines nihilistic megalomania (Cohn 1970: 176) with altruistic demonization of the enemies of the sacred Other, e.g., Jean-Antoine Boullan who "regarded himself as 'the sword of God,' charged with the task of cleansing the earth of ... impurity" (Ibid: 176–77). The difference between positive and negative mysticism is the inclusion in the latter of a strong infusion of anomie—*anarchy* in Cohn's lexicon—resulting in "total amoralism" and the evacuation of personal conscience (Ibid: 177). Individualism in itself can lead off into the most heterogeneous forms of intellectual and political life.

Transcendental idealism, extreme in its apotheosis of the Ego, leads off to socialism with Fichte and the ethics of Kantian idealism rests on a foundation of irrational faith and blind submission. And 'submission' would seem to be an unexpected quality in the domain of egoism, yet, with the Stoics, we find it alive and well in their construct of the wise man and, again, in the melancholy of the Puritans where we find that depression and sadness were "evidence of individual submission to Satan and therefore of a conscious and purposeful rejection of salvation"—"submission to diabolical temptation"

(Kushner 1989: 17).[192] Of course, the deep-seated desire for submission is but one half of the authoritarian complex that links submission of the faithful with the persecution of criminal taboo-smashers. What appears to be collective solidarity of an intense and punishing variety (sadistic atonement) as well as the appearance of a tender altruism, can mask "brutal egoism" and the mass lure of prohibited desires (Freud [1913] 1950: 90–1).[193]

Rousseau's "individualism is complemented by his authoritarian conception of society" (Durkheim 1973: 47). The extreme form of egoism, narcissism, often abandons itself in sadomasochism where the self is sacrificed to a stronger power (Adorno 1974: 65).[194] How does a depressed loner wind up propelled into the energetic coordinates of rage and destruction? Egoism leads not only to indifference or resignation, etc., but also, on the basis of social disintegration, a sense of panic and overreaction. Things that appeared to be small threats assume gigantic proportions to the isolated ego devoid of libidinal or energetic ties to others and supporting institutions (Freud [1921] 1959: 36). There exist various routes from egoism to a position in the moral geometry where violence is inflicted on self and others; one might even concede that violence is all that transpires here. An important avenue, to mention only one, is through ascetic self-torture (what Caillois calls "the road to power") representing a short-circuit into the domain of sadomasochistic destruction or, worse, its higher unity in the *piaculum*. But we should backtrack a little and note that the "disillusioned matter-of-factness" of the Epicurean can play a part as well where others are reduced to ordinary objects of no greater value than anything else in the physical and psychical environment. Here is a secret link to the inhumanity of altruism where inhibitions toward destruction fall away.

The purity of both autistic narcissism and acute fanaticism are only ideal points not found in reality in any pristine shape. Originally, Durkheim thought that the 'primitive mentality' was purely altruistic (members compacted into a horde of one-sided monstrosities). Mauss called this thesis an error of genius. Later, however, Durkheim came around to the notion that egoism and anomie were older than altruism, that "naive egoism" was the seed that supported altruism: "one finds traces of it in every primitive morality. Altruism was so weak

---

192 "The notion that suicide derived from 'miserable insanity' was clearly in part a survival of the belief that suicide is of diabolical inspiration, a view which, under the impress of the Church, held sway until some way through the eighteenth century" (Giddens 1965: 4).
193 There is nothing selfless about self-sacrifice (Nietzsche 2015: 11).
194 Malraux finds the sadism of the egoist released when indifference encounters devotion and sacrifice in the other (1961: 174).

that it could hardly have prevailed even with the assistance of religion if egoism had not lent a hand."[195] Further,

> One finds in Homer many accounts of unselfish acts; but the motives are always marked by naive egoism. If a warrior risks his life to save another, it is because such devotion is glorious or generally useful since it is a means of acquiring support which one may need.... [T]he egoistic satisfaction one feels from having triumphed over oneself [!] can become a motive *sui generis* which reinforces the tendency toward sympathy and assures its victory in the future without any further need for appeal to self-interested considerations.
> DURKHEIM 1993: 99

Returning to the relationship between narcissism and fanatical altruism (the acute form) we find that both have a problem with the ego: the narcissist seeks external supports for the ego in order to cultivate it further while the acute altruist experiences the ego as an alien and hostile resident and seeks not to develop it or support it in any way but, on the contrary, to expel the thing, the monstrosity within, via self-annihilation. In no empirical cases should we expect to find pure automatons lacking individual egos, but we should find, as in the cases of the excessively or insufficiently individuated, a problem with the self. Excesses here, deficiency there, always unsettled disequilibrium and one-sidedness—things and monsters, in other words, but never objectivity or morality.

Cooley for one supports the originality of egoism: "It is sometimes said that the individual counted for nothing in tribal life, that the family or the clan was the unit of society, in which all personalities were merged."

> From the standpoint of organization there is much truth in this; that is the group of kindred was for many purposes (political, economic, religious, etc.) a corporate unit, acting as a whole and responsible as a whole to the rest of society; so that punishment of wrong-doing, for example, would be exacted from the group rather than from the particular offender. But taken psychologically, to mean that there was a lack of self-assertion, the idea is without foundation. On the contrary, the barbaric mind exalts an aggressive and even extravagant individuality. Achilles is a fair sample

---

195 It is difficult (and maybe beside the point) to decide on the historical primacy of egoism or altruism because, in the final analysis, the two currents are never separated from one another in reality. Egoism is *ego*-morphism; altruism is *alter*-ation (Nietzsche 1968: 167).

of its heroes mighty in valor and prowess, but vain, arrogant and resentful—what we should be apt to call an individualist. The men of the Nibelungenlied, of Beowulf, of Norse and Irish tales and of our Indian legends are very much like him.

COOLEY [1909] 1962: 110

The "error of genius" in Durkheim's original assessment was, perhaps, more genius than error, as it turns out. Decades later it was discovered that the translations of Homeric poetry by modern subjects distorted the reality of the past by projecting subjectivity into actions and deeds where subjectivity was perhaps absent; the Homeric poems were depictions of acts undertaken by people who lacked egos, will, and consciousness of their own (Jaynes 1990: 67–83). Though, again, the debate is sterile.

In general, the attempt to synthesize egoism and altruism results in mysticism or suicide.[196] One of the most important connections here is the problem of revenge. Both the depressed egoist[197] and the altruistic fanatic can be animated by the desire for retribution and vengeance (especially, in the case of the altruist, in the form of piacular violence). It is important to keep in mind that, when it comes to mysticism, we never actually confront solidarity; mysticism, even if it occurs within a collectivity, is a concept applicable only to individuals—mysticism may appear to be a mass phenomenon plaguing groups now and then, but mysticism can never escape its individualistic or atomistic character. "A philosophy based on postulates taken from the mystical life can pertain only to isolated persons, or people who have left their isolation by joining a group where exactly the same convictions as theirs prevail" (Sorel 1950: 258).

Another especially important form of the egoistic-altruistic dynamic can be found in Fanon's account of an egoist bent solely on pursuing his personal interests during the Algerian revolt against the French. His *indifference* returns in the form of paranoia and guilt over his lack of solidarity towards his family and the larger liberation movement. Fearing that he has been judged a coward and

---

196 "Mysticism" is an appropriate name for one of the negative syntheses of egoism and altruism, especially the Stoic and optional altruist. For a brief discussion of the connection between contemplation, possession, and mysticism, see Riley (2002: 367). Notable in Riley's piece is the attempt to port Weber's conception of the calling into Durkheim's theory of the sacred. A connection between ecstasy and mysticism is also established by Geertz (see Riley 2002: 376).

197 The loss of object Eros for the depressed individual can be introjected in the process of identification: these people "seem to be punishing their lost objects in effigy, but their own ego is the effigy" (Lewin 1961: 27).

collaborator this egoist attempts to martyr himself; death by police is imagined as a means of atonement and reestablishing positive social identity (1963: 272–75). Here, death amounts to a symbolic rebirth and is a kind of liberation, albeit negatively.[198]

At precisely this set of coordinates, egoistic indifference is transposed to the register of altruistic carelessness. One might argue that marriage and parenthood are preferable forms of martyrdom.

In a good marriage, for example, egoism is "thoroughly suspended, not only in favor of the other, but also in favor of the general relationship …" (SGS: 129).[199] However, this altruism and collective orientation "is grounded in bases of the ego which rationalistically are inexplicable and which lie beyond its consciousness.[200] It is also expressed in the distinction between the unit and its elements. That each of them feels the relation to be something with its own life-forces, merely indicates that it is incommensurable with the personal, self-contained ego, as we usually conceive it" (SGS: 130). The sociological ego, then, is not identical with the abstract psychological ego.

Egoism should not be evaluated within the light of personalism but comprehended as an impersonal force; where we think we are free we are still subjugated by the trans-personal. In some ways, egoism is always already the back door into determinism and the dictates of some heteron. Altruism may veil a "raging egoism" and the person who believes they are an irrepressible individualist may in fact be quite the opposite. "A successful man looking back on his life believes that the plans he followed, the happy trains of thought and action that he elaborated, were his own…. He discovers that no moment of his existence was his own…. [M]odish even in death, the suicide is the slave of the same fashion that dictates to the dandy" (Fedden 1938: 290). The unregulated passions are quite often the doorway to fate and death (Royce 1914: 18; Herder 1966: 121).

> It is so easy to trip along in the dance of desire; but further along where it is desire that dances with man against his will, it is a hard dance! It is so

---

198　Liberation entails some form of "rebirth" (Freire 1993: 43).

199　Simply being married offers little protection from suicide whereas being a parent does lower the chances for self-destruction (S: 185). Left alone as a dyad, a couple will often devolve into outright warfare "But in the family triad, the winning and common care for the child may charm away many of the most besetting influences that tend to wreck home unity" (Royce 1914: 37–8).

200　Here we find the famous 'cunning of reason' at work behind the backs of individuals—far from rational choices, we have an unconscious power working to elevate the ego above and beyond itself as a member of a larger social unit.

easy to give rein to passions—a daring ride one can hardly follow with his eyes!—until the passions, having taken the reins which were given them, sweep the man away on a still wilder ride, and the man hardly dares look where they are leading him!.

    KIERKEGAARD 1940: 77

The synthesis of anomie and altruism is another composite that assumes a panoply of forms such as besiegement (S: 288)[201] and Rabelaisianism (which will be explored in the next volume). For now, we are chiefly interested in what we might refer to as the 'Phrygian' dimension of ecstasy. It is in this vicinity that the important currents of the expiation, the *piacular* rites, and revenge emerge. The image of the prophet in Weber's *Ancient Judaism* offers a good example of this combination:

> Indeed, unconfined by priestly or status conventions and quite untempered by any self control, be it ascetic or contemplative, the prophet discharges his glowing passion and experiences all the abysses of the human heart. And yet, despite all these human frailties ... it is not their private motives but the cause of Yahweh ... that reigns supreme ....
>
>   AJ: 273

The polarity of sin and expiation is a choice example of the dynamic tension between the individual acting without regard for authority, the accumulation of anxiety, and the expiation of sin and discharge of accumulated anxiety.[202] Without periodic atonement sin would lead to more sin and the individual would become supercharged with demonic powers (Hertz 1994: 62–72). Always, with atonement, we know we are dealing with sin and religious authority and forces as opposed to, say, luck (Radcliffe-Brown 1952: 136), which belongs to the domain of anomie. Regarding this fusion, anomie and altruism, we will

---

201   *The fusion of altruism and anomie is subjugation (under the yoke) like the besieged.* 'Besiege' means to sit aside from the opposed and is related to obsession. Indeed, full-blown obsession or "taboo sickness" (Freud [1913] 1950: 34) sits right next to it in our affective space. To be under siege is to be obsessed and unable to break away from the other. But fear at this moment is alloyed with hope and encouragement whereas in pure "taboo sickness" there is nothing but fear. Together, the besieged are yoked with the opposite. To be 'yoked' together is simply to be joined in a mechanical fashion rather than related in any substantive or rational manner.

202   Anxiety is a "cosmic" problem—we are incapable of standing "outside" of anxiety to comprehend it as an objective totality (May 1977: 207).

have more to say in the next volume. The blending of fatalism and altruism, however, cannot wait and for this unity we have the concept of taboo.

The disease of finitude (taboo) is the rule of evil. Where egoists are "enamoured of infinity" as Durkheim puts it, the highly repressed are blocked from getting what they want, setting up an economy of resentment and a desire for revenge that will flow into sanguinity (altruism). Anything taboo is set apart, sacred, and off limits to most. Since it partakes in the sacred, or is sacred, taboo can have integrative effects (Freud [1913] 1950: 41–3) but since the positive or pure is contaminated with the negative or impure, it must be equally considered a force of disintegration. A taboo (prohibited) object, thought, action, or feeling means separation and in separation a thing either falls out of social relations or, inversely, becomes an all-consuming power that devours social relations, a black hole of collective hopelessness and guilt. Where hope flows out of altruism and is preserved it runs in multiple directions out of taboo: superstition, ecstatic destruction, and fanaticism. Here we are in the proximity not of religious prohibitions or categorical imperatives but collective magical or utilitarian maxims (EFRL: 304–05) that abandon Spirit in things, repetitions, and capricious dreams but also demons (avatars of negative mana) with their special capacities for surplus utility (Mauss 1972: 85–6). A more sustained confrontation with 'taboo' will be taken up in volume three.

Perhaps the most difficult composition to theorize is the unity of anomie and fatalism. Here we are forced to extrapolate not a passage from one current to its opposite but a polarity and unity of opposites that Durkheim did not explicitly confront as well as we should hope.[203] As we saw, Durkheim sloughed off 'fatalism' in a footnote but then built fatalistic aspects into the other suicidogenic currents, e.g., the polarity of liberty and determinism (S: 39, 325) or the reference to oscillations between anarchy and authoritarianism (S: 380; cf. Fromm 1973: 165).[204] The understanding confronts the opposition of fate as a "counter-image of his freedom" but fate is not a limit but a completion: "freedom and fate embrace each other to form meaning" (Martin Buber, in Horne 1983: 67). In psychological terms, the surface symptomology of this couplet suggests the bi-polarity of egoism and anomie (depression alternating with mania) but the underlying mechanism, at the level of the subject, is the periodic alternation of, on the one hand, over-severe censoring and repression (over-regulation) on part of the conscience leading to depression, and, on

---

203   "In Germany, everything is forcibly suppressed; a real anarchy of the mind, the reign of stupidity itself, prevails there ..." (MECW, 3: 142).
204   As Mounier says, "... financial imperialism, wherever it feels itself menaced, will not scruple to turn against the liberties it defended while they were useful to it, and will entrust its ultimate security to reigns of terror or to inexpiable wars" (1952: 104).

the other, the elation accompanying the withdrawal of the superego and the liberation of the uninhibited ego to satisfy all its desires without guilt (Freud 1965: 76).

People are doomed when anomie is held up as a duty. As William A. White says,

> 'Each problem [man has] solved has raised the conflict [the very core of life] to a higher level so that it has finally come to pass that man has imposed upon himself the burden of the unattainable, he has set himself the task of striving for a goal that can never be reached, or if reached is instantly replaced by another still further ahead. It is this unattainable that gives to man those qualities that are termed spiritual. Man's conflicts have climbed up with him, from out the depths by their aid he has attained the heights'.
>
> in DUBLIN and BUNZEL 1933: 272

Though Durkheim lacked a sustained and condensed encounter with this current we do find much scattered about that pertains to connections between anomie and fatalism.[205] For example, no one is a greater slave than the unregulated (1961: 44) and *Fortuna* confronts the anarchist at every turn.[206] In the negative heaven of the bourgeois geometry individuals (egos) are subject to determinations whereas their sublation into the positive hell of regulated collective life, the right life, (where we find actual individuality) is one where determinacy is negated (PS: 238). Egoistic action is futile whereas individuality in action is negating and free. This is a universal insight across all philosophical systems worth mentioning. One does not do what one wants because fate or destiny is already determined, rather, one is delivered up to inevitability by virtue of acting in accordance with the ideals of the unencumbered will and deregulated conduct.[207]

As Dewey perspicaciously observes, freedom is not absolute; where we find freedom from restraint at one point we will find a corresponding restraint at

---

205 As Chateaubriand says, an "excess of liberty" leads not to more liberty but to despotism (1962: 101).
206 Depending upon the context, *Fortuna* is luck or destiny, good fortune or bad fortune. Anomie combines the sense of good and bad fortune within the distinction between progressive and regressive anomie.
207 See Puett and Gross-Loh (2016: 85) on relevant points pertaining to thoughts of the Chinese philosopher Mencius and the dynamic polarity between free will and fate. See also Kant (1998: 8) on the unlimited and limited as preconditions for one another.

another (1946: 113). "To live is to feel ourselves *fatally* obliged *to exercise our liberty*, to decide what we are going to be in this world" (Ortega y Gasset 1932: 48). It should also be indicated that Destiny is not a disembodied supernatural force but incarnated as an "effect" of institutional processes we find in schools, courts, the police, and so on. Fate is produced by institutions (Bourdieu, in Bourdieu et al. 1999: 63). For Marx, capitalism was the system par excellence for combining the duality of fatalism and anomie. "While, within the workshop, the iron law of proportionality subjugates definite numbers of workers to definite functions, in the society outside the workshop, the play of chance and caprice results in a motley pattern of distribution of the producers and their means of production among the various branches of social labour" (C: 476). The capitalist demands the "complete subjection" of the worker in production but simultaneously "denounces ... every conscious attempt to control and regulate the process of production socially, as an inroad upon such sacred things as the rights of property, freedom and the self-determining 'genius' of the individual capitalist" (C: 477). The disjunction between "iron law" and "caprice" in the same system was woven into the very heart of Protestant theology.

> Here the concept of 'psychological freedom' offers a way out: Calvin expounds the concept of a necessity (*necessitas*) which is not coercion (*coactio*) but a 'spontaneous necessity.' The ... will is necessarily corrupt and necessarily chooses evil. This does not mean, however, that man is forced 'against his will' to choose evil; his enslavement in sin is a 'voluntary enslavement' (*servitus voluntaria*). 'For we did not consider it necessary to sin, other than through weakness of the will; whence it follows that this was voluntary.' Thus despite the *necessitas* of the will, responsibility can be ascribed for human deeds. The concept of enslavement or voluntary necessity signifies one of the most important steps forward in the effort to perpetuate unfreedom in the essence of human freedom: it remains operative right up until German Idealism. Necessity loses its character both as affliction and as the removal of affliction; it is taken from the field of man's social praxis and transferred back into his 'nature.' In fact necessity is restored to nature in general and thus all possibility of overcoming it is removed. Man is directed not towards increasingly overcoming necessity but towards voluntarily accepting it.
> MARCUSE 1972: 73; cf. HEGEL 1988: 340

Durkheim goes so far as to offer us a model of the unity of negative or regressive anomie and fatalism:

Sometimes, after having temporarily succeeded in satisfying all his desires and craving for change, he suddenly dashes against an invincible obstacle, and impatiently renounces an existence thenceforth too restrictive for him. This is the case with [Goethe's] Werther,[208] the turbulent heart as he calls himself, enamoured of infinity, killing himself from disappointed love, and the case of all artists who, after having drunk deeply of success, commit suicide because of a chance hiss, a somewhat severe criticism, or because their popularity has begun to wane (S: 286).

The Chinese 'Great Leap Forward' (i.e., the abyss of mass murder) represents the fusion of *progressive* anomie and fatalism:

> The immediate catalyst for the Great Leap Forward took place in late 1957 when Mao visited Moscow for the grand celebration of the fortieth anniversary of the October Revolution (another interesting contrast to recent months, with discussion of its centenary stifled in Moscow and largely ignored in Beijing). The Soviet leader, Nikita Khrushchev, had already annoyed Mao by criticizing Stalin, whom Mao regarded as one of the great figures of Communist history.... [Additionally] the Soviet Union had just launched ... Sputnik, which Mao felt overshadowed his accomplishments. He returned to Beijing eager to assert China's position as the world's leading Communist nation. This, along with his general impatience, spurred a series of increasingly reckless decisions that led to the worst famine in history. The first signs of Mao's designs came on January 1, 1958, when the Communist Party's mouthpiece, *People's Daily*, published an article calling for 'going all out' and 'aiming higher'—code phrases for putting aside patient economic development in favor of radical policies aimed at rapid growth. Mao drove home his plans in a series of meetings over the next months, including a crucial one—from January 11 to 20 in the southern Chinese city of Nanning—that changed the Communist Party's political culture. Until that moment, Mao had been first among equals, but moderates had often been able to rein him in. Then, in several extraordinary outbursts, he accused any leader who opposed 'rash advance' of being

---

208 "What is the Fate of Man, but to suffer his appointed due and drink the cup of bitterness?.... And why should I feel ashamed in that dreadful moment when my entire self trembles on the edge of being and not-being, and the past flashes upon the dark abyss of the future like lightning, and all about me disintegrates, and the world goes to its doom with me" (Goethe 1989: 99–100).

counter-revolutionary. As became the pattern of his reign, no one successfully stood up to him. Having silenced party opposition, Mao pushed for the creation of communes—effectively nationalizing farmers' property. People were to eat in canteens and share agricultural equipment, livestock, and production, with food allocated by the state. Local party leaders were ordered to obey fanciful ideas for increasing crop yields, such as planting crops closer together. The idea was to create China's own Sputnik—harvests astronomically greater than any in human history. This might have resulted in no more harm than local officials' falsifying statistics to meet quotas, except that the state relied on these numbers to calculate taxes on farmers. To meet their taxes, farmers were forced to send any grain they had to the state as if they were producing these insanely high yields. Ominously, officials also confiscated seed grain to meet their targets. So, while storehouses bulged with grain, farmers had nothing to eat and nothing to plant the next spring. Compounding this crisis were equally deluded plans to bolster steel production through the creation of 'backyard furnaces'—small coal or wood-fired kilns that were somehow supposed to create steel out of iron ore. Unable to produce real steel, local party officials ordered farmers to melt down their agricultural implements to satisfy Mao's national targets. The result was that farmers had no grain, no seeds, and no tools. Famine set in. When, in 1959, Mao was challenged about these events at a party conference, he purged his enemies. Enveloped by an atmosphere of terror, officials returned to China's provinces to double down on Mao's policies. Tens of millions died.

JOHNSON 2018

Mao's impatience and progressive revolutionary delusions correspond remarkably well with Germany's "will mania" that lured them into WWI, which, in all, took the lives of roughly four percent of the nation's population.

Pushed to the extreme, anarchy (positive or negative) is always already a form of fatalism, or, better, inexorably leads to its opposite where "what is going to happen has already happened" (Žižek *passim*).[209] Of course, some political ideologies and religious strains are more prone to automatic polar reactions than others. In the Protestant West, anomie almost guarantees a fatalistic

---

209 "Language has completely failed Claire now. She thinks of the deal she'd made with herself—*One day, one idea for one film*—and realizes that Fate is truly fucking with her now. It's bad enough trying to live in this vacuous, cynical world, but if Fate is telling her that she doesn't even *understand* the rules of the world—well, that's more than she can bear. People can handle an unjust world; it's when the world becomes arbitrary and inexplicable that order breaks down" (Walter 2012a: 148).

response. As Harrington says, "Throughout the 19th century, there was a conservative existentialism which protested against the rationalization of life in a machine society. In England, Burke was one of its figures, in France, Baudelaire. But in Germany, industrialism was both late in coming and extraordinarily rapid once it arrived. There seemed to be no possibility of resistance, and the conservative protest acquired a distinctive quality: fatalism" (1965: 51).

If we return to the notion of right secretly belonging to the sphere of overregulation, there is no better way to get what one wants than to transform it from a desire or problem of will into a right. "If I *desire* X, there is no reason why others ought not to try and prevent my getting X; but if I have a *right* to X, others ought not to interfere with my acquiring it" (Wyschogrod 1990: 69). Once it is my right, it is my destiny and failure to arrive at the destination rests solely upon the individual's initiative and energy, unless, of course, bad luck intervenes. Neoliberalism has elevated the unity of anomie and fatalism to high art. As Lukács said of Social Democracy, it elevated as a virtue the "dualism of economic fatalism and ethical utopianism" (1971: 196). On the one hand, the world of commerce, shopping, and consumer lifestyle is one of pure anarchy, however, the world of work is one of iron-fisted determinism—as Weber vividly portrays:

> The capitalistic economy of the present day is an immense cosmos into which the individual is born, and which presents itself to him, at least as an individual, as an unalterable order of things in which he must live. It forces the individual, in so far as he is involved in the system of market relationships, to conform to capitalistic rules of action. The manufacturer who in the long run acts counter to these norms, will just as inevitably be eliminated from the economic scene as the worker who cannot or will not adapt himself to them will be thrown into the streets without a job.
> PESC: 19–20

Bageant sums up the problem succinctly and poignantly:

> ... America is just one big workhouse, with time off to shit, shower, and shop.... But you won't hear anyone complaining. America doesn't like whiners. A whiner or a cynic is about the worst thing you can be here in the land of gunpoint optimism. Foreigners often remark on the upbeat American personality. I assure them that our American corpocracy has its ways of pistol-whipping or sedating its human assets into the appropriate level of cheerfulness.... Aside from the tent camps for the homeless underneath bridges and overpasses, every habitable space has been made

private. Each has ironclad boundaries, surrounded by a force field of suspicion of strangers, and guarded by a state of hyper-vigilance directed at unknown dangers (2010: 69–71).[210]

Necessity and contingency[211] encapsulate well the polarity of fatalism and anomie in their distinct moments whereas the unity of the two lies in magic.[212] We already know that when fate bears down on a people "magics" and "mystagogics" are necessarily produced (AJ: 367)[213] and where anomie (moral laxity) is present, the pure at heart condemn the dominant institutions of pandering to folk magic.

O'Keefe does a fine job encapsulating the basic aspects of magic from Durkheim, Mauss, Weber, and Freud: magic is the employment of a professional manipulator of social forces (charisma, mana, etc.) and collective representations for purely egotistical or group (fractional) purposes (1982: 12–16). Where am I to go if I wish for an unloved member of the extended family to spontaneously burst into flames? The church has no interest in such a thing, so I have to secure an agent who can multiply powers and wrestle with demons for my benefit (Mauss 1972: 79–80). Or perhaps I wish to 'have it all' but find myself stymied by fate: the church and society do not find it disagreeable that I bow to necessity but if the 'all' is somewhere other than my coordinates within the domain of fate I will require special rites, which I neither own nor know how to operate, in order to be in two places at once.[214] Only the magician can suspend

---

210   Beyond 'whining' and ignorance there is the fact of the privatization of government in the hands of employers and the brutality privatization delivers. Workers no longer want to talk about work, working conditions, or wages, because they fear reprisals (Anderson 2017: 6).

211   Contingency "is conceivable only *sub specie temporis* (from the point of view of time), that necessity is conceivable only *sub specie aeternitatis* (from the standpoint of eternity) and that, taken together in the present, the two are impossible to distinguish. The same, I think, could be said of mystery and fact" (Comte-Sponville 2007: 84).

212   Hegel would place this couplet elsewhere: necessity (opposed to its polar extreme, contingency) entails a retreat into self. Necessity holds the self in stillness and abstract freedom. "To this extent it is a flight; but at the same time it is freedom insofar as the human being is not vanquished or bowed down by fate as something external. Whoever has this consciousness of independence, should he die, is indeed outwardly defeated but not conquered, not vanquished" (Hegel 1988: 341, 352).

213   A mystagogue is a magician or savior with a "a special *congregation* around him" (ES, 1: 447).

214   The local Episcopalians may frown upon my desire to own a private jet outfitted with gold toilets but the magicians at the non-denominational health and wealth megachurch have just what the doctor ordered. Rational people are flabbergasted by the apparent hypocrisy of megachurch culture and it would seem that, indeed, it is religion and not magic, since,

the laws of abstracted egoism and be in two places at once. Mysticism delivers me over to the wise man or the sage (Durkheim) but magic makes me dependent upon the magician or the mystagogue.[215] Magic, unlike practices and beliefs linked to the holy pure, puts faith in words and the automatic sequencing of words for enacting desired ends.[216] To obtain a personal end I need the word because the objective is really just the materialized word itself (Mauss 1972: 77). This logic can be generalized and enacted by the desperate do-it-yourselfers.

For those employed in post-secondary education, the specter of the tyrannized student reduced to mental anarchy is all too frequently encountered. Here is a common scenario: a young woman training to be a teacher in an undergraduate early childhood education program encounters a bump in the road and the spectacular run of grades is blemished with a humble C+ (an *impossibility* for this person). During the same semester an introductory course in sociology has concluded with the earning of an A+ and the student determines to jump ship to the friendlier confines of the sociology major. The fabulous run of high grades in sociology continues uninterrupted until reaching a course that demands conceptual thinking at which point the 'A Student' flounders on the rocky crag of a major writing project. The tactics that worked in the past are now counterproductive. It is revealed in conversation with her professor that she cannot receive any grade lower than a 'B' because her father will not accept any other result. The student adapts to the pressure by, and this is the phrase heard repeatedly, *memorizing everything*, at the expense of any comprehension

---

after all, there is no church of magic, as Durkheim and Mauss indicate. But megachurch logic follows the laws of magic and what appears to be a minister leading a congregation is really a mystagogue leading a gaggle of customers: I am in contact with a millionaire capitalist (the preacher) and things in contact share in a moral identity; my small-scale but nonetheless prestigious emulation (*mimesis*) of the pastor's opulent lifestyle and mannerisms means that like will produce like; and even if I am poor and impure, the very opposite qualities of the rite-leader, wealth and purity, are guaranteed to act automatically on my deficiencies (Mauss 1972: 64).

215 Magic involves a syllogistic structure (Durkheim [1912] 1915: 174): the individual magician wielding particular phratry or group instruments to manipulate universal forces for the utility-benefit of a client. But the magical rite is a spiral that begins and ends with two separate egos: the I of the magician and the I of the client, which is the opposite of the We-for-We circle of religious practices including derivative individualizations (private worship).

216 With this insight we can absorb Schopenhauer's idea of the unity of fatalism or predestination with will or anomie as 'imitation.'

whatsoever. In concept-impoverished courses where rote memorization of words and definitions, along with primitive picture thinking are effective in obtaining 'good grades,' the student presents an image of the model student pleasing to the father. Behind this facade, however, the strategy of memorizing everything and comprehending nothing has reduced knowledge to a jumble of words bolted together into strings of definitions and pictures that mean nothing. The mechanics of memorizing[217] words and definitions in the secular educational context, with no concern for an underlying comprehension, arises from the magical tradition of formulaic coercion over impersonal forces and destiny. The magical knowing of the words instead of possessing a conceptual knowledge is an attempt to forestall the death of the ego and defend the individual from society and authority (O'Keefe 1982: 14). Where there is desperate memorization we can expect to find also lucky numbers and fetish objects. The intellect has been sacrificed for good signs (a string of indices) and parental approval. When the student is barred from further studies at the graduate level (demanded by the father) because her writing samples are meaningless or, after washing out after her first semester, she returns home disgraced and, in possession of little more than the mind of a 'primitive' and perhaps even a psychotic, the woman settles into a series of dead end jobs in the service sector or simply kills herself either partially or totally. But that's not all.

The university is also the leading edge of the ideology of diversity enrichment that creates a 'magical' effect, i.e., the clash of anomie and fate.

Diversity as it is articulated under neoliberalism is, first of all, an issue of social disorganization and control. "Like corporate feminism, Diversity™ focuses on the achievements of individuals versus meaningful systemic change. It celebrates difference as long as it's not actually trying to do anything too different" (Mahdawi 2019). Real diversity is not produced by multiculturalism which "suggests a morality of live-and-let-live, a politics of side-by-side development in which members of distinct cultures preserve and protect their own culture against the incursions of other cultures" (Rorty 1998: 24). Neoliberal multiculturalism and 'diversity' represent the breakdown of teleological churning. As the US approaches unprecedented levels of inequality, the state and elites must attempt to keep a lid on things and the 'diversity' movement is one element in this program of mass demobilization as diversion whereby the exploited simultaneously avert their gaze from their white wealthy masters and turn against one another or retreat into mysticism.[218] The most broad-minded

---

217 Here 'memory' is in connection not with mindfulness but *mérmeros* (anxious).
218 The irony of liberal diversity is that liberals live in less-diverse communities than conservatives (see Hochschild 2019). It is good for the other guy insofar as I do not have to endure otherness.

tolerance of others from top to bottom would seem to be the best, most liberal thing to promote in all areas of life. "Unfortunately it is not tenable and shares all the pernicious features of an entirely unscientific *Weltanschauung* and is equivalent to one in practice. It is simply a fact that the truth cannot be tolerant, that it admits of no compromises ... and that it must be relentlessly critical if any other power tries to take over any part of it" (Freud 1965: 198).

Rednecks hate what they refer to as 'political correctness.' But as obnoxious as the phrase 'political correctness' is, there is a fleck of rationality buried beneath the annoyance. The sociological reality hidden behind the animosity is the granularization of social control. The law isn't what it used to be and, consequently, groups and "vexatious busybodies"[219] have taken it upon themselves to police the actions and expressions of other groups and individuals. Social justice untampered by good is not actual justice (SL: 112) and instead of actual justice we have battalions of self-righteous and self-appointed moral police, sometimes coagulating into pressure groups, exposing the intolerable, often imagined, and sometimes fabricated toxicity of others. Of course, most people worried about 'liberal fascism' and 'political correctness' do not have sufficient symbolic capital to worry about devaluation to begin with, nor do they have much to fear in the way of social consequences, but there is an underlying problem here that points back to the sacralization of the abstracted social atom that demands unalloyed enjoyment in the consumerist utopia.

Utopianism can be located within the currents of anomie. This might seem odd, but we cannot forget that bourgeois marketeering and the enclosures are bound up with a kind of class utopianism. When all the "factors of production" such as land and labor become separated from the people who depend on them for survival, when we are isolated from necessities like water, the inclination is to see the results as dystopic, but dystopia is only a negative utopia (see Polanyi 1944: 178). "'There is a tyranny in the womb of every utopia,' the French economist and futurist Bertrand de Jouvenel wrote" (Kapur 2016). The concept of utopia is incomplete without its opposite, dystopia, the final form that all utopias assume (Ibid.). Marxism pretty well embodies the union of utopia (revolution and communism) and dystopia (actually existing communism).

Marxism was imagined as the antidote and positive unity of fatalism and anomic voluntarism—I say 'anomic' because that is truly where 'voluntarism' runs, especially of the bourgeois pragmatic form. This is how the Italian Hegelian-Marxists viewed the situation:

---

219   A modern reappearance of the reduced *Sykophantês* (Dillon 2004).

> Marx avoided the bad choices of fatalism and voluntarism through a 'critical-practical conception.' 'From a critical consciousness of the social reality to historical praxis: this sequence signals the supersession of the antithesis of voluntarism and fatalism.' Mondolfo took *Umwälzende Praxis* (revolutionary praxis) from the theses as the vital concept fusing subjective and objective moments. Capitalism is not constituted solely of objective tendencies.
> JACOBY 1981: 56

Of course, the concept of critical or radical praxis has devolved over the years into an insulated and nearly dead jargon. Communism as it actually exists (or existed) shares decisive elements with capitalism or even is a kind of capitalism.

In the US, dominionism is a weird conjunction of apocalyptic Christianity and corporate hegemony that advocates a paradoxical mixture of economic and environmental anarchy, the imposition of a theocratic dictatorship, and the extreme repression of people who do not adhere to the dominionist ideals of probity (Worrell 2013). Unregulated capitalism produces hell on earth but the solution, here, is not regulating or dismantling capitalism, but a combination of expiation for sinful living and the punishment of a nearly infinite list of transgressors against god's grace that has brought about his wrath. What is needed, from this standpoint, is fewer gays and more god; less science and more bibles; less reasoning and more belief; and less forgiveness and more retribution (Worrell 2013). This fusion of fatalistic inevitability, evangelical fundamentalism, and corporate limitlessness produces a bountiful crop of demagogues and fundamentalist entrepreneurs. The dominionist agitator dreams of "the unification of the horrible and the wonderful, the drunkenness of an annihilation that pretends to be salvation" (Adorno [1975] 2000: 131).[220]

---

[220] The support for morally bankrupt politicians among self-professed Christian evangelicals is perplexing until we compare them to, say, terrorists dedicated to spiritual purification whereby any means whatsoever are deemed acceptable so long as the mission is completed. "While the more formidable the contradiction between real and ideal the greater the psychological reward in reconciling it, the greater too are the hazards of compromise and failure. Emotionally the most compelling struggles take place at the very point where fulfillment and tragedy meet. Holy war to reform the world according to a transcendent ideal employs the most craven means" (Aho 1994: 25). The 'love' professed by evangelical Christians is an undeveloped and unlived. Their "restriction of love to itself, its flight from all determinate modes of living even if its spirit breathed in them, or even if they sprang from its spirit, this removal of itself from all fate, is just its greatest fate" (Hegel 1948: 281). This 'love' devolves into hatred and "appalling fanaticism" (Ibid.).

The ego that throws off community transitions to necessity and consciousness, instead of finding truth, becomes "a riddle to itself" (PS: 220). These "masters of their destinies" (S: 209) become enigmatic and mysterious to themselves as society becomes increasingly alien (S: 212). We are now in the unity of fatalism and egoism. Where the ego seeks real individuality in being its own master a pulverization and smashing to bits is the result (PS: 220–21). This disintegration of the self, the loss of collective consciousness and the bloating and warping of the personal consciousness, leads to resignation or the return to self in the form of necessity.

Resignation (the self-surrender of negative ecstasy)[221] represents the principle composite unity of egoism and fatalism. Resignation is, in one sense, an end of freedom, a "surrender to destiny" (Hesse 1963: 152; cf. FMW: 128), yet, at the same time, "Resignation was ever the fount of man's strength and new hope.... Uncomplaining acceptance of the reality of society gives man indomitable courage and strength to remove all removable injustice and unfreedom" (Karl Polanyi, in Westhues 1982: 464). This was the stance of the Greeks in the face of destiny. In fact, we might do well to consider the unity of fatalism and egoism as necessity in itself where this unity comes to an actual rest and the withdrawal of the subject back into itself (Hegel 1988: 340–41) as opposed to the unrest of resignation that contains within itself a kind of practical acceptance and subjective negation of the situation, i.e., something along the lines of Bhaskar's *rejection in theory, acceptance in practice* (2008).[222] However, as we will see, the moment of asceticism lends itself too well as a representation of this unity as well as a transit point into its speculative double.[223] The mystical ascetic attempts to suffer their way out of the net of the profane world

---

221 "Even with one companion ecstasy is almost banished: you want to be alone and to feel that ..." (Hopkins 2015: 48).

222 There are moments of resigned choices and acts as well as moments of resigned *being*, as if the spring is coiling for some future action. "Saeed and Nadia knew what the buildup to conflict felt like, and so the feeling that hung over London in those days was not new to them, and they faced it not with bravery, exactly, and not with panic either, not mostly, but instead with a resignation shot through with moments of tension, with tension ebbing and flowing, and when the tension receded there was calm, the calm that is called the calm before the storm, but is in reality the foundation of a human life, waiting there for us between the steps of our march to our mortality, when we are compelled to pause and not act but be" (Hamid 2017: 138).

223 Both egoism and fatalism are moral currents that lead to profanation; the person who embraces either (or both in the form of resignation) is reduced to a brute or the equivalent of inert material. Asceticism as negative ecstasy is the attempt of the reduced being to regain contact with life (cf. Meredith 1951: 500) however the contrary currents of anomie and altruism pull the individual beyond life and into the domain of monsters.

(EFRL: 37) and reenter the sacred domain of energy and life. As we can see, this is not simply the life of "quiet desperation" that Thoreau attributed to resignation ([1854] 1960: 10).

Among the egoists, Stoics especially incline in the direction of fatalism.

> Although the Stoics argued that death was not to be feared, they were not themselves cheerleaders for a morbid preoccupation with it. Rather, as the modern application of their name implies, theirs was a message of fortitude and resignation, or of fatalism in the face of the inevitable unfolding of events.
>
> BLACKBURN 2001: 74

Resignation is a world devoid of justice and right is an illusion. "We think we have rights when we have no rights of any kind, I thought. No one has any rights, I thought. There's nothing but injustice in the world, I thought. Human beings are unjust, and injustice prevails everywhere—that's the truth, I thought" (Bernhard 1987: 93). Opposed to the extreme of resignation is ecstasy or positive resignation.

Ecstasy is a kind of moral delirium, a condition of standing outside the normal, profane sphere of life (EFRL: 228). Social life becomes intense and effervescent and, at least partially and temporarily, "does a sort of violence to the individual's body and mind and disrupts their normal functioning" (Ibid.). But this violence extends beyond the individual and easily overflows into a "theater of cruelty" (Artaud 1958: 89–94). Ecstasy is the wellspring from which charisma and the piacular spirit of self-annihilation will flow. It may be produced individually and continuously through rational techniques by the wizard or, more importantly, it is generated socially and periodically in the collective orgy, the "primordial form of religious association" (ES, 1: 401). The unity of resignation and ecstasy can be thought of as a kind of submission through suffering, or, to say the same thing, suffering is the negative unity of ecstasy and resignation. This is all vague, I realize, but the next volume will explore these abstractions more thoroughly.

In all the above combinations or composites, we find the possibility of absurd juxtapositions and what appears to be wild combinatory contradictions; in society we can locate absurdities such as moralizing devils, materialistic idealists, nihilistic utopians, and so forth—Polanyi called these collisions, for example, the combination of fanaticism and cynicism, cases of "dynamo-objective coupling" (1962: 232). And every pathological coordinate, every subjective position or economy type, ends up aiming at and relying on one thing: the miracle.

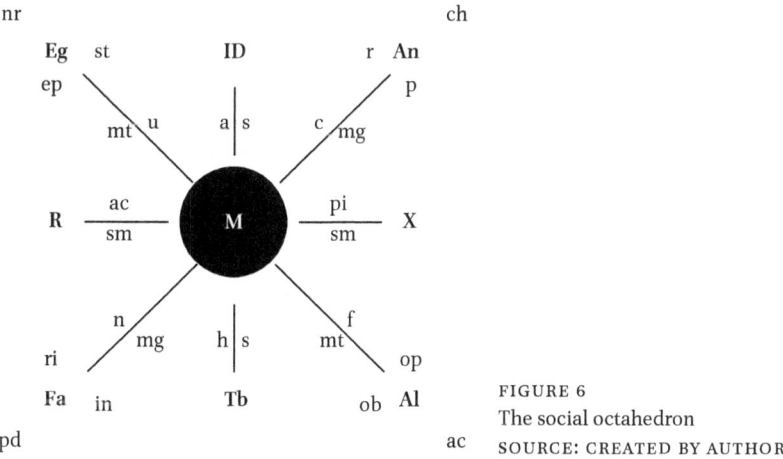

FIGURE 6
The social octahedron
SOURCE: CREATED BY AUTHOR

Eg = egoism and its three forms: narcissism (nr), Stoicism (st), and Epicureanism (ep); ID = Infinity Disease or the fusion of the Infinity of dreams (egoism) and the infinity of desires (anomie); An = anomie in its three forms: regressive or negative (r), progressive or positive (p), and chronic anomie; R = resignation with its primary active impulse, asceticism (a); X = ecstasy with its primary active impulse, the piacular spirit (p); the unity of resignation and ecstasy is in submission (sm) or suffering of the besieged; Al = altruism with its three forms: the primary, obligatory (ob), optional (op), and acute (ac); Fa = fatalism is here accompanied by its three moments of right (ri), inevitability (in), and predestinationism (pd) which will be crucial in the volume on the Protestant Reformation and the commodity; Tb = taboo or a kind of disease of the finite is linked to heteronomy (h) and the fusion of taboo with infinity and its relationship to autonomy (a) is superstition (s) or the rule of things or evil encouraging the flight of mysticism or regress into magic; The necessity (n) of fatalism and the contingency (c) of anomie are unified in magical practices (m) and the utilitarianism (u) of egoism unites the fanaticism (f) of altruism are united in mysticism (mt). At the center is the miracle, i.e., the void.

A diagram, as Goethe says, is little more than a hieroglyphic that hinders comprehension as much as it promotes it (1840: xxix). Missing (in Figure 6, above) are the thousands of colors and shades of life observable in a disaggregating society and one can easily substitute many concepts for those I have used. Confusions may be curtailed if we recall that what we are looking at is not a 'square' but a misshapen view of a hyperbolic rectangle generated out of the notion of the Möbius-lemniscate. From the standpoint of the syllogism we are trying to provide a shape to the constellation of synthetic *a priori* judgments radiating outward from the surface of the loop, striving to work themselves out of an impasse, groping for concepts and mediating grounds from which to develop itself, but Spirit, rather than working up a solid ground, finds itself trapped in a what appears to be closed circles to some groups and individuals and infinite lines to others.[224]

We are viewing this imaginary space from the coordinates of an imagined fourth spatial dimension (to misappropriate an image from Mauss) normally reserved for the Idea (reason that seeks to relate the fragments of life into a conceptual whole).[225] This is the absolute after the downfall. Though, where we might expect nothing but disarray and fragmentation, we have, instead, a form that can be affirmed so far as it contains the right 'ingredients' even if the overall 'recipe' is toxic. Reviewing the "Formal Intermezzo" from the first volume will assist in grasping this in its origins as a single strand of assemblage energy that has been preserved and resists dissolution even though it is undergoing deformation and disintegration. It is a moral power and has all that is required to regenerate itself. However, where we should have relations we have only links and transitions. What is missing in all cases is the real concept, and where we have supplied the negative conceptual unifications, the results are more horrifying than the notions and judgments. In other words, life flows from one extreme to another, from one judgment to another, but misapprehending the middle term. These are notions that pass themselves off as judgments and judgments that confuse rationalizations for reason. Means become

---

224 Superficially, this diagram may suggest a Greimas schema but this matrix is better grasp by looking at the description at the end of *The Sociogony*. In the next volume, we will explore the inner departments of this thing and work on a few empirical problems pertaining to violence.

225 The absolute is not a hyper-rationalized totality like we find in conspiracy theories (Wilson 1982: 604) and not every piece of reality has to be conceptually related into one mind. Rather, it is sufficient (a quite herculean task, actually) for Spirit to know its own work when it encounters it. And clearly, even though most people are and will forever be sunk in error and confusion, the trend toward negative enlightenment (disenchantment) continues. The task, though, is not merely negative but also positive disenchantment, i.e., the de-mystification of social life and the negation of magics, mysticism, and other forms of superstition and the revaluation of law over anarchy and the quicksilver dreams of infinity.

Depression	Discouraged	
Repression	?	
Oppression	Encouraged	

FIGURE 7
The concealment of 'recourage'
SOURCE: CREATED BY AUTHOR

ends and the ends are fatal. The moral geometry of neoliberalism is the opposite of the Schellingian dialectic whereby all contradictions end in the unity and reconciliation of contradictions (see Kroner 1961: 286) but this is also not Žižekland where contradictions merely persist in an eternal deadlock of symptom enjoyment. With Hegel we can see that contradictions are the product of a one-sided point of view and with Durkheim that oppositions are engineered in such a way that the conceptual unity of all moral currents are rendered invisible either through conscious effort (e.g., myths) or through the work of time. For example, in *Suicide* we discover the work of time in concealing precise affective coordinates that seem almost like a conspiracy of repression. Egoism is characterized by depression and fatalism by oppression. We can extrapolate that at the point of resignation and asceticism we have repression. Under altruism we find encouragement and, with anomie, discouragement. But, as we see (Figure 7) it appears that the English language has failed us at resignation's mirror opposite:

There is a hole or a riddle where there should be a word. This word did exist in English from the 16th through the 19th centuries before vanishing. 'Recourage' exists as an insignificant blip in the complete Oxford English Dictionary (the only dictionary that contains it as far as I know) and has not been used in an English language book in well over 100 years as far as I can ascertain.[226] Apparently, one can be encouraged or discouraged but once courage has abandoned us we can expect only sanguinity and bloodshed. We can only do so much here without familiarity with what came before in *The Sociogony* and what lies ahead in *Ecstasy and Resignation*.

---

226 "Language is only the instrument of science, and words are but the signs of ideas: I wish, however, that the instrument might be less apt to decay, and that signs might be permanent, like the things which they denote" (Johnson 1816: 37).

6   Positive Hell and Heavenly Negativities

Let us imagine for a moment a perfect society, a utopia where genuine individuals are happy and creative, where the advance over Chaos and the Dark has been made (Emerson 1950: 147). There are no elites hoarding all the money, nor are there dregs living in subhuman conditions. In this utopia all the energetic currents (S: 299) generated through human interaction synthesize into an objective social whole, a kind of ethical totality or absolute, where everyone is 'plugged in' and 'turned on' to the general social project through their integration in the social division of labor and participation on a wide number of social circles. Hegel called something like this an "immaculate world" where social "powers" cross and intermingle "in such a way that each preserves and brings forth the other" ([1807] 1977: 278). In this imaginary utopia we are not confronted "with the sorry spectacle of a collision between passion and duty" (Hegel [1807] 1977: 279) but a condition of universal *agape* (brotherly and self-emptying love), isonomic balance, and actual individuality within the organic division of labor. This place does not have a flat ontic structure that one associates with tumbling molecules, overlapping or clashing subjective interests, the multitude,[227] or interconnected webs spreading out along a plane. The structure of the good society involves objective criteria and objective associations that result in the crystallization of super-structural elements that rise up "over and against" individuals and smaller circles (Simmel 1955: 135). Then, some disturbance hits this utopia with sufficient force to lead to a partial disturbance of the whole; where there had been an equilibrium "a great void" opens (S: 377)[228] and begins to devour institutions and individuals are lured[229]

---

227 "Although many men are often referred to as a 'multitude' ... if one were to consider the matter more accurately, 'multitude' is not a collective word, or one that denotes a one consisting of many.... [R]ather, it actually denotes nothing but many things, abstracting from the question of whether they are of the same or different kinds, gathered together or dispersed" (Pufendorf 1994: 211). Although 'conservatives' are typically too mentally debilitated to articulate their points with any degree of rationality, they nonetheless have a legitimate beef with neoliberal 'multiculturalism.' Multiculturalism, like 'diversity' (diversion), does not contribute to a plural society but to conflict between jumbled groups and disconnected and disoriented individuals fighting over the scraps of money and resources the elite have not managed to soak up entirely.

228 The void that opens at the heart of society is permanent and an essential feature of society (EFRL: 322).

229 "For a moment he felt as if the silver-mine, which had killed his father, had decoyed him farther than he meant to go; and with the roundabout logic of emotions, he felt that the worthiness of his life was bound up with success. There was no going back" (Conrad [1904] 1961: 58).

to their doom.[230] The purely negative currents (S: 299) that had previously been fused into a positive alloy, the tetrarchy of morbid and impersonal powers (Worrell 2014) canceled upward into the energetic structure of the 'positive hell' of a normal society (cf. Hegel [1807] 1977: 278), now operate as separate and confederated powers of dissolution and anarchy. We have arrived at the moment of *Untergang*—downfall, destruction, sinking, declination. The negation of the individual is registered in the rate of suicide, etc., while the remainder of society is reduced to lurching about in mysticism,[231] magic, miracles, luck, mania, depression, and rage.

Once the concept is lost, a person or group seldom idles for long at one coordinate. A person resigned to fate on Monday may, by the end of the week, set out on a quest for revenge and love (O'Neill 1932: 714–15). The velocity at which a person whirls around the vortex of life is wildly variable, from the whimsical shifts in moods to lifelong trajectories mapped out only at the end in retrospect. Mary Shelley gives us a good description of the person thrown about willy-nilly.

> Nothing is more painful to the human mind than, after the feelings have been worked up by a quick succession of events, the dead calmness of inaction and certainty which follows and deprives the soul both of hope and fear. Justine died, she rested, and I was alive. The blood flowed freely in my veins, but a weight of despair and remorse pressed on my heart which nothing could remove. Sleep fled from my eyes; I wandered like an evil spirit, for I had committed deeds of mischief beyond description horrible, and more, much more (I persuaded myself) was yet behind. Yet my heart overflowed with kindness and the love of virtue. I had begun life with benevolent intentions and thirsted for the moment when I should put them in practice and make myself useful to my fellow beings. Now all was blasted; instead of that serenity of conscience which allowed me to look back upon the past with self-satisfaction, and from thence to gather promise of new hope's, I was seized by remorse and the sense of guilt, which hurried me away to a hell of intense tortures such as no language can describe.

---

230 The specter of a society completely off kilter and lacking all regulation is an ideal-typical limit. As Dewey says, "It is nonsense to suppose that we do not have social control *now*. The trouble is that it is exercised by the few who have economic power, at the expense of the liberties of the many and at the cost of increasing disorder, culminating in that chaos of war which the representatives of liberty for the possessive class identify with true discipline" (1946: 114).

231 "Jaspers has underlined the staggering question presented to every man by the ultimate negations of suicide and of mysticism, the one a negation of life itself, the other of the world" (Mounier 1952: 47).

This state of mind preyed upon my health, which had perhaps never entirely recovered from the first shock it had sustained. I shunned the face of man; all sound of joy or complacency was torture to me; solitude was my only consolation—deep, dark, deathlike solitude ([1818] 1992: 85).

As exhaustive as Durkheim is I have not found in his own works an illustration or literary reference to an example of the four primary forces functioning simultaneously within a given system in a way that offers the picture of a 'career' within the negative heaven. One work, however, goes further than anything else I know of in bringing the currents together in a succinct and illuminating way that is directly relevant to the Durkheimian project: Huysmans' *Against Nature*, where the author captures the neurotic misery of the deregulated egoist, Des Esseintes, attempting (and failing miserably) to construct a solitary world of his own, free from the corruption and influence of society.

After finally disintegrating into a near-fatal physiological state the protagonist's doctor orders Des Esseintes back to Paris and its vibrant social life of frivolity and distractions. After consulting with multiple doctors, Des Esseintes faces the unavoidable fact of returning and drowning in bourgeois insipidness. Facing the inevitability of the situation closing around him he explodes furiously, propelling him into an identification with the anachronistic object of bourgeois scorn, the Church. Literally every element we could wish for is tightly compressed into a compact denouement:

> 'May you crumble into dust, Society; old world, may you expire!' exclaimed Des Esseintes, filled with indignation at the ignominious spectacle he was conjuring up; his protest shattered the nightmare that oppressed him. 'Ah!' he said; 'to think that all this is not a dream! To think that I shall be rejoining the depraved and servile rabble of this age!' He turned for help and comfort to Schopenhauer's consoling precepts; he repeated to himself the painful axiom of Pascal's: 'The soul sees nothing that, upon reflection, it does not find distressing,' but these words echoed in his mind like meaningless noise; his ennui broke them up, stripping them of all significance, all consolatory power, all gentle, effective potency.
>
> He finally realized that the arguments of pessimism were incapable of giving him comfort, that only the impossible belief in a future life would give him peace.
>
> A fit of rage, like a fierce gale, swept away his efforts at resignation, his attempts at indifference. He could no longer deceive himself, there was nothing, nothing left, everything had been brought down; the bourgeoisie sat about on the ground, as though on a Sunday outing, stuffing

themselves from paper bags, amid the majestic ruins of the Church which had become a place of assignation, a pile of debris, defiled by contemptible gibes and infamous jokes. Surely, in order to prove their existence beyond any doubt, surely the terrible God of Genesis and the pale Crucified Christ would revive the cataclysms of the past, reignite the rain of fire that once consumed those cities of the damned, those abodes of death of long ago? Was it possible that this filth would continue to flow and with its pestilence swamp this old world in which nothing now grew save seeds of iniquity and harvests of shame?

.... Exhausted, Des Esseintes collapsed into a chair. 'In two days' time I shall be in Paris,' he exclaimed; 'it really is all over; the waters of human mediocrity, like a tidal wave, are rising up to the sky and will engulf this haven whose sea-walls I have with my own hands most unwillingly breached. Ah! My courage fails me and I am sick at heart! Lord, take pity on the Christian who doubts, on the unbeliever who longs to believe, on the galley-slave of life who is setting sail alone, at night, under a sky no longer lit, now, by the consoling beacons of the ancient hope!' ([1884] 1998: 180–81).

His hitherto dimly perceived bond of sympathy and perverse fascination with the Church and otherworldly asceticism is revealed, in a flash, under the pressure of a fated re-emersion into the stupidity of Parisian life; this egoist is literally transported to the doorstep of institutionalized discipline and self-abandonment. The 'progressive' anomic of a wealthy stoic lifestyle mixed with hedonism slowly degenerates into a 'regressive' draining of resources and a physiological breakdown. It is the being cornered, caught between a rock and a hard place, that triggers the rage (what Durkheim identifies with "active" and "regressive" phases of anomie) that will metamorphose Des Esseintes into his polar opposite form and make possible, at least imaginatively, his transit into a world of discipline and self-renunciation.

Another example, going right to the denouement, is the 'victorious defeat' we find in Maugham's *Of Human Bondage*, where freedom from family and to do whatever one wants produces the unwanted feeling of "desolate emptiness."

> He realised that he had deceived himself; it was no self-sacrifice that had driven him to think of marrying, but the desire for a wife and a home and love; and now that it all seemed to slip through his fingers he was seized with despair. He wanted all that more than anything in the world.... He thought of his desire to make a design, intricate and beautiful, out of the

myriad, meaningless facts of life: had he not seen also that the simplest pattern, that in which a man was born, worked, married, had children, and died, was likewise the most perfect? It might be that to surrender to happiness was to accept defeat, but it was a defeat better than many victories (1915: 765).

Unlike the abandonment of the self to the monastery, we find the protagonist embracing the normal social pattern of obligations and finding some kind of 'Durkheimian liberty.' We do not require fame and adventure, immortality or wealth, and no "rationale outside" of social life (S: 211). Our calling or specialization within the social division of labor as well as our integration with secondary associations and our obligations toward others, especially toward our offspring, lowers the propensity for self-destruction (S: 198). But many are not so fortunate to find a place to practice their vocations.

Other systems of life represent not a hair-raising excursion around the rim of the abyss, nor a fortified outpost along some frontier but a concoction so toxic, drawing upon multiple countervailing currents, that it represents the monsterization of life. The Methodism that was instrumental to the development of the moral economy of the English working class, was so deeply inhuman and self-destructive that "A more appalling system of religious terrorism, one more fitted to unhinge a tottering intellect and to darken and embitter a sensitive nature, has seldom existed" (Lecky, in Thompson 1963: 374).

Societies and selves tend to oscillate, sometimes quickly and violently, from one form of existence to some new form or even a polar opposite. Today's revolution is tomorrow's restoration; fellow travelers whipsaw into rabid anti-communists; Trotskyists in the spring, Nixonites in the fall; one generation of conservatives produces the next generation's progressives; yesteryear's communist regime is today's capitalist hothouse. Everyone is looking for a way out, the escape hatch to freedom. However, without the concept, there is no free life in the negative heaven of disintegration and freedom is "not a gift that mankind, groaning under the weight of necessity, receives from Fate as a reward for its steadfast endurance" (Lukács 1971: 250). Excitement, enjoyment, pleasures galore are all possibilities, but not freedom, at least in the positive sense of the concept. As the downfall surges, we look around for symbols of stability and the state is, for liberals, a bulwark against finality. But Marx was right: whatever else it may be, in the final analysis, the state is the executive branch of the bourgeoisie and the embodiment of everything evil. Everything that is immoral (murder, brutality, corruption, greed, waste, bribery, deception, lies, dishonesty, stupidity, incompetence, indifference, and theft) keeps the state in perpetual motion. Everything we prohibit and hate among our neighbors, family members, and friends, are the actual tasks of the state. As Freud says, the state attempts to monopolize the wrong and exerts a seduction on the hearts and minds of individuals to emulate its wrongs ([1915] 1959: 294). We recoil from the chasm of disintegrating life, but the pull is irresistible.

In the absence of institutional support, we have the experience of dangling above an abyss, clinging to a wall above a crevasse. Some learn to climb without ropes like virtuosos; others are successful with the assistance of specialized equipment and support teams. The Nietzschean 'leap' is impossible. Not even Zarathustra has legs long enough to successfully traverse the hole at the center of the neoliberal whirlpool and, even if it were possible, the long-legged would only succeed in landing in another dimension of negativity. Even *monsters* with strides impossibly *longer* than their legs find the gap too wide (Montaigne 1842: 556).

We look to art for examples of hovering life and examples of defeating the spirit of gravity. Look no further than the 'Dream Ballet' sequence in the film adaptation of *Oklahoma!* (Zinnemann [1955] 1999) where the transcendental third, represented by the music, enables Laurey, played in the dream sequence by Bambi Lin, to soar into the sky as if her counterpart ('dream Curley' played by James Mitchell) is not only *not* the source of her buoyancy but an actual source of limitation and restraint. Of course, it is the performance of both actors that produces the effect that only the partner, the equivalent other is being carried away by the imaginary universal. Short of hovering or soaring, *we* have what is left of institutional bridges and glass-bottom elevations that produce anxiety. "Looked at quite simply, the prominent manifestations of Nightmare are seen to be an overmastering dread and terror of some external oppression against which all the energies of the mind appear vainly to be fighting. They are thus pre-eminently mental manifestations, the central one being a morbidly acute feeling of *Angst*" (Jones 1931: 40).

Bibliography

Achenbach, Joel. 2017. "Why Drugs are Getting Harder to Contain." *The Washington Post*, 24 October. Online: (www.washingtonpost.com/national/wave-of-addiction-linked-to-fentanyl-worsens-as-drugs-distribution-evolve/2017/10/24.html).

Adams, Marilyn McCord. 1983. "Introduction." Pp. 1–33 in *Predestination, God's Foreknowledge, and Future Contingents*, 2nd ed., by William Ockham, tr. M. Adams and N. Kretzmann. Indianapolis: Hackett.

Adler, Alfred. 1954. *Understanding Human Nature*. Greenwich: Fawcett.

Adorno, Theodor W. 1950. "Democratic Leadership and Mass Manipulation." Pp. 418–35 in *Studies in Leadership*, ed. Alvin W. Gouldner. New York: Harper.

Adorno, Theodor W. [1964] 1973. *The Jargon of Authenticity*, tr. Knut Tarnowski and Frederic Will. Evanston: Northwestern University Press.

Adorno, Theodor W. 1973. *Negative Dialectics*, tr. E.B. Ashton. New York: Continuum.

Adorno, Theodor W. 1974. *Minima Moralia*, tr. E.F.N. Jephcott. London: Verso.

Adorno, Theodor W. [1975] 2000. *The Psychological Technique of Martin Luther Thomas*. Stanford: Stanford University Press.

Adorno, Theodor W. 1976. "Sociology and Empirical Research." Pp. 68–86 in *The Positivist Dispute in German Sociology* by Theodor W. Adorno, Hans Albert, Ralf Dahrendorf, Jürgen Habermas, Harald Pilot, and Karl R. Popper. London: Heinemann.

Adorno, Theodor W. 1997. *Aesthetic Theory*, tr. Robert Hullot-Kentor. Minneapolis: University of Minnesota Press.

Adorno, Theodor W. 1989. *Kierkegaard*, tr. Robert Hullot-Kentor. Minneapolis: University of Minnesota Press.

Adorno, Theodor W. 1993. *Hegel: Three Studies*, tr. Shierry Nicholsen. Cambridge: The MIT Press.

Adorno, Theodor W. 1998. *Critical Models*, tr. Henry W. Pickford. New York: Columbia University Press.

Adorno, T.W., Else Frenkel-Brunswik, Daniel J. Levinson, and R. Nevitt Sanford. 1950. *The Authoritarian Personality*. New York: W. W. Norton.

Adorno, Theodor W. and Hellmut Becker. 1983. "Education for Autonomy." *Telos* 55: 103–10.

Aho, James A. 1994. *This Thing of Darkness*. Seattle: University of Washington Press.

Alain. [1934] 1974. *The Gods*, tr. Richard Pevear. New York: New Directions.

Algren, Nelson. [1949] 1999. *The Man with the Golden Arm*. New York: Seven Stories Press.

Altamura, Chris. 2019. "The Sorrows of Modern Subjectivity: Capital, Infinity Disease, and Werther's Hysterical Neurosis." *Fast Capitalism* 16.2. Online: (https://fastcapitalism.journal.library.uta.edu/index.php/fastcapitalism).

Altemeyer, Bob. 2006. *The Authoritarians*. Online: (http://home.cc.umanitoba.ca/~altemey).

Alter, Robert. 2019. "Introduction to the Five Books." Pp. xliii–xlix in *The Hebrew Bible*, Vol. 1, tr. Robert Alter. New York: W. W. Norton.

Althusser, Louis. 1970. "Ideology and Ideological State Apparatuses." Online: (www.marxists.org/reference/archive/althusser/1970/ideology.htm).

Alvarez, A. 1972. *The Savage God*. New York: Random House.

Amator patriae (anon.). 1829. *An Appeal to Capitalists and the Rest of the Community of the British Empire, on the State of its Trading and Commercial Interests, and Submitting a Remedy for the Evils to which they are Subjected*. London: Printed and sold for the author by Holdsworth and Ball.

Amin, Samir. 1994. *Re-Reading the Postwar Period*. New York: Monthly Review Press.

Amin, Samir. 1997. *Capitalism in the Age of Globalization*. London: Zed Books.

Amin, Samir. 2004. *The Liberal Virus*. New York: Monthly Review Press.

Amis, Martin. 1984. *Money: A Suicide Note*. New York: Penguin.

Anderson, Elizabeth. 2017. *Private Government*. Princeton: Princeton University Press.

Anton, Anatole. 1974. "Commodities and Exchange." *Philosophy and Phenomenological Research* 34(3): 355–83.

Antonio, Robert J. 1995. "Nietzsche's Antisociology: Subjectified Culture and the End of History." *American Journal of Sociology* 101(1): 1–43.

Antonio, Robert J. 2003. "Introduction: Marx and Modernity." Pp. 1–50 in *Marx and Modernity*, ed. Robert J. Antonio. Malden: Blackwell.

Antonio, Robert J. 2017. "Immanent Critique and the Exhaustion Thesis: Neoliberalism and History's Vicissitudes." Pp. 655–76 in *The Palgrave Handbook of Critical Theory*, ed. Michael J. Thompson. New York: Palgrave.

Appleby, Julie. 2017. "Obesity-Linked Diagnoses on the Rise Among Kids and Teens." National Public Radio, 12 January. Online: (www.npr.org/sections/health-shots/2017/01/12/509374443/obesity-linked-diagnoses-on-the-rise-among-kids-and-teens).

Apuleius. 1994. *The Golden Ass*, tr. P.G. Walsh. Oxford: Oxford University Press.

Aquinas, Thomas. 1947. *Summa Theologica*. Grand Rapids: Christian Classics.

Aquinas, Thomas. 2000. *Treatise on Law*, tr. Richard J. Reagan. Indianapolis: Hackett.

Arendt, Hannah. 1968. *The Origins of Totalitarianism*. New York: Harcourt.

Aristotle. 1984. *Complete Works of Aristotle*, volume 2. Princeton: Princeton University Press.

Aron, Raymond. 1954. *The Century of Total War*. New York: Doubleday.

Aron, Raymond. 1964. *German Sociology*. New York: The Free Press.

Aron, Raymond. 1965. *Main Currents in Sociological Thought*, Vol. 1. New York: Doubleday.

Aron, Raymond. 1967. *Main Currents in Sociological Thought*, Vol. 2. New York: Doubleday.

Aron, Raymond. 1968. *Progress and Disillusion*. New York: The New American Library.
Artaud, Antonin. 1958. *The Theater and its Double*, tr. Mary Richards. New York: Grove.
Asch, Solomon. 1961. "Issues in the Study of Social Influences on Judgment." Pp. 143–58 in *Conformity and Deviation*, ed. Irwin A. Berg and Bernard M. Bass. New York: Harper.
Auden, W.H. 2002. *The Complete Works*, Vol. 2. Princeton: Princeton University Press.
Auden, W.H. 2008. *The Complete Works*, Vol. 3. Princeton: Princeton University Press.
Augustine. 1876. *Works*, Vol. 15 (3). Edinburgh: T. and T. Clark.
Augustine. 1972. *City of God*. New York: Penguin.
Aurelius, Marcus. 1945. *Marcus Aurelius and His Times*. New York: Walter J. Black.
Aurelius, Marcus. 1983. *The Meditations*, tr. G.M.A. Grube. Indianapolis: Hackett.
Avineri, Shlomo. 1976. "How to Save Marx from the Alchemists of Revolution." *Political Theory* 4(1): 35–44.
Bacevich, Andrew J. 2009. *The Limits of Power*. New York: Holt.
Bageant, Joe. 2007. *Deer Hunting with Jesus*. New York: Three Rivers Press.
Bageant, Joe. 2010. *Rainbow Pie*. Melbourne: Scribe.
Baldwin, James M (ed.). 1902. *Dictionary of Philosophy and Psychology*. New York: Macmillan.
Balzac, Honoré de. [1846] 1991. *Cousin Bette*, tr. James Waring. New York: Knopf.
Barker, Nicola. 2017. *H(a)ppy*. London: William Heinemann.
Barnes, Harry Elmer and Howard Becker. 1938. *From Lore to Science*. Boston: D. C. Heath.
Barnes, Jonathan. 2001. Early Greek Philosophy. New York: Penguin.
Barrett, Lisa Feldman. 2017. How Emotions are Made. Boston: Houghton.
Barry, Keith. 2019. "Higher Speed Limits Led to 36,760 More Deaths, Study Shows." *Consumer Reports*, 4 April. Online: (www.consumerreports.org/car-safety/higher-speed-limits-led-to-36760-more-deaths).
Barth, Karl. 1933. *The Epistle to the Romans*. London: Oxford University Press.
Barthes, Roland. 1976. *Sade, Fourier, and Loyola*, tr. Richard Miller. Berkeley: University of California Press.
Barthes, Roland. 1982. *Empire of Signs*, tr. Richard Howard. New York: Hill and Wang.
Barzun, Jacques. 1964. *Science: The Glorious Entertainment*. New York: Harper.
Bataille, Georges. [1962] 1991. *The Impossible*, tr. Robert Hurley. San Francisco: City Lights.
Bataille, Georges. 2004. *Divine Filth*, tr. Mark Spitzer. Creation.
Baudelaire, Charles. 1993. *Poems*, tr. Richard Howard. New York: Knopf.
Baudelaire, Charles. 2002. *On Wine and Hashish*, tr. Andrew Brown. London: Hesperus Press.
Baudrillard, Jean. 1983a. *Simulations*, tr. Paul Foss, Paul Patton, and Philip Beitchman. New York: Semiotext(e).

Baudrillard, Jean. 1983b. *In the Shadow of the Silent Majorities*, tr. Paul Foss, John Johnston, and Paul Patton. New York: Semiotext(e).
BBC News. 2019. "Joseph Stalin: Why so Many Russians Like the Soviet Dictator." BBC, 18 April. Online: (www.bbc.com/news/world-europe-47975704).
Bebinger, Martha. 2019. "Fentanyl-Linked Deaths: The U.S. Opioid Epidemic's Third Wave Begins." National Public Radio, 21 March. Online: (www.npr.org/sections/health-shots/2019/03/21/704557684/fentanyl-linked-deaths-the-u-s-opioid-epidemics-third-wave-begins).
Bechdel, Alison. 2006. *Fun Home*. New York: Houghton Mifflin Harcourt.
Bechtold, Thomas. 2019. "Sociopoetics in the Work of Shakespeare." *Fast Capitalism* 16.2. Online: (https://fastcapitalism.journal.library.uta.edu/index.php/fastcapitalism).
Becker, Ernest. 1973. *The Denial of Death*. New York: The Free Press.
Beiser, Frederick. 2002. *German Idealism*. Cambridge: Harvard University Press.
Belasco, Amy. 2014. "The Cost of Iraq, Afghanistan, and Other Global War on Terror Operations Since 9/11." Congressional Research Service. Online: (www.fas.org/sgp/crs/natsec/RL33110.pdf).
Bell, Daniel. 1976. *The Cultural Contradictions of Capitalism*. New York: Basic Books.
Bellah, Robert N., Richard Madsen, William M. Sullivan, Ann Swidler, and Steven M. Tipton. 1985. *Habits of the Heart*. New York: Harper.
Benjamin, Walter. [1963] 1998. *The Origin of German Tragic Drama*. London: Verso.
Benjamin, Walter. 1996. *Selected Writings*, volume 1. Cambridge: Harvard University Press.
Berger, Bennett M. 1995. *An Essay on Culture*. Berkeley: University of California Press.
Berger, Peter. 1967. *The Sacred Canopy*. New York: Anchor.
Berger, Peter. 1969. *A Rumor of Angels*. New York: Anchor.
Berger, Peter, Brigitte Berger, and Hansfried Kellner. 1973. *The Homeless Mind*. New York: Vintage.
Berger, Peter and Thomas Luckmann. 1966. *The Social Construction of Reality*. New York: Anchor.
Berger, Peter and Stanley Pullberg. 1965. "Reification and the Sociological Critique of Consciousness." *History and Theory* 4(2): 196–211.
Bergson, Henri. 1920. *Mind-Energy*, tr. H. Wildon Carr. New York: Henry Holt.
Berkeley, George. 1843. *Works*, volume 1. London: Thomas Tegg.
Berlant, Lauren. 2011. *Cruel Optimism*. Durham: Duke University Press.
Berlet, Chip and Matthew N. Lyons. 2000. *Right-Wing Populism in America*. New York: The Guilford Press.
Berman, Jillian. 2018. "Student Debt Just Hit $1.5 Trillion." Marketwatch, 12 May. Online: (www.marketwatch.com/story/student-debt-just-hit-15-trillion-2018-05-08).
Bernal, J.D. 1949. *The Freedom of Necessity*. London: Routledge and Kegan Paul.
Bernhard, Thomas. 1979. *Correction*, tr. Sophie Wilkins. New York: Vintage.

Bernhard, Thomas. 1987. *Woodcutters*, tr. David McLintock. New York: Vintage.
Besnard, Philippe. 2000. "The Fortunes of Durkheim's *Suicide*." Pp. 97–125 in *Durkheim's Suicide*, eds. W.S.F. Pickering and Geoffrey Walford. London: Routledge.
Besnard, Philippe. 2005. "Durkheim's Squares: Types of Social Pathology and Types of Suicide." Pp. 70–9 in *The Cambridge Companion to Durkheim*, eds. Jeffrey C. Alexander et al. Cambridge: Cambridge University Press.
Bettelheim, Bruno and Morris Janowitz. 1964. *Social Change and Prejudice*. New York: The Free Press.
Bhaskar, Roy. 2008. *Dialectic: The Pulse of Freedom*. New York: Routledge.
Bichell, Rae Ellen. 2016. "Suicide Rates Climb in the U.S., Especially Among Adolescent Girls." National Public Radio, 22 April. Online: (www.npr.org/sections/health-shots/2016/04/22/474888854).
Biniek, Jean F. and William Johnson. 2019. "Spending on Individuals with Type 1 Diabetes and the Role of Rapidly Increasing Insulin Prices." Health Care Cost Institute. Online: (www.healthcostinstitute.org/research/publications/entry/spending-on-individuals-with-type-1-diabetes-and-the-role-of-rapidly-increasing-insulin-prices).
Binion, Rudolph. 2005. *Past Impersonal*. Dekalb: Northern Illinois University Press.
Blackburn, Simon. 2001. *Being Good*. Oxford: Oxford University Press.
Bloch, Ernst. 1988. *The Utopian Function of Art and Literature*. Cambridge: The MIT Press.
Bloch, Marc. 1953. *The Historian's Craft*. New York: Vintage.
Bloch, Marc. 1961. *The Royal Touch*, tr. F.E. Anderson. New York: Dorset.
Bloch, Marc. 1966. *French Rural History*, tr. Janet Sondheimer. Berkeley: University of California Press.
Bloch, Marc. 1968. *Strange Defeat*, tr. G. Hopkins. New York: W. W. Norton.
Board of Governors of the Federal Reserve System. 2019. "Distribution of Household Wealth in the U.S. Since 1989." Online: (www.federalreserve.gov/releases/z1/dataviz/dfa/distribute/chart/#range:1989.3,2019.1).
Boas, Franz. 1916. *The Mind of Primitive Man*. New York: Macmillan.
Boétie, Etienne de la. [1552–53] 1975. *The Politics of Disobedience: The Discourse of Voluntary Servitude*. Montreal: Black Rose Books.
Bosanquet, Bernard. 1912. *The Principle of Individuality and Value*. London: Macmillan.
Bosanquet, Bernard. 1913. *Mind and its Object*. Manchester: Manchester University Press.
Bosanquet, Bernard. 1920. *What Religion Is*. London: Macmillan.
Bosanquet, Bernard. [1923] 1965. *The Philosophical Theory of the State*. New York: St Martin's.
Bottomore, Tom. 1981. "A Marxist Consideration of Durkheim." *Social Forces* 59(4): 902–17.

Bouglé, Celestin. [1926] 1970. *The Evolution of Values.* New York: Augustus M. Kelley.
Boulding, Kenneth E. 1964. *The Meaning of the Twentieth Century.* New York: Harper.
Bourdieu, Pierre. 1977. *Outline of a Theory of Practice.* Cambridge: Cambridge University Press.
Bourdieu, Pierre. [1980] 1990. *The Logic of Practice.* Stanford: Stanford University Press.
Bourdieu, Pierre. 1990. *In Other Words.* Stanford: Stanford University Press.
Bourdieu, Pierre. 1991. *Language and Symbolic Power.* Cambridge: Harvard University Press.
Bourdieu, Pierre. 2005. *The Social Structures of the Economy.* Malden, MA: Polity Press.
Bourdieu, Pierre et al. 1999. *The Weight of the World.* Stanford: Stanford University Press.
Boutmy, Emile. 1902. *Élélments d'une Psychologie Politique du Peuple Américain.* Paris: Librairie Armand Colin.
Bracton, Henricus de. 1879. *Legibus et Consuetudinibus,* ed. Travers Twiss. London: Longman.
Brandon, Emily. 2014. "The Ideal Retirement Age—and Why You Won't Retire Then." *U.S. News and World Report.* 12 May. Online: (money.usnews.com/money/retirement/articles/2014/05/12/the-ideal-retirement-age-and-why-you-wont-retire-then).
Breckman, Warren. 2013. *Adventures of the Symbolic.* New York: Columbia University Press.
Brinton, Daniel. 1902. *The Basis of Social Relations.* New York: G. P. Putnam's Sons.
Brooks, Phillips. 1893. *The Mystery of Iniquity.* London: Macmillan.
Brown, Courtney. 1987. "Voter Mobilization and Party Competition in a Volatile Electorate." *American Sociological Review* 52(1): 59–72.
Brown, Norman O. 1959. *Life Against Death.* London: Routledge and Kegan Paul.
Browne, Thomas. 1658. *Pseudodoxia Epidemica.* London: Printed for Edward Dod.
Buber, Martin. 1965. *The Knowledge of Man.* New York: Harper.
Büchner, Georg. 2010. *Danton's Death.* London: Bloomsbury.
Bureau of Labor Statistics. 2019. "Union Members Summary." 18 January. Online: (www.bls.gov/news.release/union2.nro.htm).
Burke, Jason. 2015. "The Story of Radicalisation." *The Guardian,* 26 November. Online: (www.theguardian.com/world/2015/nov/26/radicalisation-islam-isis-maysa-not-thinking-my-thoughts-not-myself).
Burroughs, William S. [1959] 2001. *Naked Lunch.* New York: Grove.
Burton, Robert. [1621–1638] 2001. *The Anatomy of Melancholy.* New York: New York Review of Books.
Byron, G.G. 1880. *The Poetical Works of Lord Byron.* New York: A.L. Burt.
Byron, G.G. 1982. *Selected Letters and Journals,* ed. Leslie Marchand. Cambridge: Harvard University Press.
Cacioppo, John T. and William Patrick. 2008. *Loneliness.* New York: W. W. Norton.

Cacioppo, Stephanie, John. P. Capitanio, and John T. Cacioppo. 2016. "Toward a Neurology of Loneliness." *Psychological Bulletin* 140(6): 1464–504.

Caillois, Roger. 1959. *Man and the Sacred*. Urbana: University of Illinois Press.

Caillois, Roger. 2003. *The Edge of Surrealism*, ed. Claudine Frank. Durham: Duke University Press.

Cain, James M. [1934] 1997. *The Postman Always Rings Twice*. Pp. 1–95 in *Crime Novels: American Noir of the 1930s and 40s*. New York: The Library of America.

Caird, John. 1885. *The Social Philosophy and Religion of Comte*. Glasgow: James Maclehose.

Caird, John. 1893. *Hegel*. Edinburgh and London: William Blackwood and Sons.

Calmes, Jackie. 2016. "Hiring Hurdle: Finding Workers who can Pass a Drug Test." *New York Times*, 17 May: (www.nytimes.com/2016/05/18/business/hiring-hurdle-finding-workers-who-can-pass-a-drug-test.html).

Calvin, John. [1559] 1981. *Institutes of the Christian Religion*, tr. Henry Beveridge. Grand Rapids, MI: Wm. B. Eerdmans.

Calvino, Italo. 1974. *Invisible Cities*, tr. William Weaver. San Diego: Harcourt.

Camus, Albert. 1955. *The Myth of Sisyphus and Other Essays*, tr. Justin O'Brien. New York. Vintage.

Capra, Fritjof. 1982. *The Turning Point*. New York: Bantam.

Carlyle, Thomas. [1836] 1987. *Sartor Resartus*. Oxford: Oxford University Press.

Carlyle, Thomas. 1900. *Critical and Miscellaneous Essays*, Vol. 1. New York: Scribner's Sons.

Carter, Gregg. 2017. *Gun Control in the United States*, 2nd Ed. Santa Barbara: ABC-CLIO.

Carus, Paul. [1900] 1996. *The History of the Devil and the Idea of Evil*. New York: Gramercy.

Case, Anne and Angus Deaton. 2015. "Rising Morbidity and Mortality in Midlife Among White Non-Hispanic Americans in the 21st Century." *Proceedings of the National Academy of Sciences of the United States of America*, 112(49): 15078–5083. Online: (www.pnas.org/content/112/49/15078.full).

Cassano, Graham. 2019. "The Master's Race: Phallic Whiteness in 'The Young Savages.'" *Fast Capitalism* 16.2. Online: (https://fastcapitalism.journal.library.uta.edu/index.php/fastcapitalism).

Cassirer, Ernst. 1944. *An Essay on Man*. New York: Doubleday Anchor.

Cassirer, Ernst. 1946. *Language and Myth*. New York: Harper.

Cassirer, Ernst. 1955a. *The Philosophy of Symbolic Forms*, Vol. 1. New Haven: Yale University Press.

Cassirer, Ernst. 1955b. *The Philosophy of Symbolic Forms*, Vol. 2. New Haven: Yale University Press.

Cassirer, Ernst. 1996. *The Philosophy of Symbolic Forms*, Vol. 4, The Metaphysics of Symbolic Forms. New Haven: Yale University Press.

Cassirer, Ernst. 2013. *The Warburg Years*, tr. S.G. Lofts with A. Calcagno. New Haven: Yale University Press.

Cather, Willa. [1913] 2000. *O Pioneers!* Westvaco.

Cavan, Ruth Shonle. [1928] 1965. *Suicide*. New York: Russell.

Center for Behavioral Health Statistics and Quality. 2015. "Results from the 2014 National Survey on Drug Use and Health." Rockville, MD: Substance Abuse and Mental Health Services Administration. Online: (www.samhsa.gov/data/sites/default/files/NSDUH-DetTabs2014/NSDUH-DetTabs2014.pdf).

Centers for Disease Control and Prevention. 2014. "Short Sleep Duration Among US Adults." Online: (www.cdc.gov/sleep/data_statistics.html).

Centers for Disease Control and Prevention. 2015. "Vital Signs: Demographic and Substance Use Trends Among Heroin Users—United States, 2002–2013." Online: (www.cdc.gov/mmwr/preview/mmwrhtml/mm6426a3.htm).

Centers for Disease Control and Prevention. 2016. "Death Rates for Motor Vehicle Traffic Injury, Suicide, and Homicides Among Children and Adolescents aged 10–14 Years—United States, 1999–2014." Online: (http://www.cdc.gov/mmwr/volumes/65/wr/mm6543a8.htm).

Centers for Disease Control and Prevention. 2018. "Vital Signs: Trends in Emergency Department Visits for Suspected Opioid Overdoses." Online: (www.cdc.gov/mmwr/volumes/67/wr/mm6709e1.htm).

Centers for Disease Control and Prevention. 2018b. "Mortality in the United States, 2017." Online: (www.cdc.gov/nchs/data/databriefs/db328-h.pdf).

Certeau, Michel de. 1984. *The Practice of Everyday Life*, tr. Steven Rendall. Berkeley: University of California Press.

Champagne, Claudia M. 1991. "Adam and His 'Other Self' in *Paradise Lost*: A Lacanian Study in Psychic Development." *Milton Quarterly* 25(2): 48–59.

Chance, Sue. 1992. *Stronger than Death*. New York: W. W. Norton.

Chandler, Raymond. 1995. *Later Novels and Other Writings*. New York: Library of America.

Chasseguet-Smirgel, Janine. 1985. *Creativity and Perversion*. London: W.W. Norton.

Chateaubriand, François-René de. 1962. "Progress." Pp. 99–107 in *Catholic Political Thought*, ed. Bela Menczer. Notre Dame: University of Notre Dame Press.

Chaze, Elliott. [1953] 2016. *Black Wings has My Angel*. New York: New York Review of Books.

Chesterton, G.K. 1986. *Collected Works,* volume 1. San Francisco: Ignatius Press.

Chinoy, Sahil. 2019. "What Happened to America's Political Center of Gravity?" *The New York Times*, 26 June. Online: (www.nytimes.com/interactive/2019/06/26/opinion/sunday/republican-platform-far-right.html).

Chisholm, Paul. 2018. "A Spike in Liver Disease Deaths Among Young Adults Fueled by Alcohol." National Public Radio, 18 July. Online: (www.npr.org/sections/health-shots/2018/07/18/630275042/a-spike-in-liver-disease-deaths-among-young-adults-fueled-by-alcohol).

Chopin, Kate. 1899. *The Awakening*. Chicago: Herbert S. Stone and Co.

Choron, Jacques. 1972. *Suicide*. New York: Charles Scribner's Sons.

Cioran, E.M. 1974. *The New Gods*, tr. Richard Howard. Chicago: The University of Chicago Press.

Clawson, Dan. 1980. *Bureaucracy and the Labor Process*. New York: Monthly Review Press.

Cleckley, Hervey. 1988. *The Mask of Sanity*, 5th ed. Cleckley.

Coffman, Keith. 2017. "Oregon College Shooter Wrote of Kinship with Mass Killers in Manifesto." *Reuters*, 8 September. Online: (www.reuters.com/article/us-usa-shooting-oregon/oregon-college-shooter-wrote-of-kinship-with-mass-killers-in-manifesto-iDUSKCN1BJ2QK).

Cohn, Nate. 2019. "Huge Turnout is Expected in 2020." *The New York Times*, 15 July. Online: (www.nytimes.com/2019/07/15/upshot/2020-election-turnout-analysis.html).

Cohn, Norman. 1970. *The Pursuit of the Millennium*. New York: Oxford University Press.

Colt, George Howe. 1991. *The Enigma of Suicide*. New York: Summit Books.

Comte-Sponville, Andre. 2004. *The Little Book of Philosophy*. London: Heinemann.

Comte-Sponville, Andre. 2007. *The Little Book of Atheist Spirituality*. New York: Viking.

Congreve, Richard. 1874. *Essays: Political, Social, and Religious*. London: Longmans.

Conrad, Joseph. [1904] 1961. *Nostromo*. New York: Heritage Press.

Cooke, George Willis. 1920. *The Social Evolution of Religion*. Boston: Stratford Co.

Cooley, Charles Horton. [1909] 1962. *Social Organization*. New York: Schocken.

Cornford, F.M. [1912] 2004. *From Religion to Philosophy*. Mineola: Dover.

Cousin, Victor. 1853. *Course of the History of Modern Philosophy*, tr. O.W. Wright. New York: D. Appleton.

Cox, Gary. 2012. *The Existentialist's Guide to Death, the Universe, and Nothingness*. London: Continuum.

Cox, Jeff. 2019. "Government Debt Hits Record $66 Trillion, 80% of Global GDP, Fitch Says." CNBC, 23 January. Online: (www.cnbc.com/2019/01/23/government-debt-tab-hits-66-trillion-80percent-of-global-gdp-fitch-says.html).

Creighton, James Edwin. 1925. *Studies in Speculative Philosophy*. New York: Macmillan.

Crifasi, Cassandra K., John Meyers, Jon Vernick, and Daniel Webster. 2015. "Effects of Changes in Permit-to-Purchase Handgun Laws in Connecticut and Missouri on Suicide Rates." *Preventative Medicine* 79: 43–9.

Crigger, Megan and Laura Santhanam. 2015. "How Many Americans Have Died in U.S. Wars?" PBS Newshour, 24 May. Online: (www.pbs.org/newshour/nation/many-americans-died-u-s-wars).

Croce, Benedetto. 1915. *What is Living and What is Dead of the Philosophy of Hegel.* London: Macmillan.

Croce, Benedetto. 1917. *Logic as the Science of the Pure Concept.* London: Macmillan.

Dahms, Harry F. 2011. *The Vitality of Critical Theory: Current Perspectives in Social Theory* 28. Bingley: Emerald.

Dante Alighieri. 1995. *The Divine Comedy,* tr. Allen Mandelbaum. New York: Knopf.

Darwin, Charles. 1897. *The Descent of Man.* New York: Appleton.

Davies, Christie and Mark Neal. 2000. "Durkheim's Altruistic and Fatalistic Suicide." Pp. 36–52 in *Durkheim's Suicide,* eds. W.S.F. Pickering and Geoffrey Walford. London: Routledge.

Davis, Kingsley. 1936. "The Application of Science to Personal Relations." *American Sociological Review* 1(2): 236–47.

Davis, Wade. 1985. *The Serpent and the Rainbow.* New York: Simon and Schuster.

Davy, Georges. 1957. "Introduction." Pp. xliii–lxxiv in *Professional Ethics and Civic Morals* by Emile Durkheim. London and New York: Routledge.

Debord, Guy. 1983. *Society of the Spectacle.* Detroit: Black & Red.

Debord, Guy, Attila Kotanyi, and Raoul Vaneigem. [1962] 1981. "Theses on the Paris Commune." Pp. 314–17 in *Situationist International Anthology,* edited by Ken Knabb. Berkeley: Bureau of Public Secrets.

Department of Veteran Affairs. 2015. "America's Wars." Online: (www.va.gov/opa/publications/factsheets/fs_americas_wars.pdf).

Descartes, Rene. 1954. *Philosophical Writings,* eds. Elizabeth Anscombe and Peter Thomas Geach. Wokingham, UK: Van Nostrand Reinhold.

DeSilver, Drew. 2018. "For Most US Workers, Real Wages Have Barely Budged in Decades." Pew Research Center, 7 August. Online: (www.pewresearch.org/fact-tank/2018/08/07/for-most-us-workers-real-wages-have-barely-budged-for-decades).

Desmond, William. 2008. *Cynics.* Berkeley: University of California Press.

Dewey, John. 1903. *Ethical Principles Underlying Education.* Chicago: The University of Chicago Press.

Dewey, John. 1929. *The Quest for Certainty.* New York: Capricorn.

Dewey, John. 1946. *Problems of Men.* New York: Philosophical Library.

Dewey, John. 1978. *The Middle Works, 1899–1911, Volume 6: 1910–1911.* Carbondale: Southern Illinois University Press.

Dillon, John M. 2004. *Morality and Custom in Ancient Greece.* Bloomington: Indiana University Press.

Dostoyevsky, Fyodor. [1863] 1955. *Winter Notes on Summer Impressions,* tr. John Calder. Surrey, UK: Alma Books.

Dostoyevsky, Fyodor. 1912. *The Brothers Karamazov,* tr. Constance Garnett. New York: The Modern Library.

Dostoyevsky, Fyodor. 1994. *Crime and Punishment, The Gambler,* and *Notes from the Underground.* London: Chancellor Press.

Douglas, Jack D. 1967. *The Social Meanings of Suicide.* Princeton: Princeton University Press.

Drapeau, C.W. and J.L. McIntosh. 2015. *U.S.A. Suicide 2014.* Washington, DC: American Association of Suicidology. Online: (www.suicidology.org).

Draut, Tamara. 2018. "Is This Your Image of the Working Class? You Need to Update it." *The Guardian,* 9 May. Online: (www.theguardian.com/commentisfree/2018/may/09/american-working-class-what-it-looks-like-today).

Droge, Arthur and James D. Tabor. 1992. *A Noble Death.* New York: Harper.

Dublin, Louis and Bessie Bunzel. 1933. *To Be or Not To Be: A Study of Suicide.* New York: Harrison Smith and Robert Haas.

Du Bois, W.E. Burghardt. 1935. *Black Reconstruction in America.* New York: Harcourt, Brace and Co.

Dumézil, Georges. 1970. *Archaic Roman Religion,* tr. Philip Krapp. Baltimore: The Johns Hopkins University Press.

Durkheim, Emile. [1893] 1984. *The Division of Labor in Society,* tr. W.D. Halls. New York: The Free Press.

Durkheim, Emile. [1897] 1951. *Suicide,* tr. J. Spaulding and G. Simpson. New York: The Free Press.

Durkheim, Emile. [1901] 2006. "Technology." Pp. 31–2 in *Marcel Mauss: Techniques, Technology and Civilization,* ed. Nathan Schlanger. New York: Durkheim Press/Berghahn.

Durkheim, Emile. [1912] 1915. *The Elementary Forms of the Religious Life,* tr. Joseph Ward Swain. New York: The Free Press.

Durkheim, Emile. [1912] 1995. *The Elementary Forms of Religious Life,* tr. Karen E. Fields. New York: The Free Press.

Durkheim, Emile. [1914] 1960. "The Dualism of Human Nature and its Social Conditions." Pp. 325–40 in *Emile Durkheim, 1858–1917, A Collection of Essays,* ed. Kurt H. Wolff. Columbus: The Ohio State University Press.

Durkheim, Emile. 1915. *Germany Above All.* Paris: Librairie Armand Colin.

Durkheim, Emile. 1957. *Professional Ethics and Civic Morals,* tr. Cornelia Brookfield. London and New York: Routledge.

Durkheim, Emile. 1958. *Socialism.* New York, NY: Collier.

Durkheim, Emile. 1960. *Montesquieu and Rousseau.* Ann Arbor: The University of Michigan Press.

Durkheim, Emile. 1961. *Moral Education,* tr. Everett K. Wilson and Herman Schnurer. Mineola: Dover.

Durkheim, Emile. 1973. *On Morality and Society.* Chicago: The University of Chicago Press.

Durkheim, Emile. 1974. *Sociology and Philosophy*, tr. D.F. Pocock. New York: The Free Press.

Durkheim, Emile. 1977. *The Evolution of Educational Thought: Lectures on the Formation and development of Secondary Education in France*, tr. Peter Collins. London: Routledge and Kegan Paul.

Durkheim, Emile. 1978. *On Institutional Analysis* ed. and tr. Mark Traugott. Chicago: University of Chicago Press.

Durkheim, Emile. 1981. "The Realm of Sociology as a Science." *Social Forces* 59(4): 1054–070.

Durkheim, Emile. 1982. *The Rules of Sociological Method*, ed. Steven Lukes and tr. W.D. Halls. New York: The Free Press.

Durkheim, Emile. 1983. *Pragmatism and Sociology*, tr. J.C. Whitehouse and ed. John B. Allcock. Cambridge: Cambridge University Press.

Durkheim, Emile. 1993. *Ethics and the Sociology of Morals*, tr. Robert T. Hall. Buffalo: Prometheus.

Durkheim, Emile. 2004. *Durkheim's Philosophy Lectures: Notes from the Lycée de Sens Course, 1883–1884*, eds. Neil Gross and Robert Alun Jones. Cambridge: Cambridge University Press.

Durkheim, Emile. 2006. *On Suicide*, tr. Robin Buss. New York: Penguin.

Durkheim, Emile and Marcel Mauss. [1903] 1963. *Primitive Classification*, tr. and ed. Rodney Needham. Chicago: University of Chicago Press.

Durkheim, Emile and Marcel Mauss. [1913] 2006. "Note on the Concept of Civilization." Pp. 35–9 in *Marcel Mauss: Techniques, Technology and Civilization*, ed. Nathan Schlanger. New York: Durkheim Press/Berghahn.

Duveen, Gerard. 2001. "Introduction: The Power of Ideas." Pp. 1–17 in *Social Representations* by Serge Moscovici. New York: New York University Press.

Eagleton, Terry. 2016. *Materialism*. New Haven: Yale University Press.

Eco, Umberto. 1983. *The Name of the Rose*, tr. William Weaver. New York: Knopf.

Eco, Umberto. 1984. *Semiotics and the Philosophy of Language*. Bloomington: Indiana University Press.

Eco, Umberto. 2016. *Chronicles of a Liquid Society*, tr. R. Dixon. New York: Houghton Mifflin Harcourt.

Edmonds, David and John Eidinow. 2001. *Wittgenstein's Poker*. New York: HarperCollins.

Elliott, Justin and Laura Sullivan. 2015. "How the Red Cross Raised Half a Billion Dollars for Haiti and Built Six Homes." *ProPublica*, 3 June. Online: (www.propublica.org/article/how-the-red-cross-raised-half-a-billion-dollars-for-haiti-and-built-6-homes).

Ellis, Havelock. 1911. *The World of Dreams*. New York and Boston: Houghton Mifflin.

Ellis, Ralph and Keith Allen. 2017. "Overdose Cases Spike in Louisville." CNN, 13 February. Online: (www.cnn.com/2017/02/11/health/overdoses-spike-in-louisville/index.html).

Emerson, Ralph Waldo. [1837] 1981. "The American Scholar." Pp. 51–71 in *The Portable Emerson*, ed. Carl Bode. New York: Penguin.

Emerson, Ralph Waldo. 1950. *The Selected Writings of Ralph Waldo Emerson*. New York: The Modern Library.

Engber, Daniel. 2015. "The Strange Case of Anna Stubblefield." *The New York Times*, 20 October. Accessed 27 January 2016. Online: (www.nytimes.com/2015/10/25/magazine/the-strange-case-of-anna-stubblefield.html).

Epictetus. 2004. *Enchiridion*. Mineola: Dover.

Erasmus. [1509] 1913. *The Praise of Folly*, tr. John Wilson. London: Oxford University Press.

Eysenck, Hans. [1967] 2006. *The Biological Basis of Personality*. New Brunswick: Transaction.

Fahmy, Dalia. 2018. "Key Findings About America's Belief in God." Pew Research Center. Online: (www.pewresearch.org/fact-tank/2018/04/25/key-findings-about-americans-belief).

Fanfani, Amintore. 1935. *Catholicism, Protestantism and Capitalism*. London: Sheed and Ward.

Fanon, Frantz. 1963. *The Wretched of the Earth*. New York: Grove Press.

Farrar, James. 1912. *Chats with Children of the Church*. New York: Funk and Wagnalls.

Fasenfest, David. 2017. "The Downward Healthcare Slide: Tearing the Social Fabric." *Critical Sociology* 43(6): 815–18.

Fedden, Henry Romilly. 1938. *Suicide*. London: Peter Davies Ltd.

Fellman, Gordon. 1998. *Rambo and the Dalai Lama*. Albany: SUNY Press.

Fenichel, Otto. [1945] 1996. *The Psychoanalytic Theory of Neurosis*. New York: W. W. Norton.

Feuerbach, Ludwig. 1986. *Principles of the Philosophy of the Future*. Indianapolis: Hackett.

Fichte, Johann Gottlieb. 1847. *The Vocation of the Scholar*, tr. W. Smith. London: Chapman.

Fichte, Johann Gottlieb. 1848. *The Vocation of Man*, tr. William Smith. London: Chapman.

Findlay, J.N. 1958. *Hegel: A Re-Examination*. New York: Collier.

Findlay, J.N. 1970. *Ascent to the Absolute*. New York: Humanities Press.

Fink, Bruce. 1995. *The Lacanian Subject*. Princeton: Princeton University Press.

Fink, Bruce. 1997. *A Clinical Introduction to Lacanian Psychoanalysis: Theory and Technique*. Cambridge: Harvard University Press.

Fischer, David Hackett. 1989. *Albion's Seed*. New York and Oxford: Oxford University Press.

Fitzgerald, F. Scott. 1922. *Tales of the Jazz Age*. New York: Charles Scribner's Sons.

Flaubert, Gustave. 1957. *Madame Bovary*, tr. Francis Steegmuller. New York: Knopf.

Fore, William F. 1970. *Image and Impact*. New York: Friendship Press.

Frankfurt Institute for Social Research. 1972. *Aspects of Sociology*. Boston: Beacon.

Franklin, Benjamin. 2008. *The Way to Wealth*. Best Success Books.

Freeman, Joseph. 1936. *An American Testament*. New York: Farrar and Rinehart.

Freire, Paulo. 1993. *Pedagogy of the Oppressed,* revised edition. New York: Continuum.

Freud, Sigmund. [1900] 1965. *The Interpretation of Dreams*. New York: Avon.

Freud, Sigmund. [1901] 1952. *On Dreams*. New York: W. W. Norton.

Freud, Sigmund. [1910] 1959, "Contributions to the Psychology of Love: A Special Type of Choice of Object Made by Men." Pp. 192–202 in *Collected Papers*, Vol. 4. New York: Basic Books.

Freud, Sigmund. [1910] 1961. *Leonardo da Vinci and a Memory of His Childhood*. New York: W. W. Norton.

Freud, Sigmund. [1912] 1959, "Contributions to the Psychology of Love: The Most Prevalent Form of Degradation in Erotic Life." Pp. 203–16 in *Collected Papers*, Vol. 4. New York: Basic Books.

Freud, Sigmund. [1913] 1950. *Totem and Taboo*. New York: W. W. Norton.

Freud, Sigmund. [1914] 1959. "On Narcissism: An Introduction." Pp. 30–59 in *Collected Papers*, Vol. 4. New York: Basic Books.

Freud, Sigmund. [1915] 1959. "Thoughts for the Times on War and Death." Pp. 288–317 in *Collected Papers*, Vol. 4. New York: Basic Books.

Freud, Sigmund. [1917] 1959. "Mourning and Melancholia." Pp. 152–70 in *Collected Papers*, Vol. 4. New York: Basic Books.

Freud, Sigmund. [1917] 1966. *Introductory Lectures on Psycho-Analysis*. New York: W. W. Norton.

Freud, Sigmund. [1919] 1959. "The Uncanny." Pp. 368–407 in *Collected Papers*, Vol. 4. New York: Basic Books.

Freud, Sigmund. [1921] 1959. *Group Psychology and the Analysis of the Ego*. New York: W. W. Norton.

Freud, Sigmund. [1923] 1960. *The Ego and the Id*. New York: W. W. Norton.

Freud, Sigmund. [1925] 1959. "Negation." Pp. 181–85 in *Collected Papers*, Vol. 5. New York: Basic Books.

Freud, Sigmund. [1926] 1959. *Inhibitions, Symptoms, and Anxiety*. New York: W. W. Norton.

Freud, Sigmund. [1927] 1959. "Fetishism." Pp. 198–204 in *Collected Papers*, Vol. 5. New York: Basic Books.

Freud, Sigmund. [1927] 1961. *The Future of an Illusion*. New York: Norton.

Freud, Sigmund. [1930] 1961. *Civilization and its Discontents*. New York: W. W. Norton.

Freud, Sigmund. [1931] 1959. "Libidinal Types." Pp. 247–51 in *Collected Papers*, Vol. 5. New York: Basic Books.

Freud, Sigmund. [1938] 1959. "Some Elementary Lessons in Psycho-Analysis." Pp. 376–82 in *Collected Papers*, Vol. 5. New York: Basic Books.

Freud, Sigmund. 1939. *Moses and Monotheism*. New York: Vintage.

Freud, Sigmund. [1940] 1969. *An Outline of Psycho-Analysis*. New York: W. W. Norton.

Freud, Sigmund. 1950. *The Question of Lay Analysis*. New York: W. W. Norton.

Freud, Sigmund. 1951. *Psychopathology of Everyday Life*. New York: New American Library.

Freud, Sigmund. 1960. *Jokes and Their Relation to the Unconscious*. New York: W. W. Norton.

Freud, Sigmund. 1962. *Three Essays on the Theory of Sexuality*. New York: Avon.

Freud, Sigmund. 1963. *The History of the Psychoanalytic Movement*. New York: Collier.

Freud, Sigmund. 1965. *New Introductory Lectures on Psycho-Analysis*. New York: W. W. Norton.

Freud, Sigmund. 2002. *The Schreber Case*. New York: Penguin.

Freud, Sigmund. 2012. *The Letters of Sigmund Freud and Otto Rank*, eds. E.J. Lieberman and R. Kramer, tr. G.C. Richter. Baltimore: The Johns Hopkins University Press.

Freyer, Hans. [1928] 1998. *Theory of Objective Mind*, tr. Steven Grosby. Athens: Ohio University Press.

Freytas-Tamura, Kimiko. 2017. "Amid Opiate Overdoses, Ohio Coroner's Office Runs out of Room for Bodies." *The New York Times*, 2 February. Online: (www.nytimes.com/2017/02/02/us/ohio-overdose-deaths-coroners-office.html).

Friedman, Milton. 1962. *Capitalism and Freedom*. Chicago: The University of Chicago Press.

Fromm, Erich. 1941. *Escape from Freedom*. New York: Henry Holt and Company.

Fromm, Erich. 1957. "The Authoritarian Personality." Online: (www.marxists.org/archive/fromm/works/1957/authoritarian.htm).

Fromm, Erich. 1968. *The Revolution of Hope*. New York: Harper.

Fromm, Erich. 1970. *The Crisis of Psychoanalysis*. Greenwich: Fawcett Publications.

Fromm, Erich. 1973. *The Anatomy of Human Destructiveness*. New York: Holt, Rinehart and Winston.

Fromm, Erich. 1976. *To Have or to Be?* New York: Continuum.

Fromm, Erich. 1981. *On Disobedience*. New York: The Seabury Press.

Fromm, Erich. 1984. *The Working Class in Weimar Germany*. Cambridge: Harvard University Press.

Fry, John. 1811. *Canticles*. London: J. Hatchard.

Frydl, Kathleen. 2016. "The Oxy Electorate." *Medium*, 16 November. Online: (https://medium.com/@kfrydl/the-oxy-electorate-3fa62765f837).

Furedi, Frank. 2013. *Authority*: A Sociological History. New York: Cambridge University Press.

Fustel de Coulanges, Numa Denis. [1873] 1956. *The Ancient City*. New York: Doubleday.

Galen, Clemens Graf von. 1941. "Sermon Delivered by Bishop Clemens August Count of Galen on July 13, 1941, at the Church of St. Lambert, Muenster." Online: (http://www.priestsforlife.org/preaching/vongalen07-13.htm).

Galston, William. 2018. "In Defense of a Reasonable Patriotism." The Brookings Institution. Online: (www.brookings.edu/research/in-defense-of-a-reasonable-patriotism).

Gangas, Spyros. 2007. "Social Ethics and Logic: Rethinking Durkheim Through Hegel." *Journal of Classical Sociology* 7(3): 315–38.

Gaspar, Carlos. 2007. "Raymond Aron and the Origins of the Cold War." Pp. 175–94 in *Political Reason in the Age of Ideology*, eds. Bryan-Paul Frost and Daniel J. Mahoney. New Brunswick: Transaction Publishers.

Gay, Peter. 1993. *The Cultivation of Hatred*. New York: W. W. Norton.

Geiger, Abigail and Gretchen Livingston. 2018. "8 Facts About Love and Marriage in America." Pew Research Center, 13 February. Online: (www.pewresearch.org/fact-tank/2018/02/13/8-facts-about-love-and-marriage).

Gellner, Ernest. 1974. *Legitimation of Belief*. Cambridge: Cambridge University Press.

George, Henry. [1879] 1956. *Progress and Poverty*. New York: R. Schalkenbach Foundation.

Gerth, Hans and C. Wright Mills. 1953. *Character and Social Structure*. New York: Harcourt.

Giddens, Anthony. 1965. "The Suicide Problem in French Sociology." *The British Journal of Sociology* 16(1): 3–18.

Gierke, Otto. 1934. *Natural Law and the Theory of Society*, tr. E. Barker. Cambridge: Cambridge University Press.

Gill, Indermit. 2019. "Joyless Growth in China, India, and the United States." The Brookings Institution. Online: (www.brookings.edu/blog/future-development/2019/01/22).

Gillespie, Michael Allen. 2008. *The Theological Origins of Modernity*. Chicago: University of Chicago Press.

Gilman, Charlotte Perkins. [1915] 1998. *Herland*. Mineola: Dover.

Goerner, Sally. 2016. "Why Extreme Inequality Causes Economic Collapse." 15 February. Capital Institute. Online: (www.capitalinstitute.org/blog/why-extreme-inequality-equals-economic-collapse/).

Goethe, J.W. [1809] 1971. *Elective Affinities*, tr. R.J. Hollingdale. New York: Penguin.

Goethe, J.W. [1808] 1961. *Faust*, tr. Walter Kaufmann. New York: Anchor Books.

Goethe, J.W. 1840. *Theory of Colours*, tr. C.L. Eastlake. London: John Murray.

Goethe, J.W. 1976. *Faust*, tr. Walter Arndt and ed. Cyrus Hamlin. New York: W. W. Norton.
Goethe, J.W. 1983. *Selected Poems*, ed. Christopher Middleton. London: John Calder.
Goethe, J.W. 1984. *Faust*, tr. Stuart Atkins. Princeton: Princeton University Press.
Goethe, J.W. 1989. *The Sorrows of Young Werther*, tr. Michael Hulse. New York: Penguin.
Goffman, Erving. 1963. *Behavior in Public Places*. New York: The Free Press.
Goffman, Erving. 1967. *Interaction Ritual*. New York: Pantheon.
Goffman, Erving. 1974. *Frame Analysis*. Boston: Northeastern University Press.
Gogol, Nikolai. [1842] 1996. *Dead Souls*, tr. R. Pevear and L. Volokhonsky. New York: Knopf.
Goux, Jean-Joseph. 1990. *Symbolic Economies*. Ithaca: Cornell University Press.
Gracián, Baltasar. [1647] 2015. *How to Use Your Enemies*, tr. J. Robbins. New York: Penguin.
Gramsci, Antonio. 1971. *Selections from the Prison Notebooks*. New York: International Publishers.
Granet, Marcel. 1951. *Chinese Civilization*. New York: Barnes and Noble.
Grant, Bridget F. et al. 2017. "Prevalence of 12-Month Alcohol Use, High-Risk Drinking, and DSM-IV Alcohol Disorder in the United States, 2001–2002 to 2012–2013." *Journal of the American Medical Association Psychiatry*, 1 September. Online: (http://jamanetwork.com/journals/jamapsychiatry/article-abstract/2647079).
Green, T.H. [1895] 1924. *Lectures on the Principles of Political Obligation*. London: Longmans, Green, and Co.
Greene, Graham. 1929. *The Man Within*. New York: Penguin.
Grene, David and Richmond Lattimore (eds.). 1960. *Greek Tragedies*, Vol. 1. Chicago: The University of Chicago Press.
Grinspoon, Lester. 1971. "Opium, not Alcohol, is the Demon." *The New York Times*, 24 October. Online: (www.nytimes.com/1971/10/24/archives/artificial-paradise-by-charles-baudelaire-translated-by-ellen-fox.html).
Groddeck, Georg. [1949] 1961. *The Book of the It*. New York: Vintage.
Grossman, Henryk. [1934] 2006. "The Beginnings of Capitalism and the New Mass Morality." *Journal of Classical Sociology* 6(2): 201–13.
Hacker, Jacob S. and Paul Pierson. 2016. *American Amnesia*. New York: Simon and Schuster.
Haidt, Jonathan. 2012. *The Righteous Mind*. New York: Vintage.
Halbwachs, Maurice. [1930] 1978. *The Causes of Suicide*, tr. Harold Goldblatt. London: Routledge and Kegan Paul.
Halbwachs, Maurice. 1958. *The Psychology of Social Class*, tr. Claire Delavenay. Glencoe: The Free Press.

Halbwachs, Maurice. 1962. *Sources of Religious Sentiment*, tr. John A. Spaulding. New York: The Free Press.

Halevy, Elie. 1965. *The Era of Tyrannies*, tr. R.K. Webb. New York: NYU Press.

Hall, Stuart. 1997. "Representation, Meaning and Language." Pp. 15–64 in *Representation*, ed. Stuart Hall. London: Sage.

Hamid, Mohsin. 2017. *Exit West*. New York: Riverhead/Penguin.

Haraway, Donna J. 2016. *A Cyborg Manifesto*. Minneapolis: University of Minnesota Press.

Hardimon, Michael O. 1994. *Hegel's Social Philosophy: The Project of Reconciliation*. Cambridge: Cambridge University Press.

Hardy, Thomas. [1894–95] 2006. *Jude the Obscure*. Mineola: Dover.

Harman, Graham. 2011. *The Quadruple Object*. Winchester, UK: Zero Books.

Harmetz, Aljean. 1977. *The Making of The Wizard of Oz*. New York: Limelight Editions.

Harper, Jake. 2017. "A Drugmaker Tries to Cash in on the Opioid Epidemic, One State Law at a Time." National Public Radio, 12 June. Online: (www.npr.org/sections/health-shots/2017/06/12/523774660/a-drugmaker-tries-to-cash-in-on-the-opioid-epidemic-one-state-law-at-a-time).

Harrington, Michael. 1965. *The Accidental Century*. Baltimore: Penguin.

Harrison, Jane Ellen. 1962. *Epilegomena to the Study of Greek Religion* and *Themis*. New Hyde Park: University Books.

Harvey, David. 1990. *The Condition of Postmodernity*. Cambridge: Blackwell.

Hearn, Frank. 1985. *Reason and Freedom in Sociological Thought*. London: Allen and Unwin.

Hecht, Jennifer Michael. 2013. "Stopping Suicide." *The Chronicle of Higher Education*, 2 December. Online: (http://chronicle.com/article/Stopping-Suicide/143279).

Hechtkopf, Kevin. 2005. "Lottery Fortune as Cookie Crumbles." *CBSNews*. Online: (www.cbsnews.com/news/lottery-fortune-as-cookie-crumbles).

Hegel, G.W.F. [1801] 1977. *The Difference Between Fichte's and Schelling's System of Philosophy*, tr. H.S. Harris and Walter Cerf. Albany: SUNY Press.

Hegel, G.W.F. [1802–1804] 1979. *System of Ethical Life* and *First Philosophy of Spirit*, ed. and tr. H.S. Harris and T.M. Knox. Albany: SUNY Press.

Hegel, G.W.F. [1807] 1967. *The Phenomenology of Mind*, tr. J.B. Baillie. New York: Harper.

Hegel, G.W.F. [1807] 1977. *Phenomenology of Spirit*, tr. A.V. Miller. Oxford: Oxford University Press.

Hegel, G.W.F. [1807] 2008. *Phenomenology of Spirit*, tr. Terry Pinkard. Unpublished.

Hegel, G.W.F. [1812] 1969. *Science of Logic*, tr. A.V. Miller. Atlantic Highlands, NJ: Humanities Press International.

Hegel, G.W.F. [1821] 1991. *Elements of the Philosophy of Right*, tr. H.B. Nisbet. Cambridge: Cambridge University Press.

Hegel, G.W.F. [1830] 1991. *The Encyclopedia Logic, Part 1 of the Encyclopedia of Philosophical Sciences with the Zusätze*, tr. T.F. Geraets, W.A. Suchting, and H.S. Harris. Indianapolis/Cambridge: Hackett Publishing.

Hegel, G.W.F. [1840] 1974. *Lectures on the Philosophy of Religion*, volume 1, tr. E.B. Speirs and J. Burdon Sanderson (Reprint). New York: The Humanities Press.

Hegel, G.W.F. [1840] 1995a. *Lectures on the History of Philosophy*, Vol. 2, tr. E.S. Haldane and Frances H. Simson. Lincoln: University of Nebraska Press.

Hegel, G.W.F. [1840] 1995b. *Lectures on the History of Philosophy*, Vol. 3, tr. E.S. Haldane and Frances H. Simson. Lincoln: University of Nebraska Press.

Hegel, G.W.F. [1892] 1995. *Lectures on the History of Philosophy*, volume 1, tr. E.S. Haldane. Lincoln: University of Nebraska Press.

Hegel, G.W.F. 1948. *Early Theological Writings*. Philadelphia: University of Pennsylvania Press.

Hegel, G.W.F. 1956. *The Philosophy of History*, tr. J. Sibree. Mineola: Dover.

Hegel, G.W.F. 1975a. *Aesthetics*, Vol. 1, tr. T.M. Knox. Oxford: Oxford University Press.

Hegel, G.W.F. 1975b. *Aesthetics*, Vol. 2, tr. T.M. Knox. Oxford: Oxford University Press.

Hegel, G.W.F. 1975c. *Lectures on the Philosophy of World History: Introduction*, tr. H.B. Nisbet. Cambridge: Cambridge University Press.

Hegel, G.W.F. 1983. *Hegel and the Human Spirit*, tr. Leo Rauch. Detroit: Wayne State University Press. Online: (www.marxists.org/reference/archive/hegel/jlindex.htm).

Hegel, G.W.F. 1984. *Hegel: The Letters*, tr. Clark Butler and Christiane Seiler. Bloomington: Indiana University Press.

Hegel, G.W.F. 1986. *The Philosophical Propaedeutic*, tr. A.V. Miller. Oxford and New York: Basil Blackwell.

Hegel, G.W.F. 1987. *Lectures on the Philosophy of Religion*, Vol. 2. Berkeley: University of California Press.

Hegel, G.W.F. 1988. *Lectures on the Philosophy of Religion*, abridged. Berkeley: University of California Press.

Hegel, G.W.F. 2002. *Miscellaneous Writings of G. W. F. Hegel*, ed. Jon Stewart. Evanston: Northwestern University Press.

Hegel, G.W.F. 2007. *Philosophy of Mind*, tr. W. Wallace and A.V. Miller. Oxford: Oxford University Press.

Helmore, Edward. 2018. "US Suicide Rate Has Risen Nearly 30% Since 1999, Federal Study Finds." *The Guardian*, 8 June. Online: (www.theguardian.com/us-news/2018/jun/08/us-suicide-rate-has-risen-nearly-30-since-1999-federal-study-finds).

Helmore, Edward. 2019. "Disney and Soros Among Super-Rich Urging US Government: Tax Us More." *The Guardian*, 24 June. Online: (www.theguardian.com/business/2019/jun/24/disney-soros-wealth-tax-call-for-higher-taxes-us).

Henrich, Dieter. 1967. *Hegel im Kontext*. Frankfurt am Main: Suhrkamp Verlag.

Heraclitus. 2001. *Fragments*, tr. Brooks Haxton. New York: Penguin.

Herder, Johann Gottfried. 1966. *Outlines of a Philosophy of the History of Man*. New York: Bergman Publishers.

Herder, Johann Gottfried. 1993. *Against Pure Reason*, ed. and tr. Marcia Bunge. Fortress Press: Minneapolis.

Herf, Jeffrey. 1984. *Reactionary Modernism*. Cambridge: Cambridge University Press.

Hertz, Robert. 1994. *Sin and Expiation in Primitive Societies*, tr. Robert Parkin. Oxford: British Centre for Durkheimian Studies.

Hess, Moses. 1845. "The Essence of Money." Online: (www.marxistsfr.org/archive/hess/1845/essence-money.htm).

Hesse, Hermann. [1925] 1965. *Demian*. New York: Harper.

Hesse, Hermann. 1963. *Steppenwolf*. New York: The Modern Library.

Hesse, Hermann. 1971. *If the War Goes On …*, tr. Ralph Manheim. New York: Farrar, Straus and Giroux.

Higgins, Kathleen. 1990. "Nietzsche and Postmodern Subjectivity." Pp. 189–215 in *Nietzsche as Postmodernist*, ed. Clayton Koelb. Albany: SUNY Press.

Hilbert, Richard A. 1986. "Anomie and the Moral Regulation of Reality: The Durkheimian Tradition in Modern Relief." *Sociological Theory* 4(1): 1–19.

Hirschler, Ben. 2017. "World's Eight Richest as Wealthy as Half Humanity, Oxfam Tells Davos." *Reuters*, 15 January. Online: (www.reuters.com/article/us-davos-meeting-inequality-IDUSKBN150009).

Hobbes, Thomas. 1651. *Leviathan*. London: Andrew Crooke. Online: (socserv2.socsci.mcmaster.ca/econ/ugcm/3ll3/hobbes/Leviathan.pdf).

Hobbes, Thomas. 1889. *Behemoth*, ed. F. Tönnies. London: Simpkin, Marshall, and Co.

Hocart, A.M. [1936] 1970. *Kings and Councillors*. Chicago: The University of Chicago Press.

Hochschild, Arlie. 2019. "Think Republicans are Disconnected from Reality? It's Even Worse Among Liberals." *The Guardian*, 21 July. Online: (www.theguardian.com/commentisfree/2019/jul/21/democrats-republicans-political-beliefs-national-survey-poll).

Hocking, William Ernest. 1918. *Morale and its Enemies*. New Haven: Yale University Press.

Hocking, William Ernest. 1926. *Man and the State*. New Haven: Yale University Press.

Hocking, William Ernest. 1956. *The Coming World Civilization*. New York: Harper.

Hodge, Robert and Gunther Kress. 1988. *Social Semiotics*. Ithaca: Cornell University Press.

Hodgkin, Luke. 2005. *A History of Mathematics*. Oxford: Oxford University Press.

Hofstadter, Douglas. 1995. *Fluid Concepts and Creative Analogies*. New York: Basic Books.

Hofstadter, Douglas. 2007. *I am a Strange Loop*. New York: Basic Books.

Hölderlin, Friedrich. 2008. *Hyperion*, tr. Ross Benjamin. New York: Archipelago Books.

Holzner, Burkart. 1968. *Reality Construction in Society*. Cambridge: Schenkman.
Homer. 1944. *The Odyssey*, tr. Samuel Butler. Roslyn: Walter J. Black.
Honneth, Axel. 1995. *The Struggle for Recognition*, tr. Joel Anderson. Cambridge: Polity Press.
Hook, Sidney. 1934. "Karl Marx and Moses Hess." Online: (www.marxistsfr.org/history/etol/writers/hook/1934/12/hess-marx.htm).
Hopkins, Gerard Manley. 2015. *As Kingfishers Catch Fire*. New York: Penguin.
Hopkins, John. 1884. "Specimens of the Classification of Cases for 'Phantasms of the Living.'" *Journal of the Society for Psychical Research* 1: 114–23.
Horkheimer, Max. 1972. *Critical Theory*. New York: Continuum.
Horkheimer, Max. 1978. *Dawn and Decline*. New York: Seabury.
Horkheimer, Max and Theodor W. Adorno. [1944] 1972. *Dialectic of Enlightenment*, tr. John Cumming. New York: Continuum.
Horne, James. 1983. *The Moral Mystic*. Waterloo: Canadian Corporation for Studies in Religion.
Horney, Karen. 1939. *New Ways in Psychoanalysis*. New York: W. W. Norton.
Horney, Karen. 1945. *Our Inner Conflicts*. New York: W. W. Norton.
Howard, Jacqueline. 2017. "Why are Fewer Americans Trying to Lose Weight?" CNN, 10 April. Online:(www.cnn.com/2017/04/10/health/weight-loss-giving-up-diet-obesity-study/index.html).
Hubert, Henri and Marcel Mauss. 1964. *Sacrifice*. Chicago: The University of Chicago Press.
Hudis, Peter. 2012. *Marx's Concept of the Alternative to Capitalism*. Leiden: Brill.
Hughes, Dorothy B. 1947. *In a Lonely Place*. New York: New York Review Books.
Hughes, H. Stuart. 1977. *Consciousness and Society: The Reorientation of European Social Thought: 1890–1930*, revised edition. New York: Vintage Books.
Hume, David. 1896. *A Treatise of Human Nature*. Oxford: Clarendon Press.
Huxley, Aldous. [1932] 1946. *Brave New World*. Cutchogue, NY: Buccaneer Books.
Huysmans, Joris-Karl. [1884] 1998. *Against Nature*, tr. Margaret Mauldon. Oxford: Oxford University Press.
Inglehart, Ronald. 2018. *Cultural Evolution*. New York: Cambridge University Press.
Ingraham, Christopher. 2019. "Wealth Concentration Returning to 'Levels Last Seen During the Roaring Twenties,' According to New Research." *The Washington Post*, 8 February. Online: (www.washingtonpost.com/us-policy/2019/02/08/wealth-concentration-returning-levels-last-seen-during-roaring-twenties-according-new-research).
Institute of Social Research. 1944. "Ten Years on Morningside Heights: A Report on the Institute's History: 1934–1944." Unpublished prospectus. Columbia University.
Institute of Social Research. 1945. *Antisemitism Among American Labor*. Unpublished, four-volume report. Columbia University.

International Air Transport Association. 2016. "Collaboration Needed to Stem Unruly Passenger Incidents." 28 December. Online: (www.iata.org/pressroom/pr/Pages/2016-09-28-01).

Irwin, Terence. 2009. *The Development of Ethics*, Vol. 3. Oxford: Oxford University Press.

Isenberg, Nancy. 2016. *White Trash*. New York: Viking.

Ivimey, Muriel. 1946. "What is a Neurosis?" Pp. 61–92 in *Are You Considering Psychoanalysis?*, ed. Karen Horney. New York: W. W. Norton.

Jacoby, Russell. 1981. *Dialectic of Defeat*. Cambridge: Cambridge University Press.

James, William. [1907] 1995. *Pragmatism*. New York: Dover.

James, William. 1909. *A Pluralistic Universe*. London: Longmans, Gren, and Co.

James, William. 1918. *The Principles of Psychology*, volume 1. Mineola: Dover.

Jameson, Fredric. 1973. "The Vanishing Mediator: Narrative Structure in Max Weber." *New German Critique* 1: 52–89.

Jameson, Fredric. 1990. *Late Marxism*. London: Verso.

Jameson, Fredric. 1991. *Postmodernism*. Durham: Duke University Press.

Jameson, Fredric. 2009. *Valences of the Dialectic*. London: Verso.

Jankélévitch, Sophie. 2012. "*Le Suicide* and Psychological Suffering." Pp. 31–48 in *Suffering and Evil*, eds. W.S.F. Pickering and Massimo Rosati. New York: Durkheim Press/Berghahn.

Jaspers, Karl. 1986. *Basic Philosophical Writings*, ed. and tr. Edith Ehrlich, Leonard H. Ehrlich, and George B. Pepper. Amherst: Prometheus Books.

Jaynes, Julian. 1990. *The Origin of Consciousness in the Breakdown of the Bicameral Mind*. Boston: Houghton Mifflin.

Jenkyns, Richard. 2007. "Introduction." Pp. vii–xxiii in *The Nature of Things* by Lucretius. New York: Penguin.

Johnson, Ian. 2018. "Who Killed More: Hitler, Stalin, or Mao?" *The New York Review of Books*, 5 February. Online: (www.nybooks.com/daily/2018/02/05/who-killed-more-hitler-stalin-or-mao).

Johnson, Samuel. 1816. *The Works of Samuel Johnson*, Vol. 2. London: Nichols, Sons, and Bentley.

Johnston, Adrian. 2008. *Žižek's Ontology*. Evanston: Northwestern University Press.

Jones, Ernest. 1931. *On the Nightmare*. London: Hogarth Press.

Jones, Ernest. 1961. *The Life and Work of Sigmund Freud*. Garden City: Doubleday.

Jones, Susan Stedman. 1998. "The Concept of Belief in the *Elementary Forms*." Pp. 53–65 in *On Durkheim's* Elementary Forms of Religious Life, eds. N.J. Allen, W.S.F. Pickering, and W. Watts Miller. London: Routledge.

Jones, Susan Stedman. [2000] 2006. "Representations in Durkheim's Masters: Kant and Renouvier." Pp. 37–58 in *Durkheim and Representations*, ed by W.S.F. Pickering. London: Routledge.

Jones, Susan Stedman. 2001. *Durkheim Reconsidered*. Cambridge: Polity.

Jones, W.T. 1969. *The Medieval Mind: A History of Western Philosophy*, Vol. 2, 2nd ed. San Diego: Harcourt.

Jones, W.T. 1970. *A History of Western Philosophy, Volume 1: The Classical Mind*, 2nd ed. San Diego: Harcourt.

Joseph, Andrew. 2016. "26 Overdoses in Just Hours." *STAT*, 22, August. Online: (www.statnews.com/2016/08/22/heroin-huntington-west-virginia-overdoses).

Jung, Carl. 1969. *The Archetypes and the Collective Unconscious*, 2nd ed. Princeton: Princeton University Press.

Kaag, John. 2016. *American Philosophy: A Love Story*. New York: Farrar, Straus and Giroux.

Kaag, John. 2017. "Me for the Woods." *The Paris Review*, 30 June. Online: (www.theparisreview.org/blog/2017/06/30/me-for-the-woods).

Kant, Immanuel. 1929. *Critique of Pure Reason*, tr. Norman Kemp Smith. New York: St. Martin's Press.

Kant, Immanuel. 1951. *Critique of Judgement*, tr. J.H. Bernard. New York: Hafner.

Kant, Immanuel. 1964. *Groundwork of the Metaphysics of Morals*, tr. H.J. Paton. New York: Harper & Row.

Kant, Immanuel. 1983. *Perpetual Peace and Other Essays*, tr. Ted Humphrey. Indianapolis: Hackett.

Kant, Immanuel. 1991. *The Metaphysics of Morals*, tr. Mary Gregor. Cambridge: Cambridge University Press.

Kant, Immanuel. 1998. *Religion Within the Boundaries of Mere Reason*, tr. and ed. by Allen Wood and George Di Giovanni. Cambridge: Cambridge University Press.

Kapur, Akash. 2016. "The Return of the Utopians." *The New Yorker*, 3 October. Online: (www.newyorker.com/magazine/2016/10/03/the-return-of-the-utopians).

Katz, Josh. 2017. "The First Count of Fentanyl Deaths in 2016: Up 540% in Three Years." *The New York Times*, 2 September. Online: (www.nytimes.com/interactive/2017/09/02/upshot/fentanyl-drug-overdose-deaths.html).

Katz, Michael B. 1986. *In the Shadow of the Poorhouse*. New York: Basic.

Kaufmann, Walter. 1958. *Critique of Religion and Philosophy*. Princeton: Princeton University Press.

Kaufmann, Walter. 1965a. *Hegel: A Reinterpretation*. Notre Dame: University of Notre Dame Press.

Kaufmann, Walter. 1965b. *Hegel: Text and Commentary*. Notre Dame: University of Notre Dame Press.

Kaufmann, Walter. 1980b. *Discovering the Mind: Freud, Adler, and Jung*. New Brunswick: Transaction.

Kaye, F.B. 1924. "Introduction: Mandeville's Thought." Pp. xvii–xxxii in *The Fable of the Bees* by Bernard Mandeville, Vol. 1. Oxford: Clarendon Press.

Kerrigan, William. 1983. *The Sacred Complex*. Cambridge: Harvard University Press.

Khazan, Olga. 2015. "Middle-Aged White Americans are Dying of Despair." *The Atlantic*, 4 November. Online: (www.theatlantic.com/health/archive/2015/11/boomers-deaths-pnas/413971).

Khazan, Olga. 2016. "Why are so Many Middle-Aged White Americans Dying?" *The Atlantic*, 29 January. Online: (www.theatlantic.com/health/archive/2016/01/middle-aged-white-americans-left-behind-and-dying-early/433863).

Kierkegaard, Søren. 1940. *For Self-Examination*. Minneapolis: Augsburg Publishing House.

Kimmel, Michael. 2013. *Angry White Men*. New York: Nation Books.

Kindy, Kimberly and Dan Keating. 2016. "Risky Alone, Deadly Together." *The Washington Post*, 31 August. Online: (www.washingtonpost.com/sf/national/wp/2016/08/31/2016/08/31/opiods-and-anti-anxiety-medication-are-killing-white-american-women).

King, D. Brett and Michael Wertheimer. 2005. *Max Wertheimer and Gestalt Theory*. New Brunswick: Transaction Publishers.

King, Jerry. P. 1992. *The Art of Mathematics*. Mineola: Dover.

King, Stephen D. 2017. *Grave New World*. New Haven: Yale University Press.

Kliff, Sarah. 2016. "Why Obamacare Enrollees Voted for Trump." *Vox*, 13 December. Online: (www.vox.com/science-and-health/2016/12/13/13848794/kentucky-obamacare-trump).

Klussman, Uwe. 2013. "Stalin Cult Alive and Well in Russia." *Der Spiegel*, 5 March. Online: (www.spiegel.de/international/europe/sixty-years-after-death-josef-stalin-still-revered-by-some-russians-a-886933.html).

Knausgaard, Karl Ove. 2018. "A Literary Road Trip into the Heart of Russia." *The New York Times Magazine*, 14 February. Online: (www.nytimes.com/2018/02/14/magazine/a-literary-road-trip-into-the-heart-of-russia).

Koepping, Klaus-Peter. 1983. *Adolf Bastian and the Psychic Unity of Mankind*. St. Lucia: University of Queensland Press.

Kogon, Eugen. 1950. *The Theory and Practice of Hell*. New York: Berkley Publishing.

Kojève, Alexandre. [1947] 1969. *Introduction to the Reading of Hegel*. Ithaca: Cornell University Press.

Kolhatkar, Sheelah. 2017. "National Disaster." *The New Yorker*, 18 September: 21.

Komlos, John and Marieluise Baur. 2003. "From the Tallest to (One of) the Fattest: The Enigmatic Fate of the American Population in the 20th Century." CESifo Working Paper No. 1028. Online: (www.cesifo-group.de/pls/guestci/download/CESifo%20Working%20Papers%202003/CESifo%20Working%20Papers%20September%202003/CESifo1_wp1028.pdf).

Konnikova, Maria. 2012. "When Authors Disown Their Work, Should Readers Care?" *The Atlantic*, 28 August. Online: (www.theatlantic.com/entertainment/archive/2012/08/when-authors-disown-their-work-should-readers-care/261615/).

Koselleck, Reinhart. 1985. *Futures Past*, tr. Keith Tribe: Cambridge: The MIT Press.
Kotwal, Karishma. 2016. "80 Deaths in 3 Months in 'Suicide Village' Badi." *Times of India*, 6 May. Online: (www.timesofindia.indiatimes.com/city/bhopal/80-deaths-in-3-months).
Kounang, Nadia. 2017. "US Heroin Deaths Jump 533 Percent Since 2002." CNN, 8 September. Online: (www.cnn.com/2017/09/08/health/heroin-deaths-samhsa-report/index.html).
Kracauer, Siegfried. 1995. *The Mass Ornament*. Cambridge: Harvard University Press.
Kracauer, Siegfried. 1998. *The Salaried Masses*. London: Verso.
Kracauer, Siegfried. 1999. "The Hotel Lobby." *Postcolonial Studies* 2(3): 289–97.
Kracauer, Siegfried. 2003. "Hollywood's Terror Films: Do They Reflect an American State of Mind." *New German Critique* 89: 105–11.
Kracht, Christian. 2015. *Imperium*, tr. Daniel Bowles. New York: Farrar, Straus and Giroux.
Krakauer, Jon. [1990] 2009. *Eiger Dreams*. Guilford: The Lyons Press.
Krakauer, Jon. 2004. *Under the Banner of Heaven*. New York: Anchor.
Kramer, Lawrence (ed.). 2011. *Hart Crane's 'The Bridge.'* New York: Fordham University Press.
Kravitz, Derek. 2016. "Red Cross 'Failed for 12 Days' After Historic Louisiana Floods." ProPublica, 3 October. Online: (www.propublica.org/article/red-cross-failed-for-12-days-after-historic-louisiana-floods).
Krier, Dan. 2005. *Speculative Management*. Albany: State University of New York Press.
Krier, Dan. 2008. "Critical Institutionalism and Finance Globalization: A Comparative Analysis of American and Continental Finance." *The New York Journal of Sociology* 1: 130–86.
Krier, Dan. 2017. "Debt, Value, and Economic Theology." *Continental Thought and Theory* 1 (2). Online: (https://ir.canterbury.ac.nz/bitstream/handle/10092/13076/Krier-CTT-v1-2-2017.pdf).
Krier, Dan and Tony Feldmann. 2016. "Social Character in Western Pre-Modernity: Lacanian Psychosis in Wladyslaw Reymont's *The Peasants*." Pp. 175–216 in *Capitalism's Future*, edited by Dan Krier and Mark P. Worrell. Leiden and Boston: Brill.
Krier, Dan and Mark P. Worrell. 2017. "The Social Ontology of Capitalism." Pp. 1–11 in *The Social Ontology of Capitalism*, eds. Dan Krier and Mark P. Worrell. New York: Palgrave.
Krier, Dan and Mark P. Worrell. 2017b. "The Organic Composition of the Big Mother." *Continental Thought and Theory* 4. Online: (http://ctt.canterbury.ac.nz).
Kristof, Nicholas. 2017. "How to Reduce Shootings." *The New York Times*, 6 November. Online: (www.nytimes.com/interactive/2017/11/06/opinion/how-to-reduce-shootings.htm).
Kroner, Richard. 1961. *Speculation and Revelation in Modern Philosophy*. Philadelphia: Westminster Press.

Kureishi, Hanif. 2017. *The Nothing*. London: Faber and Faber.
Kushner, Howard I. 1989. *Self-Destruction in the Promised Land*. New Brunswick: Rutgers University Press.
Lacan, Jacques. 1988. *The Seminar of Jacques Lacan, Book II: The Ego in Freud's Theory and in the Technique of Psychoanalysis, 1954–1955*, tr. S. Tomaselli. New York: W.W. Norton.
Lacan, Jacques. 1993. *The Seminar of Jacques Lacan, Book III: The Psychoses, 1955–1956*, tr. Russell Grigg. New York: W.W. Norton.
Lacan, Jacques. 2002. *Écrits*, tr. Bruce Fink. New York: W.W. Norton.
Lacan, Jacques. 2008. *My Teaching*, tr. David Macey. London and New York: Verso.
Lacan, Jacques. 2014. *The Seminar of Jacques Lacan, Book X: Anxiety*, tr. A.R. Price. Cambridge: Polity.
Lacan, Jacques interviewed by Emilio Granzotto. 1974. "There Can Be No Crisis of Psychoanalysis." *Panorama*. Online: (www.versobooks.com/blogs/1668-there-can-be-no-crisis-of-psychoanalysis-jacques-lacan-interviewed-in-1974).
Lachs, John. 2012. *Stoic Pragmatism*. Bloomington: Indiana University Press.
Lasswell, Harold D. 1933. "The Psychology of Hitlerism." *The Political Quarterly* 4(1–4): 373–84.
Lawrence, D.H. 2001. *Lady Chatterley's Lover*. New York: Random House/Modern Library.
Leach, William. 1993. *Land of Desire*. New York: Pantheon.
Lears, T.J. Jackson. 2003. *Something for Nothing*. New York: Viking.
Le Bon, Gustave. 1913. *The Psychology of Revolution*. London: Unwin.
LeDuff, Charlie. 2018. *Sh*tshow*. New York: Penguin.
Lee, Jennifer. 2005. "Who Needs Giacomo? Bet on the Fortune Cookie." *The New York Times*, 11 May. Online: (nytimes.com/2005/05/11/nyregion/who-needs-giacomo-bet-on-the-fortune-cookie.html).
Lefebvre, Henri. [1968] 2009. *Dialectical Materialism*, tr. John Sturrock. Minneapolis: University of Minnesota Press.
Levi-Strauss, Claude. 1963. *Structural Anthropology*. New York: Basic.
Levy, Ernst. 1985. *A Theory of Harmony*. Albany: SUNY Press.
Levy–Bruhl, Lucien. 1899. *History of Modern Philosophy in France*. Chicago: Open Court.
Lewin, Bertram D. 1961. *The Psychoanalysis of Elation*. New York: Psychoanalytic Quarterly.
Lichtman, Richard. 1982. *The Production of Desire*. New York: The Free Press.
Lieberman, Lisa. 2003. *Leaving You*. Chicago: Ivan R. Dee.
Lilla, Mark. 2016. *The Shipwrecked Mind*. New York: The New York Review of Books.
Lilla, Mark. 2017. *The Once and Future Liberal*. New York: Harper Collins.
Lipka, Michael. 2014. "Latinos in the U.S. Have a Strong Belief in the Spirit World." Pew Research Center. Online: (www.pewresearch.org/fact-tank/2014/05/15/latinos-in-the-u-s-have-a-strong-belief-in-the-spirit-world/).

Lipps, Theodor. 1903. *Leitfaden der Psychologie*. Leipzig: Verlag von Wilhelm Engelmann.

Lipsitz, George. 1998. *The Possessive Investment in Whiteness*. Philadelphia: Temple University Press.

Littlefield, Henry M. 1964. "The Wizard of Oz: Parable on Populism." *American Quarterly* 16(1): 47–58.

Locke, John. [1706] 1966. *Of the Conduct of the Understanding*. New York: Teachers College Press.

Longinus. 1890. *On the Sublime*, tr. H.L. Havell. London: Macmillan.

Lowenthal, Leo and Norbert Guterman. 1949. *Prophets of Deceit*. New York: Harper and Brothers.

Löwith, Karl. 1964. *From Hegel to Nietzsche*. New York: Columbia University Press.

Löwith, Karl. 1995. *Martin Heidegger and European Nihilism*. New York: Columbia University Press.

Luckmann, Thomas. 1967. *The Invisible Religion*. New York: Macmillan.

Luckmann, Thomas. 1987. "Comments on Legitimation." *Current Sociology* 35(2): 109–17.

Lukács, Georg. 1926. "Moses Hess and the Problems of Idealist Dialectics." Online: (www.marxistsfr.org/archive/lukacs/works/1926/moses-hess.htm).

Lukács, Georg. 1971. *History and Class Consciousness*. Cambridge: The MIT Press.

Lukács, Georg. 1978a. *The Ontology of Social Being, 1, Hegel*. London: Merlin.

Lukács, Georg. 1978b. *The Ontology of Social Being, 2, Marx*. London: Merlin.

Lukács, Georg. 1978c. *The Ontology of Social Being, 3, Labour*. London: Merlin.

MacCabe, Colin. 1985. *Tracking the Signifier*. Minneapolis: University of Minnesota Press.

Machiavelli, Niccolò. [1532] 2005. *The Prince*, tr. Peter Bondanella. New York: Oxford University Press.

MacPherson, C.B. 1962. *The Political Theory of Possessive Individualism*. Oxford: Oxford University Press.

Macy, Beth. 2018. *Dopesick*. New York: Hachette.

Mahdawi, Arwa. 2019. "Don't get Your Hopes Up about Chicago's First Black Lesbian Mayor." *The Guardian*, 6 April. Online: (www.theguardian.com/world/commentisfree/2019/apr/06/lori-lightfoot-chicago-mayor-criticism-progressive-record).

Malabou, Catherine. [1996] 2005. *The Future of Hegel*. New York: Routledge.

Malinowski, Bronisław. 1948. *Magic, Science and Religion*. New York: Doubleday.

Malraux, Andre. 1961. *Man's Fate*, tr. Haakon M. Chevalier. New York: Random House.

Man, Hendrick de. 1985. *The Psychology of Marxian Socialism*. New Brunswick: Transaction.

Mandeville, Bernard. [1732] 1924. *The Fable of the Bees*. Oxford: Clarendon Press.

Mann, Erika. 1938. *School for Barbarians*. Mineola: Dover.

Mann, Thomas. [1924] 1952. *Buddenbrooks*, tr. H.T. Lowe-Porter. New York: Vintage.

Mann, Thomas. [1927] 1955. *Magic Mountain*, tr. H.T. Lowe-Porter. New York: Heritage Press.
Mann, Thomas. 1931. *Mario and the Magician*, tr. H.T. Lowe-Porter. New York: Knopf.
Mann, Thomas. 1936. *Stories of Three Decades*, tr. H.T. Lowe-Porter. New York: Knopf.
Mann, Thomas. 1948. *Doctor Faustus*, tr. H.T. Lowe-Porter. New York: Knopf.
Mann, Thomas. 1951. *The Holy Sinner*, tr. H.T. Lowe-Porter. New York: Knopf.
Mann, Michael. 1986. *The Sources of Social Power*. Cambridge: Cambridge University Press.
Mannheim, Karl. 1982. *Structures of Thinking*. London: Routledge and Kegan Paul.
Mao Zedong. 1927. "Report on an Investigation of the Peasant Movement in Hunan." Online: (www.marxists.org/reference/archive/mao/works/red-book/ch02.htm).
Marcuse, Herbert. 1941. *Reason and Revolution*. Atlantic Highlands: Humanities Press.
Marcuse, Herbert. 1972. *From Luther to Popper*. London: Verso.
Maris, Ronald W. 1981. *Pathways to Suicide*. Baltimore: The Johns Hopkins University Press.
Maritain, Jacques. 1939. "Integral Humanism and the Crisis of Modern Times." *The Review of Politics* 1(1): 1–17.
Marsh, James L. 1999. *Process, Praxis, and Transcendence*. Albany: SUNY Press.
Marx, Gary T. 1990. "Reflections on Academic Success and Failure." Online: (http://web.mit.edu/gtmarx/www/success.html).
Marx, Karl. [1844] 1964. *The Economic and Philosophic Manuscripts of 1844*, ed. Dirk J. Struik and tr. Martin Milligan. New York: International Publishers.
Marx, Karl. [1857] 1973. *Grundrisse*, tr. Martin Nicolaus. New York: Penguin.
Marx, Karl. 1859. *Zur Kritik der Politischen Ökonomie*. Berlin: Duncker. Online: (www.mlwerke.de/me/me13/me13_003.htm).
Marx, Karl. [1859] 1970. *A Contribution to the Critique of Political Economy*, tr. S.W. Ryazanskaya. New York: International Publishers.
Marx, Karl. 1867. *Das Kapital: Kritik der politischen Ökonomie*. Hamburg: Verlag von Otto Meissner.
Marx, Karl. [1867] 1976. *Capital: A Critique of Political Economy*, Vol. 1, tr. Ben Fowkes. New York: Penguin.
Marx, Karl. [1869] 1963. *The Eighteenth Brumaire of Louis Bonaparte*. New York: International Publishers.
Marx, Karl. [1884] 1978. *Capital: A Critique of Political Economy*, Vol. 2, tr. David Fernbach. New York: Penguin.
Marx, Karl. [1894] 1981. *Capital: A Critique of Political Economy*, Vol. 3, tr. David Fernbach. New York: Penguin.
Marx, Karl. 1904. *A Contribution to the Critique of Political Economy*, tr. N.I. Stone. Chicago: Charles H. Kerr.
Marx, Karl. 1906. *Capital*, tr. Samuel Moore and Edward Aveling. Chicago: Charles Kerr.

Marx, Karl. 1935. *Value, Price, and Profit*. New York: International Publishers.
Marx, Karl. 1963. *Theories of Surplus Value, Part 1*. Moscow: Progress Publishers.
Marx, Karl. 1969. "Feuerbach." Online: (www.mlwerke.de/me/me03/me03_017.htm#I_I).
Marx, Karl. 1973. *The Revolutions of 1848*. New York: Penguin.
Marx, Karl. 1974. *The Ethnological Notebooks of Karl Marx*, second edition, ed. L. Krader. Assen: Van Gorcum.
Marx, Karl. 1978. "The Value-Form." *Capital and Class* 4, Spring: 130–50. Online: (www.marxists.org/archive/marx/works/1867-c1/appendix.htm).
Marx, Karl and Friedrich Engels. [1848] 1972. "The Communist Manifesto." Pp. 331–62 in the Marx-Engels Reader, edited by Robert C. Tucker. New York: W.W. Norton.
Marx, Karl and Friedrich Engels. [1848] 1977. *Manifesto of the Communist Party*. Moscow: Progress Publishers.
Marx, Karl and Friedrich Engels. 1968. *Selected Works*. New York: International Publishers.
Marx, Karl and Friedrich Engels. 1970. *The German Ideology*. New York: International Publishers.
Marx, Karl and Friedrich Engels. 1972. *The Marx–Engels Reader*, ed. Robert C. Tucker. New York: W.W. Norton.
Marx, Karl and Friedrich Engels. 1975–2004. *Collected Works*, volumes 1–50. New York: International Publishers.
Marx, Karl and Friedrich Engels. 1978. *The Socialist Revolution*. Moscow: Progress Publishers.
Marx, Karl and Friedrich Engels. 2008. *On Religion*. Mineola: Dover.
Masis, Julie. 2016. "World's Longest Workday?" Public Radio International, 27 July. Online: (www.pri.org/stories/2016-07-27/worlds-longest-workday-it-may-not-be-where-you-think-it).
Massing, Paul W. 1949. *Rehearsal for Destruction*. New York: Harper.
Maugham, William Somerset. 1915. *Of Human Bondage*. New York: The Modern Library.
Maupassant, Guy de. [1883] 1999. *A Life*, tr. R. Pearson. New York: Oxford University Press.
Maupassant, Guy de. [2004] 2015. *Femme Fatale*, tr. S. Miles. New York: Penguin.
Mauss, Marcel. [1909] 2003. *On Prayer*, tr. Susan Leslie. New York: Durkheim Press/Berghahn Books.
Mauss, Marcel. [1920/1950] 2006. "The Nation." Pp. 41–48 in *Marcel Mauss: Techniques, Technology and Civilization*, ed. Nathan Schlanger. New York: Durkheim Press/Berghahn.
Mauss, Marcel. 1972. *A General Theory of Magic*. New York: W.W. Norton.
Mauss, Marcel. 1979. *Sociology and Psychology*, tr. B. Brewster. London: Routledge & Kegan Paul.

Mauss, Marcel. 1990. *The Gift*, tr. W.D. Halls. New York: W.W. Norton.
Mauss, Marcel. 2005. *The Nature of Sociology*, tr. William Jeffrey. New York: Durkheim Press/Berghahn Books.
May, Rollo. 1977. *The Meaning of Anxiety*, revised edition. New York: W.W. Norton.
Mayo, Elton. 1945. *The Social Problems of an Industrial Civilization*. Boston: Division of Research, Graduate School of Business Administration, Harvard University.
Mazlish, Bruce. 1972. "The Tragic Farce of Marx, Hegel, and Engels: A Note." *History and Theory* 11(3): 335–37.
McCall, Brian M. 2017. "The New Protestant Bargain." Pp. 175–95 in *Luther and his Progeny*, ed. John C. Rao. Kettering: Angelico Press.
McCarthy, Cormac. [2006] 2012. *The Road*. New York: Knopf.
McCarthy, Cormac. 2010. *The Sunset Limited*. New York: Vintage.
McCloskey, David. 1976. "On Durkheim, Anomie, and the Modern Crisis." *The American Journal of Sociology* 81(6): 1481–488.
McGreal, Chris. 2016. "Financial Despair, Addiction, and the Rise of Suicide in White America." *The Guardian*, 7 February. Online: (www.theguardian.com/us-news/2016/feb/07/suicide-rates-rise-butte-montana-princeton-study).
McNeill, William H. 1963. *The Rise of the West*. Chicago: The University of Chicago Press.
Mead, George Herbert. 1899. "The Working Hypothesis in Social Reform." *The American Journal of Sociology* 5(3): 367–71.
Mead, George Herbert. [1932] 1977. "The Objective Reality of Perspectives." Pp. 342–54 in *George Herbert Mead on Social Psychology*. Chicago: University of Chicago Press.
Mead, George Herbert. [1934] 1962. *Mind, Self, and Society*. Chicago: The University of Chicago Press.
Melville, Herman. [1851] 1988. *Moby-Dick*. New York: Knopf.
Melville, Herman. [1856] 2009. "Bartleby the Scrivener." in *Billy Budd, Sailor and Selected Tales*. New York: Oxford University Press.
Melville, Herman. [1857] 1990. *The Confidence-Man*. New York: Penguin.
Melville, Herman. 1892. *Moby-Dick*. Boston: St. Botolph Society.
Menninger, Karl. 1938. *Man Against Himself*. New York: Harcourt.
Meredith, George. 1951. *The Egoist*. New York: The Modern Library.
Merleau-Ponty, Maurice. 1968. *The Visible and the Invisible*, tr. Alphonso Lingis. Evanston: Northwestern University Press.
Merleau-Ponty, Maurice. 1973. *Adventures of the Dialectic*, tr. Joseph Bien. Evanston: Northwestern University Press.
Merton, Robert. 1957. *Social Theory and Social Structure*. Glencoe: The Free Press.
Mészáros, István. 2010. *Social Structure and Forms of Consciousness*, Vol. 1, *The Social Determination of Method*. New York: Monthly Review Press.

Mészáros, István. 2011. *Social Structure and Forms of Consciousness*, Vol. 2, *The Dialectic of Structure and History*. New York: Monthly Review Press.

Mettler, Katie. 2016. "At Suicide Hotlines, the First 24 Hours of Trump's America Have Been Full of Fear." *The Washington Post*, 10 November. Online: (www.washingtonpost.com/news/morning-mix/wp/2016/11/10/at-suicide-hotlines-the-first-24-hours-of-trumps-america-have-been-full-of-fear).

Metzl, Jonathan M. 2019. *Dying of Whiteness*. New York: Basic Books.

Michels, Robert. 2001. *Political Parties*, tr. Eden and Cedar Paul. Kitchener, Ontario: Batoche.

Michener, James A. 1965. *The Source*. New York: Fawcett Crest.

Milgram, Stanley. 1974. *Obedience to Authority*. New York: Harper.

Miliband, Ralph. 1969. *The State in Capitalist Society*. New York: Basic Books.

Mill, John Stuart. 1881. *The Principles of Political Economy*. London: Longmans, Green and Co.

Miller, Arthur. 1950. *Death of a Salesman*. New York: Viking.

Miller, Claire Cain. 2018. "Americans are Having Fewer Babies." *The New York Times*, 5 July. Online: (www.nytimes.com/2018/07/05/upshot/americans-are-having-fewer-babies.html).

Miller, Henry. 1945. *The Air-Conditioned Nightmare*. New York: New Directions.

Miller, Henry. 1961. *Tropic of Cancer*. New York: Grove Press.

Miller, John W. 1982. *The Midworld of Symbols and Functioning Objects*. New York: W.W. Norton.

Miller, W. Watts. 1996. *Durkheim, Morals, and Modernity*. Montreal: McGill-Queen's University Press.

Mills, C. Wright. 1956. *The Power Elite*. Oxford: Oxford University Press.

Mills, C. Wright. 1959. *The Sociological Imagination*. New York: Oxford University Press.

Mills, C. Wright. 1962. *The Marxists*. New York: Dell.

Mills, C. Wright. 1966. *Sociology and Pragmatism*. New York: Oxford University Press.

Mills, Charles W. 1998. "Dark Ontologies." Pp. 131–68 in *Autonomy and Community*, eds. Jane Kneller and Sidney Axinn. Albany: SUNY Press.

Milton, John. [1667] 2000. *Paradise Lost*. New York: Penguin.

Mintz, Susannah B. 2003. *Threshold Poetics*. Newark: University of Delaware Press.

Mirabile, Francesca and Daniel Nass. 2018. "What's the Homicide Capital of America?" *The Trace*, 27 September. Online: (hwww.thetrace.org/2018/04/highest-murder-rates-us-cities-list/).

Moliere. 2001. *The Misanthrope, Tartuffe, and Other Plays*, tr. Maya Slater. Oxford: Oxford University Press.

Monnat, Shannon. 2016. "Deaths of Despair and Support for Trump in the 2016 Presidential Election." The Pennsylvania State University, Department of Agricultural

Economics, Sociology, and Education Research Brief. Online: (http://aese.psu.edu/directory/smm67/Election16.pdf).

Montaigne. 1842. *The Complete Works of Michel de Montaigne* tr. W. Hazlitt. London: Templeman.

Montesquieu. 2002. *The Spirit of Laws.* Amherst: Prometheus.

Moore, Brian J., Carol Stocks, and Pamela L. Owens. 2017. "Trends in Emergency Department Visits, 2006–2014." Agency for Healthcare Research and Quality. Online: (www.hcup-us.ahrq.gov/reports/statbriefs/sb227-Emergency-Department-Visit-Trends.pdf).

More, Thomas. [1516] 1999. *Utopia,* in *Three Early Modern Utopias,* ed. Susan Bruce. Oxford: Oxford University Press.

Mounier, Emmanuel. 1952. *Personalism.* Notre Dame: University of Notre Dame Press.

Moyn, Samuel. 2019. "How to be a Marxist." *Jacobin,* 1 April. Online: (https://jacobinmag.com/2019/04/this-life-review-martin-hagglund-socialism).

Mumford, Lewis. 1973. *Interpretations and Forecasts: 1922–1972.* New York: Harcourt.

Munkelt, Richard A. 2017. "Religious Evolution and Revolution in the Triumph of *Homo Economicus.*" Pp. 143–74 in *Luther and his Progeny,* ed. John C. Rao. Kettering: Angelico Press.

Murakami, Haruki. 2014. *The Strange Library,* tr. Ted Goossen. New York: Knopf.

Murphy, Robert F. 1971. *The Dialectics of Social Life.* New York: Basic Books.

Murray, Gilbert. 1915. *The Stoic Philosophy.* London: Watts.

National Law Center. 2015. "Homelessness in America." Online: (www.nlchp.org/documents/Homeless_Stats_Fact_Sheet).

National Public Radio. 2019. "Dialogue and Exchange." Online: (www.npr.org/programs/ted-radio-hour/558307433).

Neill, A.S. 1960. *Summerhill: A Radical Approach to Child Rearing.* New York: Hart.

Nelson, Leonard. [1917] 1957. *Critique of Practical Reason.* Frankfurt: Verlag.

Nielsen, Donald A. 2005. *Horrible Workers.* Lanham, MD: Lexington Books.

Nietzsche, Friedrich. [1887] 1974. *The Gay Science,* tr. Walter Kaufmann. New York: Vintage.

Nietzsche, Friedrich. 1909. *The Complete Works of Friedrich Nietzsche,* Vol. 12. Edinburgh: T.N. Foulis.

Nietzsche, Friedrich. 1967. *Ecce Homo,* tr. Walter Kaufmann. New York: Vintage.

Nietzsche, Friedrich. [1967] 1989. *On the Genealogy of Morals* and *Ecce Homo,* tr. Walter Kaufmann. New York: Vintage.

Nietzsche, Friedrich. 1968. *Will to Power,* tr. Walter Kaufmann. New York: Vintage.

Nietzsche, Friedrich. 1982. *The Portable Nietzsche,* ed. and tr. Walter Kaufmann. New York: Penguin.

Nietzsche, Friedrich. 1986. *Human, All too Human,* tr. R.J. Hollingdale. Cambridge: Cambridge University Press.

Nietzsche, Friedrich. 2002. *Beyond Good and Evil*, tr. J. Norman. Cambridge: Cambridge University Press.

Nietzsche, Friedrich. 2015. *Aphorisms on Love and Hate*, tr. Faber and Lehmann. New York: Penguin.

Nordland, Rod and Fahim Abed. 2018. "Afghan Military Deaths Since 2015." *The New York Times*, 15 November. Online: (www.nytimes.com/2018/11/15/world/asia/afghanistan-military-death-toll.html).

Northwestern Mutual. 2018. "1 in 3 Americans Have Less Than $5000 in Retirement Savings." 8 May. Online: (news.northwesternmutual.com/2018-05-08-1-In-3-Americans-Have-Less-Than-5-000-In-Retirement-Savings).

Nossiter, Adam. 2019. "35 Employees Committed Suicide. Will Their Bosses go to Jail?" *The New York Times*, 9 July. Online: (www.nytimes.com/2019/07/09/world/europe/france-telecom-trial.html).

Novalis. 1997. *Philosophical Writings*, ed. and tr. Margaret Stoljar. Albany: State University of New York Press.

Nutt, Amy Ellis. 2016. "Loneliness Grows from Individual Ache to Public Health Hazard." *The Washington Post*, 31 January. Online: (www.washingtonpost.com/national/health-science/loneliness-grows-from-individual-ache-to-public-health-hazard/2016/01/31).

Nye, Robert A. 1984. *Crime, Madness, and Politics in Modern France*. Princeton: Princeton University Press.

Oberhauser, Ann M., Daniel Krier, and Abdi Kusow. 2019. "Political Moderation and Polarization in the Heartland: Economics, Rurality, and Social Identity in the 2016 US Presidential Election." *The Sociological Quarterly* 60(2): 224–44. Online: (https://doi.org/10.1080/00380253.2019.1580543).

O'Connor, James. 1984. *Accumulation Crisis*. New York: Basil Blackwell.

O'Donnell, Jayne. 2019. "US Deaths from Alcohol, Drugs and Suicide hit Highest Level Since Record-Keeping Began." *Courier Journal*, 5 March. Online: (www.courier-journal.com/story/news/2019/03/05/suicide-alcohol-drug-deaths-centers-disease-control-well-being-trust/3064189002/).

O'Keefe, Daniel Lawrence. 1982. *Stolen Lightning*. New York: Continuum.

O'Neill, Eugene. 1932. "Mourning Becomes Electra." Pp. 683–867 in *Nine Plays*. New York: The Modern Library.

Ortega y Gasset, José. 1932. *The Revolt of the Masses*, tr. anon. New York: W.W. Norton.

Ortega y Gasset, José. [1941] 1961. *History as a System*, tr. Helen Weyl. New York: W.W. Norton.

Ortega y Gasset, José. 1957. *Man and People*, tr. Willard Trask. New York: W.W. Norton.

Oxfam. 2016. "An Economy for the One Percent." Online: (http://policy-practice.oxfam.org.uk/publications/an-economy-for-the-1-how-privilege-and-power-in-the-economy-drive-extreme-inequ-592643).

Packard, Vance. 1959. *The Status Seekers*. New York: David McKay Co.

Paoletti, Giovanni. 2012. "Some Concepts of 'Evil' in Durkheim's Thought." Pp. 63–80 in *Suffering and Evil*, ed. W.S.F. Pickering and Massimo Rosati. New York: Durkheim Press/Berghahn.

Park, Robert Ezra. 1950. *Race and Culture*. Glencoe: The Free Press.

Parker, Kim, Rich Morin, and Juliana M. Horowitz. 2019. "Looking to the Future, Public Sees and America in Decline on Many Fronts." Pew Research Center, 21 March. Online: (https://www.pewsocialtrends.org/2019/03/21/public-sees-an-america-in-decline).

Parker-Pope, Tara. 2013. "Suicide Rates Rise Sharply in U.S." *The New York Times*, 2 May. Online: (www.nytimes.com/2013/05/03/health/suicide-rate-rises-sharply-in-us).

Parrington, Vernon L. 1927. *The Colonial Mind*. New York: Harcourt, Brace, and Co.

Parrington, Vernon L. 1958. *The Beginnings of Critical Realism in America*. New York: Harcourt, Brace, and World.

Pascal, Blaise. 1941. *Pensées*, tr. W.F. Trotter. New York: The Modern Library.

Paterson, W. Romaine. 1907. *The Nemesis of Nations*. London: J.M. Dent and Co.

Peirce, C.S. [1892] 1992. "Man's Glassy Essence." Pp. 334–51 in *The Essential Peirce*, Vol. 1, eds. Nathan Houser and Christian Kloesel. Bloomington: Indiana University Press.

Penn, William. 1905. *Some Fruits of Solitude*. London: Headley Brothers.

Pessoa, Fernando. 2001. *The Book of Disquiet*, tr. Richard Zenith. New York: Penguin.

Pessoa, Fernando. 2012. *Philosophical Essays*. New York: Contra Mundum Press.

Peters, F.E. 1967. *Greek Philosophical Terms*. New York: New York University Press.

Pew Research Center. 2011. "Global Survey of Evangelical Protestant Leaders." Online: (www.pewforum.org/2011/06/22/global-survey-beliefs/).

Pew Research Center. 2015. "Parenting in America." Online: (www.pewsocialtrends.org/2015/12/17/1-the-american-family-today).

Pew Research Center. 2017. "Religious Belief and National Belonging in Central and Eastern Europe." Online: (www.pewforum.org/2017/05/10/religious-beliefs/).

Pew Research Center. 2019. "Little Public Support for Reductions in Federal Spending." Online: (www.people-press.org/2019/04/11/little-public-support-for-reductions-in-federal-spend).

Philipps, Dave. 2015. "Study Finds no Link Between Military Suicide Rate and Deployments." *The New York Times*, 1 April. Online: (www.nytimes.com/2015/04/02/us/study-finds-no-link-between-military-suicide-rate-and-deployments.html).

Pickering, Andrew. 1984. *Constructing Quarks: A Sociological History of Particle Physics*. Chicago: The University of Chicago Press.

Pickering, W.S.F. 2000. "Reading the Conclusion." Pp. 66–80 in *Durkheim's Suicide*, eds. W.S.F. Pickering and Geoffrey Walford. London: Routledge.

Pickering, W.S.F. [2000] 2006a. "Representations as Understood by Durkheim." Pp. 11–23 in *Durkheim and Representations*, ed. W.S.F. Pickering. London: Routledge.

Pickering, W.S.F. [2000] 2006b. "What do Representations Represent?" Pp. 98–117 in *Durkheim and Representations*, ed. W.S.F. Pickering. London: Routledge.

Pickering, W.S.F. 2012. "Reflections on the Death of Emile Durkheim." Pp. 11–27 in *Suffering and Evil*, eds. W.S.F. Pickering and Massimo Rosati. New York: Durkheim Press/Berghahn.

Piketty, Thomas. 2014. *Capital in the Twenty-First Century*. Cambridge: Belknap/Harvard.

Pinkard, Terry. 1996. *Hegel's Phenomenology*. Cambridge: Cambridge University Press.

Pinkard, Terry. 2000. *Hegel*. Cambridge: Cambridge University Press.

Pinkard, Terry. 2002. *German Philosophy*. Cambridge: Cambridge University Press.

Plato. 1945. *The Works of Plato*, tr. Benjamin Jowett. New York: Tudor.

Polanyi, Karl. 1944. *The Great Transformation*. Boston: Beacon.

Polanyi, Michael. 1962. *Personal Knowledge*. Chicago: University of Chicago Press.

Poliakov, Leon. 1975. *The History of Anti-Semitism, 1: From the Time of Christ to the Court Jews*, tr. Richard Howard. Philadelphia: University of Pennsylvania Press.

Pollin, Robert. 2003. *Contours of Descent*. London: Verso.

Pope, Whitney. 1976. *Durkheim's Suicide: A Classic Analyzed*. Chicago: The University of Chicago Press.

Porter, Lewis. 1998. *John Coltrane*. Ann Arbor: The University of Michigan Press.

Proal, Louis. 1905. *Passion and Criminality*, tr. A.R. Allinson. London: Imperial Press.

Puett, Michael and Christine Gross-Loh. 2016. *The Path*. New York: Simon and Schuster.

Pufendorf, Samuel. 1994. *The Political Writings of Samuel Pufendorf*, ed. C. Carr, tr. M. Seidler. New York: Oxford University Press.

Pylas, Pan. 2019. "Wealth Inequality 'Out of Control,' Oxfam Warns." Associated Press, 21 January. Online: (www.bostonglobe.com/business/2019/01/20/wealth-inequality-out-control-oxfam-warn).

Queenan, Joe. 2008. "I'm Non-Sticking with You." *The Guardian*, 11 April. Online: (www.theguardian.com/film/2008/apr/12/culture.features).

Quincey, Thomas De. [1827] 2015. *On Murder Considered as One of the Fine Arts*. New York: Penguin.

Radcliffe-Brown, A. 1952. *Structure and Function in Primitive Society*. New York: The Free Press.

Rainie, Lee. 2013. "Cell Phone Ownership Hits 91% of Adults." Pew Research Center, 6 June. Online: (pewresearch.org/fact-tank/2013/06/06/cell-phone-ownership-hits-91-of-adults).

Reich, Wilhelm. [1933] 1972. *Character Analysis*. New York: Farrar, Straus and Giroux.

Reich, Wilhelm. 1970. *The Mass Psychology of Fascism*. New York: Noonday.

Reich, Wilhelm. 1974. *Listen Little Man*. New York: Noonday.
Remmling, Gunter W. 1967. *Road to Suspicion*. New York: Appleton-Century-Crofts.
Ricoeur, Paul. 1981. *Hermeneutics and the Human Sciences*, ed. and tr. by John B. Thompson. Cambridge: Cambridge University Press.
Ricoeur, Paul. 1991. *From Text to Action*, tr. Kathleen Blamey and John B. Thompson. Evanston: Northwestern University Press.
Riley, Alexander T. 1999. "Whence Durkheim's Nietzschean Grandchildren? A Closer Look at Robert Hertz's Place in the Durkheimian Genealogy." *European Journal of Sociology* 40(2): 304–30.
Riley, Alexander T. 2002. "The Sacred Calling of Intellectual Labor in Mystic and Ascetic Durkheimianism." *European Journal of Sociology* 43(3): 354–85.
Rinofner-Kreidl, Sonja. 2004. "What is Wrong with Naturalizing Epistemology?" Pp. 41–68 in *Husserl and the Sciences*, ed. Richard Feist. King Edward, Ottawa, Ontario: University of Ottawa Press.
Roché, Henri-Pierre. [1953] 2006. *Jules et Jim*, tr. Patrick Evans. London: Marion Boyars.
Rodrick, Stephen. 2019. "All-American Despair." *Rolling Stone*, 30 May. Online: (www.rollingstone.com/culture/culture-features/suicide-rate-america-white-men).
Rokeach, Milton. 1961. "Authority, Authoritarianism, and Conformity." Pp. 230–57 in *Conformity and Deviation*, ed. Irwin A. Berg and Bernard M. Bass. New York: Harper.
Rolfe, Frederick. 1953. *The Desire and Pursuit of the Whole*. New York: New Directions.
Romo, Vanessa. 2018. "California STDs Raging at All Time Highs For Third Year in a Row." National Public Radio, 15 May. Online: (www.npr.org/sections/thetwo-way/2018/05/15/611307046/california-stds-raging-at-all-time-highs-for-third-year-in-a-row).
Rorty, Richard. 1998. *Achieving our Country*. Cambridge: Harvard University Press.
Rosenkranz, Karl. [1844] 2002. "The Full Report of Rosenkranz Concerning the Triangle of Triangles." Pp. 264–69 in *Miscellaneous Writings of G.W.F. Hegel*, ed. Jon Stewart. Evanston: Northwestern University Press.
Roth, Michael. 1987. *Psycho-Analysis as History*. Ithaca: Cornell University Press.
Roth, Philip. 2004. *The Plot Against America*. Boston and New York: Houghton Mifflin Co.
Rousseau, Jean-Jacques. [1762] 1968. *The Social Contract*, tr. Maurice Cranston. New York: Penguin.
Rousseau, Jean-Jacques. [1762] 1978. *On the Social Contract*, tr. Judith R. Masters. New York: St. Martin's Press.
Rousseau, Jean-Jacques. 1898. *Emile*, tr. Eleanor Worthington. Boston: D.C. Heath.
Royce, Josiah. 1892. *The Spirit of Modern Philosophy*. Boston and New York: Houghton Mifflin.

Royce, Josiah. 1909. *The Philosophy of Loyalty*. New York: Macmillan.
Royce, Josiah. 1914. *War and Insurance*. New York: Macmillan.
Royce, Josiah. 1948. *California*. New York: Knopf.
Royce, Josiah. 1969. *The Basic Writings of Josiah Royce*, Vol. 1, ed. John J. McDermott. Chicago: The University of Chicago Press.
Royce, Josiah. 1982. *The Philosophy of Josiah Royce*, ed. John Roth. Indianapolis: Hackett.
Royce, Josiah. 2005. *The Basic Writings of Josiah Royce*, Vol. 2: *Logic, Loyalty, and Community*, ed. John J. McDermott. New York: Fordham University Press.
Rudolph, Kara, Elizabeth Stuart, Jon Vernick, and Daniel Webster. 2015. "Association Between Connecticut's Permit-to-Purchase Handgun law and Homicides." *American Journal of Public Health* 105(8): e49–354. Online: (https://ajph.aphapublications.org/doi/pdf/10.2105/AJPH.2015.302703).
Ruskin, John. 2015. *Traffic*. New York: Penguin.
Sable-Smith, Bram. 2018. "Insulin's High Cost Leads to Lethal Rationing." National Public Radio, 1 September. Online: (www.npr.org/sections/health-shots/2018/09/01/641615877/insulins-high-cost-leads-to-lethal-rationing).
Sade, Marquis de. 1966. *The 120 Days of Sodom and Other Writings*, tr. Austryn Wainhouse and Richard Seaver. New York: Grove.
Sade, Marquis de. 2006. *Philosophy in the Boudoir*, tr. Joachim Neugroschel. New York: Penguin.
Sahlins, Marshall. 1972. *Stone Age Economics*. New York: Aldine de Gruyter.
Sainsbury, Peter. 1955. *Suicide in London*. New York: Chapman and Hall.
Samuelson, Paul. 1986. *The Collected Scientific Papers of Paul A. Samuelson*, Vol. 5, ed. Kate Crowley. Cambridge: The MIT Press.
Santayana, George. 1913. *Winds of Doctrine*. London: J.M. Dent and Sons.
Santayana, George. [1936] 1949. *The Last Puritan*. New York: Charles Scribner's Sons.
Sappho. 1986. *Sappho*, tr. Mary Barnard. Berkeley: University of California Press.
Saroyan, William. [1939] 2004. "Preface to *The Time of Your Life*." Pp. 8–10 in *Words on Plays*. San Francisco: American Conservatory Theater.
Sartre, Jean-Paul. [1946] 1976. *No Exit*. New York: Vintage.
Sartre, Jean-Paul. 1950. *Baudelaire*, tr. Martin Turnell. New York: New Directions.
Sartre, Jean-Paul. 1976. *Critique of Dialectical Reason*, Vol. 1: *Theory of Practical Ensembles*, new edition, tr. Alan Sheridan-Smith. London: Verso.
Sassen, Saskia. 1996. *Losing Control?* New York: Columbia University Press.
Schachtel, Ernest G. 1959. *Metamorphosis*. New York: Basic Books.
Schäffle, Albert. 1890. *The Quintessence of Socialism*, tr. Bernard Bosanquet. London: Swan Sonnenschein.
Scharf, B.R. 1970. "Durkheimian and Freudian Theories of Religion: The Case of Judaism." *The British Journal of Sociology* 21(2): 151–63.

Schelling, Friedrich. [1813] 1997. *Ages of the World*, tr. Judith Norman. Ann Arbor: The University of Michigan Press.
Schiller, Friedrich. 1966. *On the Sublime*. New York: Frederick Ungar.
Schiller, Friedrich. 1967. *On the Aesthetic Education of Man*. Oxford: Clarendon Press.
Schneider, Michael. 1975. *Neurosis and Civilization*. New York: Seabury.
Schnitzler, Arthur. [1926] 1999. *Dream Story*, tr. J.M.Q. Davies. New York: Penguin.
Schroeder, Jeanne L.. 1998. *The Vestal and the Fasces*. Berkeley: University of California Press.
Schwarz, Peter. 2017. "Raoul Peck's *The Young Karl Marx*." World Socialist Web Site. Online: (www.wsws.org/en/articles/2017/03/15/marx-m15.html).
Scott, James C. 2017. *Against the Grain*. New Haven: Yale University Press.
Scott-Holland, Canon H. 1894. "Children's Questions: Sermon Preached in St. Paul's Cathedral, 21 January." *The Church of England Pulpit and Ecclesiastical Review* 37: 61–65.
Scutti, Susan. 2017. "Suicide Rate Hit 40-Year Peak among Older Teen Girls in 2015." CNN, 3 August. Online: (www.cnn.com/2017/08/03/health/teen-suicide-cdc-study-bn).
Scutti, Susan. 2019. "ERs 'Flooded' with Mentally Ill Patients with no Place Else to Turn." CNN, 4 January. Online: (www.cnn.com/2019/01/03/health/er-mental-health-patients-eprise/index.html).
Seelye, Katherine. 2015. "In Heroin Crisis, White Families Seek Gentler War on Drugs." *The New York Times*, 30 October. Online: (www.nytimes.com/2015/10/31/us/heroin-war-on-drugs-parents.html).
Seligman, Adam B.. 2000. *Modernity's Wager*. Princeton: Princeton University Press.
Sellars, John. 2006. *Stoicism*. Berkeley: University of California Press.
Sennett, Richard. 1980. *Authority*. New York: Knopf.
Sennett, Richard. 2006. "Introduction." Pp. xi–xxiv in *On Suicide*, tr. Robin Buss. New York: Penguin.
Shad, Jeffrey. 1989. "Michael Mann. The Sources of Social Power." *Comparative Civilizations Review*, 21(21). Online: (https://scholarsarchive.byu.edu/ccr/vol21/iss21/7).
Shakespeare, William. 1956. *Measure for Measure*. New York: Penguin.
Shakespeare, William. 1963. *Love's Labor's Lost*. New York: Penguin.
Shakespeare, William. 1973. *Coriolanus*. New York: Penguin.
Shakespeare, William. 1999. *Much Ado About Nothing*. New York: Penguin.
Shakespeare, William. 2000. *Macbeth*. New York: Penguin.
Shakespeare, William. 2001. *Hamlet*. New York: Penguin.
Shand, Alexander F. 1914. *The Foundations of Character*. London: Macmillan.
Sharaf, Myron. 1983. *Fury on Earth: A Biography of Wilhelm Reich*. New York: DaCapo.
Shaw, Bernard. 1933. *The Political Madhouse in America and Nearer Home*. London: Constable and Co.
Shelley, Mary. [1818] 1992. *Frankenstein*. New York: Knopf.

Sherif, Muzafer. 1961. "Conformity-Deviation, Norms, and Group Relations." Pp. 159–98 in *Conformity and Deviation*, ed. Irwin A. Berg and Bernard M. Bass. New York: Harper.

Shihipar, Abdullah. 2019. "The Opioid Crisis Isn't White." *The New York Times*, 26 February. Online: (www.nytimes.com/2019/02/26/opinion/opioid-crisis-drug-users.html).

Shiller, Robert. 2015. *Irrational Exuberance*, 3rd ed. Princeton: Princeton University Press.

Siddique, Haroon. 2017. "Baby Boomers Warned Over Alcohol Intake as Hospital Admissions Soar." *The Guardian*, 3 May. Online: (www.theguardian.com/society/2017/may/03/baby-boomers-warned-over-alcohol-intake-as-hospital-admissions-soar).

Simmel, Georg. [1907] 1990. *The Philosophy of Money*. London and New York: Routledge.

Simmel, Georg. [1921–1922] 1984. "On Love (A Fragment)." Pp. 153–92 in *Georg Simmel: On Women, Sexuality, and Love*, tr. and ed. Guy Oakes. New Haven: Yale University Press.

Simmel, Georg. 1950. *The Sociology of Georg Simmel*, tr. and ed. Kurt H. Wolff. New York: The Free Press.

Simmel, Georg. 1955. *Conflict* and *The Web of Group Affiliation*. New York: The Free Press.

Simmel, Georg. 1959. *The Sociology of Religion*. New York: Philosophical Library.

Simmel, Georg. 1971. *On Individuality and Social Forms*, ed. Donald N. Levine. Chicago: University of Chicago Press.

Simon, Bennett. 1979. "Hysteria—The Greek Disease." Pp. 175–215 in *The Psychoanalytic Study of Society*, ed. W. Muensterberger and L. Boyer. New Haven: Yale University Press.

Simon, M. 1914. "To Melt or Not to Melt." *The Maccabaean Magazine* 24(1): 180–81.

Simpson, George. 1937. *Conflict and Community*. Ph.D. dissertation, Columbia University.

Singer, Peter. 1983. *Hegel*. Oxford: Oxford University Press.

Skinner, E. Benjamin. 2008. *A Crime So Monstrous*. New York: The Free Press.

Slonimsky, Nicolas. [1947] 1975. *Thesaurus of Scales and Melodic Patterns*. New York: Amsco.

Slotkin, Richard. 1992. *Gunfighter Nation*. Norman: University of Oklahoma Press.

Smith, Adam. [1776] 1937. *The Wealth of Nations*. New York: The Modern Library.

Smith, Cyril. 1994. "Karl Marx and the Origins of 'Marxism.'" Online: (www.marxists.org/reference/archive/smith-cyril/works/millenni/smith4.htm).

Smith, David Norman. 1988. "Authorities, Deities, and Commodities: Classical Sociology and the Problem of Domination." Ph.D. dissertation, University of Wisconsin–Madison.

Smith, David Norman. 1994. *The Realm of the Social.* New York: McGraw–Hill.

Smith, David Norman. 1998. "Faith, Reason, and Charisma: Rudolf Sohm, Max Weber, and the Theology of Grace." *Sociological Inquiry*, 68: 32–60.

Smith, David Norman. 2001. "Anomie, Solidarity, and Conflict: French Sociology and the Limits of Dialogue." *The Sociological Quarterly* 42(1): 69–78.

Smith, David Norman. 2006. "Time is Money: Commodity Fetishism and Common Sense." Pp. xix–lxiii in *The Hegemony of Common Sense* by Dean Wolfe Manders. New York: Peter Lang.

Smith, David Norman. 2013. "Charisma Disenchanted: Max Weber and His Critics." *Current Perspectives in Social Theory* 31: 3–74.

Smith, David Norman. 2014. "Slashing at Water with a Knife? Durkheim's Struggle to Anchor Sociology in First Principles." *Contemporary Sociology* 43(2): 165–71.

Smith, David Norman. 2016. "Capitalism's Future: Self-Alienation, Self-Emancipation and the Remaking of Critical Theory." Pp. 11–62 in *Capitalism's Future* eds. Daniel Krier and Mark P. Worrell. Leiden: Brill.

Smith, David Norman. 2017. "Theory and Class Consciousness." Pp. 369–423 in *The Handbook of Critical Theory*, ed. Michael J. Thompson. New York: Palgrave.

Smith, David Norman. 2019a. "Authoritarianism Reimagined: The Riddle of Trump's Base." *The Sociological Quarterly*. Online: (https://doi.org/10.1080/00380253.2019.1593061).

Smith, David Norman. 2019b. "Max Weber's Odyssey." *Fast Capitalism* 16.2. Online: (https://fastcapitalism.journal.library.uta.edu/index.php/fastcapitalism).

Smith, Douglas. 2016. *Rasputin*. New York: Farrar, Straus and Giroux.

Smith, Norman Kemp. 1992. *Commentary to Kant's 'Critique of Pure Reason,'* 2nd ed. Atlantic Highlands, NJ: Humanities Press.

Smith, Sarah. 2016. "After Mississippi Flooding, Red Cross Stumbles Again." *ProPublica*, 19 May. Online: (www.propublica.org/article/after-mississippi-flooding-red-cross-stumbles-again).

Smith, Tony. 1993a. *Dialectical Social Theory and its Critics*. Albany: SUNY Press.

Smith, Tony. 1993b. "Marx's *Capital* and Hegelian Dialectical Logic." Pp. 15–36 in *Marx's Method in* Capital, ed. Fred Moseley. Atlantic Highlands: Humanities Press.

Smith, William Robertson. 1927. *Lectures on the Religion of the Semites*, 3rd ed. New York: Macmillan.

Solovyov, Vladimir. 1918. *The Justification of the Good*, tr. N. Duddington. London: Constable.

Sorel, Georges. 1950. *Reflections on Violence*, tr. T.E. Hulme. Mineola: Dover.

Southern Poverty Law Center. 2019. "Hate Groups Reach Record High." Online: (www.splcenter.org/news/2019/02/19/hate-groups-reach-record-high).

Spirkin, Alexander. 1983. *Dialectical Materialism*. Online: (www.marxists.org/reference/archive/spirkin/works/dialectical-materialism/ch05-s07).

Steiner, Franz. 1956. *Taboo*. London: Cohen and West.
Stekel, Wilhelm. 1929. *Sadism and Masochism*, tr. Louise Brink. New York: Horace Liveright.
Stevenson, Robert Louis. [1886] 1992. *Dr. Jekyll and Mr. Hyde and Other Stories*. New York: Knopf.
Stewart, Ian. 2019. "Report: Americans are now More Likely to Die of an Opioid Overdose than on the Road." National Public Radio, 14 January. Online: (www.npr.org/2019/01/14/684695273/report-americans-are-now-more-likely-to-die-of-an-opioid-overdose-than-on-the-ro).
Storr, Anthony. 1989. *Freud*. Oxford: Oxford University Press.
Strahan, S.A.K. 1893. *Suicide and Insanity*. London: Swan Sonnenschein and Co.
Strauss, Valerie. 2016. "Hiding in Plain Sight: The Adult Literacy Crisis." *The Washington Post*, 1 November. Online: (www.washingtonpost.com/news/answer-sheet/wp/2016/11/01/hiding-in-plain-sight-the-adult-literacy-crisis).
Strenski, Ivan. 2006. *The New Durkheim*. New Brunswick: Rutgers University Press.
Suicide Prevention Resource Center. 2008. "Suicide Risk and Prevention for Lesbian, Gay, Bisexual, and Transgender Youth." Online: (http://www.sprc.org/sites/default/files/migrate/library/SPRC_LGBT_Youth.pdf).
Sullivan, Henrietta. 1871. *Mediation*. Andover: Warren F. Draper.
Sullivan, Paul. 2017. "Who are the Richest of the Rich?" *The New York Times*, 19 February. Online: (www.nytimes.com/2017/02/19/your-money/who-are-the-richest-of-the-rich.html).
Sumner, William Graham. [1906] 1940. *Folkways*. New York: Mentor.
Suzman, James. 2017. *Affluence without Abundance*. New York: Bloomsbury.
Talmon, J.L. 1967. *Romanticism and Revolt*. San Diego: Harcourt.
Taylor, Steve. 1990. "Suicide, Durkheim, and Sociology." Pp. 225–36 in *Current Concepts of Suicide*, ed. David Lester. Philadelphia: Charles Press.
Thompson, E.P. 1963. *The Making of the English Working Class*. New York: Vintage.
Thoreau, Henry David. [1854] 1960. *Walden*. New York: New American Library.
Tocqueville, Alexis de. [1835] 1956. *Democracy in America*. New York: Mentor.
Tocqueville, Alexis de. 1856. *The Old Regime and the Revolution*, tr. John Bonner. New York: Harper.
Tönnies, Ferdinand. 1988. *Community and Society*. New Brunswick: Transaction.
Transamerica Center for Retirement Studies. 2015. "Retirement Throughout the Ages." Online: (www.transamericacenter.org/docs/default-source/resources/center-research/16th-annual/tcrs2015_sr_retirement_throughout_the_ages.pdf).
Transportation Security Administration. 2017. "TSA Week in Review: July 24th–31st– New Firearm Discovery Record Set." Online: (www.tsa.gov/blog/2017/08/02/tsa-week-review-july-24th-31st-new-firearm-discovery-record-set).
Tranströmer, Tomas. 2006. *The Great Enigma*, tr. Robin Fulton. New York: New Directions.

Traubel, Horace. 1910. "As to Books and Writers." *The Conservator* 9: 136–41.
Troeltsch, Ernst. [1911] 1931. *The Social Teaching of the Christian Churches*, Vol. 2. Chicago: University of Chicago Press.
Troeltsch, Ernst. 1922. *Historism and its Problems*, tr. James Luther Adams, et al. Unpublished English translation of *Historismus*. Tübingen: Verlag von J.C.B. Mahr (Paul Siebeck).
Trotsky, Leon. 1939. "The ABC of Materialist Dialectic." Online: (www.marxists.org/archive/trotsky/1939/12/abc.htm).
Trueblood, David. 1942. *The Logic of Belief*. New York: Harper.
Twain, Mark. 1872. *The $30,000 Dollar Bequest and Other Stories*. New York: Greystone.
Twain, Mark. 1883. *Life on the Mississippi*. Boston: james R. Osgood and Co.
Twain, Mark. 1917. *A Connecticut Yankee in King Arthur's Court*. New York: Greystone.
Tylor, Edward B. [1873] 1958. *The Origins of Culture, Part 1 of 'Primitive Culture,'* 2nd ed. New York: Harper.
United Nations Development Programme. 2015. "Human Development Report." Online: (http://hdr.undp.org/sites/default/files/2015_human_development_report.pdf).
Unnithan, N. Prabha, Hugh P. Whitt, Lin Huff-Corzine, and Jay Corzine. 1994. "Charting the Currents of Lethal Violence." Pp. 161–370 in *The Currents of Lethal Violence*, eds. N. Prabha Unnithan, Lin Huff-Corzine, Jay Corzine, and Hugh P. Whitt. Albany: State University of New York Press.
Vacherot, Étienne. 1870. *La Science et la Conscience*. Paris: Germer Bailliere.
Vai, Steve. 2019. *Vaideology*. Milwaukee: Hal Leonard.
Varty, John. 2000. "Suicide, Statistics and Sociology." Pp. 53–65 in *Durkheim's Suicide*, ed. W.S.F. Pickering and Geoffrey Walford. London: Routledge.
Veblen, Thorstein. 1912. *The Theory of the Leisure Class*. New York: Macmillan.
Veblen, Thorstein. 1914. *The Instinct of Workmanship*. New York: B.W. Huebsch.
Verheggen, Theo. 1996. "Durkheim's 'Représentations' Considered as 'Vorstellungen.'" *Current Perspectives in Social Theory* 16: 189–219.
Vincent, Marvin R. 1879. *Stranger and Guest*. New York: Anson D.F. Randolph and Co.
Voegelin, Eric. 2000. *The World of the Polis*. Columbia: University of Missouri Press.
Voltaire. 1962. *Philosophical Dictionary*, tr. Peter Gay. New York: Harcourt.
Vygotsky, Lev. 1978. *Mind in Society*. Cambridge: Harvard University Press.
Wahl, Jean. 2017. *Transcendence and the Concrete: Selected Writings*, eds. Alan D. Schrift and Ian Alexander Moore. New York: Fordham University Press.
Wallace, David Foster. 2003. *Everything and More*. New York: W.W. Norton.
Walter, Jess. 2009. *The Financial Lives of the Poets*. New York: Harper.
Walter, Jess. 2012a. *Beautiful Ruins*. New York: Harper.
Walter, Jess. 2012b. "In the Time of Galley Slaves." Pp. 6–12 (Appendix) in *Beautiful Ruins*. New York: Harper.

Wamsley, Laurel. 2017. "Three-Star Chef Asks Michelin Guide to Leave Him Out." National Public Radio, 21 September. Online: (www.npr.org/sections/thetwo-way/2017/09/21/552691774/three-star-chef-asks-michelin-guide-to-leave-him-out-i-will-be-able-to-feel-free).

Wang, Wendy and Kim Parker. 2014. "Record Share of Americans have Never Married." Pew Research Center. Online: (www.pewsocialtrends.org/2014/09/24/record-share-of-americans-have-never-married/).

Wartofsky, Marx W. 1977. *Feuerbach*. London: Cambridge University Press.

Weber, Marianne. 1988. *Max Weber*, tr. Harry Zohn. New Brunswick: Transaction.

Weber, Marianne. 2003. "Authority and Autonomy in Marriage." *Sociological Theory* 21(2): 85–102.

Weber, Max. [1905] 2002. *The Protestant Ethic and the Spirit of Capitalism*, tr. Peter Baehr and Gordon C. Wells. New York: Penguin.

Weber, Max. [1909] 1984. "Energetic Theories of Culture." tr. Jon Mark Mikkelsen and Charles Schwartz. *Mid-American Review of Sociology* 9(2): 33–58.

Weber, Max. [1922] 1991. *The Sociology of Religion*. Boston: Beacon.

Weber, Max. [1930] 2001. *The Protestant Ethic and the Spirit of Capitalism*, tr. Talcott Parsons. London: Routledge.

Weber, Max. 1946. *From Max Weber: Essays in Sociology*, eds. Hans H. Gerth and C. Wright Mills. New York: Oxford University Press.

Weber, Max. 1949. *The Methodology of the Social Sciences*. New York: The Free Press.

Weber, Max. 1952. *Ancient Judaism*. New York: The Free Press.

Weber, Max. 1958. *The Rational and Social Foundations of Music*. Carbondale: Southern Illinois University Press.

Weber, Max. 1978. *Economy and Society*. Berkeley: University of California Press.

Weber, Max. 1981. *General Economic History*. New Brunswick: Transaction Publishers.

Weber, Max. 2000. *The Religion of India*, tr. Hans Gerth and Don Martindale. New Delhi: Munshiram Manoharlal.

Wells, H.G. 1934. *Marxism Versus Liberalism*. Online: (www.marxists.org/reference/archive/stalin/works/1934/07/23.htm).

Wesep, H.B. 1920. *The Control of Ideals*. New York: Knopf.

Westhues, Kenneth. 1982. *First Sociology*. New York: McGraw-Hill.

Westphal, Kenneth R. 2018. *Grounds of Pragmatic Realism*. Leiden: Brill.

Westphal, Merold. 1990. *History and Truth in Hegel's Phenomenology*. New Jersey: Humanities Press International.

Wharton, Edith. 1924. *Old New York*. New York: Scribner.

Whitehead, Alfred North. 1978. *Process and Reality*. New York: The Free Press.

Whitman, Walt. 1847–1854. "Talbot Wilson" Notebook. The Walt Whitman Archive. Online: (https://whitmanarchive.org/manuscripts/notebooks/transcriptions/loc.00141.html).

Whitman, Walt. [1892] 1992. *Leaves of Grass*. New York: Book of the Month Club.
Whitt, Hugh P. 1994. "Old Theories Never Die." Pp. 7–34 in *The Currents of Lethal Violence*, ed. N. Prabha Unnithan, Lin Huff-Corzine, Jay Corzine, and Hugh P. Whitt. Albany: State University of New York Press.
Wilde, Oscar. [1890] 1995. *The Picture of Dorian Gray*. Köln: Könemann.
Wilde, Oscar. [1891] 2003. "The Soul of Man Under Socialism." Pp. 1174–197 in *Complete Works of Oscar Wilde*. New York: Harper-Collins.
Wilde, Oscar. [1892] 2011. *Lady Windermere's Fan*. Mineola: Dover.
Willett, John (ed). 1992. *Brecht on Theatre*. New York: Hill and Wang.
Willich, August. 1973. "We Will Make of Hell a Well Organized Unionfoundry." Pp. 258–66 in *The American Hegelians*, ed. William Goetzmann. New York: Knopf.
Willsher, Kim. 2016. "'World's Best Chef' Benoit Violier Found Dead." *The Guardian*, 1 February. Accessed 1 February, 2016. Online: (www.theguardian.com/world/2016/feb/01/worlds-best-chef-benoit-violier-found-dead).
Wilson, Edmund. [1940] 1967. *To the Finland Station*. New York: New York Review of Books.
Wilson, Eric. 2008. *Savage Republic*. Leiden: Martinus Nijhoff.
Wilson, Stephen. 1982. *Ideology and Experience*. East Brunswick: Associated University Presses.
Wollstonecraft, Mary. [1792] 1983. *Vindication of the Rights of Woman*. New York: Penguin.
Woolf, Virginia. [1929] 2001. *A Room of One's Own*. Peterborough: Broadview Press.
Worrell, Mark P. 1995. "Getting to Know You: Marx and Nietzsche in the Age of Postmodernism." *Humanity and Society* 20(4): 109–12.
Worrell, Mark P. 1998. "Authoritarianism, Critical Theory, and Political Psychology: Past, Present, and Future." *Social Thought and Research* 21(1–2): 3–33.
Worrell, Mark P. 1999. "The Veil of Piacular Subjectivity: Buchananism and the New World Order." *Electronic Journal of Sociology* 4(3). Online: (www.sociology.org/content/vol004.003/buchanan.html).
Worrell, Mark P. 2008. *Dialectic of Solidarity*. Chicago: Haymarket.
Worrell, Mark P. 2009a. "A Faint Rattling: A Research Note on Marx's Theory of Value." *Critical Sociology* 35(6): 887–92.
Worrell, Mark P. 2009b. "The Cult of Exchange Value." *Fast Capitalism* 5.2. Online: (www.uta.edu/huma/agger/fastcapitalism/5_2/Worrell5_2.html).
Worrell, Mark P. 2009c. "The Ghost World of Alienated Desire." *Critical Sociology* 35(3): 119–22.
Worrell, Mark P. 2009d. "Joseph Freeman and the Frankfurt School." *Rethinking Marxism* 21(4): 498–513.
Worrell, Mark P. 2011. *Why Nations Go to War*. New York: Routledge.

Worrell, Mark P. 2013. *Terror: Social, Political, and Economic Perspectives*. New York: Routledge.

Worrell, Mark P. 2014. "The Commodity as the Ultimate Monstrosity." *Fast Capitalism* 11.1. Online: (www.uta.edu/huma/agger/fastcapitalism/11_1/worrell11_1.html).

Worrell, Mark P. 2015a. "Imperial Homunculi: The Speculative Singularities of American Hegemony." *Current Perspectives in Social Theory* 33: 217–41.

Worrell, Mark P. 2015b. "Discarding Simmel: Public Property, Neoliberalism, and Potlatch Capitalism." *Logos* 14(1). Online: (www.logosjournal.com).

Worrell, Mark P. 2017a. "The Social Psychology of Authority." Pp. 463–80 in *Handbook of Critical Theory*, ed. Michael J. Thompson. New York: Palgrave.

Worrell, Mark P. 2017b. "The Sacred and the Profane in the General Formula for Capital: The Octagonal Structure of the Commodity and Saving Marx's Sociological Realism from Professional Marxology." Pp. 75–119 in *The Social Ontology of Capitalism*, eds. Dan Krier and Mark P. Worrell. New York: Palgrave Macmillan.

Worrell, Mark P. 2019. *The Sociogony: Social Facts and the Ontology of Objects, Things, and Monsters*. Leiden: Brill.

Worrell, Mark P. and Jamie Dangler. 2011. "Cafe Narcissism Redux." Pp. 72–92 in *Journal of No Illusions: The Legacy of Telos*, eds. Tim Luke and Ben Agger. New York: Telos Press.

Worrell, Mark P. and Dan Krier. 2012. "The Imperial Eye." *Fast Capitalism* 9.1. Online: (www.uta.edu/huma/agger/fastcapitalism/9_1/worrellkrier9_1.html).

Worrell, Mark P. and Dan Krier. 2018. "Atopia Awaits!" *Critical Sociology* 44(2): 213–39.

Worrell, Mark P. and Dan Krier. 2018b. "Totems, Fetishes, and Enchanted Modernity: Hegelian Marxism Confronts Idolatry." *Logos* 17(1). Online: (www.logosjournal.com).

Wray, Matt, Tatiana Poladko, and Misty Vaughan Allen. 2001. "Suicide Trends and Prevention in Nevada." University Nevada Las Vegas Center for Democratic Culture. Online: (http://cdclv.unlv.edu/healthnv_2012/suicide.pdf).

Wundt, Wilhelm. 1897. *Ethics: An Investigation of the Facts and Laws of the Moral Life*. London: Swan Sonnenschein.

Wyschogrod, Edith. 1990. *Saints and Postmodernism*. Chicago: The University of Chicago Press.

Zamyatin, Yevgeny. [1924] 1993. *We*, tr. Clarence Brown. New York: Penguin.

Zarembo, Alan. 2015. "Suicide Rate of Female Military Veterans is Called 'Staggering.'" *Los Angeles Times*, 8 June. Online: (www.latimes.com/nation/la-na-female-veteran-suicide-20150608).

Zinnemann, Fred (Director). [1955] 1999. *Oklahoma!* (DVD). Los Angeles: 20th Century Fox.

Žižek, Slavoj. 1989. *The Sublime Object of Ideology*. London: Verso.
Žižek, Slavoj. 1991. *Looking Awry*. Cambridge: The MIT Press.
Žižek, Slavoj. 1993. *Tarrying with the Negative*. Durham: Duke University Press.
Žižek, Slavoj. 2000a. *The Fragile Absolute*. London: Verso.
Žižek, Slavoj. 2000b. *The Ticklish Subject*. London: Verso.
Žižek, Slavoj. 2000c. "From *History and Class Consciousness* to *The Dialectic of Enlightenment* ... and Back." *New German Critique* 81: 107–23.
Žižek, Slavoj. 2000d. *The Art of the Ridiculous Sublime*. Seattle: University of Washington Press.
Žižek, Slavoj. 2001. *Enjoy Your Symptom*, 2nd ed. New York: Routledge.
Žižek, Slavoj. 2001b. *On Belief*. London: Routledge.
Žižek, Slavoj. 2002. *For They Know not What They Do*, 2nd ed. London: Verso.
Žižek, Slavoj. 2003. *The Puppet and the Dwarf*. Cambridge: the MIT Press.
Žižek, Slavoj. 2005. *Interrogating the Real*. London: Continuum.
Žižek, Slavoj. 2006a. *How to Read Lacan*. New York: W.W. Norton.
Žižek, Slavoj. 2006b. *The Parallax View*. Cambridge: The MIT Press.
Žižek, Slavoj. 2008a. *In Defense of Lost Causes*. London and New York: Verso.
Žižek, Slavoj. 2008b. *Violence*. New York: Picador.
Žižek, Slavoj. 2010a. *Living in the End Times*. London and New York: Verso.
Žižek, Slavoj. 2010b. "Thinking Backward: Predestination and Apocalypse." Pp. 185–210 in *Paul's New Moment: Continental Philosophy and the Future of Christian Theology* by Milbank et al. Grand Rapids, MI: Brazos Press.
Žižek, Slavoj. 2012. *Less Than Nothing*. London: Verso.
Žižek, Slavoj. 2012b. "Don't Act. Just Think." *Big Think*. 3 July 2010. Online: (https://bigthink.com/dont-act-just-think).
Žižek, Slavoj. 2012c. The Year of Dreaming Dangerously. London: Verso.
Žižek, Slavoj. 2014. *The Most Sublime Hysteric*, tr. Thomas Scott-Railton. Cambridge: Polity Press.
Žižek, Slavoj. 2014b. *Absolute Recoil*. London and New York: Verso.
Žižek, Slavoj, interviewed by Katie Forster. 2016. "Slavoj Žižek: We Are All Basically Evil, Egotistical, Disgusting." *The Guardian*, 10 December. Online: (www.theguardian.com/lifeandstyle/2016/dec/10/slavoj-zizek-we-are-all-basically-evil-egotistical-disgusting).
Žižek, Slavoj. 2019. "Making Use of Religion? No, Thanks!" *Los Angeles Review of Books*, 3 June. Online: (https://thephilosophicalsalon.com/making-use-of-religion-no-thanks).
Žižek, Slavoj. 2019b. "Was I Right to Back Donald Trump Over Hillary Clinton? Absolutely." *The Independent*, 26 June. Online: (https://www.independent.co.uk/voices/trump-hillary-clinton-populist-right-left-democratic-party-civil-war-a8975121.html).

Zweig, Stefan. [1929] 2012. *Casanova, Stendhal, Tolstoy*. New Brunswick: Transaction Publishers.

Zweig, Stefan. [1943] 2013. "A Chess Story." Pp. 91–150 in *The Collected Novellas of Stefan Zweig*, tr. Anthea Bell. London: Pushkin Press.

Index

Absolute Spirit   52, 102
addictions   87, 88, 90, 94, 100
alcohol   80, 87–89, 99, 104
alienation   18–19, 24, 29, 40, 48, 75, 106, 125, 136, 138, 154–55
  compound   19, 189
altruism   109, 116–17, 121, 124–25, 131–32, 153, 158–61, 163–64, 189–91, 196–97, 200–203, 205–10, 224–25
  acute   161
  blended   204
  fanatical   206
  obligatory   160, 163
  optional   200
  premodern   160
  principle of   46–47
ambivalence   31, 169
anarchy   17, 127, 131, 165, 168–70, 179–81, 184–87, 201, 204, 210, 214, 224, 227
anomie   16–17, 64, 100, 116–18, 123–27, 162–65, 167–68, 179–81, 189, 191–93, 195, 199–200, 204–5, 209–12, 214–19, 223–25
  chronic   17, 22, 27, 179, 223
  imaginary   178
  positive   180
  regressive   171, 181, 188, 211–12
anti-authoritarianism   29
antinomianism   151
antisemitism   27–28
anxiety   4, 26, 200, 209, 231
asceticism   144, 146, 221, 223, 225, 229
assemblage effervescence   134
Aufheben   49, 60
austerity   63, 84, 93, 97
authoritarianism   9, 11–12, 28–33, 72, 74, 187, 210
authority   5–6, 8–13, 20, 22–23, 25, 29–31, 33, 35, 65, 73, 81–82, 147, 203
  negative   82
  positive   82
  rational   34
  traditional   168
autonomy   13, 16, 31, 45, 62–64, 127, 137, 140, 147, 165, 184–86

bourgeois   31
  individual   44
  liberal   127
autotelism   138

barbarism   167, 187
besiegement   209
blood sacrifice   115
bondage   9, 19, 24–25, 34, 68, 150, 199
bourgeois ataraxia   141
bourgeoisie   7, 75, 152, 170, 174, 228, 230
Bretton Woods   172
brutality   50, 84, 230
business   4, 17, 71, 74, 110, 197
  profitable   114

callings   16, 68, 127
Calvin   110, 148, 187
Calvinism   110, 133, 187
cannibalism   199
capital   3–4, 6–7, 19–21, 26–27, 49, 52, 54, 56–59, 68, 72, 106, 114–15, 193–94
  absolute of   108
  competitive logic   173
  constant   67
  organic composition of   27, 107
  symbolic   219
capital accumulation   26, 56
capital fetishism   75
capitalism   1, 4, 6–7, 18, 21–22, 39, 42, 56–60, 74–75, 101, 104, 179–80, 194, 220
  consumer   130
  contemporary   174
  depoliticizing   168
  dismantling   220
  imaginary   74
  mature   13
  modern   63
  really-existing   74
chance   106, 125, 169, 181, 183, 208, 212
  games of   45, 101
chaos   18, 64, 107, 168, 176, 181, 226–27
character structure   29–30
charisma   1, 28, 73, 165, 216, 222

INDEX 281

charity   148, 159, 174
chrematistics   166
Christianity   52, 127, 137, 141, 162, 220
civilization   101, 128–29, 192, 198
classes   5–6, 8, 21, 23, 25, 81, 83, 89, 93, 114, 117, 123–24, 181–82
class solidarity   5, 8
coercion   1, 10–12, 15, 23, 212
collective consciousness   7, 15, 64, 76, 80–81, 102–5, 113, 125, 159, 221
collective representations   5, 8, 40, 47, 77, 110, 137, 216
collective unconsciousness   101
commodities   5–6, 19, 48, 52, 56–58, 69, 73, 106, 108, 111, 152, 154
commodity fetishism   130, 135
communism   5, 27, 72, 153, 183, 219–20
concept   1, 4, 11, 17, 18, 31, 33, 38, 44, 46, 50–51, 53–56, 64–65, 67, 73–75, 103–5, 114, 116–17, 130–31, 165–66, 212, 219–20, 223, 230
   absolute   184
   actualized   38, 50
conflict   20, 51, 65, 78, 94–95, 107, 131, 143, 211, 221, 226
conformity   11–12, 36, 49, 67, 83
conscience   13, 22, 46–47, 76, 82, 104–5, 107, 127, 140, 152, 210
   bad   104
   collective   9, 51, 111
   personal   204
consciousness   3, 15–16, 18, 20, 24, 39–43, 50, 52–53, 77, 84, 103–5, 116, 121–22, 141, 207–8
contagion   196
credit   33, 101, 110–11
cunning of reason   208
cynicism   146–47, 165, 222

death   3–4, 24–26, 52, 62–65, 79–81, 83–85, 88–91, 113–16, 126, 128, 140, 162–63, 167, 178, 208
death drives   84, 122
debt   84, 96–97, 114
demagoguery   27, 63
demagogues   25–27, 28, 74, 220
democracy   11, 30, 36, 76, 119, 215
demonization   28, 49, 66, 119

demonologies   1, 28, 187
demons   40, 48, 103, 187, 210, 216
depression   19, 81, 142, 149, 169–70, 181, 194, 204, 210, 225, 227
dé-règlement   17
deregulation   26, 68, 93–94, 101, 127, 164–66, 168, 171, 181, 194
destiny   17, 128, 148, 169–70, 182, 185, 198, 211–12, 215, 218, 221
destructiveness   33, 45, 52, 134
determinism   14, 76, 113, 182, 187, 208, 210
devaluation   161, 163, 171–72, 182, 219
devils   31, 119, 121
diabetes   87, 98, 149
dialectics   11, 43, 47, 53, 57, 59, 118, 126, 132, 154
discipline   39, 49, 66, 126, 132, 196, 229
disenchantment   102, 141, 224
disintegration   4, 10, 60, 64, 66, 120, 151, 154, 159, 221, 224, 230
disobedience   12, 25, 32–36, 81–82, 155, 184
diversity   11, 63, 131, 218, 226
domination   10–12, 183
dominionism   220
dreams   64, 70, 102, 105, 107–9, 134, 140–42, 147, 149, 173–75, 178–79, 181, 201
dreamwork   40, 102, 106–7, 109, 121
drugs   80, 88–89, 92, 126
duality   62–63, 68, 72, 154, 212
Durkheim, E   5–9, 12–14, 16–17, 40, 49–53, 59–61, 72–74, 78–79, 102–6, 114–19, 121–23, 125–26, 130–31, 134–35, 137–39, 178–82, 187–89, 205–7, 210–12, 216–17
dynamism   18, 121
dystopia   219

economy   75–77, 86, 115, 174–75, 210
ecstasy   1, 19, 118, 161, 174, 196, 203–4, 207, 209, 222–25
   apathetic   92
   negative   221
education   42, 46, 61, 64, 78, 99, 101, 104, 137, 152
effervescence   84, 104, 122
ego   45–46, 64–65, 106–7, 121–23, 130, 133–34, 136, 140–43, 157, 159–60, 200–201, 203–4, 206–8, 217–18, 221
Ego-altruistic suicide   189

egoism   116–17, 121–25, 128, 132, 135–40,
    145–46, 151–53, 158–60, 162, 164–65,
    191–92, 195–96, 200, 204–6, 208, 221, 223
  aristocratic   153
  bourgeois   94
  sociological   137
egoism and altruism   189–90, 196–97, 200,
    203, 207
egoism and anomie   47, 116, 118, 126, 131, 189,
    191, 195, 205, 210
empiricism   3, 60, 103, 117
enemies   28, 58, 78, 119, 128, 131, 155, 204, 214
energies   19, 21, 44–45, 77–78, 104–5, 107, 110,
    128–29, 134, 141, 143, 145, 152
  assemblage   224
  diabolical   20
  moral   73, 77, 85, 110, 134
  physical   77
ennui   70, 131, 164, 228
enthusiasm   161, 180, 201
Epicureanism   144, 165, 223
equilibrium   80, 122, 129, 131, 173, 196–97, 226
  dynamic   132, 197
  mechanical   132
  social   121
estrangement   12, 19, 138, 142, 152–53, 196
evil   64, 66, 69, 72–74, 80, 122, 154, 156,
    172–73, 176, 187–88, 201, 204, 210, 212
exchange-value   6, 40, 42, 58, 106, 194

faith healing   2
fake news   27
fanaticism   20, 68–69, 152, 161, 203, 210, 222,
    224
  acute   205
  appalling   220
  religious   94
fantasy   26, 94, 108, 139, 178, 192, 200–201
fatalism   64, 116–17, 121, 124–25, 131, 133,
    168–69, 181–82, 186, 188–89, 191,
    200–201, 210–16, 219–22, 224–25
fate   106, 114, 124, 182–83, 185, 188, 208,
    210–14, 216, 218, 220, 227, 230
fetishism   6, 36, 104, 114, 139
fetish objects   103, 201, 218
fetish splitting   77
forces   10, 12, 33, 36, 109–10, 112, 115, 120,
    122–23, 125–26, 131, 133–35, 209–10

divine   73
electromagnetic   124
market   150
physical   124
polar   189
  sacred   118
  spiritual   126
Fordism   76, 98
freedom   7–8, 14–17, 24–26, 34–35, 46, 62,
    64–65, 84, 127, 144–45, 166, 183–84,
    194–95, 210–12, 229–30
  abstract   216
  concrete   166
  positive   7, 16, 19, 183, 194
Freud, S.   22, 28, 40–41, 46, 50–51, 64–66,
    68–70, 76–77, 83–86, 102–5, 107–9,
    118–19, 121–22, 145–46, 187–89, 196–97,
    205, 209–11

geometry   173, 193
  moral   200, 205, 225
Glass-Steagall Act   171
globalization   85, 101
God   4, 6, 110–11, 127–28, 144, 148, 153–54, 156,
    166–67, 172, 175–76, 188, 191
gold   1, 6, 168, 172, 216
grace   40, 110, 114, 220
Great Depression   26, 170
Great Leap Forward   213
Greimas schema   223
group selection process   113
guilt   34, 108–9, 114, 119, 155, 182, 207, 210–11,
    227

hallucinations   103–4
happiness   141, 174–75, 191, 230
  personal   146
  social   62
hate   70–72, 74–75, 78–79, 106, 146, 171, 190,
    230
hedonism   187, 229
Hegel, G. W. F.   8–9, 11–14, 16, 38–40, 42–43,
    45–46, 50, 52–54, 58–60, 65–68, 103–5,
    111, 131, 133, 156, 159–60, 165–68, 175–76,
    181–84, 225–27
heroin   88–90, 92
heterogony   152
heteronomy   45, 137, 165, 184–85, 224

heterotelism 138
Homo duplex 62–63, 135–36
human sacrifice 6, 57, 59, 82, 109, 114
hypnosis 55, 103, 108

Id 105, 223
Idea 38–39, 50–55, 58, 67, 79, 86, 105, 117, 122, 124, 127, 224–25
idealism 108, 138, 202
    empirical 112
ideals 108, 137, 171, 211
    negative 141
    pathological 86
identification 21, 50, 132, 155, 158, 199, 207, 228
identity 50, 52, 71, 108, 113, 155, 162, 198
    corporate 131
    moral 207
    narcissist-fanatic 198
    personal 8, 137
    positive social 208
    speculative 33, 117, 197–98
ideology 36, 45, 52, 71, 86, 105, 107, 130, 146, 152, 185
    bourgeois 152, 184
    political 214
impurity 3, 68, 161, 204
    social 9, 29
incarceration 86, 91, 92
indifference 60, 62, 133, 139–40, 142–43, 145–46, 191, 195, 205, 207, 228, 230
individualism 11, 47, 83, 130, 135–38, 169, 195, 198, 204–5
individuality 15, 17, 46–47, 52, 55–56, 60, 127, 133, 135–37, 191, 194, 211
inequality 52, 63, 93–94, 168, 218
    income 94
    reducing 78
    righteous 74
inevitability 16, 36, 64, 106, 142, 169, 182, 188, 211, 224, 228
    fatalistic 220
infinity 35, 45–46, 59, 62–63, 165, 175–76, 188, 191, 193–94, 213, 223–24
infinity disease 94, 152, 162, 191–93, 200, 223
instincts 18, 127, 175, 197
instrumentalization 19, 141, 177
intelligence 123, 132, 152, 175, 196

isolation 10, 19, 49, 84, 94, 137, 139, 148–49, 152, 188, 194
    egoistic 150
    social 113, 149
    worshiping 139

jazz 41, 50, 88
Jesus 116
jokes 102–3, 107–8, 229

Kantianism 161, 173, 204

labor 19, 24–25, 27, 40, 48–49, 57, 106–7, 114–15, 144–45, 219, 226
    abstract 40, 48
    concrete 40, 48
    forced divisions of 108, 127
labor power 27, 57, 89, 95, 107, 136, 168, 174
labor process 12, 58, 84, 107–8
labor products 6, 19, 67, 106
    alienated 6
laws 14, 16, 26–27, 34–35, 47, 63–64, 80, 137, 139–40, 164, 166, 168, 181–82, 184, 217
leadership 5, 21–22, 28, 55, 69, 73, 76, 105, 116, 195, 213
    charismatic 116
    narcissistic 68
    religious 180
lemniscate 134, 223
limitlessness 17, 36, 64, 165–67, 170, 180, 187, 194–95

madness 21, 63, 108, 147, 176, 181
magic 1–4, 45–46, 70, 80, 88, 167, 178, 186, 198, 200, 216–17, 224, 227
malaise 15, 26, 27
mana 7, 40, 44, 52, 103, 114, 200, 210, 216
mania 17, 71, 133, 139, 161, 165, 187, 194, 210, 227
Marx, Karl 5–8, 12–13, 15–16, 19–20, 35, 48–49, 51–53, 56–59, 64, 67, 89, 103, 106, 118, 183
Marxheimianism 4, 8
Marxism 5, 8, 12, 53, 219
    cultural 27, 75
masochism 28–29
mass murder 7, 73, 86, 180, 213
master-slave relation 24–25

miracles   1–2, 4, 8, 61, 63, 70, 184, 193, 222, 224, 227
Möbius band   134
money   3, 6–7, 11–12, 17, 19, 57, 59, 69, 106, 167–68, 173, 176, 193–94, 226
monsters   8, 18, 78, 114, 162, 187, 206, 221, 231
   autistic   162
   bipolar   162
   schizoid   162
monstrosities   12, 83, 191–92, 206
   dictatorial   76
   one-sided   205
   socio-historical   19
   terrifying   72
moral economy   6, 21, 32–33, 105–7, 120, 135, 230
   conscious   107
   universal   75
moral forces   86, 120, 166, 189
   invisible   117
   real collective   117
morality   20, 22, 47, 51, 106, 117, 165, 183, 206, 218
morbid effervescence   17, 174
mourning   77, 143
multiculturalism   73, 218, 226
mystagogues   216–17
mysticism   2, 4, 129, 138, 186, 191, 203–4, 207, 217–18, 224, 227
myth   102, 105, 133, 154, 158, 167, 183, 225

narcissism   17, 22, 76, 105, 128, 160, 180, 192, 198, 205–6, 223
necessity   33, 35–36, 52–53, 58–59, 62, 81–82, 84, 106–7, 182–85, 212, 216, 219, 221, 224
   alien   54
   historical   183
   internalized   184
   logical   39, 94
   mechanical   183
   moral   36, 65, 183
   natural   183
   political   83
   profane   84
negations   35, 41, 47–48, 58, 65, 104, 106–8, 111–12, 120, 123, 190–91, 224, 227
Nemesis   77, 79, 130
neoliberalism   22, 63, 68, 93, 110–11, 215, 218, 225
neuroses   67, 102, 108, 119

Nietzsche   54, 69–70, 140, 144, 163, 174, 180–81, 185, 200–201, 205–6
nominalism   11, 103, 147
nomos   77, 146

obedience   12, 23, 30–32, 35–36, 81–82, 86, 129, 153, 199
obesity   98, 149
object choice   21, 78
objectification   18, 49, 80
objectivation   18
objective phantoms   52, 104
objectivity   12, 49, 53, 55, 67, 74, 143, 193, 206
   concrete   47
   ontological   39
   passive   43
   universal   66
objects   40, 48–49, 82–83, 105, 108, 175–76, 178, 180, 190, 193, 196, 199, 202
obligations   4, 31, 47, 142, 160, 182, 192, 195, 230
   collective   184
   formal   143
   reciprocal   63
obligatory altruistic suicide   163
octahedron (social)   124, 126, 134
October Revolution   213
Operation Enduring Freedom   91
opinion   14, 28, 60, 73, 79, 121, 122, 182
opinion research   73
opioid deaths   89, 91, 92
organicism   86, 118
overdoses   86, 90, 91, 92
overproduction   173–74
overregulation (fatalism)   125, 141, 196, 210, 215
Oxfam   94–95
OxyCons   89
OxyContin   89, 90

pain   31, 85, 89, 107, 141, 145, 155, 172, 188, 199
   chronic   94
   epidemic of   89
paranoia   189, 193, 207
passions   34, 123, 138, 140, 146, 166, 174–76, 179, 192, 209, 226
   anarchic   107
   collective   121, 123
   exalted   140
   unregulated   208

INDEX

patriarchy   11, 101
patriotism   180
personality   46–47, 56, 125, 128, 137–38, 140, 176, 184, 196–97, 203, 206
polarities   36, 106, 124, 133, 140, 172, 179, 189, 196, 197, 209–10, 216
possession   19, 52, 93, 125, 146, 153–54, 173–74, 176–77, 186, 194, 196
power   3, 5–7, 9–11, 28–29, 51–52, 55–56, 64–65, 73–74, 77, 95, 121, 170, 176–78, 183, 205
powerlessness   133, 203
praxis   32, 47, 49, 53–56, 131, 166
   conscious   49
   historical   220
   radical   220
   sacred (misnomer)   6
   teleological   79, 104
predestinationism   19, 182, 187–88, 224
prejudice   12, 20, 22, 28, 32, 40, 72–74, 146, 175
   measuring   75
prestige   2, 29, 116, 151, 200
progressive anomie   94, 132, 174, 201–2, 213, 229
projection   67, 91, 104, 138, 153, 161
proletariat   5, 7, 50, 89, 93, 183
Pronoia   138
propaganda   27, 100, 107
   antisemitic   75
   conservative   70
property   40–41, 46, 58, 171, 185, 212, 214
   private   6, 74, 135, 161
prophets   85, 180, 209
punishment   21, 28, 31, 34–36, 70–72, 78, 106, 149, 155, 159, 164, 182, 187
puritans   67, 69, 136, 152, 170, 204

Rabelaisianism   209
racism   27, 63, 72
Reaganomics   93
Reagan Revolution   168
realism   108
   common-sense   202
   naïve   111
reason   2–4, 9, 11–15, 31–35, 42–45, 51–54, 64–66, 68, 80–81, 100, 102, 116, 124–25, 127–28, 141, 166, 175–77, 181, 185, 224–25
   abstract   175
   transcendental   140
   universal   141

reciprocity   139, 152, 198
recognition   25, 35, 65, 145, 154
   mutual   24
   partial   143
recourage   225
Reflective Determinations   38–39, 41, 43, 45, 47, 49, 51, 53, 55, 57, 59, 61
regulation   17–18, 52, 68, 79, 101, 133, 165, 168, 181, 197, 227
reification   12, 18, 28, 39, 105, 167
religion   2, 5–6, 20, 27, 73, 75, 119, 122, 189, 200, 203, 206
representations   18, 40–41, 43, 47, 104, 135, 151, 190, 221
   authoritative   47, 70
   logical   70
   mythological   155
   political   72
   profane   40
   sacred   104
repression   22, 65, 109, 115, 210, 220, 225
resignation   19, 55, 122, 125, 141, 146, 148, 159, 221–23, 225, 228
   hopelessness   125
   positive   222
retirement   94, 97
   early   145
retribution   187, 207, 220
revenge   3, 8, 26–27, 77, 139, 207, 209–10, 227
revenge monsters   163
revolution   8, 21, 35, 51, 58, 61, 126, 168, 171, 183, 219
   nominalist   11
   proletarian   4
   social democratic   8
revolutionaries   8, 23–24, 33–34, 58, 78, 146
rights   71, 128, 184–85, 212, 222
   abstract   184
   human   143
   inalienable   127
   individual   184
   one-sided   184
   personal   183–84
   sacred   184
   subjective   184
   totalitarian conception liquidates   185
   voting   78
   wealth-accumulation   184
rights and necessity   184–85

rites   77, 104, 182, 196
    piacular   209
    special   216
ritual conduct   102
ritual effervescence   77
rituals   79, 110, 137
ritual tribute   121

sacralization   143, 185, 219
sacredness   7, 17, 50, 196
sacrifice   7, 11, 13–14, 46, 60, 67, 85, 89,
    109–10, 114–16, 119
sadism   28–29, 92, 139, 205
    political   11
    social   28
sadness   85, 124, 140, 149, 158, 204
sadomasochism   28, 29, 205
sage   140, 202–3, 217
    neo-Platonic   203
sageism   140, 198, 202–3
scapegoats   107
scepticism   138, 142, 146, 197
self-destruction   3, 7, 80–84, 93, 100, 111, 115,
    121, 123, 125, 127, 129, 163
    collective   23
    ecstatic   55
    moderate   110
    total   113
    voluntary   87, 170
self-sacrifice   116, 205, 229
servitude   11, 23, 25, 52, 144–45, 161
simulated schizophrenia   142
slavery   19, 24–25, 145, 181
    partial   184
sleep deprivation   97–98
social forces   81, 84, 86, 104, 120, 137, 216
social organization   5, 7, 30, 40, 44, 51, 68, 72,
    78, 120, 124, 151, 155
social psychology   12, 23, 30, 32, 34, 77, 158
solidarity   1, 7, 11, 15, 27, 34–35, 51–52, 122,
    128, 133–34, 202, 207
solitude   124, 148–52, 188, 228
soul   38, 47, 137, 153, 158, 160, 162, 178, 227–28
spirit   39–40, 42, 46, 49–52, 59, 120–21,
    169–70, 173, 176–77, 192, 194, 220, 223–24
Stoic egoism   139–40
Stoic indifference   144
Stoic intellectualism   196
Stoicism   139, 141–42, 144, 165, 202–3, 223

Stoics   117–18, 128, 138–42, 145, 191, 198, 202,
    204, 222
sublation   47, 49–50, 60, 104, 125, 131, 136, 184,
    191, 211
submission   12, 23, 29, 71, 81, 85, 183, 185, 195,
    204–5, 222, 224
suicide   36, 79–83, 85–89, 108, 110–12, 114–19,
    121–25, 129, 131, 133–34, 163, 189, 205,
    207–8, 227
    altruistic   7, 115–16
    anomic   127
    ego-anomic   189, 191
    obligatory   163
    optional   116
    partial   114
    virtual   114
suicide rates   79, 81, 87, 117, 121, 123, 125, 227
superstition   1–4, 9, 186–87, 191, 210, 224
surplus labor   27, 67, 107
surplus labor products   50
surplus punishment   71
surplus value   7, 20, 52, 58, 107, 114, 168, 193
sybaritism   199, 201
syllogism   11–12, 19, 44, 47–49, 53, 55, 57–60,
    65–66, 103, 110, 131
    disjunctive   59–60, 133
    wrong   19, 58
symbols   29, 43, 69, 76–77, 81, 104, 129, 139,
    196, 230

taboo   4, 40, 85, 88, 186, 188, 191, 194, 200, 210,
    224
taboo energies   48
taboo sickness   209
teleological activity   15, 32, 43, 46, 66, 102,
    113, 131, 182
telos   39, 49, 55, 131, 173
terror   24–25, 33, 90, 93, 115, 161, 196, 210, 214,
    231
terrorism   161, 230
terrorists   69, 115, 119, 203, 220
Themis   130
totality   19, 56, 60, 104, 133–34, 157
    ethical   226
    hyper-rationalized   224
    objective   209
    rational   39
    self-reproducing   56
totems   6, 44, 52

INDEX   287

transdescendance 191
triads 62, 131, 133
    egoism-anomie-altruism 182
    synthetic 182
Trump 3, 22, 33, 71, 73, 89, 123
Trumpism 22, 76, 89
Trump's base 3, 72, 73, 76
Tyche 86
tyranny 10, 36, 64, 73, 81, 144–45, 219
tyrants 9–10, 14, 36, 198

ultrasociality 130
understanding 3, 7, 12, 15, 39, 42, 52, 102, 105, 116, 168
unemployment 26, 91, 96
unfreedom 154, 221
unhappiness 178, 188
uselessness value 106
utilitarianism 62, 143, 201, 203, 210, 224
utilitarian purposiveness 50, 135
utilitarian rationalizations 144
utopia 4, 219, 226
    communist 4, 50
    consumerist 219
    negative 219
    post-capitalist 16
Utopianism 219

values 7–8, 20–21, 40, 42–44, 46–48, 51–52, 61–63, 65–67, 105–7, 121–23, 166–67, 172, 174
variables
    psychological 75
    social 117
vengeance 77, 207
viciousness 119, 170, 198
victims 71, 83, 86, 115, 119, 164, 200
    sacred 86
villains 71, 119
violence 45, 66, 100, 119, 168, 205, 222–23
    large-scale 169
    piacular 207
vocation 68, 127
    religiously-tinged 68

voters 72, 78, 79, 89
voting 32, 72, 78
voting patterns 32

wages 19, 36, 72, 95–96, 101, 194, 216
wage slavery 13, 136
wage stagnation 26, 171
war 20, 33–34, 36, 81, 83, 86, 89–90, 92–93, 97–98, 100, 162, 166, 180, 183, 208
    civil 95
    holy 220
    hyperbolic 64
    permanent 68, 166
    total 64
wealth 10, 17, 22–23, 93–95, 101, 107, 110, 146, 150, 174, 178–79, 192–93
    absolute 173
    abstract 91
    imagined 179
    multiform 176
    relative 173
    total 93
    unlimited 28
wealth distribution 95
Weber, Max 1, 5–6, 13, 15–16, 115, 118, 127–28, 135, 182, 187, 215–17
We-for-We circle 217
will-mania 185, 195
wizards 69, 88, 222
workers 4–5, 7–8, 19, 21, 25, 84, 97, 145, 169, 171, 174, 212, 215–16
World War I 34
World War II 34, 87, 90, 95

Yahweh 209
yoga 2

Zarathustra 105, 231
Zeus 155
zombies 126, 161–63

www.ingramcontent.com/pod-product-compliance
Lightning Source LLC
Chambersburg PA
CBHW071334080526
44587CB00017B/2828